Courtroom Talk and Neocolonial Control

Language, Power and Social Process   22

Editors

Monica Heller
Richard J. Watts

Mouton de Gruyter
Berlin · New York

Courtroom Talk and Neocolonial Control

by

Diana Eades

Mouton de Gruyter
Berlin · New York

Mouton de Gruyter (formerly Mouton, The Hague)
is a Division of Walter de Gruyter GmbH & Co. KG, Berlin.

Library of Congress Cataloging-in-Publication Data is available at http://catalog.loc.gov.

ISBN 978-3-11-020482-7 hb
ISBN 978-3-11-020483-4 pb

Bibliographic information published by the Deutsche Nationalbibliothek

The Deutsche Nationalbibliothek lists this publication in the Deutsche
Nationalbibliografie; detailed bibliographic data are available in the Internet
at http://dnb.d-nb.de.

Acknowledgements

Over the many years that it has taken me to write this book, I have benefited greatly from stimulating discussions with scholars and legal professionals on a great number of the issues it deals with. I owe special thanks to Michael Cooke, Susan Philips, Susan Ehrlich, Shonna Trinch, Jeff Siegel, Janet Holmes, Mack O'Barr, John Conley, and Greg Matoesian. During my time at the University of Hawai'i, I benefited from the wisdom and questions of Neil Milner, Jon Goldberg-Hiller, David Johnson, Andrew Aarno, Meda Chesney-Lind, and Gabi Kasper, as well as graduate students in the Department of Second Language Studies, especially Steven Talmy and Matt Prior. On specific legal details, I have been assisted by Ann-Marie Donnelly, Ron Finney, Tim Carberry, Tony Keyes, David Brereton, Greg Shadbolt, Andrew Boe, Chris Cunneen, Mark Findlay, and David Yarrow. The manuscript was reviewed by Kate Auty, Susan Ehrlich and a third reviewer: I am most grateful to these three people for their careful and helpful comments and suggestions. All remaining errors are entirely my responsibility.

Thanks are also due to Monica Heller, who has been a most attentive, encouraging and helpful series editor, to Marcia Schwartz for her enthusiastic and efficient editorial assistance, and to Vicki Knox for meticulous proofreading.

Throughout the incubation of this book, I have enjoyed fantastic support – intellectual, emotional and material – from my husband and live-in linguist, Jeff Siegel. It is to him that I dedicate this book.

Any author royalties which derive from the sale of this book will be donated to the Aboriginal Legal Service in Brisbane, in recognition of their important work in the struggle against neocolonial domination.

Contents

Part II: Evidence given in unequivocal terms?

Part IV: Conclusions

List of tables

List of transcript extracts

Transcription conventions

<u>Underlining</u>	indicates emphatic stress
SMALL CAPITALS	indicate raised volume
°	before and after an utterance indicates that it is spoken in a very low volume
=	indicates latched utterances, i.e. no pause between the end of one utterance and the start of the next
[	indicates talk overlapping with that of another speaker, marked at the point in each utterance where overlap begins
-	indicates a pause within a turn of less than 0.5 of a second
A number	in parentheses indicates the length of a pause in seconds e.g. (3.2)
Parentheses	around a word or phrase indicates transcriber doubt
(xxxxxx)	indicates an inaudible utterance
Double parentheses	are used to enclose transcriber's description of paralinguistic or other activity by the speaker, e.g. ((laughs))
DC	defence counsel
M	magistrate
Pros	prosecutor
Bold	type indicates particular segments of the transcript being highlighted in my analysis. It is used only in extracts where one particular utterance pertains to the discussion more than the rest of the utterances in that extract, as for example in the extracts in Section 2.2 of Chapter 4. In many of the extracts, there are several utterances which pertain to the discussion, and it is considered unhelpful to use bold type (e.g. in Chapters 7–9).
Regular English spelling	is used throughout, except for a few places where a word or phrase is pronounced in a clearly abbreviated or nonstandard way (e.g. in a number of DC

turns the first utterance is *Nd*, a clearly abbreviated form of *and*).

Personal names   (which are pseudonyms) are mainly used for the three witnesses, as they are the only personal names that occur with any frequency in the data. Any other personal names in the transcript extracts are also pseudonyms. Identifying locality names have been changed, with the exception of major towns and cities.

Abbreviations

ABC	Australian Broadcasting Commission
AE	Aboriginal English
ALS	Aboriginal Legal Service
CA	Conversation Analysis
CDA	Critical Discourse Analysis
CJC	Criminal Justice Commission
DC	Defence counsel
Fitzgerald Inquiry	Commission of Inquiry into Possible Illegal Activites and Associated Police Misconduct
M	Magistrate[1]
NISATSIC	National Inquiry into the Separation of Aboriginal and Torres Strait Islander Children from their Families
Pros	Prosecutor
QPS	Queensland Police Service
RCIADC	Royal Commission into Aboriginal Deaths in Custody
SE	Standard English
"the court"	the presiding magistrate or judge in a particular case

Part I

Aboriginal participation in the criminal justice system

Chapter 1
Introduction

Late one night in a Brisbane shopping mall, three Aboriginal boys aged 12, 13 and 14 were approached by six armed police officers and told to get into three separate police vehicles. They were then driven 14 kilometres out of town to a swampy industrial wasteland, in the suburb of Pinkenba. After threatening to chop off their fingers and throw the boys in the river, the police drove off, leaving the boys to find their own way back.

Aboriginal community members in Brisbane said that such occurrences had happened before, and anecdotal evidence from a number of Australian cities suggests that such a practice is not restricted to this occurrence or this location. But for the first time, this event led to the police officers involved facing criminal charges for "unlawful deprivation of liberty", which could have resulted in imprisonment. This book focuses on the cross-examination in the first stage in the trial process in this case, known as the Pinkenba case. This was the committal hearing in the Brisbane Magistrates' Court (*Crawford v Venardos & Ors* 1995), in which the prosecution had to establish that there was a case strong enough to put to a jury in a District Court trial. This book will examine in detail the linguistic strategies used to discredit the evidence of the three boys, which were so successful that the magistrate not only dropped the charges against the police officers, but also devoted a considerable part of his decision to delivering a negative evaluation of the characters of the boys.

Why write a whole book about one courtroom hearing – especially one at the lowest level in the criminal justice process? The short answer to this question lies in the fact that the cross-examination of the boys was extreme in terms of linguistic manipulation, and that an examination of these linguistic strategies shows just how far the legal system can go in the "delivery of justice". A critical sociolinguistic exploration of this case sheds light on a central issue in sociolegal studies, namely how the criminal justice system fails to deliver justice. The longer answer to the question lies in the way in which sociolinguistics can show the workings of the control which has been exercised by the state over Aboriginal people for more than two hundred years. This book will show that central to this control is the way that talk is used, both in the construction of Aboriginal people as a threat to public safety, and in the legitimisation of police removal of Aboriginal people from public places. A critical sociolinguistic analysis of the Pinkenba case, focusing on the cross-examination in this hearing, puts both of these uses of talk under the spotlight, exposing mechanisms which enable the continuing oppression of Aboriginal Australians.

It is important to clarify from the outset the terms "Aboriginal" and "Indigenous" as they are currently used in Australia. The term "Indigenous Australians" refers to descendants of the original inhabitants, both Aboriginal people, whose ancestry comes the Australian continent, and Torres Strait Islanders, from the islands between Queensland and Papua New Guinea. As Aboriginal people and Torres Strait Islanders share many experiences and results of the colonial past and neocolonial present, many surveys and statistical reports combine both groups in the category of "Indigenous". However, there are many differences in social and cultural life, as well as history, between the two groups (Mye 1994: 1089–1090), and it is Aboriginal people and their experiences which are a major focus of this book. Further, Aboriginal people number many more than Torres Strait Islanders, and they have assumed the greatest prominence in court cases involving Indigenous people (CJC 1996: xi). Thus, except where referring to issues or quoting from research, such as census analysis, which does not separate the two groups of Indigenous Australians, I use the term Aboriginal, rather than Indigenous.

1.   Colonialism and neocolonialism in Australia

Archeological evidence indicates that Aboriginal peoples have inhabited Australia for at least 60,000 years (Thorne 2005: 38). The British invasion of Aboriginal lands began in the late eighteenth century, and in 1788 the first British colony was established in the area now known as Sydney. At this time, the continent was populated by Aboriginal societies with complex sociocultural organisation, and there were about 250 distinct languages (McConvell and Thieberger 2005). "Informed guesswork" currently suggests that the Aboriginal population at the time of British settlement was about 500,000 (Taylor 2005: 66). Such was the arrogance and ethnocentrism of British settlers and colonial rulers, that the country was legally considered to be *terra nullius* (an unoccupied country, literally "the land of no-one"). This legal doctrine was only overturned by the High Court of Australia in 1992 (Altman and Palmer 2005). So, although the leaders of the initial British settlement were instructed to deal with the Indigenous population with "amity and kindness" (Barton 1889: 483, cited in McRae et al. 1997: 33), their colonial preoccupation with the annexation of land soon resulted in conflict with its Aboriginal owners. Historical research depicts the time between 1788 and the 1840s as one characterised by brutal frontier conflict (Rowse 2005). As we will see in Chapter 3, the police played a central role in these frontier conflicts.

From the beginning of British colonial rule, the Indigenous inhabitants were subject to British control, yet they were not offered the same protection as other subjects. Thus, their land could be taken without compensation, as there was no legal recognition of their land ownership, and they could be removed from their own land to any area which the government chose. In the 1860s, a new phase of colonial rule began, with the enacting of the first "protective" legislation, which resulted in a large percentage of Aboriginal people around the country being rounded up and transported to settlements or reserves, where they were forced to live under state regulation. From this time on, many families were separated, and children placed in state care, as we will see in Chapter 3. The first Aboriginal settlement in Queensland was established in 1905, some 250 kilometres north-west of the state capital of Brisbane. Originally named Barambah Station, it has been called Cherbourg since 1932 (Hegarty 2000: 11). Cherbourg is the birthplace of two of the boys in this case, and the home of many members of their extended families. The legislation controlling the movements and lives of Aboriginal people on settlements and reserves throughout Australia was not repealed until the mid-late twentieth century, with Queensland being the last state to do so in 1984 (Rowse 2005). Thus, many adults of the generation of grandparents, and even parents, of the boys in this case still required written permission from a White manager to get married, and even to leave the Aboriginal reserve of Cherbourg, if only for a day, and they were not allowed to drink alcohol.

The colonial dispossession of Aboriginal people from their land, and the legacies of this dispossession are experiences shared with Indigenous people in many other first world countries. Australian Aborigines experience living conditions and indicators typical of people in third world countries. Thus, a recent government report (SCRGSP 2005: 1) found a "large gap between Indigenous people and the rest of the population" in all of the key indicators, including health, education, employment, home ownership, and criminal justice. For example, the average life expectancy for Indigenous Australians is 17 years shorter than for other Australians (ibid.: 5). The linguistic impact of colonisation has also been drastic. Of the approximately 250 distinct Indigenous languages spoken at the time of British invasion and colonisation in the late 18th century, most are no longer spoken on a daily basis (McConvell and Thieberger 2005: 78). There are still a number of communities in the remote northern and central areas of Australia where people speak one of the "traditional" languages as their first language.[2] Of particular concern for the participation in the legal system of speakers of these "traditional" languages are the complexities involved in the training and work of interpreters. These and related issues have been examined by Cooke 1995a, 1995b, 1995c, 1996, 1998, 2002, Edwards 2004, Goldflam 1995, Mildren 1997, 1999, and Walsh 1994. Two English-lexified creoles are also widely spoken in the remote north of Australia. Kriol is spoken predominantly in parts of the Northern Territory and Western Australia, and Torres Strait Creole is spoken predominantly in the Torres Strait Islands and on the northern tip of Queensland. But for the great majority of Aboriginal people, including those who live in southeast Queensland, the location of the Pinkenba case, their first language is Aboriginal English, which will be introduced in Section 4 below.

Arguably, the colonial situation extended nationally at least until 1967, when full rights as citizens were finally extended to all Indigenous Australians, and they began to be counted in the census (although for Aborigines on Queensland reserves the colonial situation did not end until 1984, as explained above). It may seem that Indigenous Australians are now in a postcolonial situation, given that they have citizenship and "formal equality" with other Australians (Cunneen 1996: 18). But the way in which government power, through the criminal justice system, systematically oppresses Indigenous Australians, makes the use of the term "neocolonial" particularly apt. This is a term widely used in political science writing to describe a postcolonial situation in which a former colonial power continues to dominate its former colonial subjects (Bealey 1999: 222). As Cunneen (2001: 232) puts it, the concept of neocolonialism "recognises the fact that the relationship between Indigenous people and the dominant society is still manifestly colonial, although the modality of colonial power may have changed with the formal emphasis on equality and citizenship". We will see in Chapter 3 that central to the ongoing inequality between the coloniser and colonised in Australia are continuities in policing.

Much has been written about Aboriginal Australians in the criminal justice system, with greatest attention focusing on the excessive rate at which Aboriginal people are taken into police custody and imprisoned. In Section 6 of Chapter 3, we will consider the Royal Commission into Aboriginal Deaths in Custody, which focused national attention on this. We will see that this wide-ranging investigation concluded that a host of historical, social, cultural and economic issues are involved. Despite considerable recognition being given to the Royal Commission's findings and its more than 300 recommendations (Johnston 1991a), the rate at which Aboriginal people are taken into police and prison custody remains alarmingly high. Recent statistics show that Australian Aborigines are twenty times more likely to come into contact with the criminal justice system than non-Aboriginal people (Findlay et al. 2005: 326). The overall national imprisonment rate for Indigenous people is 11 times the rate for non-Indigenous people, while for juveniles that figure goes up to 20 times (SCRGSP 2005: 3.79). This continuing high over-imprisonment rate is a clear indication that there are serious problems with the participation of Aboriginal people in the criminal justice system. The underlying realities are complex and multi-faceted: the Royal Commission's wide-ranging sociolegal analysis high-lighted the ongoing control of the state over Indigenous Australians, through such practices as selective policing and over-policing. Particularly disturbing, as we will see in Chapter 3, is the criminalisation of Aboriginal young people, to a large extent through public order offences, such as "disturbing the peace" (e.g. Cunneen 2001; Cunneen and White 2002). This criminalisation can be seen in part as the outcome of bitter asymmetrical struggles between Aboriginal communities and the police force.

Sociologists, political scientists and sociolegal scholars argue that the crimi-nal justice system continues to fail Aboriginal people in a number of ways, and that a wide range of factors are implicated in this failure. This book asks why, in the words of criminology professor Fay Gale and her colleagues, "Aboriginal people have no reason to believe in the capacity of our legal system to provide protection or justice, nor in the willingness or ability of the administrators of justice to act in an even-handed manner" (Gale et al. 1990: 1). Criminologists such as Gale and Cunneen have provided rich historical, sociological and crimi-nological evidence of the ways in which the criminal justice system particularly fails Aboriginal people, as we will see in Chapter 3. This book addresses the question put by Gale et al. in rather a different way, focusing on linguistic detail in one particular case. In doing this, it aims to add to the discussion of <u>why</u> the criminal justice system continues to fail in this way, by taking a detailed look at <u>how</u>. Thus, this book takes up the call by leading sociolegal and linguistic anthropology scholars Conley and O'Barr (1998) for the analysis of the actual mechanisms through which the legal system fails to deliver justice. We will see that talk matters, and the sociolinguistic analysis of talk can make a powerful contribution to our understanding of how neocolonial control continues to work.

This case is unusual in that the defendants are police officers, and the pros-ecution witnesses are Aboriginal young people – something of a reversal of the typical involvement of Aboriginal young people in the criminal justice system. But, in another way, this case is a version of a familiar story about police re-moval of Aboriginal young people. Issues involved in the removal of Aboriginal people, particularly children, for most of the twentieth century, have become salient in national discourse in Australia, particularly since the National Inquiry into the Separation of Aboriginal and Torres Strait Islander Children from their Families (NISATSIC 1997). There is now a growing recognition that the ubiq-uitous problems that affect Aboriginal communities, such as alcohol related violence and child abuse, have to be understood as part of the legacy of these "stolen generations". The internationally acclaimed feature film *Rabbit Proof Fence* (2002, directed by Phillip Noyce) presents some of the experiences of the stolen generations. This film may leave the impression that state intervention in the lives of Aboriginal people is a thing of the past. This book will show that this intervention continues, and it has become so naturalised that even the legal process legitimises it. And another recent Australian feature film presents some of the earlier colonial experiences of Aboriginal people when they were being chased off their traditional lands, as the invaders took over, namely *The Tracker* (2002, directed by Rolf DeHeer). *Rabbit Proof Fence* and *The Tracker* show some of the forces which legitimised the police removal of Aboriginal people in the earlier historical periods they depict – including blatant racism, colonial expansion, and the legal doctrine of *terra nullius*. Detailed sociolinguistic analysis of the courtroom talk in the Pinkenba case will show how these colonial removal practices are legitimised now, for example through the construction of Aboriginal people as a law and order problem, and through the construction of the use of "four-letter words" as an offence requiring police intervention, and even at times, imprisonment.

2.   The Pinkenba case: what happened

Let us now turn to what happened after the police drove the three Aboriginal boys to Pinkenba and abandoned them in the industrial wasteland there. After taking hours to find their way back to the Valley, they met a relative in a park and they told her what had happened. Her anger at their treatment by the police led to her contacting the Aboriginal Legal Services organisation. As a result, an investigation into the incident was conducted by the Criminal Justice Commission (CJC). This investigation found that the police did not have any lawful reason for taking the boys anywhere without their consent (CJC 1996: 2), and recommended that criminal charges be laid against the six police officers. Thus, the police officers were charged that they had unlawfully deprived each of the boys of *his personal liberty by carrying him away in a motor vehicle against his will*. It is important to know that the boys had not been charged with any offence that night, nor were they taken to any police station, and they were not in custody or under arrest. According to a statement from the police union to the media, the boys were "taken down to Pinkenba to reflect on their misdemeanours" (ABC 1996).

The first stage in the trial process was the committal hearing held in the Magistrate's Court in Brisbane in February 1995. The purpose of this hearing was for a magistrate to hear the prosecution case, in order to decide if there was sufficient evidence for a trial, which would be heard in the District Court with a judge and a 12 member jury. There was considerable public interest in this case, as it involved such serious allegations against the police officers, and the committal hearing was attended by a large contingent of reporters, as well as onlookers.

Under the British system of justice which forms the basis of the Australian system, the accused were "innocent until proven guilty beyond reasonable doubt", and they had no need to give any evidence. Apart from the three boys, there was brief evidence from only two people. The examination-in-chief of the CJC investigator who had interviewed the boys lasted about one minute, and consisted of eight questions about two minor corrections to her statement. Her cross-examination lasted twenty minutes, and was mainly about three instances of the use by one of the boys of a specific swear word in her interview with him (to be discusssed in Section 4 of Chapter 6). After the boys' evidence was concluded she had two minutes of re-cross-examination and one minute of re-examination. There was also nine minutes evidence from a surveillance video monitor operator about the technology involved in the Valley Mall, where the police approached the boys. But most of the four day hearing consisted of evidence from the three boys, which included lengthy cross-examination by each of the two counsel who represented three of the police officers. The case centred on the issue of whether or not the boys had travelled in the police cars against their will: no doubt was ever raised that they were approached and told to get in the police cars, and that they were taken to the industrial wasteland and abandoned there. The defence case was that the boys *gave up their liberty* and that *there's no offence of allowing a person to give up his liberty*,[3] and therefore that *the deprivation of liberty was not unlawful* (as quoted by the magistrate in his decision, 24 Feb 1995).

3.   Introducing the boys and their Aboriginality

The three boys, who will be referred to with the pseudonyms David Pender, Albert Carter and Barry Coley were aged 12, 13 and 14 years respectively when the incident took place in May 1994. At the time of their evidence in the committal hearing, which forms the focus of this book, they were 13, 13 and 15 years old respectively.[4] The boys had grown up in extended Aboriginal families in southern Queensland. Two of them had spent most of their lives in Cherbourg, the rural Aboriginal community 250 kilometres northwest of Brisbane, which was the first Aboriginal settlement in Queensland (see Section 1 above, and Section 1.2 of Chapter 3). The oldest of the three boys had spent most of his time in Brisbane, having been born in a rural town about 750 kilometres west of Brisbane. At the time of the alleged abduction they were not regularly attending school, and they could be described as "part-time street kids". That is, although they were in the habit of staying with different relatives in Brisbane and Cherbourg, at times they stayed in the city or Valley, sleeping in disused buildings, and meeting friends in parks and pin-ball parlours. At other times, they stayed in a youth refuge. Each of the boys had a criminal record, which included such offences as "unlawful use of motor vehicle", "break enter and steal" and "destruction of property" (smashing street lights). The oldest of the boys, Barry, was in the Brisbane juvenile detention facility at the time of the hearing, as a result of a street robbery of a young woman in which he had participated, which had occurred several months after the Pinkenba event.

Based on my two days of interviews with, and observations of the boys, in early June 1994 (to be explained in Section 6 below), I formed the opinion that the boys' communication styles were typical of many young Aboriginal people in cities and towns in southeast Queensland. Being raised in Aboriginal families and communities, most of their interaction with non-Aboriginal society was in schools, where they had not been regular or successful participants.

It is important to the understanding of this case to set out some relevant aspects of contemporary Aboriginal social and cultural life in southeast Queensland. In doing so, I am mindful of the danger of essentialisation. It is not my intention to present Aboriginal society and culture as homogeneous, static or reified. It is now widely recognised in sociolinguistic research that "participants' identities are fundamentally multi-faceted" (Sarangi 1994: 416), and that we need a "non-essentialist and action-oriented perspective" on "culture" which "enables analysts interested in intercultural miscommunication to take on board the complexities related to the uses and functions of 'culture' in contemporary societies" (see also Shea 1994; Kubota 1999). Interactional sociolinguistics, which is an important part of my approach, is less at risk of overgeneralising and stereotyping than other approaches because of its focus on interactions between individuals (see Scollon and Scollon 1995: 154–163).

There are many ways of being Aboriginal, and there is much that is shared between Aboriginal and non-Aboriginal people of the same socioeconomic class and regional identity, for example. But, Keen's (1988: 10) finding almost two decades ago is still pertinent today, in my view. He found that there is "a great variety in Aboriginal styles of life, but the gulf between these and the social life of other Australians is even greater".

One of the main difficulties in describing aspects of contemporary Aboriginal social and cultural life in southeast Queensland is that there is little published research on this topic. In the last two decades there has been no substantive ethnographic account of Aboriginal societies in Southeast Queensland, or indeed of any Aboriginal society in the non-traditionally-oriented southern and eastern areas of Australia (but see Malin 1997; Malin et al. 1996). This does not mean however, that we can ignore cultural beliefs and practices of Aboriginal society in southeast Queensland in this book. And nor should we, given the central relevance of the Aboriginal identity of the boys to the Pinkenba case.

The ethnographic observations below, and in various places throughout the book, are based on several sources. Following my initial ethnographic fieldwork in an extended Aboriginal family in southeast Queensland over a three-year period in the early 1980s (Eades 1983), I have continued observations and involvements with Aboriginal people from that area, in varying capacities. These include enduring personal friendships, specific research related to individual legal cases, and wide-ranging reading of accounts of the lives, views, expectations, and experiences of Aboriginal people from that area in diverse print media, such as newspapers, newsletters and biographies (e.g. Bell 1997; Hegarty 2000, 2003; Huggins and Huggins 1994). And given the many continuities in Aboriginal culture around Australia (Keen 1988), observations and reading about Aboriginal people in other localities can also help in understanding contemporary Aboriginal social and cultural life in Brisbane. Where I cite research from other parts of Australia (e.g. Malin 1997) or dated research from southeast Queensland (e.g. Eckermann 1977; Koepping 1977), I do so only to provide some additional support for my observations in contemporary southeast Queensland, and not in the absence of such observations.

As in many other Australian cities and towns, Aboriginal people in southeast Queensland live in a variety of localities and types of housing. In the cities, most do not live in discrete communities, but they are mainly clustered in poorer neighbourhoods. In Brisbane, the highest density of Aboriginal population live in the southern outer suburbs (Taylor 2005: 73–74), which include Woodridge and Riverview, two of the suburbs where David had been staying with relatives before the Pinkenba event. Houses are often overcrowded by non-Aboriginal standards, and this can probably be attributed both to financial necessity and to preference, as people fulfil reciprocal obligations to relatives, and enjoy their support (see Barwick 1988: 28).

Aboriginal people in southeast Queensland today belong to overlapping kin-based networks in which they typically share residential and travel arrangements, as well as social activities, personal loyalties, responsibilities and rights. Barwick's (1974: 154) summary of Aboriginal identity three decades ago is still pertinent: "To be Aboriginal is to be born to, to belong to, to be loyal to a family". Some twenty years later, *The Encyclopedia of Aboriginal Australia* (Howie-Willis 1994b: 356), talks of family as "an essential factor in defining Aboriginality" (see also Peterson et al. 2005: 90). When people talk about being Aboriginal, they invariably talk about Aboriginal family relationships. Family involves a wide network of people, many of whom are related only distantly in non-Aboriginal terms.

Aboriginal people place a high priority on visiting family and spending time with a wide range of relatives, as well as widely sharing money and goods within this kin network. It is common for people to move between relatives in different towns. This "high rate of mobility" can also involve other factors, such as seeking employment, housing or access to health care (Taylor 2005: 75). Taking care of children is generally seen as the responsibility of a wider range of kin than within the nuclear family. It is common for children to be in the care of an aunt, or uncle, or grandparent, or older sibling, for example (see Keen 1988: 12–13). It is also common for children to move between different relatives. Within Aboriginal societies, such movement of children is frequently seen as responsible child-rearing, which enables children to build relationships within the wider family. Further, the movement of children between relatives can be quite dynamic and flexible, responding to a variety of contingencies. This is readily criticised, for example by teachers and welfare workers, as deficient parenting, and as denying children "security" and "stability", which are typically defined in middle-class Anglo terms.[5]

Several researchers have written about Aboriginal child rearing practices in the last three decades. Barwick (1974, 1988) worked with urban and rural families in Victoria, Eckermann (1977) with urban families in southeast Queensland, Hamilton (1981) with traditionally-oriented families in remote northern Arnhem Land in the Northern Territory, and more recently Malin et al. (1996, 1997) with urban families in Adelaide, the capital of South Australia. There are many similarities in the findings of all of this research, and they resonate with my observation of contemporary practices in urban and rural Queensland (and New South Wales). Malin's (1997: 142–143) summary of the home socialisation of Adelaide Aboriginal children is consistent with the findings in other parts of Australia, and is pertinent to the situation in Brisbane and southeast Queensland:

> In sum, the important aspects of child-rearing in the Aboriginal families of this study included encouraging autonomy by expecting that children would be self-reliant, able to make decisions for themselves regarding their basic needs, be naturally observant, practically competent, and prepared to seek help and attention from their peers as much as from adults ... To balance this individual independence, the parents encouraged their childen to be affiliative – that is, to be affectionate and nurturant with those younger than themselves, to maintain an awareness of the whereabouts of everyone, to help those needing it and to trust that their peers will be similarly dependable.

As Malin points out, there are significant differences between these expectations and the resulting practices on the one hand, and those of non-Aboriginal families on the other, where autonomy and self-reliance of children is not as highly valued or supported.

4. Aboriginal English in southeast Queensland

An important part of Aboriginal identity throughout much of Australia is found in the Aboriginal ways in which people speak English, known collectively as "Aboriginal English" (also AE). Nationwide, there is considerable variation in the dialectal varieties of Aboriginal English, with the "heaviest" (or furthest from Standard English, hereafter SE) varieties being spoken most in more remote areas, and the "lightest" (or closest to SE) being spoken most in urban and metropolitan areas. Aboriginal English has "a complex history of multiple origins" (Malcolm and Kaldor 1991: 68) including depidginisation in some areas, as well as the Aboriginalisation of English, and possibly decreolisation in some remote areas.

My work over two decades, to be introduced in Section 1.2 of Chapter 2, has highlighted the importance of including pragmatic features in defining language varieties. Because even where there is considerable overlap between SE and AE, and grammatical and phonological differences between them are not great, there can be significant pragmatic differences, which have implications for intercultural communication (e.g. Eades 1984, 1988, 1991, 1993). There may well also be semantic differences, following recent work on Aboriginal English in Western Australian, which shows the role of Aboriginal cultural schemas in the semantic system of the English lexicon (e.g. Malcolm and Sharifian 2002; Sharifian 2005).

It is the pragmatic features of AE which are most relevant to the Pinkenba case, as we will see. For example, much information seeking in Aboriginal interactions is carried out indirectly, avoiding direct questions. Important personal information is often sought in a reciprocal manner, where a person may give some information or hint at certain matters, as a kind of unspoken invitation to the interlocutor to provide information. Further, as we will see in Chapter 4, silence is positively valued in Aboriginal conversations, so that its use is not generally considered to be an indication of a failure of communication. While most of my research and applied work has been carried out in southeast Queensland, there is reason to believe that there is much that is shared between AE varieties around Australia (see, for example, Cooke 1996; Hiley 1996; Lavery 1992; Malcolm 1994; Malcolm et al. 1999; Mildren 1999).

I have written in a number of places about the importance for the legal system of significant differences between AE and SE in the role of questions in information-seeking (e.g. Eades 1992, 1994a, 1996a, 2003b). There can be no denying that questions are central to the legal system at all stages, and indeed to many other mainstream institutions, events and practices, including interviews, questionnaires and quizzes, as well as in many interpersonal relationships. On the other hand, much information-seeking in Aboriginal societies avoids direct questions. The significance of this contrast was underlined in a 10-part ABC television drama in 1994 titled *Heartland*. The series focused on Aboriginal and non-Aboriginal interactions in a fictional New South Wales coastal town, located about 500 kilometres south of Brisbane. The story centred around a legal case which shared many similarities with the Condren case, to be discussed in Section 1.1 of Chapter 2. The protagonist was an Aboriginal police liaison officer, played by internationally-acclaimed Ernie Dingo. His "love interest" was a local white woman, played by the not-yet-famous Cate Blanchett. The series included much perceptive material on Aboriginal social and cultural life and intercultural communication, partly through Blanchett's character's well-meaning attempts to become a part of Dingo's character's community. In one scene, Blanchett's character happily tells Dingo's character that she has heard that the local Aboriginal people have given her an Aboriginal name – *waadjin* – and she wants to know what it means. Dingo's character translates it for her as *little questioner*. Interestingly, any Aboriginal person watching the series would know that *waadjin* is a widely used Aboriginal English word, which simply means *white woman*.[6] But this meaning was, to my knowledge, never made available (for non-Aboriginal viewers) during the television series. Dingo's character's translation of the AE word for *white woman* as *little questioner* highlights the widespread Aboriginal complaint that *whites ask too many questions*. And this widespread complaint encapsulates a significant difference between Aboriginal and non-Aboriginal varieties of English, which is relevant to any Aboriginal involvement in the legal system.

Turning specifically to the use of English by the boys in the Pinkenba case, my observations of them in Aboriginal peer group interactions and in individual interviews (see below), as well as in the Pinkenba hearing, led me to conclude that they were speakers of a "light" variety of Aboriginal English. That is, much of their talk shared features with other varieties of Australian English. The following examples of AE grammar, pronunciation and lexicon come from the boys' talk during my observations, conversations and interviews with them some eight months prior to the Pinkenba hearing, as explained below in Section 6. The features mentioned in the discussion of Extract 1 can be found in general descriptions of AE (e.g. Malcolm and Kaldor 1991; Eades 1992; Malcolm et al. 1999).

Extract 1.   From conversations between David, Albert and Barry, June 1994

[telling me about a concert the boys had attended starring the famous African American rap artist Ice Cube]
a) *Das his autograph dere la- Ice Cube.*
'That's Ice Cube's autograph.'

[talking about people in Cherbourg]
b) *Dey all cheeky up dere.*
'All those people are wild.'

[identifying a worker]
c) *E name Jim.*
'His name's Jim.'

[asking me about my accommodation for the night we are planning to spend in Cherbourg]
d) *Where you stay up dere?*
'Where are you staying up there?'

All of these examples illustrate the widespread AE use of alveolar stops corresponding to SE interdental fricatives, e.g. in *das* (a), *dey* (b), and *dere* (a, b, d).
The AE word *dere* (seen in Examples (a), (b) and (d) is widely used both as a
location adverb (as with SE *there*), and with demonstrative function, translating
SE "that, those". The AE double subject construction is exemplified in Example (a). This example also illustrates an AE discourse marker, clause-final *la*
which functions like clause-final *eh* and question tags to involve the interlocutor
(possibly a contraction of English *look*). Examples (b) and (c) exemplify the
verbless equational/descriptive sentence structure, which is the most persistent
AE grammatical feature, found in even very light varieties of AE. Example (b)
also contains the word *cheeky* which typically means "wild", "dangerous" or
even "violent" in AE (Arthur 1996: 92), in contrast to its general Australian English meaning of "impudent" or "insolent". Example (c) illustrates the deletion
of word-initial *h*, as well as the expression of possession by the juxtaposition
of possessor with possessed. Example (d) illustrates the widespread AE question structure which involves no statement inversion or auxiliary insertion. The
example also shows the finite verb form functioning as a progressive.

Because these three boys speak such a "light" variety of Aboriginal English, which shares many features with other varieties of Australian English,
there would be unlikely to be major problems of communication in the areas
of phonology, morphosyntax and lexicosemantics. Further, they said so little in
their courtroom evidence, that it might seem that Aboriginal English is barely
relevant to this book. Indeed, there was very little distinctive AE in the linguistic
form of their answers in court, of which we will see many examples in Parts II
and III below. (And, as we will see in Section 8.1 of Chapter 6, at least 60%
of their answers in cross-examination were *yes*, *yeh*, *mm*, *no*, *nuh*, *I dunno* or
I don't know). This might lead to the erroneous conclusion that the boys' English is just like that of other speakers of Australian English. My observations,

conversations and interviews with them in May 1994 indicated that when given the chance to give more than minimal answers, whether in peer interaction or in an interview with a SE speaker, they used many features of linguistic form that are characteristic of AE. But, more relevant than the linguistic form of the boys' answers, was the fact that the boys had had little chance to develop bicultural competence, which is essential to successful participation in interviews, particularly in the legal system (see Eades 1992, 1994a). That is, we can assume that they were using Aboriginal ways of communicating which involve significant cultural differences from mainstream English, and which disadvantaged them in the interview situation, as we will see throughout Parts II and III. As I explained in radio interviews after the hearing, although these boys were "streetwise", and much was made of this in the media as well as in cross-examination, they were not "interview-wise". And, as we will see in Chapter 4, some of the most significant differences between "light" Aboriginal English and other varieties of Australian English are relevant to the minimal answers given by the boys to many of the cross-examination questions in this case.

5.   Child witnesses in an adult court

In Queensland and Victoria, anyone under the age of 17 is defined as a child in the criminal justice system, while in the rest of Australia, people retain legal status as a child for twelve months more (Cunneen and White 2002: 268). This means that if the boys in this case had been defendants, they would have been most likely to give their evidence in a Children's Court. At the time of the Pinkenba hearing, hearings in Children's Court were closed hearings, magistrates in these courts were generally trained and experienced to deal with children, and there were support services which recognised some of the needs of children. Where children admitted guilt or were found guilty, they could participate in a restorative justice process known as Youth Justice Conferencing. This was introduced into Queensland by the *Juvenile Justice Act 1992*, and modelled on restorative justice approaches developed in New Zealand and Canada, and used in other Australian jurisdictions. Youth Justice Conferencing includes the offender and the victim as well as their support people, in addition to a prosecutor or police officer. Like other restorative justice processes it emphasises the restoration of balance to individuals and the community, in contrast to the punitive and/or welfare approaches which typify approaches to juvenile justice (Cunneen and White 2002: 358–359).

But, as child victim-witnesses in the prosecution of adult defendants, the boys in the Pinkenba case had no choice but to appear in the regular adult court. They would have been eligible to be treated as "special witnesses" under Section 21A of the Queensland *Evidence Act 1977*. According to this section it should have been possible for them to give evidence-in-chief without being able to see the defendants, or in another room, or even by videotape. However, it seems that these provisions are rarely utilised (ABC 1999), and they would not have provided any protection from the cross-examination.

While most of the research on child witnesses has looked at issues directly concerned with child sexual abuse cases, and there has been a particular focus on quite young children, there are nevertheless some important findings from this area of research which need to be taken into account in the consideration of the 13- and 15-year-old witnesses in this case. The most comprehensive linguistic research is that of Walker (e.g. 1999) whose extensive analysis of a wide range of psycholinguistic and linguistic studies, including those which she conducted herself, led her to conclude (ibid.: 2) that even "very young children can tell us what they know if we ask them the right questions in the right way". While much of the research involved children of younger ages than the boys in the Pinkenba case, Walker (ibid.: 5) believes that "adolescents [aged roughly 11–18] are . . . in some ways at greater risk than young children of misjudgment" by adults. Some of the reasons which led to this conclusion include the findings that adolescents . . . :

    . . . Still have difficulty with complex negation . . .
    . . . Are likely to lose track of long, complex questions . . .
    . . . Are reluctant to ask for clarification of a question or acknowledge that they
        don't understand.

The complexity of cross-examination questions addressed to child victim-wit-nesses was the focus of an Australian study in the mid-1980s (Brennan and Brennan 1988; Brennan 1994, 1995). This study found a number of linguis-tic strategies which caused comprehension difficulties for child witnesses, in-cluding negative rhetorical questions, juxtaposition of topics, nominalisation and unclear anaphora. Part of their study involved an experiment which tested children's comprehension of questions through asking them to repeat questions selected from databases of courtroom questions. The study concluded that "chil-dren six to fifteen years of age fail to hear as sensible language around half of what is addressed to them during cross-examination" (Brennan 1995: 71).

The analysis of questions addressed to the child witnesses in the Pinkenba case will provide some examples in which the syntactic structure of questions raises concerns about possible comprehension difficulties. But perhaps the most disturbing implication for this case from research on child witnesses relates to suggestibility. As we will see in Section 1.2 of Chapter 4, a wide range of studies have found that it is easier to mislead children than adults. While this may not be a surprising finding, it appears to have been completely ignored in this hearing.

6.   My involvement in the Pinkenba case

At this point, it is important to introduce my involvement in the case specifically, and in issues concerning Aboriginal English in the legal process more generally. Following my ethnography of communication PhD research with an extended Aboriginal family in southeast Queensland (Eades 1983), my interest in Aboriginal English in the legal process began in the mid 1980s, when I gave expert linguistic evidence in the case of *R v Condren*. This linguistic evidence related to the allegedly fabricated confession of a speaker of Aboriginal English (Eades 1993, 1995a), and it will be briefly discussed in Section 1.1 of Chapter 2. My work on this case drew my attention to the widespread lack of understanding among legal professionals about the subtle ways in which Aboriginal ways of using English differ from mainstream English. This realisation, combined with growing legal concerns about better communication with Aboriginal people, led to the publication of my handbook for lawyers titled *Aboriginal English and the Law: Communicating with Aboriginal English Speaking Clients: A Handbook for Legal Practitioners* (Eades 1992). This lawyers' handbook, which was published by the Queensland Law Society, will be discussed in Section 1.2 of Chapter 2. It received considerable publicity, as did its relevance to a high-profile 1993 appeal case, that of Robyn Kina (see Eades 1996a, to be discussed in Section 7.2 of Chapter 3). Since the early 1990s I have taken up numerous invitations to present workshops and lectures to lawyers, magistrates and judges in several Australian states, on the topic of communicating with Aboriginal speakers of English in the legal process.

Because of this work, I was approached by Aboriginal Legal Services in Brisbane in May 1994 in relation to the three boys in the Pinkenba case. I was asked to provide a report about "aspects of [the boys'] language and communication patterns, together with [my] recommendations for maximising communication with these boys, should they be required to give evidence in relation to the incidents involved in their alleged abduction" (Eades 1994b: 1). In order to write this report I spent two days with the three boys at the beginning of June. Facilitated by an Aboriginal field officer from ALS, I was able to observe the boys in a number of casual conversations with their peers, as well as with field officers and other ALS staff, and to a limited extent with some Aboriginal adults. I also conducted a formal interview with each of the boys. My resulting nine-page report summarised aspects of their communication and language use, relating it to the lawyers' handbook (Eades 1992). I found each of the boys to be "lively, bright and highly communicative" (Eades 1994b: 8). However, I found that "the language and communication skills which these boys use in their community are ... not the skills which are needed in formal legal interviews in police stations, lawyers' offices, or in giving evidence to an inquiry or a courtroom hearing" (ibid.: 9). My report made a number of specific recommendations including the following (ibid.: 6–7):

- avoid 'big words'
- ask questions with a simple structure, questioning only one proposition at a time
- wherever possible minimise the risk of gratuitous concurrence, by inviting the boys to give their own details. In particular avoid long strings of Yes-No questions (that is questions which can logically be answered with *yes* or *no*).

It is unclear how this report was used, but it seems to have assisted the CJC in its initial investigation of the boys' complaint. After the committal hearing began in February 1995, I attended the second day of the hearing (Tuesday 21 February) and was amazed by the way in which the cross-examination of the witnesses was proceeding. It appeared that significant differences between Aboriginal and non-Aboriginal ways of using English were being exploited to distort the boys' testimony, and to show them as untrustworthy and unreliable witnesses. During a morning adjournment I was introduced to the prosecutor who asked me to assist, by studying all of the boys' evidence in this hearing (from the official transcript) and by writing a report in the form of a statement. He also asked me to be ready to appear as an expert witness two days later (on Thursday 23 February).

My ten-page report, which analysed cultural and linguistic issues involved in the cross-examination of the boys, was completed and left for the prosecutor early on the morning of 23 February. When I arrived at the court that afternoon, I was informed that the Director of Public Prosecutions had decided that I should not be called as an expert witness, and that my statement was not to be used. Thus, in coming to his conclusions (delivered on Friday 24 February) about the reliability and credibility of these Aboriginal witnesses, the magistrate was, in my view, not informed about important cultural and linguistic issues which needed to be understood in order to accurately interpret the boys' answers to many of the questions in cross-examination. However, the lawyers' handbook (Eades 1992, referred to above) had been clearly visible on the Bar table during the hearing. I was disturbed, as were a number of legal professionals present at the hearing, with the realisation that it had been used by the DCs to facilitate less effective communication with the Aboriginal boys, contrary to its intended purpose (see Section 1.2 of Chapter 2 below, and Eades 2004a, 2004b).

My involvement with the case did not stop with my report. The following week (on Monday 27 February), I issued a press release, calling for a public inquiry into the case, and calling the cross-examination of the boys of "an obscene travesty of justice". This press release was reported in a number of newspapers, and my comments were rejected by one of the two defence counsel as "plain lies". This resulted in another press release from me (on Tuesday 28 February) titled "Time for the public to know what was happening in the trial".[7]

At this time (on Monday 27 February) I was also interviewed on national radio (on the morning current affairs Australian Broadcasting Commission – hereafter ABC – program *AM*) and Queensland state television (on the evening current affairs ABC program *7.30 Report*, which was later televised in other states). I also did a number of other regional radio news interviews in that week, and appeared in a television documentary the following year about Queensland police and Aboriginal people which featured the Pinkenba case (ABC 1996). In the week after the Pinkenba hearing, I pursued my calls for an inquiry into the case in a telephone call with the Attorney-General, who had, some three years earlier, launched the lawyers' handbook, with considerable enthusiasm, saying it was "an important work", which would be made available to all state government legal officers (Gagliardi 1992). There was no public inquiry, but the Criminal Justice Commission undertook an extensive research project on Aboriginal witnesses in Queensland's criminal courts (CJC 1996), which will be discussed in Section 6 of Chapter 10.

7. Data sources and transcription conventions

My analysis of this hearing is based on a number of data sources, namely:

–   the official transcript of the three days of evidence, totalling 197 pages,
–   copies of the official tape-recordings of almost the whole hearing (including the magistrate's decision),
–   my transcript of these tape-recordings,
–   notes from my direct observations of most of the three days of evidence,
–   notes from my informal discussions throughout the hearing with the prosecutor, other lawyers following the case, and members of the Aboriginal community,
–   official transcripts of pre-trial interviews of the boys by investigating officers,
–   newspaper cuttings, press releases, national radio and television interviews about the case,

– notes from my two days of participant observation with the three boys in the interim between the Pinkenba event and the hearing (discussed in Section 6 above).

Several stylistic features of my discussion of the cross-examination (Parts II, III and IV of the book) need to be explained:

– Although the plural form of the noun phrase *defence counsel* is also *defence counsel* with no overt plural marking, when using the abbreviated form DC, I use the plural form DCs, which is consistent with spoken convention, and which can help to reduce any confusion.

– In the microanalysis of the Pinkenba hearing, (Chapters 4–10), I use the historic present tense. This is consistent with other sociolinguistic publications on courtroom hearings (e.g. Ehrlich 2001; Matoesian 1993, 2001), and it parallels the conventional academic use of present tense to refer to contemporary published material, as for example in "Ehrlich (2001) argues that . . . ".

– To avoid cumbersome expression, some of the discussion in Parts II and III uses the form *Ye#* to refer generically to the answers *yeh*, *yes*, or *mm*, and the form *No#* to refer generically to the answers *no* or *nuh*.

– In Chapters 4–10, all numeric specification of times and numbers of occurrences uses digits, rather than words (e.g. 4 times, rather than four times, 12 minutes, rather than twelve minutes).

– Italics are used throughout the book when quoting any utterance from a spoken source, primarily the courtroom hearing, but also radio and television broadcasts.

– All page numbers given in the form "p1, p23" etc refer to the official transcript of the Pinkenba hearing.

Data extracts throughout the book are my transcriptions from audiotapes. Where my discussion quotes only one short turn (or a short part of one turn), this quote is generally given in the text in italics, and thus it does not appear as a numbered extract. Where I quote one long turn or two or more turns, this quotation generally appears as a numbered extract. Where these extracts are from the cross-examination (i.e. the majority of the extracts), the extract heading gives the following information:

Extract number: Interviewing DC (DC1 or DC2) to named boy (David, Albert or Barry), Day of hearing (1, 2, or 3), corresponding page of official transcript.

I use the following standard transcription conventions for data transcribed from audiotapes:

- <u>underlining</u> indicates emphatic stress
- SMALL CAPITALS indicate raised volume
- ° before and after an utterance indicates that it is spoken in a very low volume
- = indicates latched utterances, i.e. no pause between the end of one utterance and the start of the next
- [indicates talk overlapping with that of another speaker, marked at the point in each utterance where overlap begins
- - indicates a pause within a turn of less than 0.5 of a second
- a number in parentheses indicates the length of a pause in seconds e.g. (3.2)
- parentheses around a word or phrase indicates transcriber doubt
- (xxxxxx) indicates an inaudible utterance
- double parentheses are used to enclose transcriber's description of paralinguistic or other activity by the speaker, e.g. ((laughs))
- DC = defence counsel
- M = magistrate
- Pros = prosecutor
- **Bold** type indicates particular segments of the transcript being highlighted in my analysis. It is used only in extracts where one particular utterance pertains to the discussion more than the rest of the utterances in that extract, as for example in the extracts in Section 2.2 of Chapter 4. In many of the extracts, there are several utterances which pertain to the discussion, and it is considered unhelpful to use bold type (e.g. in Chapters 7–9).
- Regular English spelling is used throughout, except for a few places where a word or phrase is pronounced in a clearly abbreviated or nonstandard way (e.g. in a number of DC turns the first utterance is *Nd*, a clearly abbreviated form of *and*).
- Personal names (which are pseudonyms) are mainly used for the three witnesses, as they are the only personal names that occur with any frequency in the data. Any other personal names in the transcript extracts are also pseudonyms. Identifying locality names have been changed, with the exception of major towns and cities.

All transcription is necessarily selective and involves some degree of transcriber discretion. The following three points indicate the main points on which I have exercised this discretion:

- DC1 has a very loud voice, whereas DC2's is much quieter. All of the boys speak more quietly, especially Albert who is very quiet in a number of his answers. There is thus a continuum in the transcript between the almost whispered utterances which are indicated between two ° symbols, and the shouted utterances indicated by small capitals.

- More than 50% of the boys' answers consist of one of the single words of either apparent agreement or disagreement. I transcribe these as either *yeh*, *yes*, or *mm*, and *nuh* or *no* respectively. Differences in the length of the vowel in the *yeh* and *nuh* answers are not recorded, as this level of phonetic detail would make the analysis too complex. The official transcript distinguishes between *Yes*, *Yeh*, *Yeah*, *Yep*, *Mm* and *Mmm*, and between *No* and *Nope*. I have not been able to discern with certainty the final vowel in those answers officially transcribed as *Yep* and *Nope*. Many of the monosyllabic answers of apparent agreement/disagreement appear to have the phonetic form of consonant followed by short vowel. The choice in the official transcript to represent such answers in the form "Yep" and "Nope" is undoubtedly related to the absence in written English of the forms *Ye* and *Nu* to represent such answers. But it is arguably also tied to the successful construction of the boys as delinquents, an issue to be dealt with in Part III. In order to avoid adopting this construction, I use the forms *Yeh* and *Nuh* in my transcription. But it should be noted that distinguishing between a *No* answer and a *Nuh* answer is often somewhat impressionistic. Similarly there is a continuum between the answers in which the three syllables of *I don't know* are heard, and those in which the middle syllable receives such weak stress as to be almost elided, which I have transcribed as *I dunno*. Thus, distinguishing between an answer of *I don't know* and *I dunno* can on occasion be impressionistic.

- Extracts and quotations from the (monologic) closing addresses and magistrate's decision do not indicate the length of pauses (they are mostly in Chapter 10).

8.   Outline of the book

The aim of this book is to contribute to the understanding of how neocolonialism works, and in particular, how the criminal justice system legitimises neocolonial control over Aboriginal people, by focusing on the cross-examination in the Pinkenba hearing. Thus, a central argument of this book is that the details of courtroom talk matter, and the two central Parts of the book (Chapters 4–9 in Parts II and III) involve close analysis of many specific extracts of courtroom interaction in the Pinkenba hearing.

Before this sociolinguistic microanalysis, Chapters 2 and 3 (which make up the rest of the first Part of the book) provide an examination of issues which are essential to understanding the social consequences of this courtroom talk. Chapter 2 sets the theoretical scene, concentrating on two main areas of sociolinguistic research: studies of Aboriginal English in the legal system, and studies of courtroom talk outside Australia. An evaluation of this work leads to the outline of the critical sociolinguistics approach to be taken in this book. Central to this approach is the interrelatedness of micro-events – such as specific encounters between police and Aboriginal people, and specific courtroom interactions, on the one hand – and macro-structures – such as neocolonial control, on the other. Thus, before we examine the Pinkenba hearing, we need some analysis of the societal and institutional struggle within which it is situated. In the investigation of this struggle, Chapter 3 examines the history of the relationship between Aboriginal people and the police in Queensland from the beginning of British settlement until the Pinkenba event.

Parts II and III provide the detailed microanalysis of the verbal interaction in the Pinkenba cross-examination. Part II focuses on the most important linguistic mechanisms used to address the central issue in the hearing: whether the boys had gone willingly in the police cars to Pinkenba. The title for this Part II – "Evidence given in unequivocal terms?" – queries a conclusion from the judge who reviewed the magistrate's decision in this case – that the boys' evidence was "given in unequivocal terms". Chapter 4 looks specifically at key features of Aboriginal English pragmatics, while Chapter 5 examines lexical strategies used to distort the boys' words.

In Part III, we turn to the linguistic mechanisms, which – in addition to those already examined in Part II – were used to construct the identities of the boys, not as victims of police abuse, but as lying criminals, who are a danger on the streets of Brisbane. This identity work by the two defence counsel is central to the underlying issue in the case: whether it is acceptable for police officers to remove Aboriginal young people as they did in the Pinkenba event. It is here that we see the mechanisms which define Aboriginal people as criminals, who are the legitimate subject of removal by police, even when they have not committed any offence. After introducing and exemplifying the main mechanisms in Chapter 6, the following three chapters (7–9) work through the cross-examination of each of the boys, examining how these mechanisms were used to construct their identities, and how each of them responded to this identity work.

Part IV comprises three concluding chapters. Chapter 10 shows how the case concluded, specifically how the evidence given by the boys in cross-examination was construed in the closing addresses, interpreted in the magistrate's decision and the judicial review of this decision, and reported in the media. While the judicial decision to dismiss the charges against the police officers reveals the "success" of the linguistic mechanisms used in the cross-examination, that is *not the end of the matter*: we also see the ways in which Aboriginal Legal Services and the Criminal Justice System continued the struggle against this legitimisation of the police actions in the Pinkenba event.

Chapter 11 considers a number of developments in the Queensland criminal justice system in the decade since the Pinkenba hearing legitimised police control over Aboriginal people. These include changes to the rules of evidence, as well as in some aspects of the policing and sentencing of Aboriginal people. But we will see that police abuse of Aboriginal Queenslanders still occurs. And the struggle between Aboriginal people and the police is not limited to the state of Queensland, or indeed to Australia.

The final chapter brings together the arguments and analysis from the book to examine the power of courtroom talk in the neocolonial control exercised by the police over Aboriginal people. It starts with an examination of the naturalising and punitive effects of courtroom talk. Then it moves to an examination of the language ideologies which underlie the linguistic mechanisms allowed by the rules of evidence in the naturalisation and punishment seen in this case. It is these language ideologies, or assumptions about how language works, which are at the heart of how the extreme language practices seen in the Pinkenba hearing were not only allowed to be used, but were taken as the proper functioning of the justice system. The social consequences of this courtroom talk are disturbing. The critical sociolinguistic analysis in this book leads me to question whether the criminal justice system can ever deliver justice to Aboriginal people in cases of police abuse. But more than this, it leads me to also question whether we can expect an end to neocolonialism without far-reaching changes to the rules of courtroom evidence.

9. Situating this book

This book is situated in the growing field of language and the law (also referred to as "forensic linguistics" in the broader use of this term,[8] see Gibbons 2003). With its focus on the sociolinguistic investigation of courtroom talk, paying particular attention to cross-examination, the book takes its place in a tradition of more than three decades, which will be introduced in Section 2 of Chapter 2. But while much of this work has restricted the analysis of language use to the context of the courtroom, this book takes a critical sociolinguistics approach, which assumes that an examination of courtroom talk requires an examination of its sociopolitical contexts (to be introduced in Section 3 of Chapter 2).

Thus, Chapter 3 analyses the historical, cultural and political contexts in which the Pinkenba courtroom hearing is located. The microanalysis of this hearing in Chapters 4–9 then integrates the study of linguistic strategies in the cross-examination with understandings informed by the sociopolitical analysis. This integrated approach enables the investigation of such issues as why lawyers use certain linguistic strategies and ask certain questions and why witnesses answer the way they do, as well as the social consequences of these interactions.

At the same time, this book addresses a central issue in sociolegal studies, namely the failure of the legal system to deliver justice. Based on the assumption that the details of talk matter, courtroom talk is analysed in terms of its reciprocal relationship with structural inequality. While important work using this approach has examined gender relations (e.g. Matoesian 1993; Ehrlich 2001), this is the first major study of language use in legal contexts to focus on ethnic relations, namely between Aboriginal and non-Aboriginal Australians. It uncovers some of the actual mechanisms which reproduce the oppression of this Indigenous minority in a first world country, and should thus also be relevant to contemporary studies of race/ethnic relations.

This study also shows the contribution that sociolinguistics can make to social theory: specifically, the analysis of courtroom language use is shown to be integral to the explanation of how and why Australian Aboriginal people continue to be subjected to neocolonial domination. Detailed investigation of linguistic mechanisms can reveal precise moments in which the oppressive control of the criminal justice system is both perpetrated on specific Aboriginal people, and legitimised as general practice.

While the Pinkenba case is an extreme one, it highlights the role of language in the delivery of justice, bringing to the surface the extremes of language practices which are permitted under rules of evidence in the adversarial legal system. In examining not just how people talk in court, but also the underlying assumptions about how language works, this book challenges accepted beliefs about the legal process, e.g. the belief that repeated questioning enables the truth to emerge. It is argued that such beliefs are integral to such abuses of justice as that which took place in the Pinkenba case. It is my hope that legal scholars, students and professionals will engage with the arguments developed here, and that such engagement will impact future reform to the rules of evidence.

Note to readers without a background in sociolinguistics: Some readers may not have the patience required to follow the detailed microanalysis in Parts II and III of this book. While my argument is that the details matter, I would advise readers without a background in sociolinguistics to concentrate on Chapters 1 and 3, the conclusions in Chapters 4–9, and most of the sections in Chapters 10–12.

Chapter 2
Setting the theoretical scene[9]

Chapter 1 has outlined the aim of this book: to analyse how courtroom language works in the ongoing state control of Australian Aboriginal people through the criminal justice system, using in-depth analysis of the cross-examination of three Aboriginal boys in the Pinkenba case. My argument is that the police removal of Aboriginal boys in this case was not an isolated act of police abusing their authority and power to frighten these three boys. Rather, it was part of a struggle between Aboriginal people and the state that has been going on for nearly two centuries. In this struggle the legitimisation of the police actions was crucial, and this was achieved through the judicial decisions which resulted from the evaluation of what was said in the courtroom. Thus the sociolinguistic spotlight must shine on courtroom talk and resulting decisions to examine how the legal system facilitates the continuing control exercised by the state over the movements of Aboriginal people.

In this chapter, I first situate this study in relation to other studies of Aboriginal English in the legal process, and then in relation to other studies of language and power in the courtroom. Most earlier studies of Aboriginal speakers of varieties of English in the legal system have used interactional sociolinguistics, with its ethnographic orientation and influence from linguistic anthropology, while most earlier studies of language and power in the courtroom have used descriptive sociolinguistic analysis, sometimes including a variationist orientation. The impact of the critical turn in the social sciences has resulted in studies of courtroom talk which are not restricted to analysis of situated linguistic power, but which also analyse the talk in terms of social consequences for broader power relations. It is this work which has most impact on the analytical framework to be used in my analysis, which I will refer to as critical sociolinguistics, and which I will introduce in the last section of this chapter.

1.   Sociolinguistic studies of Aboriginal English in the legal system

1.1.   Expert evidence and fabricated confessions

The earliest analysis of Aboriginal English in the legal system concerned two criminal cases – separated by almost 30 years – in which linguistic evidence about the kind of English spoken by an Aboriginal man was part of the defence in his murder trial (see Eades 1995a, 1997, 2006 for details of these cases and the linguistic evidence presented in them). In both cases, the main evidence against the accused was his allegedly verbatim confession, produced in a typed record of an interview with police. Also, in both cases the accused told his lawyers that he did not commit the crime, or confess to it, but that he was forced into signing the typed record of interview. The linguistic evidence in both cases concluded that the allegedly verbatim "confession" could not have been an accurate transcription of exactly what the accused had said. There were too many glaring inconsistencies between the "confession" on the one hand, and the Aboriginal English speech patterns of the accused on the other, as found in other interviews with him, and as consistent with Aboriginal English generally. The linguistic evidence in the first of these two cases, that of Rupert Max Stuart in 1959, was provided by linguist and anthropologist T. G. H. Strehlow, and was not accepted by the courts or the subsequent Royal Commission. (This case has been dramatised in the 2002 feature film *Black and White*, directed by Craig Lahiff.) In the second case, that of Kelvin Condren in the mid-late 1980s, linguistic evidence, which was provided by this author, was ruled inadmissible by the highest court in Queensland (*R v Condren* 1987). But this ruling was overturned by the High Court, and the linguistic evidence was ultimately accepted. Elsewhere (Eades 1995a, 1997), I have written about judicial reactions to the linguistic evidence, highlighting the lack of understanding of dialectal variation and the social basis of language acquisition.

The Stuart and Condren cases focused attention on the way in which a linguistic analysis of differences between Aboriginal English and Standard Australian English can help to provide clues about the fabrication of the police confessions of Aboriginal people. While indirectly exposing fundamental abuses of power by police officers over Aboriginal suspects, and resulting miscarriages of justice, this work was not undertaken as part of any wider research project, but as specific linguistic expertise for each of the cases involved, from the perspective of descriptive linguistics and sociolinguistics. Fabricated confessions became a prominent issue in debates about the legal system in Australia in the 1980s, with widespread allegations that they were a regular feature of police practice in several Australian states. Indeed, fabricated confessions have been such a prominent feature of discourse surrounding the criminal justice system, that speakers of Australian English refer to such an occurrence with the single noun "verbal". The action of a police officer fabricating a confession is referred to with the single transitive verb "to verbal [someone]". The folk belief that verbals were a regular part of police practice was given credence, for the state of Queensland at least, by the evidence of senior police officers to the 1988 Fitzgerald Inquiry into Police Corruption in that state, as we will see in Section 5 of Chapter 3. Their evidence was that police regularly fabricated confessions for suspects whom they believed to be guilty (Fitzgerald 1989). But since the 1991 High Court ruling in *McKinney and Judge v The Queen*, it is now quite difficult for a confession to a serious crime to be admissible in an Australian court, unless it has been electronically recorded (see Eades 1997). Thus, this should have removed the opportunity for police to fabricate a confession.[10]

1.2. Interactional sociolinguistics and intercultural communication

My experience as an expert witness in Condren's case and another case in the mid 1980s which also involved an Aboriginal person, drew my attention to legal and judicial misconceptions about Aboriginal English. At the same time, some lawyers working with Aboriginal clients were expressing concerns about communication difficulties, which seemed related to some of my PhD findings about Aboriginal patterns of communication in southeast Queensland (Eades 1983). These lawyers' concerns, and my experiences as an expert witness, led to the focusing of research I had been doing on Aboriginal English (e.g. 1988, 1991) to its use within the legal system (e.g. 1994a). This work has been within the tradition of interactional sociolinguistics, strongly influenced by the work of John Gumperz. Gumperz' seminal work (e.g. 1982a, 1982b, 1992) makes a powerful case for the central role of interactional sociolinguistic analysis in addressing problems of intercultural communication. Thus, it was the subtle differences in communicative style which were seen as most relevant to miscommunication between Aboriginal and non-Aboriginal people in the legal process, encapsulated in the much quoted insight from Gumperz and Cook-Gumperz (1982: 13) that speakers "may have similar life styles, speak closely related dialects of the same language, and yet regularly fail to communicate".

In addressing this situation, Gumperz draws an important distinction between utterance meaning and speaker intent, between the structure of talk and the process by which interlocutors make meaning. In the analysis of speaker intent and situated interpretations, (similar to the notion of illocutionary force in pragmatic approaches), the interplay of shared sociocultural knowledge and contextualisation cues is important. As Gumperz (1992: 230) explains it, the term "contextualisation" refers to "speakers' and listeners' use of verbal and nonverbal signs [cues] to relate what is said at any one time and in any one place to knowledge acquired through past experience, in order to retrieve the presuppositions they must rely on to maintain conversational involvement and assess what is intended". Gumperz' approach draws on ethnography of communication, and Goffman's interaction analysis, with careful attention to what is actually said, as well as how it is said. Cultural norms, in the form of culturally specific presuppositions, play a central role in the analysis of communicative differences in the organisation and interpretation of talk. As Gumperz (2001b: 220) puts it: "A main purpose of [interactional sociolinguistics] is to show how diversity affects interpretation".

The influence of Gumperz' approach to understanding intercultural communication on work concerning Aboriginal English in the legal system can be seen in my earlier academic writing (e.g. Eades 1994a, 1996a, 2003a). Thus, as explained in Section 4 of Chapter 1, while "light" varieties of Aboriginal English often differ little from other varieties of Australian English in terms of phonology, grammar and word choice and meaning, it is in features of communicative style that key differences are found (e.g. Eades 1994a). Of particular relevance are the significant differences between Aboriginal English and Standard English in the role of questions in information seeking. Two of the most important features of Aboriginal English communicative style relate to cultural differences in the use and interpretation of silence, and in the tendency of Aboriginal people to freely answer *yes* in answer to questions, regardless of whether or not they agreed with the proposition being questioned. These features of Aboriginal English will be important to the Pinkenba case, and will be discussed in Chapter 4.

At the same time as writing for academic audiences, I accepted a number of invitations to present workshops and lectures to legal professionals in several states.[11] These language awareness workshops came at the time when the final and damning report of the Royal Commission into Aboriginal Deaths in Custody (Johnston 1991a, 1991b) focused national attention on the remarkable over-imprisonment of Aboriginal people (mentioned in Chapter 1, and to be discussed further in Chapter 3). The workshops were received with considerable enthusiasm, and a number of legal professionals raised questions about the extent to which legal ignorance about Aboriginal English might be a factor in the over-imprisonment rates. What role was being played by the failure of the legal system to recognise that Aboriginal communication patterns are significantly different from those of the legal process, and from mainstream Australian society generally? In the light of questions such as this, I responded with some enthusiasm to the suggestions of lawyers in the early 1990s that I write for the legal profession about Aboriginal English.

The resulting handbook for lawyers in Queensland (Eades 1992) had the general aim of providing legal professionals with some awareness and understanding about Aboriginal English which would facilitate more effective intercultural communication in the legal process. Published by the Queensland Law Society, the handbook is not a scholarly publication. But given its apparent role in the Pinkenba case (referred to in Section 6 of Chapter 1), and its connection to the sociolinguistic research, it is important to discuss it here. The handbook presents Aboriginal English in a general introductory sociolinguistic framework for understanding concepts such as language socialisation, dialect difference, communicative style, bicultural competence, cultural continuity and dialect continuum. It explains particular features of Aboriginal English pronunciation, grammar and vocabulary, and it highlights pragmatic features which are relevant to communication with speakers of this dialect in legal contexts, particularly in the courtroom. These features include ways of seeking substantial information, which avoid direct questions, as well as the use of silence, and the tendency to use gratuitous concurrence (that is freely saying *yes* to a question, regardless of belief of the truth or falsity of the proposition questioned, see Eades 2002). It was my hope that the handbook would "help lawyers communicate more effectively with Aboriginal English speaking clients" (Eades 1992: 1). An important aspect which addressed this goal was the provision of practical strategies "which can help accommodate relevant cultural differences in the legal system" (ibid.: 32), such as (ibid.: 46):

> Do not interpret silence as an Aboriginal speaker's admission of guilt or ignorance, or even as evidence of a communication breakdown. Remember that silence is often used positively by Aboriginal people to think about things and to get comfortable with the social situation.

The handbook comprises 97 pages plus references and contact details for Aboriginal organisations. The style combines short descriptive prose paragraphs, with conversational examples, bullet-pointed and boxed advice, and each chapter concludes with short numbered summary statements of the main points. The chapter titles indicate the material covered:

1. Aboriginal people in Queensland today;
2. Aboriginal English: the background;
3. Introducing the role of culture in cross-cultural communication: the legal interview;
4. Asking questions;
5. Understanding Aboriginal answers;
6. Aboriginal English pronunciation, grammar and vocabulary;
7. Specific legal issues relevant to Aboriginal English speakers;
8. Further issues.

A major theme of the handbook related to my belief that "Aboriginal people are seriously disadvantaged in those formal situations where success in an interview is crucial to an individual's rights and benefits" (ibid.: 30). I saw the handbook as one way to address Aboriginal disadvantage in the legal system and thus promote justice, by increasing awareness about language difference.

The lawyers' handbook was a similar initiative to the "language awareness" (LA) movement in schools, which began in the UK in the early 1980s in the contexts of English and foreign language education (Hawkins 1984). Moving away from deficit approaches to the teaching of Standard English, the LA approach advocates conscious attention to the structures and functions of language as an essential element in language education. The LA approach has also been advocated for teaching Standard English to speakers of creoles and minority dialects (e.g. Siegel 1999, 2006a). While LA is generally aimed at improving language and literacy education, the aim of the lawyers' handbook was to address the disadvantage of Aboriginal people in the legal process, by raising language awareness among legal professionals. In aiming to educate legal professionals, the handbook shares with LA approaches to language and literacy education the aim of raising awareness about the structures and functions of the language variety (in this case, Aboriginal English), in an atmosphere of respect and comparison of language varieties.

Critiques of the LA approach that have led to the development of critical language awareness (CLA) have pointed out that language awareness programs and materials generally "have not given sufficient attention to important social aspects of language, especially aspects of the relationship between language and power" (Fairclough 1992a: 1, see also Siegel 2006b). This criticism can also be levelled at the lawyers' handbook, whose focus on "more effective participation of Aboriginal people in the justice system" (Eades 1992: 33) arguably obscures important social aspects of language, especially in terms of power relationships. Nowhere can we see this more clearly than in a consideration of the Pinkenba case.

1.3. Limitations of the difference approach

In considering the sociolinguistic work on Aboriginal English in the legal process, a useful framework is found in Rampton's (2001a) discussion of general orientations to linguistic and cultural diversity and social inequality. Rampton's discussion categorises four main approaches, which he labels, "deficit", "difference", "domination", and "discourse".[12] The lawyers' handbook and related sociolinguistic research are situated within the "difference" approach, one which "emphasises the integrity and autonomy of the language and culture of subordinate groups, and the need for institutions to be hospitable to diversity" (Rampton 2001a: 261; see also Pennycook 2001). It is Gumperz' interactional sociolinguistic work, discussed above, which has been the major inspiration for sociolinguistic work within the difference approach, of which an excellent example is Roberts et al. (1992) on intercultural communication in gate-keeping encounters in post-industrial societies. Another well-known example is Tannen's analysis of male-female communication (e.g. 1994). This difference approach also underlies the language awareness movement, briefly introduced above.

A major criticism of the difference approach is that it ignores the "social inequality and power relations present in intercultural encounters" (Meeuwis and Sarangi 1994: 310; see also Ehrlich 2001: 122; Meeuwis 1994; Pennycook 2001: esp. Ch. 6; Rampton 2001a; Sarangi 1994; Shea 1994; Singh et al. 1988). The point made by Pennycook about the difference perspective in studies of language and gender can easily apply to the way in which this perspective has been used to account for Aboriginal English in the legal system: "The disadvantage [of this approach] was that it tended to remove the political dimension from the equation, focusing on difference as a result of differing socialization rather than unequal social power" (2001: 152–153; see also Freed 1992).

In publications on Aboriginal English in the legal system, there is generally no discussion, let alone analysis, of power relations. For example, the lawyers' handbook (Eades 1992) simply presents a descriptive account of features of Aboriginal English pragmatics, grammar, lexicon and pronunciation, highlighting possible areas of miscommunication for speakers of Standard English communicating with Aboriginal English speakers in legal contexts. In its focus on the seemingly neutral goal of "effective communication", the handbook avoids any discussion of domination, power relations or broader structural issues.

While the lawyers' handbook is not intended to be analysis, but rather to provide guidelines for intercultural communication in the legal process, scholarly writing about Aboriginal English and the law also typically ignores power relations in the involvement of Aboriginal people (e.g. Eades 1996a). If such issues are raised at all, they are only briefly mentioned. For example, Eades (1994a: 235) mentions "racism towards Aboriginal people by the community generally, and by people within the police force and judiciary specifically", as well as "the fundamental problem [of the legacy of the dispossession and colonisation of Aboriginal people]" (ibid., citing Bird 1987: 62). The philosophy is that such sociopolitical issues are separate from the sociolinguistic issues, and that, as articulated in the handbook, "Aboriginal people are disadvantaged [in the legal system] simply by the culturally different approach to information seeking" (Eades 1992: 40). The use of "simply" here was intended to indicate how easy it is to disadvantage Aboriginal people in the legal system by this cultural difference in communication, and was not intended to dismiss other ways in which this disadvantage is brought about (although it could be read in this way).

The few other works on Aboriginal English in the legal system have also been within the difference approach in sociolinguistics. Koch (1985, 1991) analyses miscommunication involving pronunciation, vocabulary and grammar, of the English used by speakers of Aboriginal English, Kriol and English as a second language, in land claim hearings in the Northern Territory. Walsh (1999) deals with similar language data, examining cultural and pragmatic features in addition to features of linguistic form, in his focus on the ways in which the English varieties in the land claim hearings are "interpreted" for the official transcript. Mildren (1999) includes Aboriginal English in his discussion of Aboriginal people in the criminal justice system, drawing on his extensive experience as a judge in the Northern Territory, as well as some of my work in relation to Aboriginal English.

But in focusing on differences, and ignoring the role of power in the way that Aboriginal people participate in the legal system, research on Aboriginal English in the legal system did not take into account the work of key Australian sociolegal scholars. As early as 1976, Eggleston's groundbreaking analysis of Aborigines in the criminal justice system pointed to political and structural inequality, as did ensuing work by sociolegal scholars such as Foley (1984), and Hazlehurst (1987). In 1991, a fairly comprehensive textbook titled *Aboriginal Legal Issues* put the point forcefully:

> Far from providing Indigenous Australians with a just and respected means of social control and protection, appropriate to their needs, the Australian criminal justice system remains an alien and discriminatory instrument of oppression, through which Indigenous people are harassed, subjected to unfair legal procedures, needlessly gaoled [jailed] and all too often die whilst in legal custody. (McRae et al. 1991: 238, also in 1997: 342)

These sociolegal scholars, who do not generally deal with language issues,[13] base their analysis of Aboriginal inequality in the legal process not on an ontology of difference, but on one in which power is central, and is situated within structural and historical contexts. This approach to social inequality is typical of Rampton's (2001a) third approach, the "domination" approach (or as it is generally called in language and gender studies, the "dominance" approach, see Freed 2003). In this approach, "the focus shifts to larger structures of *domination*, and the need is stressed for institutions to combat the institutional processes and ideologies that reproduce the oppression of subordinate groups" (Rampton 2001a: 261, emphasis in original). With its focus on structures and processes of domination at the societal level, this domination approach has not been found in the work of the small number of linguists working on Aboriginal language issues in the legal process (but it is found in the writing of Goldflam e.g. 1995, a practising lawyer, who worked for many years as a language professional in training Aboriginal interpreters).

While it is true that interactional sociolinguistics can be fairly accused of not taking power into account in its analyses, it is not true to say that it has ignored power. On the opening page of Gumperz' edited 1982 book, he and co-author Cook-Gumperz say that they are seeking "to develop interpretive sociolinguistic approaches to human interaction which account for the role that communicative phenomena play in the exercise of power and control and in the production and reproduction of social identity" (Gumperz and Cook-Gumperz 1982: 1). And more bluntly, Gumperz states that "ultimately redressing the balance of discrimination is a matter of power. But communication *is* power" (Gumperz et al. 1979: 47, emphasis in original). Further, as Blommaert et al. (2001: 8) rightly point out "equity issues have in fact been an enduring concern" in interactional sociolinguistics, as "difference and inequality are two sides of a coin" (Blommaert 2005: 69). Tannen (1994: 8) has argued that "societally determined power differences are an inextricable element of cultural difference theory and research". Arguing against the "unfortunate dichotomy" between the "cultural difference" approach and the "power" or "dominance" approach (ibid.: 9), she says that "the cultural difference framework provides a model for explaining how dominance can be created in face-to-face interaction" (ibid.: 10). But while the difference approach recognises that language plays an important role in inequality, interactional sociolinguistic studies typically do not <u>analyse</u> power relations as such: there is no analysis of societal power relations beyond the immediate contexts. Recently, Gumperz (2001a) has addressed domination more directly, incorporating the analysis of linguistic ideology in his approach to intercultural communication. But this still falls short of the approach to be advocated in this book, in that it deals with domination at the level of beliefs and attitudes, rather than actions, such as struggles over power.

2.   Courtroom talk: language and power

2.1.   Situated linguistic power

While research on Aboriginal English in the legal system has been carried out in the interactional sociolinguistic framework, focusing on intercultural communication, most sociolinguistic research on courtroom language outside Australia has focused on power and control. In fact, the earliest sociolinguistic studies of courtroom language foregrounded the importance of power. The Duke University Law and Language Program (hereafter the Duke study), co-directed by law professor John Conley and linguistic anthropologist William O'Barr, undertook a major empirical study of variations in witness speech style, and the impact of this variation on jury decision-making. While an important influence on this study was Robin Lakoff's 1975 book *Language and Woman's Place*, the Duke study found that the key variable influencing variation in witness speech style was not gender, but power. Indeed the two most widely-cited publications from this study (Conley et al. 1978 and O'Barr 1982) highlight the concept of power in their titles ("The power of language: presentational style in the courtroom" and *Linguistic Evidence: Language, Power and Strategy in the Courtroom*, respectively). Consistent with the dominant methodology in sociolinguistic research at the time, the Duke study focused on a variationist analysis which correlated different variables of speaking style (such as the use or absence of hedges) with social variables. In this study, the terms "powerful" and "powerless" speech receive little explanation, but O'Barr (1982: 70) says that "a powerful position may derive from either social standing in the larger society and/or status accorded by the court". Thus, a powerful witness is defined in terms of socio-economic status, and/or their situational status of being an expert witness. Similarly, Conley et al. (1978: 1380) say that the term "powerless" in relation to style of testimony is used "because the incidence of use of this style was more common among those with little social power".

While the emphasis in the Duke study was on courtroom talk by witnesses, starting in the 1980s a number of sociolinguists have focused on courtroom questions by lawyers. Again the issue of power has been central, with the major concern being how the structure of questions in examination-in-chief and cross-examination exercises power over witnesses. The imbalance between witness and lawyer in control over the content and form of talk has been discussed in terms of conduciveness, control, coerciveness or manipulation, and a number of scholars have produced hierarchical typologies of question form, based on the way in which the syntactic structure of the question serves to constrain the type of answer (e.g. Danet el al. 1980; Sandra Harris 1984; Woodbury 1984; Walker 1987). A significant concern of all of these studies is "control through language" (Danet et al. 1980: 223), specifically the way in which the lawyer questioning a witness in court "can impose his [sic] own interpretations on the evidence" (Woodbury 1984: 199).

Critics of these studies of question form in courtroom talk have shown that restricting courtroom linguistic analysis to syntactic structure ignores the ways in which such features as propositional content, context, intonation and the sequential placement of the question can intensify or mitigate the control exercised by questions (e.g. Dunstan 1980; Sandra Harris 1984; Lane 1990; Eades 2000). Further, Eades (2000) has pointed out the problematic assumption of isomorphism between linguistic form of questions and their function, as well as the narrow focus on question-answer pairs that ignores the wider linguistic and non-linguistic context. This study shows how lawyers' use of the question forms which had been analysed as most controlling is sometimes taken by witnesses as an open invitation for an explanation, and thus such question forms can actually function in the least controlling way.

A more fundamental problem with many of the sociolinguistic courtroom studies relates to their somewhat oversimplified notions of power and control. In these studies power has been seen in terms of one-sided situational domination of lawyers over witnesses (in Walker's 1987 terms, linguistic power). An exception is found in Harris (1989), which takes up the theorising of societal power from the work of Foucault and other social theorists, to which she brings much-needed empirical linguistic analysis. This analysis pertains to the issue of resistance to power and control, which Harris finds among defendants in a British magistrates' court, who exercise some situational power over those who question them, for example by asking "counter-questions" or by interrupting their questioner.

But Harris' study still shares with the other studies of power in the courtroom, the underlying assumption that asking questions amounts to interactional control. This assumption resonates with much Critical Discourse Analysis research in other contexts (see for example Verschueren's (2001: 77) critique of Fairclough 1992c). But, this assumption, that "questions ... are more powerful than answers", risks the problem of "reifying structure" in Matoesian's (2005b: 621) words, and in assuming isomorphism of question form and function in my terms (Eades 2000). However, unlike CDA work, studies of power in courtroom talk have not dealt with societal power structures. The focus has remained within the courtroom: it is situational inequality and imbalance that is at issue, not social inequality.

But not all sociolinguistic analysis of situational inequality in the courtroom has been restricted to the analysis of power through the asking of questions. Cotterill's (2003, 2004) analysis of the linguistic dimensions of power asymmetry in the courtroom considers a range of lexical, grammatical and discourse workings of situated conversational power, some of which will be helpful in the analysis in Chapter 5 below. And much closer to "home", Cooke's work uses sociolinguistic microanalysis to investigate miscommunication and "struggle[s] over linguistic power" (1995b: 109) as they affect Yolngu Aboriginal people in several different speech events in the legal system: including police interview, courtroom examination and cross-examination (e.g. 1995a, 1995b, 1995c, 1996, 1998, 2002). Cooke's focus is not on Aboriginal English, but on traditional Yolngu languages, as well as English learners' interlanguage, in the remote northern area of the Northern Territory. Cooke's work presents a convincing analysis of a range of linguistic ways in which power is exercised over Aboriginal witnesses in these legal contexts, particularly in situations where no interpreting assistance is provided. Examples of this "linguistic power" include the use of complex grammatical constructions, such as negative questions, which can easily trick witnesses who are not fluent speakers of English. In examining legal speech events where Yolngu do have access to interpreting assistance, Cooke demonstrates problems which relate to the limited role allowed to interpreters, and the misunderstandings among legal professionals about bilingualism and translation. His work, which makes it clear that "the imbalance against NESB [Non-English Speaking Background] Aboriginal people in the criminal justice system is grave" (1998: 336), has gone further than just exposing the ways in which language use can produce inequalities. It has been an influential force in legal and judicial circles and a strong element in convincing the Northern Territory government of the need to establish a permanent Aboriginal Interpreter Service, which began operating in 2000. This detailed and influential research focuses on struggles over linguistic power in the courtroom, and has led to strategies for "linguistic empowerment" (Cooke 1998: 253). Although it is situated within the broader political context, Cooke's analysis is of situated linguistic power.

Kress' (2001: 543) general critique of early sociolinguistic work is relevant to the courtroom studies discussed in this section: while they "created opportunities for quite fundamental critiques of society, such critiques were not developed". Situational linguistic inequality is described, but there is no exploration of the way in which language use figures in the workings of power at a broader societal level. Nevertheless, these studies have played an important role, in laying the groundwork for more nuanced sociolinguistic analyses of language and power in courtroom talk, which work with a more sophisticated and societally-located theory of power.

2.2.   The impact of the critical turn

The need for sociolinguistics to move to a more societally-located theory of power is part of Conley and O'Barr's (1998) call to both sociolinguists and sociolegal scholars to move beyond the shortcomings of their fields in isolation, and bring together insights and analyses from both fields. Conley and O'Barr argue that the interdisciplinary field of law and society (or sociolegal studies) has documented "the law's failure to deliver on its biggest promises, especially the equal treatment of all citizens", without explaining how this failure occurs (ibid.: 13). On the other hand, sociolinguistics has documented "a great deal about how social differences are encoded within language", but has generally failed to ask "whether language variation is truly consequential in social life" (ibid.: 12). But, they argue, bringing sociolinguistics and sociolegal scholarship together can uncover "how the power of law actually operates in everyday legal settings" (ibid.: 14).

To follow Conley and O'Barr's criticism of sociolinguistics, most courtroom studies to date have not addressed the question: what are the social consequences of power imbalances in the ways in which language is used, such as the ways in which questions are asked? Sociolinguists have generally limited their court-room analysis to the immediate context, seeing their expertise as limited to the analysis of face-to-face verbal interaction. Thus, in reviewing Cotterill's (2003) otherwise excellent analysis of language use in the O. J. Simpson trial, titled *Language and Power in Court*, I pointed out that the restriction of her focus to situated conversational power left many unanswered questions (Eades 2004c). For example, how did the contests over power in the Simpson courtroom connect to the broader issues of power and inequality surrounding African Americans and the criminal justice system, particularly as the Simpson trial occurred just a couple of years after the Rodney King case, which had involved officers from the same Los Angeles Police Department?[14]

To come back to Conley and O'Barr's (1998) general position, and to over-simplify it somewhat, their view is that sociolinguistic studies of language in the legal process have been largely limited to situated interactional issues, while law and society studies have been restricted to structural issues in society. (We will return to this divide in Sections 2.3 and 3 below.) The authors argue that in order to make sense of what is happening in immediate legal contexts, such as the courtroom, sociolinguists also need to engage with the work of sociolegal scholars. It is in bringing together sociolinguistic and sociolegal work that we can address what these authors see as "the most important theoretical issue in law and language: the use of linguistic methods to understand the nature of law and legal power" (ibid.: 6). Some scholars are already working within this approach, and Conley and O'Barr examine representative work in a number of legal contexts, including courtroom talk, mediation, and in non-formal legal processes in a Papua New Guinea society.

Conley and O'Barr's call to language and law scholars is part of the widespread "critical turn" in the social sciences, which began in the later part of the 20th century. While there is a range of critical approaches, they all share a major aim, expressed by Blommaert (2005: 6) as "performing analyses that ... expose and critique existing wrongs in one's society", and by Penny-cook (2001: 4) as "engaging with questions of power and inequality". Several theoretical traditions that focus on situated language use are currently experienc-ing this critical turn, including interactional sociolinguistics, discourse analysis, linguistic anthropology and applied linguistics. Insightful reviews can be found in Blommaert 2005, Blommaert and Bulcaen 2000, Blommaert et al. 2001, Kress 2001, Rampton 2001a, 2006, Pennycook 2001, and contributions to the 2001 special issue of *Critique of Anthropology*, including those by Blommaert, Bucholtz, Collins, Heller, Rampton, Slembrouck and Verschueren.

The critical turn provides us with more refined concepts than have typically been used in the sociolinguistic work on language and power in courtroom talk. Many critical theorists have taken up Gramsci's (1971) point about two different kinds of power: coercion (or "direct domination") is exercised by legislative or executive powers, or expressed through police intervention, while hegemony involves the dominant group securing the consent of the society. Van Dijk (1993: 254) succinctly expresses this distinction, when he says that "a powerful group may limit the freedom of action of others [coercion], but also influence their minds [hegemony]". And as "managing the minds of others is essentially a function of text and talk" (ibid.), the analysis of language use is central to the analysis of power. Thus, sociolinguistic attention to the ways in which power is exercised through talk involves more than the immediate interaction – for example in the courtroom – as it must be seen as part of the wider societal exercise of power.

Further, most sociolinguistic studies of courtroom talk have conceptualised power in the Marxist tradition, as unidirectional control by a dominant group (as for example in Van Dijk's position above). But scholars influenced by Foucault and poststructuralism see power not in terms of a static attribute or a monolithic oppressive power structure, but rather in terms of relationships (e.g. Matoesian 1993; Ehrlich 2001). These relationships of power are dynamic and complex. Taking up Foucault's (1991: 148) insistence that power needs to be explained, leads to "analyses of discourse [which] aim to explore how power may operate, rather than to demonstrate its existence" (Pennycook 2001: 93). Similarly, Blommaert (2005: 1–2) argues that "we need to be more specific" when we talk about power, and we should analyse "power effects, or the outcome of power, of what power does to people, groups and societies, and of how this impact comes about" (emphases in original). And it is just this exploration of how power operates as well as its impact, which Conley and O'Barr (1998) have outlined in their call for sociolinguistic studies which examine the actual mechanisms through which the legal system fails to deliver justice, and which is exemplified in the work of Matoesian (1993) and Ehrlich (2001), to be reviewed below.

Central to this exploration of how power works is the notion of discourse, for which I follow Conley and O'Barr's (1998) helpful definition and discussion. They point out that there are two senses in which this term is used, a linguistic sense and a social sense. In the linguistic sense, discourse refers to any spoken or written text which is larger than a single utterance or sentence. In its wider sense in the social sciences, following Foucault, discourse is a more abstract concept, referring to "not simply talk itself, but also the way that something gets talked about" (Conley and O'Barr 1998: 7). While the term "discourse" is widely used in the second sense, Conley and O'Barr (ibid.: 8) "have become convinced that the linguistic and social notions of discourse are merely different aspects of one and the same process of expressing social power". The central argument of their book, which has been one of the inspirations for this book, is that "the concrete linguistic technique of discourse analysis is an indispensable tool for explaining discourse in the more abstract, sociological sense" (ibid.). This interdependence of the two notions of discourse will become apparent below in the discussion in Section 2.4 below of Ehrlich's (2001) analysis of rape trials. Ehrlich's analysis of the interaction in a rape trial (discourse in the first sense) is central to her analysis of society's patriarchal construction of the crime of rape and related issues of consent (discourse in the second sense).

In exploring how people and groups work to gain and/or retain power, Fairclough (1989: 34) has pointed out that "power relations are always relations of *struggle*" (emphasis in original). While Fairclough uses the term "struggle" in a "technical sense" to refer to "the process whereby social groupings with different interests engage with one another" (ibid.), in the Pinkenba case this engagement is well described by the ordinary English use of the word "struggle". Indeed, the Pinkenba hearing is a classic episode in the struggle between the state and the Aboriginal community, as we will see in Chapter 3. The struggle or work involved in gaining or retaining power, means that there are ways in which dominated groups or individuals resist the power of the dominant group. In terms of the Pinkenba case, the police force must constantly work to retain its control over Aboriginal people, while there are a number of ways in which Aboriginal people resist this power, as we will see. And, as Matoesian highlights in his study of the domination of rape victims, much of the work involved in exercising and resisting power is done through language.

In Fairclough's (1989) terms, the Pinkenba hearing involves a struggle over power that is situated within the discourse of the courtroom. But to fully understand this courtroom power struggle, it is imperative to attend to Fairclough's point (ibid.: 70) that any given piece of discourse may simultaneously be a part of a struggle at each of the three levels of social organisation: a situational struggle, an institutional struggle and a societal struggle. To examine the power behind the discourse will require an examination of the institutional and societal struggles, which will be introduced in Chapter 3 below. Fairclough's point resonates with Blommaert's recent call to sociolinguists (2005: 35) that "if we wish to understand contemporary forms of inequality in and through language, we should look inside language *as well as outside it*, in society, and both aspects of analysis are not separable" (emphasis in original). It is this inseparability of language and its social context, summarised here by Blommaert, which is central to the work of a number of scholars engaged in critical analysis of language use, and which will be taken up in Section 3 below. The use of this approach in critical analysis of language use in the legal process, is most prominent in the work of five scholars: Susan Philips, Marco Jacquemet, Shonna Trinch, Gregory Matoesian and Susan Ehrlich.

Philips (1998) examines variation in the ways in which judges in an American trial court question defendants in the brief, non-adversarial and somewhat routinised event of the guilty plea. Philips' analysis of the linguistic details of judges' talk in this courtroom event is part of a larger analysis of the judges' ideological stances, of which her detailed ethnographic interviews are an important part. Her conclusion to this study, which centres on the linguistic mechanisms by which judges take the guilty plea, is that "judges are not just practicing a profession but practising politics and exercising power" (ibid.: 123).

Courtroom interaction between judges and defendants is also the focus of Jacquemet's (1996) study, which examines two major hearings in the attempted "clean-up" of organised crime in southern Italy in the 1980s. Jacquemet's detailed microanalysis of the hearings addresses the question of why the prosecution witnesses (the "pentiti" or informants) were believable to the judges in the initial trial, but rejected as lacking credibility and truthfulness by the appeal judges. The conclusion of his study is that "notions such as truth and credibility can be communicatively manipulated by groups in the position of dominance" (ibid.: 296). His analysis of the judicial determination of truth shows the intricate connection between courtroom talk and sociopolitical concerns of such dominant social groups.

Trinch (2003) analyses the ways in which the stories of domestic violence told by United States Latinas in interviews with their lawyers and paralegals are transformed into written narratives as affidavits, to support their applications for a protective order. Trinch concludes that the social consequence of these linguistic transformations is that ". . . the reproduction of women's powerlessness is achieved through omission, alteration, disfiguration and distortion of their stories in order to achieve a temporary and individual solution to the insidious and societal problem of violence against women" (ibid.: 278).

The critical sociolinguistic work on language in the legal process which is most relevant to this book is the work of Gregory Matoesian and Susan Ehrlich. Both of these scholars analyse courtroom talk in cases concerning the crime of rape (of adults), which has some striking parallels with the crime of "unlawful deprivation of liberty", which is at the heart of the Pinkenba case.[15] In both situations, a defendant is charged with a crime for an action which would be legal if the victim-witness had given consent. Further, in both situations, there is no other witness, so the central legal issue revolves around competing stories about whether or not the victim-witness consented. Issues involving the speech act of consent, and relative power relations between defendant and victim-witness are also parallel in abduction and rape cases.

2.3. *Matoesian: courtroom talk and the duality of structure*

Matoesian's (1993) analysis of courtroom language in rape trials is used by Conley and O'Barr to illustrate their argument about the importance of understanding the mechanisms by which the justice system fails to deliver justice. Matoesian's book addresses the question of why the introduction of rape shield laws, designed to make it easier for rape victims to give evidence, do not seem to have achieved this goal. This sociolegal question, which is seemingly about structural issues in rape trials, is answered by Matoesian's microanalysis of courtroom interaction in such trials.

Matoesian relies to a considerable extent on tools from Conversation Analysis (hereafter, CA), which he shows to be highly relevant to addressing the question of "*how* the systematic nature of talk-in-interaction emerges from and is generated by structural mechanisms" (ibid.: 47), namely the "discourse mechanisms" of rape trial discourse (ibid.: 57). The book provides a detailed development of Atkinson and Drew's (1979) original CA analysis of the "formal, structural or sequential properties of aspects of the organisation of verbal interaction in courts" (Matoesian 1993: vii). However, Matoesian "departs from orthodox CA in several key respects" (ibid.: 66), most notably in my view, in his subordination of the CA analytical tools to a critical theory framework, which includes calling upon a "structuration theoretical framework", to be discussed below. For Matoesian, sequential devices in talk-in-interaction (the typical focus of CA) are only one of three important structural mechanisms drawn on in the "reproduction of rape" during rape trials: the other two structural mechanisms are legal-institutional rules and patriarchal ideologies (ibid.: 69). Thus, his analysis of the reproduction of rape exemplifies the inseparability of language and social context, discussed above, by bringing together CA with a critical theory analysis of patriarchy in the legal system. This enables him to examine his fundamental question, namely "how rape as an enforcement of the social order is reproduced in trial talk" (ibid.: 71). His CA analysis focuses on such sequential strategies as lawyer control and manipulation of silence, and the syntax of question-answer sequences (in which he draws on the earlier hierarchies of question type, discussed above). And his more recent study of language in a rape trial

(Matoesian 2001) investigates further linguistic mechanisms, including repetition and entextualisation. This microanalysis of the situational struggle between rape victim-witnesses and defence counsel in cross-examination is embedded in Matoesian (1993) in a macro-sociological analysis of the societal struggle which is behind this courtroom discourse. This embedding of a CA analysis within a macro-sociological analysis is a significant departure for a scholar of CA, which has been criticised – rightly in my view – for generally being "resistant to making connections between ... 'micro' structures of conversation and the 'macro' structures of social institutions and societies" (Fairclough 1989: 12), and for using a "too narrow" notion of context (Verscheuren 2001: 69).

As we will see in Section 3 below, the relationship between micro- and macro-analysis (between studying social structures on the one hand, and specific interactions between individuals on the other) has been a concern for some sociolinguists since Cicourel's (1978) study of parent-child interactions and doctor-patient interviews, and Mehan's (1987) study of language and power in education. It is first found in sociolinguistic studies of language in the legal process, in Matoesian (1993), in which the analysis is based on the structuration theory of Giddens (e.g. 1987). In discussing the way in which the analysis of society has tended to focus on either structure or agency, Giddens (1987: 60) has argued that "this seeming opposition of perspectives actually disguises a complementarity", which he terms "the duality of structure". Using Giddens' duality of structure approach, also termed "structuration theory", Matoesian argues that the "micro-mode of domination" found in rape trials, as indicated in his microanalysis, amounts to the reproduction of rape: "structure is recursively drawn upon and reproduced by members in interactional performance" (1993: 198). Thus, what is happening in rape trials involves "the sequential, syntactic and discourse procedures of talk-in-interaction interact[ing] with patriarchal ideologies and methods of practical reasoning to fashion the powerful thrust of blame-implicative attributions against the victim" (ibid.: 206).

While earlier sociolinguistic studies assumed that powerful actors in the legal system used linguistic strategies to exercise control over witnesses, Matoesian presents a much more nuanced theory of power, introducing notions such as the "dialectic of control" which "captures the fact that power is always bi-directional, even in the most systematically asymmetrical relationships" (1993: 208). The point raised by Harris (1989) about witnesses moments of resistance during courtroom cross-examination, is amplified in Matoesian's study in the analysis of how witnesses reject the labels of cross-examining lawyers, for example. And because power is always bi-directional, the "reproduction of domination is never automatic. It is always something that must be worked for" (Matoesian 1993: 208).

2.4. Ehrlich: courtroom talk and ideology

Another important study which examines the reproduction of power through courtroom language practices is Ehrlich's (2001) book about language in a rape trial and a university disciplinary tribunal hearing, both of which examined the same rape allegations. While Matoesian's (1993) focus is on the ways in which courtroom language is used to revictimise rape victims ("reproducing rape"), Ehrlich's book examines rape trial talk from another perspective, namely the ways in which it defines the victim's experiences, actually constructing the social reality of rape ("representing rape").

As with Matoesian (1993), Ehrlich's book deals with the social consequences of courtroom talk, providing a powerful explanation for what we might call one of Conley and O'Barr's "how-questions": how courtroom talk perpetuates the patriarchal control of the legal system over rape victims, by controlling the ways in which these victims can talk about their experiences. Like Matoesian's study, Ehrlich's work also places microanalysis of trial (and in Ehrlich's book, also tribunal) talk at the centre of analysis. But the particular analytical tools are different: in contrast to Matoesian's use of CA for his microanalysis, Ehrlich draws on Critical Discourse Analysis (hereafter CDA), for example in the linguistic means used to attribute non-agency to the defendant and agency to the complainant in the rape trial. Just as Matoesian's use of CA is unorthodox, Ehrlich's use of CDA to analyse interactions rather than monologic texts, such as political speeches, advertisements and the like, is also somewhat unusual. In addition to CDA, Ehrlich draws on "feminist linguistic studies" (p. 35), which, as Kress (2001: 543) points out, differ from other sociolinguistic approaches in providing "explicitly political, critical descriptions of particular forms of language, or of language use".

Central to Ehrlich's analysis is the way in which courtroom talk defines consent, in its construction of the rape incidents as consensual sex. How is this achieved? Ehrlich analyses the linguistic means involved, of which a crucial part is the "substantive ideological work" done by questions in cross-examination of the complainants (2001: 76), specifically through pseudo-declaratives and embedded presuppositions (many of which are reformulations of the complainants' earlier propositions). The cross-examining lawyers' propositions which emerge through this process "'frame' the way events come to be understood: they function as an ideological filter through which the complainants' acts of resistance are characterized as 'inaction' and the events generally are (re)constructed as consensual sex." (ibid.)

Thus, ideology is an important theoretical concept in Ehrlich's book, consistent with her use of CDA analytical tools. But there is no single agreed-upon definition of ideology in CDA, let alone in the wider range of critical approaches (see discussion in Blommaert 2005: Chapter 7). Ehrlich's notion of ideology is consistent with Fairclough's position which connects mental phenomena (common-sense assumptions) and material action (ways of behaving). In Fairclough's (1989: 2) definition, ideologies are "common-sense" assumptions which "are a means of legitimizing existing social relations and differences of power, simply through the recurrence of ordinary, familiar ways of behaving which take these relations and power differences for granted". The common-sense, taken-for-granted nature of ideologies is important: as Fairclough (1989: 33) explains it, ideological power is "the power to project one's practices as universal and common-sense". The process by which practices (and beliefs) become accepted as universal and common-sense is referred to as "naturalisation" (e.g. Fairclough 1989, 1992a), a concept which will have considerable explanatory usefulness in this book. Thus, in the trial examined by Ehrlich, presupposed propositions about what the women could and should have done in the face of sexual aggression work to "naturaliz[e] a version of events that represents the complainants as having made bad choices in the context of unlimited options" (Ehrlich 2001: 92). And so, it is taken as common-sense that women can resist unwanted sexual aggression with physical resistance, an ideological position that ignores the role of the victim's fear.

The link between ideology and language in the reproduction of power relations is central to CDA: as Wodak (2001: 10) puts it, ideology "is seen as an important aspect of establishing and maintaining unequal power relations", and in Fairclough's (1989:12) words, language is "the major locus of ideology". Thus, Ehrlich's analysis of the rape trial and tribunal shows how the cross-examining lawyers' questions presuppose and assert common-sense assumptions about the choices and options that women have when confronted with sexual aggression. Such questions are the mechanisms through which patriarchal ideologies are used in the courtroom to reproduce power relations which legitimise societal violence against women.

Ehrlich's analysis (ibid.: 152) concludes with a strong echo of the structuration theory discussed above in Matoesian's work:

> To locate the problem of rape trials in discursive practices, embodied in institutional settings, is not to deny the power of law to enact rules and impose sanctions. Rather, it is to recognize the structuring potential of language, its capacity to constitute 'the objects of which it speaks' and the effects of this structuring on the particular ways rules are enacted and sanctions are imposed.

Thus, despite her use of CDA analytical tools, Ehrlich's work stands in sharp contrast to much CDA work, which has been criticised for having a "deterministic view of human agency" (Blommaert and Bulcaen 2000: 455, Pennycook

2001), as well as for being "short on detailed, systematic analysis of text or talk" (Van Dijk's 1999 summary of Schegloff's 1999 view), and sometimes involving "deference to macro-social analysis" (Rampton 2001a: 95). Rampton's criticism refers to studies in which "social theory or cultural description is drawn from elsewhere to provide "*a priori*" contextualisations and background narratives on power and institutions to which selected texts then testify" (ibid.). Ehrlich's analysis, on the other hand, like Matoesian's, is one in which macro and micro levels of analysis are interdependent. The agency of speakers is central to the microanalysis of the courtroom and tribunal interaction, but its analysis would be impossible without the critical feminist theory of the legal system and society more generally, in which it is embedded, and to which it makes an important contribution.

3.   A critical sociolinguistics approach

Having contextualised the ways in which Aboriginal English in the legal system has been researched and written about, as well as sociolinguistic analyses of language and power in courtroom talk, I now turn to the theoretical approach which underpins my analysis. This book is a response to Conley and O'Barr's (1998: 14) challenge for studies of language and law which "seek to identify the linguistic mechanisms through which power is realized, exercised, sometimes abused and occasionally subverted". It is neocolonial control over Aboriginal people which is the concern here, and which is investigated by means of a detailed analysis of the Pinkenba case.

This study is situated within the critical approach to language use, introduced in Section 2.2 above. In this section I outline the "critical sociolinguistics" approach as expounded by Heller (2001a, 2002), and Eades (2004a).[16] Central to critical sociolinguistics is the use of sociolinguistic analytical tools in the examination of "the specific role of language in the social construction of relations of difference and inequality" (Heller 2001a: 120). In Sarangi's (2001: 56) reframing of Durkheim's (1930) adage, "the social must be explained sociolinguistically". Thus, Heller's (2001b) investigation of francophone political mobilisation in Ontario has at its centre the analysis of classroom interactions between teachers and students in a French-language minority school. Consistent with the ideology of bilingualism as dual monolingualisms, the use of English or any other language is not allowed in the school. Like speaking out of turn, or speaking "impolitely", speaking in any language other than French is seen as disorderly behaviour. Thus there is a complex and recursive relationship between anglophone-francophone power relations and classroom sociolinguistic practices.

In Heller's study then, there is no separation between the structural level of anglophone-francophone power relations, and the interactional level of classroom sociolinguistic practices. The relationship between the macro-level of social structure and the micro-level of social processes (often referred to as "agency") is central to the critical sociolinguistics approach, and it is one of the major issues in social theory in the last twenty five years. We saw in Section 2.3 above that Matoesian's (1993) analysis of talk in rape trials uses Giddens' structuration or "duality of structure" model to argue that there can be no divide between macro and micro levels of society, or between structure and agency. Similarly in Section 2.4, we saw that Ehrlich's (2001) study shows the interdependence between discursive practices in rape trials and power of the legal system over rape victims. As with Heller's (2001b) investigation of language practices in francophone schools, these two studies of courtroom talk show how by "undoing the macro/micro dichotomy" (ibid.: 213) sociolinguistics can develop "a theory of language as social action" (ibid.: 232).[17]

In developing such a theory of language, sociolinguists such as Coupland (2001), Ehrlich (2001), Heller (2001a, 2001b), Matoesian (1993), Mehan (1987), Rampton (e.g. 2001, 2006), and Sarangi (e.g. 2001), both draw on and at the same time extend the social theory developed by Cicourel (e.g 1978, 1981), Collins (e.g. 1988), and Giddens (e.g. 1982, 1987), among others. Thus, the relationship between micro-events and macro-structures is not separable (as we saw in Sections 2.2, 2.3 and 2.4 above), but rather, is seen in terms of interaction (following Cicourel 1981: 54), integration (ibid.: 65) and reflexivity (Mehan 1987: 298). As Collins (ibid.: 244) succinctly expresses it, "everything macro is composed out of micro", and "anything micro is part of the composition of macro". In terms of my study, this means that neocolonial control is composed out of micro-events, which include specific encounters between police and Aboriginal people (as we will see in Chapter 3), as well as courtroom talk (which will be the focus of the chapters in Parts II and III). And this courtroom talk (as well as the encounters between police and Aboriginal people) is an integral part of the neocolonial control over Aboriginal people. Given the tools which sociolinguistics has developed for the analysis of courtroom talk, it follows then that sociolinguistics has an important role to play in the investigation of neocolonialism.

But it is not just that the micro and the macro compose each other, to use Collins' (1988) terms. Following Cicourel's (1981: 67) call, this study will identify some of the "processes and inferences that transform micro-events into macro-structures" (emphasis added). In his early work on the sociology of juvenile justice, Cicourel (1976) showed how the social construction of the structural category of delinquency is best understood by analysing the processes involved in police and probation officers' conversations with young people, and the sub-sequent production of written reports. This work was based on analysis not of recorded conversations, but rather approximations, and was not able to focus in detail on linguistic mechanisms. But more recent work which has examined the transformation of micro-events into macro-structures is based on close analysis on what was actually said, and thus the analytical tools of sociolinguistics can play a powerful role. Such transformation, which can also be seen as the repro-duction of power relations, is seen in the work of the sociolinguists referred to above. Thus for example, Mehan (1987) shows the processes and inferences by which class relations in society are reproduced in discussions between educa-tors and parents about decisions regarding student placement. Heller (2001b) shows the processes and inferences by which macro-political ideologies of bilin-gualism as parallel monolingualisms are reproduced in classroom interactions between teachers and students. Matoesian (1993) argues that the "micro-mode of domination" found in rape trials, as indicated in his microanalysis, amounts to the reproduction of rape: "structure is recursively drawn upon and repro-duced by members in interactional performance" (1993: 198). In this book we will see that inequality between coloniser and colonised is reproduced through courtroom talk.

Critical sociolinguistic work, such as the studies referred to above, exemplify Coupland's (2001: 16) point that sociolinguistics can develop the "integrationist" theoretical account of the recursive and reflexive relationship between structure and agency, which Coupland sees as "incomplete without sociolinguistics" (an argument similar to that of Conley and O'Barr 1998, discussed in Section 2.2 above). Following Coupland, we can see that, through detailed analysis of "lo-cal practices of talk", Ehrlich, Matoesian, Heller, Mehan and others have been able to develop a "much more, differentiated, and hence, arguably *better social theoretic* account [...] of structure and agency" (Coupland 2001: 16, emphasis in original). It is my aim in this book to undertake a detailed analysis of court-room talk, integrated and interacting with an analysis of larger events in the 200-year history of relations between Aboriginal people and police, in order to show how it is that neocolonialism is possible, and to demonstrate some of the mechanisms through which it works. Thus, this study will show the contribution that sociolinguistics can make to social theory: detailed analysis of linguistic mechanisms will reveal precise moments in which the oppressive control of the criminal justice system is both perpetrated on specific Aboriginal people, and legitimised as general practice. A courtroom case which tests the power of police to remove Aboriginal people from a public place is the ideal site to reveal the actual mechanisms of control. In this case, language works at two main levels to reproduce this neocolonial control: in using linguistic trickery to elicit apparent agreement from the boys to the proposition that they had agreed to be taken for a ride by the police,[18] and in using an array of linguistic mechanisms to construct Aboriginality in terms of criminality and a threat to public safety, thus legitimising police control.

I turn now to the particular analytical tools to be employed in this book. As in the work of Matoesian and Ehrlich discussed above, I do not follow a single theoretical tradition, hoping to avoid problems which can arise from what has been criticised as "slavish adherence to a single method" found among the "relatively few card-carrying critical discourse analysts or conversation analysts or natural historians of discourse or interactional sociolinguists" (Bucholtz 2001: 175). Much of my analysis uses an approach informed by interactional sociolinguistics, as well as a number of critical studies in sociolinguistics and linguistic anthropology, focusing primarily on cross-examination in the Pinkenba hearing, examining what is said in the hearing, how it is said and what happens as a result.

As a "slow motion" study of interaction (Rampton 2001b: 97), interactional sociolinguistics will enable me to focus on the detailed ways in which the power struggle is enacted between the Aboriginal boys and the defence lawyers. Part of this power struggle involves the "situated interpretation of communicative intent" (Gumperz 2001b: 223). For example, do the boys share culturally-specific presuppositions, which enable them to interpret the sarcasm in some of the cross-examination questions? And central to this power struggle is the struggle over the construction of the boys' identities: are they victims of police abuse, or lying *criminals* who *want to get even with police*?

My analysis will also draw on Critical Discourse Analysis, particularly in relation to ways in which the legal system, through this case, naturalises the police removal of Aboriginal young people. It is presented as "common-sense" that police need to remove them, given that they present a law and order problem. Further, the tools of CDA will be used in the analysis of how ideological struggle is enacted through lexical strategies (Chapter 5).

But, my analysis needs to go beyond interactional sociolinguistics and CDA, for reasons explained above. It would be impossible to make sense of the Pinkenba hearing if the sociolinguistic analysis is limited to the immediate courtroom interaction. To take just one aspect of this case: the child witnesses in this case were repeatedly harangued and harassed during their cross-examination by the two defence counsel, as we will see in Parts II and III below. The magistrate had the power to stop this kind of questioning, and magistrates and judges in other cases regularly use this power, for example telling counsel *You can't address a witness in this manner*. Why didn't the magistrate do this in the Pinkenba hearing? And why did the prosecutor make very few objections? A consideration of such questions about the interaction within the hearing cannot be adequately addressed by traditional sociolinguistic explanations. While interactional socio-linguistics would look for miscommunication caused by misinterpretation of utterances within the hearing, CDA would typically appeal to an explanation based on the obvious power imbalance between the young Aboriginal witnesses and the defence lawyers, which is part of the wider power imbalance between Aboriginal people and the state. But neither explanation would be adequate. In Heller's (2001a: 118) terms, we need an approach which can "allow us to see the connections between the moment and the big picture".

To answer these and similar questions, we need a dynamic approach, which places the struggles over power at its centre. There is clearly a significant power imbalance between the young Aboriginal witnesses and the defence lawyers. But the relationship between these two sets of interlocutors is part of a wider context, which includes institutional and grassroots resistance and change to this power relationship. Thus, to understand the struggles over power in the discourse (that is, in the courtroom hearing), we need to understand the struggles over power behind the discourse, in Fairclough's (1989) terms. To examine power behind the discourse, that is, outside the courtroom, takes us to the wider social, po-litical and historical context, for which we will need to engage with sociolegal research, as urged by Conley and O'Barr (1998). Following Rampton's (2001a: 264) general point about the need for sociolinguistic research to draw on re-search outside sociolinguistics, sociolegal research can provide key analytical concepts which take us beyond generalised statements about power structures. Two central concepts are "criminalisation" of Aboriginal young people and the "naturalisation of police control" over them (e.g. Cunneen 1994, 2001). The first of these concepts will be introduced in Chapter 3, and will be central to the analysis in the chapters in Parts III and IV, while the second will be central to the discussion in Chapter 12.

My critical sociolinguistic study of language in the legal process will be characterised by attention to:

- ongoing struggles over power, and resulting inequalities,

- microanalysis of the linguistic mechanisms involved in these struggles,

- both social structure and individual agency, and recognition of the recursive and reflexive nature of the relationship between them,

- the distant and recent historical context in which the focal interactions are situated,

- the role of language in naturalising assumptions relating to Aboriginal people,

- culturally specific presuppositions about ways of acting, including talking,

- inter- and multi-disciplinarity, recognising the need for sociolinguistic work to draw on social theory in both understanding and explaining power relations in society.

My earliest writing on the Pinkenba case (Eades 1995b, 2002, 2003a), highlighted the ways in which the cross-examining lawyers exploited the subtle differences between Aboriginal English and general Australian English. My recent work, culminating in this book, has been carried out while my theoretical perspective has been shifting – from one which highlights intercultural communication to one which examines the dynamic and reciprocal relationship between courtroom interaction and neocolonial control over Aboriginal people, as explained in this chapter. This theoretical shift has resulted in a shift of focus, from Aboriginal English in court, to linguistic practices in and out of court. Shifting the focus of analysis from use of a named language variety to situated practices by embodied individuals is also consistent with recent critiques of the "ideology of languages as separate and enumerable categories" (Makoni and Pennycook 2005: 138), and with sociolinguistic moves "away from autonomous structure and towards process and practice" (Heller 2006: 10; see also Blommaert 2005).

It is not my intention to ignore features which characterise Aboriginal English varieties, which will indeed form the basis of Chapter 4 below. However, it will be clear that dialectal difference is only one of the aspects of language use that we must attend to in the analysis of the way in which courtroom language is used in the neocolonial control of Aboriginal people.

It is never a simple matter to provide a linear and sequentially developed argument in the analysis of complex interconnected issues and practices. However, given that the writing of a book requires linearity and sequence, there will be some inevitable repetition as I build the argument of the book, namely that courtroom talk in the Pinkenba case plays a central role in ongoing neocolonial control over Aboriginal Australians. The next chapter presents an overview of the institutional and societal struggles within which the situational struggle in the Pinkenba hearing takes place.

Chapter 3
The societal and institutional struggle

Since the early nineteenth century, the relationship between Aboriginal people and the police has been characterised by bitter conflict. The first section of this chapter examines the three modes of police intervention in the lives of Aboriginal young people, focusing where possible on Brisbane and the wider southeast Queensland area within which it is located. Section 2 moves to societal issues about the role of moral panic in constructing Aboriginal young people as a "law and order problem". Section 3 examines police violence and harassment and concludes by asking whether the three boys in the Pinkenba event could have refused to go in the police cars. Section 4 then examines ways in which Aboriginal people have resisted police control over their lives, both institutionally, with the establishment of Aboriginal Legal Services, and individually, by swearing at police officers. This leads to a discussion of the central role of the criminal offence of offensive language in the criminalisation of Aboriginal people.

It is impossible to discuss the societal struggle between Aboriginal people and police without discussing institutional struggle, in which several key institutions are prominent. Right from its beginnings in 1864, the Queensland police force has played a central role in the control of the state over Aboriginal people. Major criticism of policing practices has been provided in the last two decades of the twentieth century by three government inquiries. Thus, Section 5 deals with the Queensland Commission of Inquiry into Possible Illegal Activites and Associated Police Misconduct (1989, hereafter Fitzgerald Inquiry), and the Criminal Justice Commission (hereafter CJC), which was established as a result of this inquiry. The CJC was one of the two institutions actively involved in the process of bringing the six police officers to court over the Pinkenba incident, the other being the Aboriginal Legal Service (hereafter ALS, dealt with in Section 4.1). Section 6 examines the national Royal Commission into Aboriginal Deaths in Custody (commonly abbreviated to RCIADC). The third inquiry which is relevant to the institutional struggle in this book, is the National Inquiry into the Separation of Aboriginal and Torres Strait Islander Children from their Families (1997, hereafter NISATSIC), which is dealt with in Section 1.2. While the main focus of these sections, as of the whole book, is on Aboriginal young people in Brisbane and neighbouring areas of southeast Queensland, it will be helpful at times, and necessary at others, to draw on research in other parts of Australia, and about Aboriginal people generally, not only young people.

In Section 7, we move to a predominantly narrative account of key events involving Aboriginal people and the criminal justice system in Brisbane in the six months leading up to the Pinkenba event, followed by an explanation of relevant legal facts concerning the charge against the police officers, and the committal hearing.

1. Modes of police intervention in the lives of Aboriginal young people

Cunneen (1994: 128) discusses three distinct phases or modes of intervention in the relationship between police and Aboriginal young people throughout Australia (see also Cunneen and White 2002). These three phases or modes, to be explained below, can be summarised as: i) open warfare and resistance, ii) "protective" legislation and iii) criminalisation. Given the overlapping and co-existence of these phases, Cunneen shows that they are "most usefully conceptualised as modes of intervention rather than simply as periods of time" (ibid.). While it is the experiences of Aboriginal people in southeast Queensland that are central to this book, in many ways they are typical of what was happening around the country.

1.1. Open warfare and resistance

The first British settlement in southeast Queensland began in 1825, when the area now known as Brisbane was established as the convict settlement of Moreton Bay (NISATSIC 1997: 71). The early decades of the settlement and the subsequent expansion north were characterised by widespread decimation of the indigenous population with the introduction of new diseases, as well as "extreme violence" (ibid.). For example, the Brisbane newspaper, the *Moreton Bay Courier*, in the 1840s and 1850s reported "a number of violent clashes between blacks, white police and civilians in Brisbane, including attacks on the blacks' camp near Breakfast Creek in 1852 and 1857, following alleged thefts" (Evans 1992: 84). The earliest police presence was in the form of a paramilitary force, fighting a "bloody frontier war" against Aboriginal people, in which police duties were comparable to that of the US army on the American frontier (Foley 1984: 161). Historians have documented the "essentially volatile and conflictual nature" of the Queensland frontier (Evans 2004: 154), which they have found to be "the most troublesome frontier story of all the Australian colonies" (ibid.: 160). In this initial contact between Aboriginal people and settlers, no distinction was made between Aboriginal young people and other Aboriginal people in the ways in which police, as well as vigilantes, engaged in open warfare on Aboriginal people. As Cunneen and White (2002: 157) explain, age was irrelevant during the period of open colonial warfare. "Aboriginal people were murdered *because they were Aboriginal*: that is, because they were the Indigenous people in possession of the land and because they resisted colonial expansion" (ibid.: emphasis in original).

In resisting colonial expansion, Aboriginal people attacked camps or homesteads of settlers who had taken their land and resources. In order to put down this resistance, the Queensland government established a Native Police force in 1863, recruiting Aboriginal people from other regions of Australia with no previous contact with, or loyalties to, the groups they were policing (Rowse 2005: 215). This Native Police force, led by European police officers, gained a reputation for "brutal dispersal" of Aboriginal groups (Howie-Willis 1994d: 878), and was criticised by several inquiries and investigations (Foley 1984: 162). The Native Police force was disbanded at the end of the nineteeth century, but not before it had "had the effect of institutionalising violence" (Cunneen 1994: 128).

1.2. "Protective" legislation

Following the "success" of the frontier war at the end of the nineteenth century, Queensland was the first state to enact so-called "protective legislation" for Aboriginal people (McCrae et al. 1997: 45). Under the *Aboriginals Protection and Restriction of the Sale of Opium Act 1897*, numerous aspects of the lives of Aboriginal Queenslanders were controlled by "district protectors", many of whom were police officers. Protectors could and did intervene, for example by opening mail, prohibiting dancing and other "native practices", operating bank accounts of Aboriginal people, and prosecuting people found to contravene the prohibition on intercourse between an Aboriginal and a non-Aboriginal person (Cunneen 2001: 67–68). This 1897 Act, and its replacement acts, the *Aboriginals Preservation and Protection Act 1939* and *The Torres Strait Islanders Act 1939*, also gave government officials the power to remove Indigenous people to and between missions and government settlements, and to separate children from their families (NISATSIC 1997: 72).

One moving personal account is found in Huggins and Huggins (1994: 9), the autobiography and biography of Rita Huggins, a Brisbane Elder in the 1990s. In the first chapter, Huggins tells how, when she was a small child in the 1920s, she and her family were approached by police troopers on their traditional land

600 kilometres northwest of Brisbane. These troopers were accompanied by a "huge cage with four round things on it, which ... made a deafening sound". This was the cattle truck which transported Huggins and her family 200 kilometres north to the Woorabinda Aboriginal Settlement. Here the elderly family members, considered by the government officials to be "wild bush Blacks", were "wrenched from [their relatives'] arms" (ibid.: 10), while the cattle truck drove the remainder of the family 500 or more kilometres southeast to Barambah Settlement. As we saw in Section 1 of Chapter 1, Barambah was renamed Cherbourg, and is the birthplace of two of the boys in the Pinkenba case, and the home of many of their relatives.

Huggins reports that, after they were taken to Cherbourg, "we were never to see our old people again. Dadda could never bring himself to talk about it. Our tribe was torn away – finished" (ibid.). Huggins' experience was a common one. Eckermann's (1977) study of Aboriginal people in an unnamed industrial city near Brisbane found that the earliest Aboriginal contacts with Europeans in this area "were often confined to police action, which involved forcible separation of individuals from their family group and from residence on the mission reserves" (ibid.: 312). The police thus played a "pivotal role" in this removal of Aboriginal people throughout the country (NISATSIC 1997: 491). This was additional to their frequent role as "protectors of Aborigines", particularly in remote areas where they might be the only government representative (Foley 1984: 162–163). Legislation such as the 1897 Act gave police "wide discretionary powers" over the liberty and property of Aborigines (ibid.).

Compared to other Aboriginal children, Rita Huggins was lucky – she was not separated from her parents. But many children of mixed descent were "targeted for removal from their communities" (NISATSIC 1997: 72). In Queensland in the first several decades of the twentieth century, many children were placed in dormitories on the Aboriginal settlements. This was what happened to Ruth Hegarty (2000, 2003), another woman who was a Brisbane Elder in the 1990s. Hegarty's family was persuaded to move to Barambah (Cherbourg) "temporarily" in 1930, when she was 6 months old. But when they arrived, they found that they had surrendered all their rights, and "like a rag [her] family was torn into pieces" (2000: 13). Hegarty was placed with her mother in the women's dormitory, but at four years old, she was removed from her mother to the other side of the dormitory, despite her mother's protests. Separated by a lattice screen, Hegarty and her mother were forbidden from contact with each other. She had been placed "under the 'care and protection' of the Queensland government which now classified [her] as a neglected child" (ibid: 26). A few months later, her mother was sent to work as a domestic assistant on a cattle station, as Hegarty was herself at the age of fourteen. Hegarty's life continued to be regulated by the (non-Aboriginal) Superintendent of the settlement, even requiring his permission and that of the Queensland Aboriginal Protector to marry, at the age of 21.

In Queensland, removal of Aboriginal people to settlements, between settlements, or to dormitories within settlements, involved no legal process, such as a court hearing or avenue of appeal. All that was required under the 1897 Act was an administrative decision authorised by the Minister of Native Affairs. And under the 1939 Acts, it was even easier for the government to remove Indigenous people: these Acts shifted the power of removal from the government minister to the Director of Native Affairs, who, until 1965, became guardian of all Indigenous children under the age of 21. As NISATSIC (1997: 72) explains it, the Director "had virtually total control of the lives of Indigenous children". But when the Director of Aboriginal and Islander Affairs (formerly the Director of Native Affairs) ceased to be the legal guardian of Indigenous children in 1965, many of these children continued to be removed from their families by state officials under the *Children Services Act 1965* (ibid. 1997: 622). At the same time, repressive control over the lives of all Queensland Aborigines, adults as well as children, continued under the 1965 *Aboriginal and Torres Strait Islander Affairs Act*. It was the superintendents of the government reserves (formerly called settlements) and the local police who policed behaviours that were only criminal on these reserves: for example, people could be "punished by detention for 'indiscipline' or 'immoral behaviour' " (Cunneen 2001: 74). This situation continued until the repeal of the 1965 Act in 1984.

By the end of the twentieth century, mounting concern over decades of the removal of Aboriginal children and its ongoing effects led to the National Inquiry into the Separation of Aboriginal and Torres Strait Islander Children from Their Families (NISATSIC). Widely known as the "stolen generations" inquiry, it was established in 1995, and received evidence from 777 people, of whom 535 were Indigenous people who gave evidence or submissions about their experiences of forcible removal. The Inquiry concluded that between one in three and one in ten Indigenous children were forcibly removed from their families and communities between 1910 and 1970 (NISATSIC 1997: 37). Many Aboriginal people in Queensland today, as throughout the country, have vivid memories of the trauma of being removed, or of losing children in this way. NISATSIC (ibid.: 272–273) found that "the predominant aim of Indigenous child removals was the absorption or assimilation of the children into the wider, non-Indigenous community so that their unique cultural values and ethnic identities would disappear, giving way to models of Western culture". It further found (ibid.: 270–275) that this removal of children was genocidal under the terms of the 1948 *Convention on the Prevention and Punishment of the Crime of Genocide* (ratified by Australia in 1949).

1.3.   Criminalisation

Contemporary policies of police intervention in the lives of Aboriginal young people "may be similarly genocidal in their impact, if not in their conscious intent", according to Cunneen (1994: 154). Many years of detailed criminological analysis leads Cunneen (ibid.: 135) to conclude that "Aboriginal youth are no longer institutionalized because they are Aboriginal, but rather because they are criminal". Cunneen (1994, 2001) argues that the colonial inequality enacted earlier through open warfare and "protective" legislation is now reproduced through the neocolonial criminalisation process (see also NISATSIC 1997: 540). It is significant that the verb *criminalise* is used in such discussions with people as its object, whereas the typical object of this verb is an activity, such as prostitution or use of marijuana, which is "made illegal" (Garner 2004: 402). Cunneen's convincing argument is that contemporary police intervention in the lives of Aboriginal young people has the effect of making many of them illegal because of their Aboriginality.

The extent of this criminalisation process can be seen in the alarmingly high national rate of the incarceration of Aboriginal children in juvenile institutions "at a rate which is nothing less than a national scandal" (Cunneen 1994: 134). Queensland statistics for the year following the Pinkenba hearing – 1996 – show that an Indigenous young person is 41 times more likely to be in juvenile correctional institutions than a non-Indigenous young person: the highest level of over-representation in the country (NISATSIC 1997: 496). While corresponding state figures are not available for police custody, the national over-representation factor for Indigenous young people in this form of detention in 1995 was 26 (ibid.: 492).

How does this criminalisation of Aboriginal young people work? A number of criminologists, including Cunneen (1994, 2001), Cunneen and White (1995), and Gale et al. (1990), have carefully analysed the progression of young people (Aboriginal and non-Aboriginal) through the criminal justice system. Their research shows that Aboriginal young people are disproportionately subject to police attention and intervention. Police have discretion on a number of matters, such as deciding whether to arrest, to use diversionary measures, or to issue a caution. The ways in which police discretionary decisions are made clearly discriminate against Aboriginal young people. What the research on police discretionary decisions shows is not that Aboriginal young people are involved in more criminal activity than non-Aboriginal young people, but that they are more often subject to police intervention. It is not difficult to see the extreme over-representation of Indigenous young people in police custody and subsequent detention, as a neocolonial extension of the earlier colonial removal policies and practices (e.g. Cunneen 1994; NISATSIC 1997: 540). As NISATSIC (ibid.: 491) points out: "police still have a major function in bringing about separations [of Indigenous young people from their families and communities]".

This disproportionate amount of initial police attention and intervention is described as "over-policing" (e.g. Cunneen 2001; Sanders 1999: 334), which is seen in a key Australian text on criminal justice as the cause of "the gross over-representation of Aborigines in our criminal justice system" (Findlay et al. 2005: 328; see also NISATSIC: 510). Arguing that this is a problem for all Aboriginal people (not just young people), Findlay et al. (ibid.) explain that over-policing:

> involves a proactive response by the police to behaviour which they perceive to be disorderly or offensive. This means that, when dealing with Aboriginal people, there is a tendency for police to initiate a confrontation with them. This often leads to an angry verbal or physical response from the Aborigines which results in their being charged for an offence. In contrast, the police normally take a reactive stance in respect of offending by non-Aboriginal people. That is, they tend to take action only after a report has been made by a victim or witness about a criminal incident.

Cunneen's (1994: 145) work on the over-policing of Aboriginal young people points out that this occurs particularly in public places, which is where most contact occurs between the police and young people in general. Malls, shopping centres and other public spaces have been reported by police as the most frequent locations for their contact with young people (Cunneen and White 2002: 260). Police have also reported that they experience "most difficulties with street kids, gangs, and young Aboriginal and Torres Strait Islander people" (ibid.).

In this, the police appear to be responding to wider community concerns, some of which we will see in the discussion on moral panic in the next section. As Sanders (1999: 335) puts it: "there is, of course, a widespread notion that there is a 'gang problem' and that groups of young people in public space must be up to no good". As happened in the Pinkenba case, it is not uncommon for young people to be just "hanging out" or walking when stopped by the police (Cunneen and White 2002: 259). A well recognised difference between Aboriginal and non-Aboriginal societies in the way in which outdoor spaces are used, is relevant to the over-policing of Aboriginal young people in public spaces. Much of day-to-day social interaction in Aboriginal communities across the country, takes place in outdoor areas (Eades 2000). The situation reported by Morris (1989: 173) in coastal NSW Aboriginal societies in the middle decades of the twentieth century still applies to many Aboriginal societies throughout Australia: "The enclosed private domains of family homes [are] not the principal sites of social interaction". Cunneen (2001: 184) exemplifies the way that "the search for civic tidiness in the light of opportunities for tourism" has impacted on police control of Aboriginal people.

Further, many of the offences in the criminal records of Aboriginal young people relate to behaviours which are arguably precipitated by police intervention (Cunneen and White 2002: 262), such as offensive language, resist arrest, hinder police, assault police.[19] Like the public order offences of public drunkenness and disorderly behaviour, which also figure largely in the arrests of Aboriginal people, there is generally no victim apart from the police officer, except for a notional "community" (Cunneen 2001: 29). Thus, as Cunneen and White (ibid.) argue, "Constructing a reason to take young people off the streets, therefore can be as simple as having the police approach young people in the first instance". And then, as Cunneen (2001: 133) points out, once a young person has a criminal record they become legitimate objects of increased police surveillance. Once this occurs, they are likely to engage in acts of delinquency, which as D'Souza (1990: 5) argues, "could also be regarded as acts of individual defiance". His view is that the "scale and nature of Aboriginal children's conflict with 'authority' is reflective of a historical defiance".

Thus, we see in general terms the historical and circumstantial factors which come together in the criminalisation of Aboriginal young people. In the analysis of the Pinkenba cross-examination in Parts II and III below, we will examine the specific ways in which language works in legitimising this process of criminalisation, and thus enabling it to continue to operate.

2.   Moral panic and youth crime

In their over-policing of Aboriginal young people in public spaces, police officers are not acting in a vacuum. Their actions have to be seen in the light of widespread "moral panic" over a perceived "breakdown in law and order" especially in relation to Aboriginal young people (Hil 1995: 51). The concept of "moral panic" is perhaps best known in sociolinguistics from Cameron's (1995) compelling analysis of what she calls "the great grammar crusade" in the UK in the 1980s–1990s. But in criminology research, "moral panic" is a much more widely-known concept (e.g. Cunneen 1994; Cunneen and White 2002; Hil 1995). Acknowledging Goode and Ben-Yehuda (1994), Cunneen and White (2002: 90) define moral panic as a situation in which:

- the behaviour of a social group is defined as deviant
- there is serious concern over the behaviour of, and hostility towards, the particular group

- there is a level of consensus over the negative definitions of the group and its behaviour
- there is a disproportionate and punitive response, usually by the criminal justice system, towards the group

In developing and maintaining this "level of consensus" which is part of a moral panic, the media's preoccupation with crime is central. In the Australian media, Aboriginal people are defined as the deviant group, and they are constantly being linked with crime (Jakubowicz et al. 1994: 38–39). The most detailed analysis of this topic comes from Western Australia in the late 1980s to mid 1990s (Mickler and McHoul 1998; Trigger 1995; Sercombe 1995). Trigger (1995: 109) found that newspaper reporting on Aboriginal topics was "disproportionately negative and focused on Aboriginal criminality", while "the link between juvenile crime and Aboriginal youth was insistently raised" by callers to talk-back radio (ibid.: 116). In Sercombe's (1995) study, 85% of newspaper stories that referred to Aboriginal youth were principally about crime. And Mickler and McHoul's (1998: 149) study in the capital city of Western Australia – Perth – found that newspaper reports in 1991–2 played a significant role in the creation of a "crisis atmosphere ... over juvenile crime ... with increasing reference to Aboriginal people", which was contradictory to the official crime statistics. An important media site for encouraging moral panic is talk-back radio, where the comments of "shock-jocks" support and encourage panic and prejudice. A particularly disturbing example comes from the comments of a Perth radio announcer in 1990 (Hagan 2005). The announcer's comments were in response to the news that three Aboriginal children aged between 12 and 15 were killed when the stolen car they were driving crashed while being chased by police. Radio announcer Howard Sattler's comment reportedly was: "Well, I say good riddance to bad rubbish. That's three less car thieves. I think they're dead and I think that's good" (ibid.).

The snow-balling moral panic over property crime, including car theft, and in particular, the role perceived to be played by young people in such crime, has made an impact on the wider community, as well as on the political process and legislative change. Hil (1995) provides an insightful analysis of the moral panic over juvenile justice in the context of the Queensland *Juvenile Justice Act 1992*, enacted just two years before the Pinkenba event. Hil contrasts the moral panic over "'rapidly rising' juvenile crime", in which Aboriginal juveniles are a particular focus, with an analysis of official crime statistics. This analysis shows that "rather than being the contemporary folk devils of our time, young people tend to offend, if at all, in petty and transitory ways" (ibid.: 58). But the new legislation with its "tough on crime" approach, has been criticised for "restating an antiquated and narrow neo-classical view of crime and criminal behaviour through its focus on the 'offence rather than the offender'" (ibid.: 53).

As with Mickler and McHoul (1998) in Western Australia, Hil (1995) also considers the media to have considerable responsibility in the manufacture of moral panic over juvenile crime in Queensland. He reports that newspapers in a number of Queensland cities and towns refer "with growing regularity to 'juvenile crime waves', 'thugs', 'street gangs', and young people 'out of control'" (ibid.: 59). In the analysis of the Pinkenba case in this book, we will see how the media's work in the manufacture and maintenance of moral panic over juvenile crime can be greatly assisted by the "disproportionate and punitive response ... [of] the criminal justice system" (Cunneen and White 2002: 90, quoted above). We will see the power of the actual words which are used in the courtroom interaction in this case in contributing to the moral panic about Aboriginal young people on the streets.

While moral panic about allegedly "rapidly rising" juvenile crime may help to explain over-policing to some extent, the reverse also needs to be considered: Hil (ibid.: 58) argues that a "significant factor in the increasing criminalization of working class youth, and particularly of those in Aboriginal communities, is the increased presence of police in public spaces such as streets, parks and shopping centres occupied by young people". Hil's analysis is that the 1992 Queensland legislation, hurriedly enacted one month before the state election, was "aimed at the control of 'problem populations' and the maintenance of social order" (ibid.: 67).

Moral panic over Aboriginal young people as a threat to the safety of property was at a peak in the years leading up to and following the Pinkenba case. It reached a legislative climax in the Northern Territory and Western Australia with the enactment of legislation mandating sentences of imprisonment for juvenile repeat offenders convicted of certain property crimes (Findlay et al. 2005: 286–289). In the Northern Territory, this mandatory sentencing law stipulated that a 15- or 16-year-old convicted of a third property crime (no matter how slight) would be imprisoned for 28 days. Adults, including 17-year-olds, faced a mandatory prison sentence for their first property offence. The mandatory sentencing laws applied to property crimes (but not the white collar crime of credit card fraud), rather than crimes against the person (such as assault, rape, murder). This focus on crimes against property was arguably consistent with colonial attempts to control Indigenous people through control of their access to land and resources, and it also effectively transferred "the real sentencing discretion to police and prosecution" (Santow 2000: 298). There was widespread condemnation of this legislation, including by six former judges of the High Court of Australia. Sir Gerard Brennan (a former Chief Justice of the High Court) argued that "locking up people in under-resourced prisons are [sic] cheap ways of satisfying a populist 'law and order' cry" (quoted in Stephens and Kingston

2000). The mandatory sentencing legislation was shown to contravene the UN Convention on the Rights of the Child (Santow 2000). In response to harsh criticism by the UN Committee on the Elimination of Racial Discrimination, the Australian government withdrew from cooperation with UN human rights bodies (Pritchard 2000). The Northern Territory repealed its mandatory sentencing laws in 2001, but similar laws remain current in Western Australia, at the time of writing in 2007. While international attention was focused on the mandatory sentencing laws, Amnesty International criticised Australia for the over-imprisonment of Indigenous people saying also that police "systematically mistreat" Aborigines (Jopson 2000).

3. Police violence and harassment

But, this systematic mistreatment of Aboriginal young people goes further than over-policing, and includes harassment and violence. While Queensland has produced some of the most serious evidence of police violence towards Aboriginal people, this is consistent with patterns in other states. Cunneen (1994: 142) argues that "the use of violence and harassment" is an "important part of the dynamics of policing Aboriginal young people", citing government reports, royal commission inquiries and reports to non-government human rights organisations. For example, the report of the 1991 National Inquiry into Racist Violence by the Human Rights and Equal Opportunity Commission found that "Aboriginal-police relations had reached a critical point due to widespread involvement of police in acts of racist violence, intimidation, and harassment" (cited in Cunneen 1996: 29). These reports and inquiries are complemented by a study which Cunneen (1995) carried out in three states, including Queensland, in which he interviewed 171 Aboriginal young people in detention centres about alleged police violence. In Queensland, 90% of the young people interviewed reported being assaulted by police. In an example with parallels to the Pinkenba case, one Aboriginal youth from Brisbane reported (ibid.: 126) that:

> [Police] pick you up for something you haven't done, drive you right out of town and bash you up and leave you there. That happened to me. They took all my money off me. They pick you up because they know you.

Cunneen's interviews indicated that Aboriginal young people saw police violence as "normal" (ibid.: 133). He argues (ibid.) that the regular use of violence in policing Aboriginal young people "can be seen as related to the central tasks of policing: order maintenance and gaining convictions". Further, in his analysis of the experiences of Aboriginal juveniles in custody, Cunneen argues that there are "compelling reasons for considering the use of violence against Aboriginal youth as part of an *institutionalised* form of racist violence" (ibid.: 134, emphasis in original).

Gale et al.'s (1990) study of the experiences of Aboriginal young people in South Australia resonates with the way in which their counterparts in Queensland are "hassled" by police. For example, a sixteen-year-old Aboriginal boy was seen running down a street in the city, and was stopped by police and asked why he was running. As a result of the way in which he responded to this query, he was arrested for abusive language. Further, this South Australian study provides a number of specific examples of over-policing, in which Aboriginal young people were charged with offences in a number of trivial situations, which "would seem to warrant a police caution rather than an apprehension" (ibid.: 65). One such example involved two Aboriginal children, aged 10 and 11 years, who entered the back yard of a vacant Aboriginal housing agency house, and picked oranges from a tree. "They were each charged with larceny and being unlawfully on the premises, even though an Aboriginal community worker argued with police that not only had the previous occupants invited the children to "help themselves", but also, because it was a designated Aboriginal house, the children regarded the fruit as being community property" (ibid).

It is not difficult to find Aboriginal complaints about police harassment and violence in Brisbane and neighbouring areas of southeast Queensland. For example, in her description of Aboriginal social and cultural life in an unnamed industrial city near Brisbane in the 1970s, Eckermann (1977: 299) quotes a woman who told her about the Aboriginal need to be prepared to "fight [i.e. argue] with *coppers* [police]" for their children: "those coppers, they reckon just because you're black they can pick on the kid".

And it is not just Aboriginal children and young people who have been subjected to police harassment and violence. Cheryl Buchanan, now chairwoman of the Kooma Traditional Owners Association, has been a prominent Aboriginal activist since the 1970s (Howie-Willis 1994a: 159). Talking to the journalists Forde and Forde (2005) about being a young Aboriginal person in Brisbane in the 1960s and 1970s, she said:

> We got raped by the police in those days and we couldn't do anything about it. They were the SS. The police would pick us up on a regular basis because they knew who we all were, and they'd take us out the back of Samford [then a rural location, some considerable distance from the city] and harass us or push us around for hours.

During the 1980s when I lived in Brisbane, Aboriginal people told me of occasions on which a young relative was assaulted by police, either in custody, or after being driven to an isolated area. Indeed, the widespread feeling among many Aboriginal people there, as in many other parts of Australia, is that the involvement of police in any incident or event, is a grounds for concern, if not fear. One experience from my years living in Brisbane (1977–1987) serves to illustrate this fear:

> I was at a dance organised by an Aboriginal group one Friday night in the mid-1980s at a hall in an inner Brisbane suburb. During the evening a fight broke out between some drunk men. The group of Aboriginal women I was with were not impressed with the fight, but kept socialising and dancing in another part of the hall. When a few members of the police force arrived in the hall, my women friends quickly left the hall through the back door, taking me with them, and explaining that it's not safe once the police arrive. I was struck with the contrast between their lack of fear during the fight, and their considerable fear once the police arrived (for me, it was the other way around). They later explained that you could never know who the police would pick on, and/or remove, for what reason and in what way, and to where. And they all had friends and/or relatives who had been abused by police.

A particularly low point in Aboriginal-police relations in Brisbane came in 1986, during a dance and football presentation night held by the local Aboriginal community at a hall in suburban Rosalie. Although the evening was proceeding peacefully (Lui 2000), and no incidents were reported, about a hundred police arrived at the hall. "Police provocation, including bringing dogs into the hall, sparked a riot during which indiscriminate violence was used against women, men and children" (Cunneen 2001: 111). A television camera crew produced evidence of one man "being batoned from behind around the head, neck and shoulders" (ibid.). This man was later kicked while on the ground. Cunneen reports that more than 70 people were charged with drunkenness, offensive language and resisting arrest. One police officer was charged with assault and pleaded guilty. But the judge exercised his right to dismiss the matter and no conviction was recorded against the police officer.

And in the following year – 1987 – Brisbane police intervened in an Aboriginal twenty-first birthday party in a hall in suburban Annerley. Eye-witnesses said that police "indiscriminately used batons, while other persons were kicked and had their heads banged against police vehicles" (Cunneen 2001: 93). While both the Rosalie and the Annerley incidents were reported as riots, Cunneen (ibid.) points out that on both occasions "many witnesses claimed that the so-called 'riots' occurred as a direct result of unnecessary police intervention, provocation and the use of excessive force".

While the incidents of police harrassment and violence discussed in this section predate the Pinkenba incident, they provide clear evidence of the likely fear that David, Albert and Barry would have had when approached by the police in the Valley that night in May 1994. We will see that an essential part of the defence argument in the Pinkenba hearing is that the boys knew that they could have refused to go in the police cars. The evidence presented in this chapter seriously questions how they could have exercised this right, if they indeed did know about it.

4. Aboriginal resistance to police powers

The first three sections in this chapter have presented a rather one-sided view of the relationship between Aboriginal people and the criminal justice system. While Aboriginal people are relatively powerless, they are not without agency. A more microanalytic approach to the modes of police intervention in the lives of Aboriginal people would find moments of resistance. For example, an elderly Aboriginal woman with whom I did Waka Waka language recording around Gayndah (about 100 kilometres north of Cherbourg) in the early 1980s used to talk of the times in her childhood that police would come looking for Aboriginal children to take away. Her family had an arrangement with a *gypsy* family (travelling Lebanese-Australian hawkers), to hide her and other Aboriginal children amongst their own children in their caravan on such occasions. In this way, she and other children escaped the worst of the "protection" era. An important example of contemporary resistance to police intervention is undoubtedly to be found in immediate verbal reactions: thus, swearing plays a significant role in interactions between Aboriginal people and police, as we will see in Section 4.2 below.

4.1.   Aboriginal Legal Services

While some individuals have struggled against colonial domination in every decade, the lack of permanent authority structures in Aboriginal societies, as well as the extent of linguistic and cultural diversity around the country have been among the factors which have contributed to the general lack of organised resistance against colonial powers. One of the earliest examples of institutional resistance by Aboriginal people came in the early 1970s with the establishment of Aboriginal Legal Services (ALS). The first ALS was established in Sydney in 1970, as an immediate response to "some young Aborigines deeply resenting police treatment of their people in Redfern" [an inner-Sydney suburb with a high Aboriginal population] (Eggleston 1977: 353; see also Lyons 1984: 138). Within two years an ALS was established in Brisbane, and there are now several ALSs in each state and territory, with a national secretariat (NAILSS). There are a number of slightly different names for the regional ALSs around Australia, and the Brisbane service, which was involved in the Pinkenba case, was at that time formally named "Aboriginal and Torres Strait Islanders Corporation (QEA) for Legal Services". Throughout this book, I will follow widespread Australian convention in using the acronym ALS and its plural ALSs as a common name for Aboriginal Legal Service(s).

Established by Aboriginal people, for Aboriginal people, on a state-by-state basis, ALSs are funded primarily by the federal government. Their priority tends to be with criminal cases, and there has been a general policy not to act in matters which involve litigation between two different Aboriginal parties, although this policy is not always followed. Eggleston's (1977: 357) analysis is that ALSs "actually have twin objectives. One is to provide legal assistance to Aborigines who need it. The other, equally important, is to promote Aboriginal self-determination by involving Aborigines in the running of the services". Further, many would agree with Charles (2003: 22), that the fact that they are Aboriginal organisations means that compared to mainstream legal aid services, they "can provide better services, more closely aligned with communities and their needs" and that they are "better able to provide culturally sensitive and useful services to their clients". While most lawyers who work for ALSs are non-Aboriginal people, a key to the functioning of these services is the work of Aboriginal paralegal field officers, who provide "the crucial link" (Lyons 1984: 143) between the legal service and the Aboriginal community. Given that a major concern of ALSs from the outset has been police-Aboriginal relations (e.g. O'Shane 1992: 4), there remains a tension between these services and the police.

4.2.   *Offensive language*

The ongoing struggle between Aboriginal people and the police is clearly an unbalanced one. Shouting abuse at a police officer is one small act of resistance which Aboriginal people can, and often do, engage in. But this is not just a matter for the relationship between police and Aboriginal people, as the use of "offensive language" or "obscene language" is a criminal offence in many Australian jurisdictions. Thus, police officers are empowered by legislation, enacted by democratically elected legislators, to criminalise Aboriginal people (and any others) who engage in this act of resistance, which in another country might simply be considered free speech, no matter how bad-mannered or offensive. But, it appears to be Aboriginal people who are the prime targets of the crime of "offensive language", because of the way in which police use their discretionary powers (Wilson 1978; Langton 1988; Taylor 1995). There appear to be three factors involved in this targeting.

Firstly, given the acceptance of the roles of swearing in Aboriginal societies, it is likely that Aboriginal people are typically less constrained in their use of words and expressions considered to be offensive by many non-Aboriginal people. Anthropological research sheds interesting light on cultural differences in the use of so-called "offensive language" or swearing. A 1930s study in several north Queensland traditionally-oriented Aboriginal societies found that "the use of swearing and obscenity is of frequent occurrence and plays an important role in social life" (Thomson 1935: 460). In addition to the use of "unorganized swearing" in arguments, Thomson found that "organized swearing" was obligatory in certain kin relationships, for example between a boy or man and his paternal grandfather. Discussing contemporary (non-traditionally-oriented) Aboriginal societies, Langton (1988: 202) argues that "swearing and fighting in contemporary Aboriginal society constitute dispute processing and social ordering devices derived from traditional cultural patterns". As with a number of other researchers, Langton points out that there is no gendered distinction in the use of swearing in Aboriginal societies: a person is no less, or more, a woman, when she swears, in contrast to a widespread view in mainstream Australian society.

Secondly, in addition to its uses between Aboriginal people, such as in resolving conflict, swearing can also be used as a form of resistance. Langton (1988: 219) sees it as a particular form of resistance, which has the government as its object, and thus she calls it a "tactic of sedition". Despite overwhelming power imbalance in the struggle between Aboriginal people and the police, who are carrying out the control of the state, Aboriginal people do have some agency: they can swear at police officers.

But as Aboriginal people use swearing as an act of sedition directed at police officers, these officers in turn can use their discretionary power and retaliate by arresting those who are swearing. Thus, the third factor in the targeting of Aboriginal people, which is closely connected to the first two, is that swearing provides an easy mechanism for police in the criminalising of Aboriginal people. This is well recognised by Aboriginal people, legal professionals and sociolegal scholars. Once an Aboriginal person is stopped by police officers for using offensive language, it is not difficult for a situation to develop in which the Aboriginal person is then charged with one or more of the offences of public drunkenness, resisting arrest and assaulting a police officer (even if there is no physical contact[20]). The combination of two of these offences with offensive language is such a regular occurrence in the policing of Aboriginal people throughout the country that it has the common name of "trifecta".[21] (Walsh (2005: 143) reports that other popular names for this three-part charge are "ham, cheese and tomato sandwich", and "hamburger with the lot".)

While offensive language is defined as an offence in terms of its use in or near a public place, in practice people are only charged with this offence if they say a word or words deemed to be offensive in the presence of a police officer. Thus, in a well-known 1991 case from a New South Wales town located 200 kilometres south of Brisbane, police charged a man with offensive language, when he said "Watch those two fucking poofters here, how they fucking persecute me", as two police officers walked into the take-away shop where he was waiting for food (Taylor 1995: 238). The magistrate who heard the case dismissed it, saying that the words were common usage and not offensive. Further, the magistrate reportedly "said the expression was not as upsetting as 'collateral damage' – a term now being used by the allies in the Gulf War to describe human casualties" (Larriera and Macey 1991). It is interesting to note that the accused in this case was not Aboriginal, although the magistrate, Pat O'Shane, was (and at that time she was the only Aboriginal magistrate in the country). The outrage in the New South Wales police force over O'Shane's decision led to calls for enacting a tougher penalty for swearing at a police officer in that state. This move appeared to be gaining popular and legislative momentum, until the release in March 1992 of the ABC television documentary titled *Cop it Sweet*. Screened on national television, the documentary was based on the television crew's work over a period of six weeks riding in police patrol cars in the inner Sydney suburb of Redfern, referred to in Section 4.1 above (see Taylor 1995: 240–242 for details). Using an ethnographic approach, with full permission from the police service and its officers, this television crew captured the realities of daily policing of Aboriginal people. Viewers were shocked to see police approach an Aboriginal man walking lawfully down the street one night and call out an obscenity to him. When the man returned the insult, he was arrested for obscene language, and held overnight in a police cell. This incident and others in the documentary confirmed allegations which had frequently been made about the ways in which police abused the "offence" of "offensive language" in their interactions with Aboriginal people. The documentary played an important part in ending attempted legislative changes, which had aimed to toughen the penalty for swearing at a police officer.

While the *Cop it Sweet* documentary captured police inciting an Aboriginal man to swear by initiating the swearing at him, another police tactic reported by Aboriginal people is found in the experience reported by an Aboriginal youth to Cunneen (1995: 124–125): "In Brisbane, in the Mall, me and a couple of other Murries [Aboriginal people] were just sitting down in a circle and these coppers came up and charged us for abusive language. We were just sitting there". But not all offensive language charges initiate in one of these two approaches. There are undoubtedly many occasions in which over-policing results in Aboriginal attempts to assert some control through the use of swearing, which leads to offensive language charges, which can then easily escalate to the trifecta of charges, as discussed above.

One case of offensive language which is widely discussed by members of the legal profession is the 1999 New South Wales case of *Police v Shannon Thomas Dunn*.[22] In this case magistrate David Heilpern dismissed an offensive language charge against an 18-year-old Aboriginal man who had allegedly said "Fuck off your [sic] not taking the bike" to a police officer who approached him and tried to take the bicycle he had been riding. In his lengthy judgment (*Police v Shannon Thomas Dunn* 1999: 240), Magistrate Heilpern said:

> The word "fuck" is extremely common now and has lost most of its punch. ...
> It is used in every school playground every day. ... If your children like JJJ [a
> national government-funded radio station that appeals to young listeners] and
> listen to it in the morning, one cannot help be assailed by the word "fuck" with
> regularity between mouthfuls of toast. ... In short, one would have to live an
> excessively cloistered existence not to come into regular contact with the word,
> and not to have become somewhat immune to its suggested previously legally
> offensive status.

Heilpern also pointed out that the "short research" which he had conducted on "relevant public policy issues" revealed that "Aboriginal people account for 15 times as many offensive language offences as would be expected" (ibid.: 240–241). He also cited the national report of the Royal Commission into Aboriginal Deaths in Custody (Johnston 1991b: 3: 7) to be discussed below, which cited the conclusions of one of the commissioners (Wootten 1991: 286–287), that it "is surely time that police learnt to ignore mere abuse, let alone simple 'bad language'" and concluded that offensive language charges "just become part of an oppressive mechanism of control of Aboriginals". Interestingly, the national report concluded that in Queensland "obscene language and vagrancy have a discriminatory impact on Aboriginal people" (Johnston 1991b: 2: 230).

The use of words such as *fuck* and *fucking* are commonplace in Australia. But the criminalisation of Aboriginal people through the selective policing of the use of such words can be seen as the contemporary counterpart to earlier legislation which punished Aboriginal reserve residents for crimes such as "in-discipline" or "immoral behaviour" discussed in Section 1.2 above. At the time of the Pinkenba incident, the use of "any profane, indecent or obscene language" in or near any public place was still a criminal offence in Queensland (under Section 7 of the *Vagrancy, Gaming and other Offences Act 1931*). Indeed swearing is still an offence under the 2005 *Summary Offences Act*, and in Section 5 of Chapter 11 we will see a recent instance of an Aboriginal woman going to jail for swearing. During the Pinkenba cross-examination, one of the two defence counsel made the most of two earlier episodes where he had evidence of swearing by one of the witnesses, using this to build up the negative identity of the boys, and to support an ongoing theme in police control over Aboriginal people, as we will see in Section 4 of Chapter 6.

We will see the powerlessness of the boys in the Pinkenba hearing to engage in any act of sedition when cross-examined about their use of offensive language. However, in Langton's (1988: 220) analysis of the general use of offensive language by Aboriginal adults, she argues that there can be a "supreme stroke of wit" involved. This is because, when police prosecutors take an offensive language charge to court, they have to "read out the alleged offences of 'unseemly words' directed by Aboriginal people at them". Thus, she argues, "Aboriginal people use the courtroom as their political audience in a game of irony".

5. The Fitzgerald Inquiry and the Criminal Justice Commission

Having considered some of the issues and practices involved in the societal struggle between Aboriginal people and the police, we now move to institutional aspects of this struggle. Complaints against the Queensland police from many social groups, not just Aboriginal people, reached a climax in the mid-1980s. Investigations of widespread allegations of police corruption (rather than violence) led to television and newspaper journalists uncovering a network of police involvement in illegal prostitution and gambling. This precipitated the establishment of the Commission of Inquiry into Possible Illegal Activites and Associated Police Misconduct in 1987. It is widely referred to as "the Fitzgerald Inquiry", after its Chairman, G. E. (Tony) Fitzgerald, who at that time was a well-respected barrister (and who later went on to become the president of the Queensland Court of Appeal, and a judge in the New South Wales Court of Appeal). The Fitzgerald Inquiry "rocked Queensland with almost daily revelations of corruption and malpractice at the highest levels of law enforcement and government" (Findlay et al. 2005: 86). Fitzgerald found (1989: 363) that there were "two main types of police misconduct enmeshed within police culture" in Queensland: verballing and corruption. He found verballing was "common, and engaged in by many officers who [were] otherwise honest" (ibid.). Interestingly, Fitzgerald had been the defence barrister in the Kelvin Condren appeal in which I had given sociolinguistic evidence in 1987 which supported Condren's allegations of having been verballed, as discussed in Section 1.1 of Chapter 2 above. While the Fitzgerald Inquiry did not report on any cases specifically involving

Aboriginal people, its impact on police in Queensland affected the policing of Aboriginal people, as we will see.

A number of senior police, including the then Police Commissioner, were found by the Fitzgerald inquiry to be corrupt, and resulting criminal trials led to their imprisonment. Fitzgerald's wide-ranging recommendations led to reform of the police force, in terms of structure, practices and recruitment, and to the establishment of the Criminal Justice Commission (CJC). Among its many responsibilities, the CJC was charged with overseeing reform of the police force, and monitoring the administration of criminal justice. It was thus, effectively, an external insitituion to which the Queensland police would now be answerable to some extent. It is hardly surprising then that there was considerable opposition in the police force to the Fitzgerald report, and the "widespread perception" among Queensland police that the reforms recommended in the report were "punitive" (CJC 1994c: 15).

The CJC became a major force for institutional change in Queensland with its "key goal" being the promotion of "an effective, fair and accessible criminal justice system" (CJC 1996: i). While one of the main functions of the CJC was to investigate claims of police and public sector misconduct, another of its functions was to work with the police to investigate organised and major crime. In 1997 this crime function was taken over by the newly formed Queensland Crime Commission (QCC), which was also given the task of investigating paedophilia. In 2002 these two commissions (CJC and QCC) were amalgamated to form a single body to fight crime and public sector misconduct, named the Crime and Misconduct Commission (CMC). As the main focus of this book concerns the years leading up to and surrounding the 1994 Pinkenba event, and the 1995 hearing, it is the CJC (rather than the CMC) which is of concern to this book.

In investigating individual allegations of police misconduct, the CJC had the power to recommend disciplinary charges within the Queensland Police Service, or criminal charges within the criminal justice process. It could also provide the Commissioner of the Queensland Police Service with policy directives. In its role of investigating claims of police misconduct, the CJC investigated some Aboriginal complaints against police officers. For example, in 1992, it investigated Kelvin Condren's complaint which arose from the court decision in 1990 that his 1984 murder conviction had been wrongful (discussed in Section 1.1 of Chapter 2 above). The same investigation (CJC 1992) also examined the complaints of three other Aboriginal people who alleged that they had been pressured by police into making false statements in relation to the murder for which Condren was charged and wrongly convicted. After hearing evidence from 21 witnesses in a tribunal setting, the CJC handed down its 103-page report. The report's conclusion on all of the allegations was that "the available evidence does not justify referring a report on this matter for consideration of criminal or disciplinary charges" (ibid.: 37, 44, 59, 61, 62).

I had been called to give evidence to this Inquiry, but, to my frustration, I had not been allowed to talk about the specific case of Condren's police interview, which I had analysed and given evidence on a few years earlier in his appeal, as discussed in Section 1.1 of Chapter 2 above. My evidence to the CJC investigation of his complaint was restricted to general issues about the difficulties faced by Aboriginal people in legal interviews (as dealt with in the then newly-published lawyers' handbook, Eades 1992). My evidence in Condren's appeal in 1987 had been rejected partly because it examined not only the answers attributed to Condren, but also features of Aboriginal English more generally. One of the appeal court judges had rejected any discussion of Aboriginal English features (implied to be shared with other speakers of Aboriginal English), saying (*R v Condren*: 267): "The verbal response characteristics of a class [of people] is not a matter at issue". Instead the issue was "only the alleged responses of the applicant" (ibid.). Ironically, the opposite logic was applied in the CJC investigation of his complaint. My expert opinion of the details of Condren's case and his "alleged responses" was not allowed, only the "verbal response characteristics" of Aboriginal English speakers more generally.

Chapter 9 of the ten-chapter CJC report of its investigation of Condren's complaint (CJC 1992) examines "some of the difficulties inherent in the criminal justice system's dealings with Aboriginal suspects and witnesses" (ibid.: 69). This chapter draws extensively on my work in the sections dealing with "The use of language" (ibid.: 71–72), "Concepts of time and distance" (ibid.: 72), "Deference to authority" (ibid.: 73), and "The formality of the interview" (ibid.: 74). Chapter 10 consists of "recommendations for changes in practices and procedures" (ibid.: 69), including provisions for police interviews of Aboriginal suspects that are similar to the *Anunga Rules* in the Northern Territory (to be discussed in Section 1.1 of Chapter 4). It also recommended amendments to the *Evidence Act* so that uncorroborated confessions would not be admissible. While these recommendations were valuable, they were seen as avoiding the serious issue of alleged police verballing and witness abuse which had occurred in Condren's case.

The Aboriginal community in Queensland was very disappointed that no police officer was to be disciplined or prosecuted over the Condren case. It had received very wide newspaper coverage, had been the topic of an hour-long investigative television program by one of the country's leading documentary makers (Masters 1988), and the subject of a 1990 street demonstration in Townsville. Further, in the year preceding the quashing of Condren's conviction, his case was considered by Amnesty International, and taken to the United Nations Commission for Human Rights in Geneva (Arnold 1989). Many Aboriginal people felt "let down" by the CJC, and increasingly frustrated over what they saw as a police force that was still out of control and unanswerable in relation to policing the Aboriginal community, despite the positive signs from the Fitzgerald Inquiry and the establishment of the CJC.

6.   The Royal Commission into Aboriginal Deaths in Custody

The Fitzgerald inquiry did not deal specifically with Aboriginal people, but it resulted in important consequences for the ways in which the criminal justice process impacts on Aboriginal people in Queensland, especially through the Criminal Justice Commission, as we will see. But, partly overlapping with the time period of this Queensland inquiry was a national inquiry, concerned directly with the experiences of Aboriginal people in the criminal justice system. The Royal Commission into Aboriginal Deaths in Custody (hereafter the Royal Commission, or RCIADC) was established in 1987 to investigate the alarming rate at which Aboriginal people were dying in custody, both in police custody and in prisons. In its final report overview (Johnston 1991a: 3), the Royal Commission concluded that none of the 99 Indigenous deaths in custody between 1980 and 1989 were "the product of deliberate violence or brutality by police or prison officers". It also found that "Aboriginal people in custody do not die at a greater rate than non-Aboriginal people in custody" (ibid.: 6). But the report was damning in its thorough exploration of the factors which led to the situation where "the Aboriginal population is grossly over-represented in custody" (ibid.: 6). Thus, while initially established to investigate deaths in custody, and while many of its 339 recommendations specifically addressed this issue, the report has had a wide-ranging impact at all levels of Australian society on the issues surrounding Aboriginal participation in the criminal justice system.

In addition to detailed investigation of each of the 99 deaths, the Royal Commission undertook an analysis of the "legacies of the history of two centuries of European domination of Aboriginal people" (ibid.: 7), which included the colonial history and its consequences. The report argued that "the most significant contributing factor" to the over-representation of Aboriginal people in custody is "the disadvantaged and unequal position in which Aboriginal people find themselves in the society – socially, economically and culturally" (ibid.: 15). It specifically addressed issues involved in policing, which have been discussed in Section 1.3 and 3 above, including the ways in which police discretionary powers are used, as well as abuse of police powers, for example through violence.

A major concern addressed in the five-volume final report (Johnston 1991b) relates to ways of reducing the number of Aboriginal people in custody. These include the decriminalisation of drunkenness, the cessation of arrests in cases where offensive language occurs in interventions initiated by police, and the general principle that arrest be seen as "the sanction of last resort" (ibid.: 50). Other recommendations directly relating to policing include Recommendation 60 (ibid.: 44):

> That Police Services take all possible steps to eliminate:
>
> a. Violent or rough treatment or verbal abuse of Aboriginal persons, including women and young people, by police officers; and
>
> b. The use of racist or offensive language, or the use of racist or derogatory comments in log books and other documents, by police officers.
>
> When such conduct is found to have occurred, it should be treated as a serious breach of discipline.

Special attention was given to Aboriginal youth in the criminal justice system, including recommendations that police be required to contact ALS and a relevant parent or other adult when an Aboriginal young person is taken to a police station (ibid.: 86).

The Royal Commission's investigations and its report marked a watershed in the recognition of the extent of injustice involved in the participation of Aboriginal people in the criminal justice system. Many of its recommendations have been adopted to some extent, with this varying from state to state. Despite these changes and some improvements, several reviews since the Royal Commission's report indicate that the pattern of Indigenous over-representation in custody continues at a high rate (e.g. Cunneen and McDonald 1997; McDonald and Cunneen 1997; ATSIC 1997; Cunneen et al. 2005).

7. Key events in Brisbane 1993–1995

After the consideration of the societal and institutional struggles between Aboriginal young people and police, we now focus attention on key events which took place in Brisbane leading up to and including the Pinkenba event. It is impossible to make sense of the Pinkenba hearing without understanding these events, which bring together the social groups and institutions discussed in this chapter: the Brisbane Aboriginal community, the Queensland police force, the Aboriginal Legal Service, the Criminal Justice Commission, as well as two of the state's top elected representatives, the Attorney-General and the Leader of the Opposition. We will see that understanding the situated conversational struggle which takes place in the Pinkenba cross-examination between two leading lawyers and three Aboriginal boys (to be examined in Parts II and III) involves understanding legal and political struggles of the greatest magnitude.

7.1. A death, a riot, an infiltrator and a protest

On 7 November 1993 what began as a typical encounter between police and a group of Aboriginal young people ended in yet another black death in police custody, which enraged the Aboriginal community. Daniel Yock was one of a group of 9 Aboriginal young men aged about 15–18, who were from Cherbourg, where most were members of the Wakka Wakka Dance Troupe. On 7 November, Yock and his friends had been drinking in Musgrave Park, a large park in the inner Brisbane suburb of West End. This park has for decades been an important meeting place for Aboriginal people, a fact recognised by state and local government in the recent establishment of an Indigenous Cultural Centre in the park. As Huggins and Huggins (1994: 138) described it around the time of Yock's arrest, Musgrave Park is "a common meeting place for Murries [Aboriginal people] ... there are Aboriginal people from all over the state who lob in [= arrive] looking for relatives and directions to other places. It is a place where Murries feel comfortable about having and sharing a drink ...".

As they were walking away from the park, the boys were approached by police in a nearby suburban street. A confrontation developed, and Yock was arrested for behaving in a disorderly manner (CJC 1994a: 63), the arguably trivial public order "offence" which is used in so many situations in the criminalisation of Aboriginal young people, as discussed in Section 1.3 above. Shortly after his arrest, while in custody in a police van, Yock died of heart failure.

There was much criticism of the arrest, especially given recommendations of the Royal Commission about alternatives to arrest in such circumstances (discussed in Section 6 above). Some Aboriginal leaders accused the arresting officers of causing his death. One day after his death, a demonstration outside the police headquarters led to "the worst street riot [in Brisbane] in a decade" (Fagan 1994). In the "protest which erupted into a bloody clash" (Woods 1993), about 200 Aborigines clashed with police (Walker and Fagan 1994), and 31 police officers were injured (Fagan 1994). While the violence was decried by Aboriginal leaders, in the words of ALS administrator Sam Watson, they noted that people "out there in suburbia were able to see that this time people were not going to accept any whitewash for one further Aboriginal death in custody" (Woods 1993).

This latest death in police custody, and the riot outside police headquarters, began a period of heightened conflict between Aboriginal people and police in

Brisbane. A newspaper report on 13 November (six days after Yock's death) reported outrage after an undercover policeman was found infiltrating a meeting of Brisbane Aboriginal sympathisers. The police officer infiltrator was recognised by a prominent lawyer at the meeting, who "blew his cover". This infiltrator – who was wearing a white T-shirt, jeans, boots and two earrings – "admitted ... that he was a police officer and he was undercover obtaining information for the [police] commissioner" (Anon 1993b). Talking about this incident, the secretary of the Australian National Indigenous Media Association, Tiga Bayles, said: "We are scared for our kids and that there will be another tragedy like Daniel Yock" (ibid.).

On 18 November (eleven days after Yock's death), about 4000 demonstrators held a peaceful protest, beginning in Musgrave Park, and marching several kilometres to the city, where there were "passionate" speeches on a number of Aboriginal issues, including deaths in custody, racism and land rights (Tom 1993). Many of the protesters wore T-shirts honouring "Boonie our brother" (using Yock's nickname) on the front. On the back of the T-shirts was the pointed question "Is it Justice or Just-Us?" (ibid.). In contrast to the violence of the protest on the day after his death, this protest was held in a peaceful manner, with outspoken leaders, such as Lionel Fogarty, urging that "we must show our anger, but we must do so calmly and peacefully" (Anon 1993a).

7.2.   *Sensitivity to cross-cultural communication OR* Mabo madness?

While anger over Yock's death was mounting in Brisbane in late November, another event was also drawing public attention to Aboriginal issues in the criminal justice system. This was an argument between two of Queensland's most senior elected representatives about "special treatment" for Aboriginal people in the legal system. The argument was precipitated by a case in which the involvement of police had been irrelevant, and it shows the wider societal struggle over the ways in which the criminal justice system deals with Aboriginal people. In responding to the judgment of a much-publicised criminal appeal case (*R v Kina 1993*), the Attorney-General called for the legal system *to have knowledge of and ... be sensitive to* the *problem of cross-cultural communication* (ABC 1993). Kina was an Aboriginal woman whose 1988 murder conviction was overturned on 29 November 1993, partly as a result of sociolinguistic evidence about her Aboriginal ways of communicating (see Eades 1996a, 2004a). In presenting this evidence to the appeal court, I had shown the apparent consequences for Kina's 1988 trial of her lawyers' lack of awareness of such features as Aboriginal use of silence (referred to in Section 1.2 of Chapter 2 above, and discussed in Section 2 of Chapter 4 below).

In response to the Kina judgment, the Attorney-General announced that "... the law is going to have to find ways and the legal system is going to have to find ways to make special provision frequently for Aboriginal witnesses because they have a number of particular and special features which do argue that they should be treated in that way" (King 1993). Specifically, he advocated the relevance of existing legislation concerning "special witnesses" for some Aboriginal witnesses (which was being widely used for child witnesses). This was Section 21A of the *Evidence Act* 1977 – discussed in Section 5 of Chapter 1 – in relation to which he proposed that *the legal system ought to be aware* of the possibility of considering *individual* Aboriginal witnesses as "special witnesses" on the grounds of "cultural differences", as specified in Subsection (b)(i) of Section 21A.

The Attorney-General's announcement was derided by the Opposition leader as "pandering to Aborigines" and advocating "one law for blacks, one law for whites" (King 1993). In a televised debate on the issue between the two political leaders on the 30 November (ABC 1993), the Opposition leader complained about the *regime of political correctness* in the legal system, arguing that the police were not *game enough to arrest demonstrators when the riot was on a few weeks back* (after Yock's death, discussed in Section 7.1 above). This complaint ignored the fact that it is not against the law to participate in a demonstration. The Opposition leader then connected the Attorney-General's comments to imminent state legislation which would establish a form of Aboriginal and Torres Strait Islander land rights. This proposed legislation was to complement recent federal land rights legislation, which had resulted from the controversial Mabo case – in which the legal fiction of *terra nullius*, referred to in Section 1 of Chapter 1, had been overturned by the High Court (see Altman and Palmer 2005). Thus, referring to the Attorney-General's announcement, the Opposition leader told him that *the people of Queensland ... [are] fed up with this extension of this Mabo madness that is just going to incredibly divide this community* (ABC 1993). The term *Mabo madness* was an emotionally-charged, derogatory (and alliterative) label to refer to legal recognition of Indigenous rights. Its use in this context highlights the connection between criminal justice issues and wider power struggles over control and ownership of land and resources. The Attorney-General attacked the Opposition leader's complaint, calling his arguments *deceitful*, and accusing him of *cynically trying to manipulate people into thinking that there is a conflictual situation where there indeed is not* (ABC 1993).

The fact that this public debate about Aboriginal rights, between two people at the highest level of government, was centred around the criminal justice system, is undoubtedly related to widespread general objections that governments spend too much money on Aboriginal people and programmes for them (Augoustinos et al. 1999: 368). Thus, the Opposition leader complained that "if you're an Aboriginal ... you'll get special consideration all the time" (King 1993). This chapter has shown that this so-called "special consideration" has generally been of a disadvantageous nature.

7.3.   Some police officers "think they can do whatever they please"

This more typical kind of "special consideration" for Aboriginal people was revealed just a few weeks after this high-profile debate. On 18 December 1993, a Brisbane ALS solicitor reported to a parliamentary inquiry into criminal justice that the legal service had received "numerous reports" from clients that "police held pistols to the heads of Aborigines to intimidate them" (Maher 1993). The solicitor further reported that "his clients were not inclined to follow complaints through, wanting to 'get it over and done with and be rid of the system'" (ibid.). Outside the hearing, this solicitor, Tony McEvoy, told the media that after Yock's death, the consensus in the Aboriginal community was "that the community lost all faith in the police force". The newspaper report continues: "[McEvoy] said despite the findings of the royal commission into black deaths in custody there was 'no decrease in the "unholy trilogy" of arrests for obscene language, resisting arrest and assaulting police which Aborigines were often drawn into after being provoked'" (ibid.).[23] McEvoy's evidence to the parliamentary committee also included the view that "the police force suffered 'attitudinal' and 'generational' problems in that some officers 'think they can do whatever they please'" (ibid.).

7.4.   "US and THEM": the CJC inquiry into Yock's death

Between November 1993 and February 1994, the CJC held its inquiry into Yock's death. Media reporting during the public hearing reflected, fairly accurately in my view, the contested and "confrontationist" (Solomon 1993a) nature of the inquiry hearing. In a report with the large headlines "A case of US and THEM", Solomon highlighted the fact that "feelings were running very high" because of the accusations "that the police had caused [the death in custody], directly or indirectly". As Solomon reported, the Commissioner considered a submission from ALS that some provisions be made to facilitate the boys' telling of their stories to the Commission. This request had come partly from the ALS consideration of the report which they had commissioned from me about communication issues affecting evidence from the Cherbourg boys who had been Yock's companions and witnesses to his arrest. The Commissioner (CJC 1994a: 10–11) did take into account some of the issues raised in my report, such as the manner of questioning and his evaluation of the boys' evidence (in the light of such features as gratuitous concurrence). However, the Commissioner's interruption of cross-examination of one of the boys by the barrister representing the police officers, led to this barrister's complaints that "special treatment had gone too far" (Solomon 1993b). In reporting this complaint as well as this barrister's "aggressive" cross-examination of the boys, Solomon (ibid.) observed that the barrister's approach was "dictated by the seriousness of the charges which are levelled against the police he represents".

Denying a request for the hearing to move to Musgrave Park, the Commissioner did give approval for an Aboriginal friend to sit beside the boys during their evidence (CJC 1994a: 10, referring to my report). The journalist Solomon (1993a), highlighting his theme of the "'us' and 'them' nature of the proceedings", reported that "[S]omehow [the police] managed to persuade the CJC that it was the police who were at risk in this clash between the Aboriginal and police cultures". Thus, police witnesses were allowed to have a colleague sitting next to them in the witness box, and a further dozen police were stationed around the hearing room. Solomon's analysis also points out that "one of the police witnesses even referred to the affair [Yock's death] as something that had happened to the police". Thus, this officer gave evidence that when he examined Yock at the watchhouse and found that he was not breathing, it was "just unbelievable – I just couldn't grasp how it had happened under the circumstances. ... It can happen to any officer today, tomorrow, or in three months' time. That's the scary thing" (ibid.).

7.5.   *"Fraught relations" between Brisbane Aborigines and the police*

The outcome of this "contest ... waged before the commission" (Solomon ibid.) was that, in the decision made five months after Yock's death, the CJC found that Yock and his companions had been behaving in a disorderly manner and that Yock's arrest was lawful. Further, it could not find sufficient evidence to support allegations of Yock's mistreatment following his arrest, and was not able to find sufficient evidence to put any police officers on any charge relating to his death (CJC 1994a). The CJC reported that aspects of the evidence of one of the arresting police officers was "unreliable" (ibid.: xxi), while some of the evidence of three of the Aboriginal boys was "completely erroneous" (ibid.: xxii). In none of these instances did the Commissioner find any "deliberate dishonesty" or "deliberate untruthfulness".

On 5 April 1994, the major national newspaper reported that "yesterday's verdict on the death of Daniel Yock does nothing to temper the fraught relations between Brisbane Aborigines and the police" (Walker 1994a). Brisbane Aboriginal community leaders were outraged about the CJC decision, with one, Mary Graham, saying that "the general feeling [in the Brisbane Aboriginal community] is that the police have got away with it again ... they are never going to find the justice authorities guilty of anything in this country" (Walker 1994b). While the CJC's finding was widely criticised by Aboriginal leaders (ibid.), the major Aboriginal antagonism remained focused on the police, whose actions were widely known to have contravened important recommendations from the Royal Commission into Aboriginal Deaths in Custody (discussed in Section 6 above), especially in relation to diversion from police custody (Recommendations 79–91, Johnston 1991a: 49–52), and the principle of arrest being the sanction of last resort (Recommendation 87, ibid.: 50).

The outrage expressed by the community over police behaviour and the system's acceptance of it, was matched by police outrage over Aboriginal allegations of police brutality in Yock's death. The police commissioner demanded an apology from the Aboriginal community, saying that there "was no doubt that some Aborigines were 'hell-bent' on using Mr Yock's death to incite tensions with police" (Anon 1994). These comments from the commissioner were described as "inflammatory" by one of Australia's most respected Aboriginal elders – retired Liberal Party senator Neville Bonner, who at that time was the only Aboriginal person ever to have held office in federal parliament (Walker 1994b). The administrator of the Brisbane ALS, Sam Watson, was adamant there would be no apology to the police, saying that it would be "tantamount to asking the Jewish people to apologise for Auschwitz or asking the Tasmanian people to apologise for genocide" (Walker and Fagan 1994).

One of the most outspoken Brisbane Aboriginal leaders, Lionel Fogarty, was in the forefront of protests around Yock's death. Fogarty has been well known in Queensland as an Aboriginal "radical" since the 1970s (Howie-Willis 1994c: 373), and he was also Daniel Yock's brother. Fogarty, along with many other Aboriginal people, remained convinced that his brother's death had resulted from police violence, despite the CJC's finding that there was not sufficient evidence of police violence "even on the balance of probabilities" (CJC 1994a: 77, 80, 81). One of Fogarty's statements is significant for events which would unfold just one month later. On April 6, he was reported as saying "Justice will not be done until the six officers face the courts on murder and manslaughter charges and are locked away for good" (Anon 1994).

In the "fall-out" from Yock's death, and the subsequent events, there was clearly heightened tension between the police and Aboriginal people in Brisbane. It was reported that while this relationship was "tense at the best of times", following Yock's death it had "broken down entirely in Brisbane" (Walker 1994a).

The police force reportedly conducted a "top-rung" investigation into the riot which had taken place outside police headquarters on the day after Daniel Yock's death (see Section 7.1 above). It appears, from the report of this investigation (Fagan 1994), that considerable blame was attributed to those officers who had good relations with members of the Indigenous community. The investigation was "harshly critical" of police officers doing liaison work with the Indigenous community, saying critically of two of them that they were "mentally and emotionally conditioned to the perceived plight of the Aboriginal and Torres Strait Islander people" (ibid.). The tone attributed to this investigation indicates the combative and "get tough" spirit which appeared to pervade much of the Brisbane police force in early 1994 in its relationship to the Aboriginal community.

Discussing the release of the CJC report clearing police in Yock's death and Aboriginal refusals to apologise for blaming police, on 6 April 1994, journalist Walker (1994a) wrote, somewhat ominously, "Just what will happen on the streets of Brisbane now remains to be seen".

7.6.   The Pinkenba event

Five weeks later, David, Albert and Barry were *walking around* the Valley Mall area when they were removed to Pinkenba by six Brisbane police officers (as outlined in Section 2 of Chapter 1). The Valley Mall area where they were taken from was an area being newly upgraded for tourism. We have seen in Section 1.3 above that this is the kind of public space which has been increasingly the focus of police control over Aboriginal people. Arguably, removing the boys from the Valley that night was ultimately related to policing strategies which not only promote tourism, but also "are premised on the idea of promoting such spaces as 'consumer' spaces and doing whatever is necessary to facilitate consumption" (Cunneen and White 2002: 245).

After being "dumped" at Pinkenba, and eventually finding their way back to the City, the boys met up with an *aunty*, who was so outraged by their story that she took them to the ALS office. Following individual interviews with ALS, and with the assistance of ALS and the support of relatives, the boys made a complaint to the CJC, which then conducted an investigation. The CJC investigation involved interviewing the boys separately in the ALS office, and on different occasions taking each of them separately by car to retrace the trip to Pinkenba and the events there. This car trip to Pinkenba and retelling there were tape-recorded, as was the initial CJC interview. The CJC investigation recommended that charges be laid against the six police officers. This recommendation was made to the Director of Public Prosecutions (DPP) which is a statutory office, responsible for the carriage of criminal prosecutions at various levels of the court. As a result, the police officers were charged with "deprivation of liberty".

The boys thus told their story in several individual interviews: first with ALS, and then in the week or so following, in two different interviews each with the CJC. The following details are consistent with all three boys' accounts in their evidence-in-chief, the evidence given in court in support of the charge of unlawful deprivation of liberty:

> The boys were approached in the Valley Mall by the six armed police officers who told them to get into three separate vehicles (David and Albert into a car, and Barry into a paddywagon, a police transport vehicle used for prisoners and detained people). They were driven 14 kilometres out of town to Pinkenba, and told to get out of the cars, in a clearing in a bushy swampy area, near a creek with a small footbridge. It was dark, except for the reflection of a large flame from an oil refinery, and airport lights in the distance. The police officers threatened to throw them in the creek, telling them it was cold in the water. One police officer took Albert out of sight of the other two boys into some bushes, and threw a rock into the water. At this sound, the other officers told David and Barry *there goes Albert*, meaning that he had been thrown in the creek. The police officers also pointed to a board which had something on it, saying that was where people had had their fingers chopped off. The police officers made the boys take their shoes off, which they then threw in the bushes. The police officers then drove off, and the boys found their shoes and started to walk back into town. They headed for a light, which was a building like a service station, where a security guard called them a taxi, and gave them $5 for the fare. Two police officers came up and spoke to them near the service station. The taxi took them about five kilometres, as far as the suburb of Hamilton, and they got off there (after the $5 had been used up). They stayed in a bus shelter for some time, sleeping for part of that time. While they were there, two other police officers came and spoke to them. Later they walked back to town, where they met up with the aunty who contacted ALS.

Each of the boys reported something different as their perception of what they saw, in the dark, on the board, where the police had referred to people's fingers being *chopped off*. To David it looked like *bird shit*, to Albert a *crawfish claw*, and to Barry *skin fish* (which appears to mean the skin of a fish).

I have had access to the transcripts from the CJC investigative interviews carried out separately with each of the boys, and have been able to confirm the overwhelming consistency for each boy of the details given in both interviews that he had with the CJC, with his evidence-in-chief and cross-examination. There are a few details which are not reported by each of the three boys. Thus, David is the only one of the boys who reported that the police had said there were piranhas in the creek. His report of this is consistent in both his CJC interviews, his examination-in-chief and his cross-examination. Both David and Albert told the CJC investigator that one police officer *slapped* Albert in the head, seemingly when he first refused to obey the order to take off his shoes, saying *fuck that.*

However, there was no assault charge against any officer. The only charge against the police officers was deprivation of liberty, so that the details of what happened at Pinkenba were not relevant to the charge – the only issue was whether the boys had gone willingly in the cars. As we will see in the chapters in Part III, this did not stop the DCs from making much of reported inconsistencies between the boys' initial interviews to the ALS (to which I have not had access), and their later retellings of this story. While it is a central strategy in cross-examinations generally to exploit any inconsistencies in different retellings of a witness's story, as we will see in Chapter 6, it must be remembered that there can be many reasons for such discrepancies. Further, it is the boys' accounts to the CJC investigators which formed the basis for the criminal charges.

There was a striking imbalance in the institutional resourcing of the committal hearing. The Queensland Police Union, which defended the actions of the six police officers in the media, hired two of the most experienced and highly paid barristers in the state to defend them. These barristers were both Queen's Counsel (known as QCs, or "silks"), a prestigious title, earned by appointment by the state Attorney-General, on the basis of a barrister's reputation and experience. Queen's Counsel charge more than other barristers, and usually only take on difficult and complex cases (Bowen 1994: 808–809). In contrast, the prosecutor, who was from the Office of the DPP (Director of Public Prosecutions) and had been a suburban police officer until about two years prior, had much less courtroom experience. While the magistrate was the final judge in the hearing, in terms of training, status and income he would be regarded as junior to the two DCs.

7.7.   *Not unlawful deprivation of liberty*

The charges against the six police officers were laid in accordance with Section 355 of the Queensland Criminal Code:

> 355. DEPRIVATION OF LIBERTY Any person who unlawfully confines or detains another in any place against the other person's will or otherwise unlawfully deprives another of the other person's personal liberty is guilty of a misdemeanour and is liable to imprisonment for three years.

"Deprivation of liberty" is less serious than the other "offences against liberty", namely "kidnapping" which involves force (and for which the penalty is imprisonment up to seven years), and "kidnapping for ransom" which can result in up to 14 years imprisonment.

The first stage in the trial process for an indictable offence such as this is a committal hearing, whose purpose is for a magistrate to "test the prosecution case and determine whether it provides sufficient evidence to justify moving on to trial" (Findlay et al. 2005: 130). In this, it fulfils some of the functions of the United States Grand Jury trial. However, in the Australian committal process there is no jury. Intended as a check on the prosecution's power, the committal places no obligation on the defence to provide any evidence. Findlay et al. (ibid.: 132–133) explains that the purposes of a committal hearing include eliminating weak cases, disclosing the prosecution case, identifying guilty pleas early in the process, clarifying the issues of the case, and testing the prosecution case in a public venue.

Apparently coincidentally, in the same month that the Pinkenba event took place, May 1994, the CJC released a report to the parliament titled *Report on a Review of Police Powers in Queensland: Volume IV Suspects' Rights, Police Questioning and Pre-Charge Detention* (CJC 1994b). This report provides helpful clarification for understanding both the legal status of the Pinkenba event, and typical police practices relevant to it. On the first point, the report (ibid.: 659) explains the two categories of suspects under Queensland law:

– persons who have been lawfully arrested – that is, a police officer has had reasonable grounds to suspect or believe that the person has committed an offence

– "voluntary attendees" – that is, persons whom a police officer suspects of involvement in an offence but who have not been arrested, either because there is not sufficent evidence to reach the standard required to make an arrest, or because the police officer has considered it more convenient not to make an arrest.

The report further explains that the "important distinction between the two groups is the act of arrest, which deprives a person of his or her liberty" (ibid.). Thus, "lawful deprivation of liberty" is carried out by means of arrest. But, if a person is arrested they have to be advised of their legal rights, for example the right to silence, and the right to a lawyer. Because the boys in this case were not under arrest, there was no legal requirement to advise them of any rights. Further, there is no evidence to suggest that they were advised of their right to refuse to get in the police cars.

Related to this point, the CJC found (ibid.: 678) that police "generally do not see it as their responsibility to inform voluntary attendees that they are free to leave at any time if they wish". Further, it found (ibid.: 683) that "many suspects are unsure as to their rights, status and obligations when in police 'company'. This is a very unsatisfactory situation, as rights are of little value unless people are aware of these rights and in a position to exercise them". It recommended (ibid.: 680) that:

> when a police officer requests a suspect to go to, and/or remain at, any place designated by the police officer, <u>the officer should inform the person that he or she is either under arrest, or is not under arrest and is therefore free to leave police company at any time unless and until arrested</u>. If the police officer makes a decision at any time that the person is no longer free to leave, the person should be informed immediately that he or she is under arrest. (emphasis added)

In rejecting a submission by the Queensland Police Service (QPS) which sought a new kind of "pre-arrest detention power", the CJC (ibid.: 685) said that "It is artificial to call a deprivation of liberty a 'detention' rather than an 'arrest': a citizen is either free or is not free. A detention as proposed by the QPS is simply an arrest by another name, in that it deprives a person of his or her liberty."

Thus, to the CJC (ibid.) it was simple. If a person is under arrest, they are lawfully deprived of their liberty. If not, they are free to leave "police company". Either way, the CJC argued, they should be informed. Exactly what happened when the police approached the three boys that night in the Valley was the major question for the committal hearing, as we will see. The prosecution case was that the boys went in the police cars against their will. There was no mention throughout the hearing, or the resulting judicial decisions (discussed in Chapter 10), of the term "voluntary attendees". The defence case, which was accepted by the magistrate in his decision, was that it was a *deprivation of liberty* which was *not unlawful*. There was no evidence, from either prosecution or defence, that the boys were under arrest. Thus, it seems that the defence succeeded in persuading the magistrate of some nebulous category similar to that denied one year before the hearing by the CJC: lawful deprivation of liberty that is not arrest. And, as we will see in Section 5 of Chapter 10, this argument was also accepted by the judge whose review of the magistrate's decision was delivered almost one year later.

8.   Conclusion

In this chapter, we have seen some of the ways in which the Queensland criminal justice system has maintained and continues to maintain a colonial and neocolonial power relationship over Aboriginal people. Societal and institutional struggles over this relationship came to a head over the death of Daniel Yock while he was in police custody, and the subsequent finding that cleared police of any blame in his death.

To many people, it appeared that what happened to the three boys in the Pinkenba event was a major strategic victory for the police in what was increasingly being seen since Yock's death as the war between the police and the Aboriginal community (e.g. Solomon 1993a). Indeed, in his song lamenting Yock's death and asking *how long will these killings go on?*, Aboriginal singer-songwriter Kev Carmody sings *Our young dancer is dead, young warrior is dead* (emphasis added). So the fact that the Aboriginal community then succeeded in having criminal charges laid against six police officers could have been seen as an Aboriginal victory in this ongoing war. Thus, the committal hearing was vested with enormous symbolic and political significance, and public attention. It was not a routine case in a lower court, but a key event in the worsening struggle between Aboriginal people and the police force. The struggle had moved from the streets to the courtroom, where the major weapon is undoubtedly language.

Community interest in the case was evidenced by the extensive media coverage of the hearing, and the fact that it was held in the largest courtroom available, which was filled to capacity (about 100 visitors) throughout the hearing. The front half of the public gallery appeared to comprise mainly family and friends of the accused police officers. This included high school-aged boys, seemingly children of the accused police officers, in school uniforms, in pointed contrast to the fact that the three Aboriginal witnesses were not at all regular in their school attendance, a point which was overtly raised in the cross-examination of both David and Albert. Relatives and friends of the three Aboriginal boys, as well as Aboriginal community leaders, occupied the back half of the gallery, together with other members of the public and legal professionals who came for parts of the hearing.

The next two parts of the book turn to the situational struggle in the Pinkenba case, with a detailed microanalysis of the cross-examination of the three Aboriginal boys who were taken for a ride by the police officers. These chapters are driven by the general question which has emerged from these three introductory chapters about Aboriginal participation in the criminal justice system, that is:

– What contribution can sociolinguistics make to the understanding of how neocolonialism works?

This general question will be addressed by answers to two specific questions about language use in the Pinkenba courtroom hearing, namely:

– How was language used in this hearing to gain the boys' apparent consent to the defence argument that they had gotten willingly into the police cars?

– How was language used in this hearing
  generally to feed the moral panic about Aboriginal young people on the streets?, and

specifically to construct David, Albert and Barry not as victims of police abuse, but as lying *criminals* who are a threat to public safety, and legitimately taken for a ride by the police?

The answers to these questions involve the critical sociolinguistic approach, discussed in Section 3 of Chapter 2, in which the interaction in the Pinkenba courtroom hearing is analysed both in microscopic detail, and in terms of the larger events and structures which have been introduced in this chapter.

Part II

Evidence given in unequivocal terms?

Chapter 4
Features of Aboriginal English communicative style[24]

The analysis of language use in the Pinkenba cross-examination starts with a focus on features of Aboriginal English communicative style. We saw in Section 4 of Chapter 1 that the boys are speakers of a "light" variety of Aboriginal English, and in their conversations outside the strict constraints of the courtroom, they use such grammatical features of Aboriginal English as verbless descriptive sentences (e.g. *Dey all cheeky up dere*), and the expression of possession with the juxtaposition of possessor with possessed (e.g. *E name Jim*). But in the courtroom hearing, the boys say so little, that we hear very little in terms of grammar and vocabulary which is distinctive to Aboriginal English. In terms of accent, there are some distinctively Aboriginal English pronunciations, which on a few occasions cause confusion. For example, David's answer to a question requiring him to describe a specific location in the Valley starts with *There's a turn-off*. It takes 18 turns before the DC2 and the magistrate work out what he has said, with DC2 hearing *tin roof* and the magistrate hearing *ten off* (p87 of the official transcript).

Because the Aboriginal English speakers – David, Albert and Barry – say very little in this hearing, much of the analysis in this chapter concerns ways in which the two DCs exploit features of Aboriginal English communicative style (or pragmatics) in their questions. But even though the boys' answers are short, as we will see throughout the chapters in Parts II and III, the most significant pragmatic differences between "light" Aboriginal English and other varieties of Australian English are highly relevant to these answers. The three pragmatic features of Aboriginal English discussed in this chapter are gratuitous concurrence (Section 1), silence (Section 2) and the avoidance of eye contact (Section 3).

1. Gratuitous concurrence

More than one-third of the answers for each of the three boys to cross-examination questions consist of the single word *yes* or its variants *yeh*, or *mm* (see Table 2 in Section 8.1 of Chapter 6, where these answers are indicated as *Ye#*). To what extent do such answers provide knowing and voluntary agreement to the propositions questioned? Any consideration of such answers must take place within an understanding of the interactional phenomenon known as "gratuitous concurrence", which is widely regarded as a pervasive problem in interviews of Aboriginal Australians. This section will start by explaining what gratuitous concurrence is, how it has been recognised in earlier literature, and its consequences in legal contexts generally in which Aboriginal people participate. Section 1.2 will investigate the role of gratuitous concurrence in cross-examination generally, and the limited legal measures that can be used to mitigate its impact. Section 1.3 looks at how gratuitous concurrence is used in the Pinkenba cross-examination, discussing four key extracts. Further examples will occur in each of the remaining chapters that present data from the cross-examination in this case.

1.1.   Introducing gratuitous concurrence

Communication difficulties affecting Aboriginal people in the legal system have been noted for many decades, for example by linguists and anthropologists, and a few legal professionals. Much of the discussion of these communication difficulties relates to questions and their answers. A common theme is that found in the remarks of the linguist Strehlow (1936: 334), more than seventy years ago: "the White man putting the questions will usually receive answers which are calculated either to avoid trouble or to excite his pleasure: he will be given the information which he desires to get". A decade later, the anthropologist Elkin (1947: 176) observed that for Aboriginal people in court, "their fundamental aim is to satisfy the questioner, to tell him what they think he wants to be told". This pattern of telling the questioner what the interviewee "thinks he wants to be told" is explained more fully by Justice Kriewaldt (1960), who was a judge of the Northern Territory Supreme Court between 1950 and 1960. Speaking in general terms about Aboriginal witnesses in his summing-up to the jury in a 1959 case, Kriewaldt said:

> ... it has been my experience that the answer 'yes' when given by an Aboriginal to a question put to him has very little meaning. It frequently means simply that the Aboriginal has not understood the question, but because he does not want the question to go unanswered he says 'yes'. It may mean that the Aboriginal, not knowing what the answer is, thinks an affirmative answer is likely to be more acceptable to the questioner than a negative answer. The answer which counsel get when asking questions of an Aboriginal which can be answered 'yes' or 'no' I sometimes feel is of little value. (*R v Aboriginal Dulcie Dumaia* 1959 NTJ: 697)

This pattern of answering questions is widely believed to be relevant to the ways in which Aboriginal people plead, as seen in the report from a Central Australian Aboriginal leader, Lester (1973), that Aboriginal people "who are frightened of the court will often plead guilty, even when they are innocent, so as to get finished and out of court quickly".

Concern about this way of answering questions in police interviews (among other issues) was addressed by a 1976 judgment in the Supreme Court of the Northern Territory, which set out guidelines for police interrogation of Aboriginal people (*R v Anunga*; see also McRae et al. 1997: 371–372). Widely known as the Anunga Rules, these nine guidelines have formed the basis of similar guidelines in other Australian jurisdictions. While they include such factors as the need for an interpreter, the Anunga Rules recognise the difficulties caused by the tendency of Aboriginal people to agree to propositions in Yes/No-questions. Thus for example, the Rules include this direction in relation to "formulation of questions": "Great care should be taken in formulating questions so that so far as possible the answer which is wanted or expected is not suggested in any way".

Although noted by members of the legal profession for some decades, research attention to the widespread Aboriginal tendency to agree to questions is more recent. The ethnomethodologist Kenneth Liberman coined the term "gratuitous concurrence" (1980, 1981, 1985) in his work with Aboriginal people in remote central Australia. Although Liberman worked with speakers of traditional Aboriginal languages, his work on gratuitous concurrence is relevant to interviews with Aboriginal people around Australia, regardless of the language spoken. Following Liberman's work, I have defined gratuitous concurrence (e.g. Eades 2002: 166) as the conversational pattern, or tendency "frequently used by Aboriginal people, of saying 'yes' in answer to a question (or 'no' to a negative question), regardless of whether the speaker actually agrees with the proposition, and at times, even if the speaker does not understand the question".

Liberman examined gratuitous concurrence in intercultural communication in the legal system in contrast with interaction patterns within Aboriginal groups. This led him to the significant conclusion that gratuitous concurrence cannot be explained only in terms of responses to colonisation and subjugation. Liberman found that Aboriginal discourse patterns favour decision-making by consensus, which involves considerable time and indirectness, as people work to keep surface harmony, and work "behind the scenes" to deal with disagreements. This is also relevant to many Aboriginal English speakers in rural and urban Australia, who tend not to use direct questioning on important personal issues, and who often express strong opinions with some distance or indirectness. As Liberman (1981: 248) points out, such "communicative structures contrast sharply with structures of European discourse, particularly those in a court of law". He argues (ibid.) that gratuitous concurrence is:

> a strategy of accommodation [that Aboriginal people have developed] to protect themselves in their interaction with Anglo-Australians. ... Aborigines have

found that the easiest method to deal with White people is to agree with whatever it is that the Anglo-Australians want and then to continue on with their own business. Frequently, one will find Aboriginal people agreeing with Anglo-Australians even when they do not comprehend what it is they are agreeing with.

The extent to which gratuitous concurrence can result in obvious communication breakdown is highlighted in Coldrey's (1987: 83–85) example from a police interview of an Aboriginal man in the Northern Territory.

While the term gratuitous concurrence has been coined to refer to this widespread feature of Aboriginal communicative style, it is likely that it is found in many other intercultural communication situations around the world (Gibbons 2003; Berk-Seligson 2002, 2008). Liberman (1985: 198) says that gratuitous concurrence "is a pervasive phenomenon of intercultural conversation", and "a frequent strategy of oppressed peoples". It is undoubtedly more prevalent in situations of power asymmetry, which characterise interactions in the legal process. Thus, in describing gratuitous concurrence as a feature of Aboriginal English, I do not mean to suggest that it is found only in this language variety (just as in describing the grammatical feature of verbless equational/descriptive sentences as a feature of Aboriginal English in Section 4 of Chapter 1, I do not mean to suggest that it is not found in a number of other languages and dialects.)

Gratuitous concurrence can also function in conversations in a similar way as minimal responses do in many languages. Also referred to as response tokens or feedback markers, such minimal responses – such as *mm*, *yeh*, *OK* and *uh-huh* in English – generally indicate conversational involvement of listeners rather than agreement (see Shuy 1990 on their use in undercover FBI operations). The striking thing about the Australian Aboriginal use of gratuitous concurrence, as observed over many decades, is its use in interviews. Here, it is common for Aboriginal people to respond to questions with answers which appear to indicate agreement, such as *yes*, and *yeh*. The analysis in this book will exemplify the extent of the problem which can arise from a literal interpretation of such answers as indicating agreement.

Although the examples cited in the early literature have been primarily with Aborigines who speak traditional Aboriginal languages, the phenomenon of gratuitous concurrence is also widely recognised by people working with Aboriginal English speaking people in non-traditionally-oriented societies. Examples of this way of responding in interviews are also widely talked about among Aboriginal people. One example comes from Ruth Hegarty, a well-known Aboriginal woman from southeast Queensland, who was born in 1929 and lived in Cherbourg between 1930 and 1966 (whose experiences of government "protection" were referred to in Section 1.2 of Chapter 3). In the first volume of her autobiography (Hegarty 2000: 136), published when she was 71 years old,

Hegarty describes how she and other Cherbourg girls responded to the "humiliating" and "demeaning" personal questions from the administrator of the reserve, in the awful interviews they "put [the] dormitory girls through when [they] came back to Cherbourg pregnant":

> Nosey and demeaning questions about who we had been seeing and what we had been doing. ... I remembered how humiliating it was, all those years ago, having to stand in front of the administrator while he asked those questions – very personal questions. ... Many of the girls were put through this, and often they would just say "yes" to anything to get the interview over and done with.

Recent research with Aboriginal English speaking people in the legal process has found that gratuitous concurrence is an important factor in the misunderstanding and miscommunication which is common between Aboriginal and non-Aboriginal speakers of English in many lawyer interviews, police interviews and courtroom hearings (e.g. Eades 1992, 1994a). An experienced Aboriginal Legal Service solicitor expressed the view to me that gratuitous concurrence is the major problem in effective communication with Aboriginal clients. Several legal professionals and members of the Aboriginal community interviewed by the Criminal Justice Commission (CJC 1996: 21–22) echoed this view, giving a number of different explanations for why they believe that Aboriginal people so readily use gratuitous concurrence. Some of the explanations given (ibid.) include:

- the "desire to please and be seen as agreeable"
- "fear of persons in authority"
- "not wanting to make a scene"
- "they do not think the police or courts will believe them if they tell their side of the story"
- "they do not wish to admit that they do not know what has been asked of them"

Gratuitous concurrence is widely recognised as occurring in all legal contexts: interviews with lawyers, and the police, and in courtroom evidence. A number of lawyers have expressed to me their concerns regarding police interviewing of Aboriginal suspects, where the tendency to use gratuitous concurrence can be escalated by physical or verbal intimidation, no matter how slight. Here the crucial factors of police power and intimidation can combine with the Aboriginal person's fear, and desire for gratuitous concurrence, often with disastrous consequences. Once a suspect in a police interview, or a witness in a court hearing, has agreed to a proposition, then this becomes a binding agreement. To renege on such an agreement to a proposition is not just seen as contradictory or contrary, as it might be in ordinary conversation, but it can establish the witness or suspect as a liar, as we will see below.

It is important to point out that all of the reports referred to above, of Aboriginal communication patterns which can be labelled gratuitous concurrence, have described the language use of Aboriginal adults. We will see many examples which seem to be gratuitous concurrence in the answers of the 13- and 15-year-old witnesses in the Pinkenba case. But it must be remembered that gratuitous concurrence is not restricted to child witnesses.

1.2.   Gratuitous concurrence in cross-examination

The discourse structure of courtroom hearings creates many opportunities for a witness to use gratuitous concurrence. A number of studies of courtroom questioning generally have demonstrated that the majority of questions put to witnesses contain already completed propositions (Sandra Harris 1984), and that "witnesses can hardly be thought to tell their stories in their own words" (Luchjenbroers 1997: 501). To a considerable extent, witnesses' contributions in court are limited to providing answers to narrowly framed questions.

Within courtroom hearings, gratuitous concurrence is particularly favoured by the aims and strategies of cross-examination, which generally attempts to weaken the credibility of the witness, by showing either that the witness is unreliable and untrustworthy in some way, or that the witness's story is contradictory or inconsistent, or both. If a witness can be shown to give contradictory evidence in court, on any matter, then how could this witness be trusted to give reliable and trustworthy evidence on the issues being investigated in court? Sociolinguistic literature on question types, reviewed in Section 2.1 of Chapter 2 above, has found a strong preference for Yes/No-questions in cross-examination (see Cotterill 2003: 127).

A particular strategy which is frequently used in cross-examination to demonstrate a witness's unreliability, involves getting a witness to agree to damaging propositions. This strategy, which involves Yes/No-questions, is ideally suited to gratuitous concurrence, and thus creates a situation where Aboriginal people are particularly vulnerable. Yes/No-questions in cross-examination typically include a number of leading questions. While leading questions are a specific type of Yes/No-question, they are defined in legal terms, not grammatically. A leading question is one which suggests a particular answer, or assumes the existence of a fact which is in dispute (*Butterworth's Concise Australian Legal Dictionary* 1998). As Tiersma (1999: 164) explains it: "a leading question suggests that there is only one correct answer, and in essence tries to 'lead' the witness to that answer". There are rules of evidence which limit the use of leading questions in examination-in-chief, but they are a major tool of cross-examination. While leading questions can clearly trigger gratuitous concurrence, it should be noted that this communication pattern is not limited to leading questions – it can occur in answer to any Yes/No-question.

Undoubtedly, there are now a number of legal professionals who are aware of the Aboriginal strategy of gratuitous concurrence, and who exploit it in their questioning of Aboriginal witnesses. So, if an Aboriginal witness is susceptible to gratuitous concurrence, it is not at all difficult for a cross-examining counsel to get the witness to "agree"' to conflicting propositions. Thus it is possible for this strategy to work even more strongly, either in favour of, or against, the Aboriginal witness. From the legal perspective, answering *yes* (or one of its variants, such as *yeh* and *mm*) to a question signals agreement to the proposition being questioned. But with an Aboriginal witness, how can we know if such an answer is a genuine agreement on one hand, or, on the other hand, an answer of gratuitous concurrence, which should not be interpreted literally?

It is impossible to know exactly what is in any witness's mind, and thus to say with certainty about any answer to a specific question: *the witness answered yes but he/she did not agree with the proposition*. Thus, in my analysis, I avoid claiming that any specific answer is gratuitous concurrence. But it seems quite reasonable to assert that for many Aboriginal witnesses, *yes* <u>may</u> signal something like *I know I have to cooperate with your questioning, and I hope that this answer will help bring the questioning to an end*. On the other hand, it <u>may</u> signal agreement to a proposition. Thus, this would strongly suggest that it can be dangerous to rely for important decisions on literal interpretations of *yes*, *yeh* or *mm* answers from Aboriginal witnesses to cross-examination questions which can easily elicit gratuitous concurrence. As we will see, this is a central issue in the way in which the evidence of the Aboriginal boys in the Pinkenba case was interpreted.

My observations over a number of years indicate that certain factors appear to increase the likelihood of gratuitous concurrence: namely repeated and pressured questioning, particularly if over a lengthy period of time; lack of opportunity for the person being questioned to take control of discourse; and pressure from the questioner, for example by shouting. These are all factors which can be found in courtroom cross-examination, as we will see in the examples in this chapter. Some lawyers who work with Aboriginal clients are well aware of the likelihood of their clients using gratuitous concurrence in court. On several occasions, I have observed lawyers' attempts to help their clients practise the use of other (i.e. not gratuitous concurrence) ways of responding to lawyer questions. Thus, lawyers sometimes interview their clients in their office in the styles of examination-in-chief, followed by cross-examination. Even when their clients seem relatively confident and articulate, it can be easy to lead them into agreeing to conflicting propositions when such strategies are used (and even about relatively uncomplicated matters, such as what they had done that day prior to the interview with the lawyer).

Recent legal publications which discuss the problem caused by gratuitous concurrence in legal interviewing of Aboriginal people (both speakers of traditional languages as well as speakers of Aboriginal English) see this as a type of "suggestibility" – the term commonly used in legal contexts to refer to a person's capability of being influenced by suggestion generally, and easily led in cross-examination specifically. This includes the writings of a judge of the Supreme Court of the Northern Territory in a law journal (Mildren 1997) and a linguistics journal (Mildren 1999), and the report of the Queensland Criminal Justice Commission (discussed above), titled *Aboriginal Witnesses in Queensland's Criminal Courts* (CJC 1996). It should be pointed out that these publications postdate the Pinkenba case, and in fact the CJC report, to be discussed in Section 6 of Chapter 10, was commissioned following the outcry over this case.

A wide range of interviewees (legal professionals, as well as Aboriginal community members) told the CJC researchers about the problems with Aboriginal people "agree[ing] with things for the sake of harmony", … "agree[ing] with statements put to them because they feel overwhelmed by the criminal justice system", … and "say[ing] anything they thought was required to remove themselves from the situation" (CJC 1996: 21). The report took account of this Aboriginal tendency to gratuitous concurrence in its recommendations, and pointed to provisions already existing, in both common law and legislation, which could be used in such situations. The report pointed out that "… under the common law the court has a discretion to disallow leading questions where the witness has proven to be – or is likely to be – highly suggestible" (ibid.: 52), citing Justice Barry in *Mooney v. James* (1949) and Justice Mildren in *R v Kenny Charlie* (1995). As early as 1949, in the first of these two cases, Justice Barry stated:

> … there is no absolute right to put leading questions in cross-examination. The basis of the rule that leading questions may be put in cross-examination is the assumption that the witness's partisanship, conscious or unconscious, in combination with the circumstance that he is being questioned by an adversary will produce a state of mind that will protect him against suggestibility. (*Mooney v James* 1949: 28)

Putting this judgment together with that of Justice Kriewaldt in *R v Aboriginal Dulcie Dumaia* (1959), discussed in Section 1.1 above, we might expect that courts would often disallow leading questions in the cross-examination of

Aboriginal witnesses. But the CJC found however, that this judicial "discretion to disallow the use of leading questions is rarely exercised by the courts" (1996: 21).

Justice Mildren of the Northern Territory Supreme Court is one judge who takes this issue seriously: he reports (1999: 147) that in his court, lawyers who are unable to "get out of the habit of putting every question in leading form" usually get "poor results" for their client, because:

> the direction given at the beginning of the trial warns the jury to beware of gratuitous concurrence and if this occurs I usually draw attention to it in my summing up.

Concerns over the suggestibility of witnesses in cross-examination were addressed by revisions to the Evidence Acts for both the Australian Federal Courts (Commonwealth *Evidence Act* 1995) and the courts of the state of New South Wales (New South Wales *Evidence Act* 1995). In both of these jurisdictions, discretion is now given to the presiding magistrate or judge, so that leading questions can be disallowed in cross-examination "if the court is satisfied that the facts would be better ascertained if leading questions were not used" (CJC 1996: 53). In following this lead, a year after the Pinkenba hearing, the CJC report (ibid., see Section 6 of Chapter 10 below) recommended a similar amendment to the Queensland *Evidence Act*. Going further than the Commonwealth *Evidence Act*, the CJC report (ibid.) recommended that in "determining whether to disallow the question, the court should be required to take into account, among other things, the extent to which the witness's cultural background or use of language may affect his or her answers". We will see in Section 3 of Chapter 11, that this recommendation was adopted in 2003 amendments to the Queensland *Evidence Act*.

Some of the particular concerns raised in research on child witnesses in court (see Section 5 of Chapter 1) are directly relevant to the issue of gratuitous concurrence in the Pinkenba hearing. In reviewing the literature on the evidence of children in court, Thompson (1999: 679) reports that a number of researchers have found that "children are more susceptible to leading questions than adults", that "children can be misled more easily than adults" (ibid.: 681), and that the "extent of the child's suggestibility is determined in large measure by the behaviour of the interviewer" (ibid.: 683). Particularly relevant to the Pinkenba case is Thompson's report (ibid.: 682) that a number of researchers have found that "children who are asked the same question more than once in the same interview are prone to change their answers". This seems to be particularly the case if they are told they had not done very well in their answers and they should try again. As we will see in the examples below, it is common for both of the defence counsel in this case to reject the initial answer to a key Yes/No-question, and pressure the witness until he gives an acceptable answer.

1.3. Yes answers in the Pinkenba cross-examination

We have seen that there are several features common to any cross-examination which are conducive to gratuitous concurrence, namely:

- the talk is entirely structured in terms of questions and their answers,
- a large number of the questions are Yes/No-questions,
- questions are asked in adversarial style by an authority figure,
- the cross-examining lawyer is in control of the discourse, and the witness is powerless to initiate or take control,
- the witness is required, both pragmatically and legally, to answer every question.

This section focuses on <u>specific</u> strategies used in the cross-examination in the Pinkenba case to elicit agreement which appears highly likely to be gratuitous concurrence, on the central legal issue of the case (whether or not the boys got into the police cars of their free will), focusing on:

- complex questions in which several different propositions are questioned at once,
- pressured prosodic features such as shouting,
- witness silence being interrupted by repeated question tags.

The examples discussed will also reveal instances of other linguistic strategies to be examined in future chapters, including contested lexical items and legal jargon (Chapter 5) and the use of pseudo-declarative questions (Chapter 6). The general discussion of gratuitous concurrence above has focused on answers of *yes* or its variants, such as *yeh* and *mm*. From here, I will use the form *Ye#* to refer generically to the answers *yes*, *yeh* and *mm*, and the form *No#* to refer generically to the answers *no* and *nuh*. (See discussion in Section 7 of Chapter 1.)

The most important defence strategy is to get the prosecution witness(es) to agree to damaging propositions. As the above general discussion on gratuitous concurrence has indicated, this is generally not at all difficult in cases with Aboriginal witnesses, and indeed the cross-examination in this case is riddled with apparent gratuitous concurrence. The most disturbing instances occur with DC1, the lawyer who often shouts and uses much overt harassment. DC2 is, in contrast, generally quietly spoken, although he uses a number of subtle strategies to lead the witnesses to agree, in situations which are quite likely to produce gratuitous concurrence. The contrast between the two DCs' styles and stances suggests they are playing the equivalent of the "good cop, bad cop" strategy. It was suggested to me that if the case had gone to trial, these two DCs might well have reversed their "good cop, bad cop" roles, in order to further trick and scare the boys at the next stage of the process.

Extract 2 occurs at the end of the first day of the hearing. David, the youngest witness, has been giving evidence for more than 3 hours, most of which has been in cross-examination. He has shown signs of being overwhelmed by the experience, even crying on a number of occasions.

Extract 2. DC2 to David, Day 1, p81

1. DC2:	It's not that you were <u>forced</u> to go in any police car- it's the fact that you were <u>left</u> out at Pinkenba- that's what you're complaining about- isn't it? (2.0) that's right- isn't it- David- co<small>RRECT</small>?
2. David:	Yeh.
3. DC2:	(3.4) Your worship is that a convenient time? [i.e. to stop proceedings for the day]
4. M:	Yes I was thinking about that Mr- uh- Hiller.

Turn 1 is a typical example of the questioning style of the less aggressive defence counsel, DC2. It questions two propositions, with the requirement for a single answer: (1) *you are complaining not about being forced to go in any police car,* and (2) *you are complaining about being left out at Pinkenba.* There is little chance for the witness to think about his answer (2 seconds being quite a short silence for Aboriginal English speakers, see Section 2 below) before being pressured by repeated question tags, the final one with raised volume. These are all strategies conducive to the elicitation of gratuitous concurrence from Aboriginal witnesses. After the witness's *yeh,* which is taken as agreement to this crucial double-barrelled proposition about the central legal issue of the trial, DC2 calls for an adjournment, thereby maximising the impact of his final exchange with the witness.

It is impossible to know whether the witness does actually agree with the crucial question in Turn 1 of Extract 2, but we have seen above several reasons which would urge caution about giving a literal interpretation to his answer in Turn 2.

On the second day of the hearing, David's cross-examination by DC2 continues. In Extract 3, we see DC2 again using complex questions, in which more than one proposition is being questioned:

Extract 3. DC2 to David, Day 2, p97–98

1. DC2:	David- let me just try to summarise if I can- what you- what you've told us (3.1) you told us yesterday that the <u>real</u> problem wasn't anything that happened getting into the car or <u>in</u> the car- but the fact that you were left at Pinkenba- that right?

2. David: (1.5) Mm.

3. DC2:   Mm- that's the truth isn't it?
4. David: Mm.

5. DC2:   (4.3) You see- you weren't de<u>priv</u>ed of your liberty at all- uh in going out
              there- it was the fact that you were <u>left</u> there that you thought was wrong?
6. David: (1.2) °Yeh°.

7. DC2:   Eh?
8. David: Yeh.

9. DC2:   (3.5) You got <u>in</u> the car (2.1) without being forced- you went <u>out</u> there
              without being forced- the <u>prob</u>lem began when you were <u>left</u> there?
10. David: (1.5) [Mm.

11. Pros: [With respect Your Worship- there are <u>three</u> elements to that question
              and I ask my friend to break them down.

12. M: Yes- just break it up one by one Mr Humphrey.

13. DC2:   You got in the car without being forced David- didn't you?
14. David: (1.5) No.

15. DC2:   You told us- you've told us a ((laughs)) number of times today you did.
16. David: (1.3) They forced me.

In Turn 1, DC2 asks a complex question with a double proposition of the form
The <u>real</u> problem wasn't X- it was Y- that right?. After a brief silence the witness
agrees, with *Mm*. In Turn 5, DC2 introduces legal language, actually presenting part of the charge against the officers, in terms that are quite likely to be
unfamiliar to the witness, namely *you weren't deprived of your liberty* . . . . This
Turn 5 questions two propositions in the form *X didn't happen to you, it was Y
that you thought was wrong?* The witness's answer (in Turn 6) is a very short
and quiet *°Yeh°*. Turn 9 questions three separate propositions, which the witness
agrees to with *Mm*. This is the third question in this short extract in which more
than one proposition is questioned, and it is not clear whether the witness's reply
of *Mm* is an agreement with all three propositions, or just one, or two of them,
or whether it is simply gratuitous concurrence. After the prosecutor's request to
the magistrate to direct DC2 to question one proposition at a time, we see an
exchange (Turns 13–16) in which the witness clearly disagrees with one of the
three propositions in the Turn 9 question – whether or not he had been forced
into the police car – which is the most important issue in the whole case.

    What this extract shows is a witness appearing to freely agree to ques-
tions containing multiple propositions. When one of these multiple questions is

broken down, and just one of the propositions is questioned, the witness does not agree to it. Further, his disagreement with the proposition comes as a complete sentence *They forced me* (Turn 16): a relatively rare occurrence for this witness whose answers are overwhelmingly single words, such as *yeh* and *no*. Such a contrast should urge caution in a literal interpretation of the *Ye#* answers on this point. This extract shows the important role that can be played by multiple question forms in the elicitation of gratuitous concurrence. But as the next extract highlights, it is only one of the factors in cross-examination conducive to the elicitation of gratuitous concurrence.

Extracts 2 and 3 illustrate strategies used by DC2 to gain agreement to the crucial defence proposition: that the boys got into the police cars of their own free will. The strategies of DC1 were more aggressive, as we will see in Extracts 4 and 5 below. Extract 4 occurs when DC1 is taking the second witness, Albert, through the statement produced during his interview with lawyers and a field officer of Aboriginal Legal Services on the day after the incident occurred, some ten months prior to the hearing. In this statement, Albert had apparently used the verb *grab* in his account of what happened when the police first came up to them in the mall, saying *They grabbed the three of us- two grabbed Barry- two grabbed me*. Now in court, in his evidence-in-chief earlier that day, Albert has not said that they were *grabbed*, but rather that they were *told to get in the police cars*, and that they did. In his cross-examination on this inconsistency, DC1 reads out the section of the interview with ALS in which Albert had said they were *grabbed*, and then proceeds to make much of the inconsistency. This recontextualising of a statement that a witness has made during the investigation is a frequent occurrence during cross-examinations generally (Cotterill 2002), and will be discussed in Section 4 of Chapter 6. At this stage, it is sufficient to draw attention to the assumption in cross-examination that a witness will always tell their story in the same words, and the disjunction between this assumption and the realities of narrativising practices (see Schiffrin 2006).

Extract 4.   DC1 to Albert, Day 2, p136–137

1. DC1:	... Now LISTEN to me- that didn't happen at all- did it? (2.0) that you were <u>grabbed</u>- it DIDN'T HAPPEN- did it?
2. Albert:	°No°.
3. DC1:	Beg your pardon?
4. M:	He said no.
5. DC1:	Well WHY did you <u>say</u> that it did? (27.1) well- WHY?(12.2) I'll suggest this answer to you- that you were TRYING TO MAKE THINGS LOOK WORSE FOR THE POLICE - is that the correct answer? (27.8) is that the correct answer?

6. Albert: (1.4) °No°.

7. DC1:   Beg your pardon?
8. Albert: No.

9. DC1:   Well- WHAT IS the answer? (2.4) why did you <u>lie</u> about it? (33.4) WHY did you LIE?

10. Pros: With respect- inconsistent answers don't necessarily imply lies and the witness hasn't yet accepted that either of them is a lie- I'd ask my friend to uh=

11. DC1:   =All right- well- I can take half an hour trying to get an answer from him (2.7) I think you <u>told</u> me that that didn't HAPPEN- what you <u>claim</u> there- [to solicitor] °didn't he say that didn't happen°- so if it didn't HAPPEN- IS IT A LIE THAT YOU'VE TOLD THERE?

12. Albert: Yes.

[partly inaudible utterance of DC1 in aside to his assistant]

13. DC1:   All right- well now why did you <u>lie</u>?
14. Albert: I don't know.

15. DC1:   YOU LIED TO MAKE THINGS LOOK BAD FOR THE POLICE- DIDN'T YOU? (1.2) DIDN'T YOU?

16. Albert: (3.5) °Yes°.

In Turn 5 of this extract DC1 puts the proposition that the reason that Albert had said that they were *grabbed* (by the police) was *to make things look worse for the police*. In his reply (Turn 6), Albert denies this proposition, and indeed one might think of a number of different reasons why a child might have said something different in the earlier interview (such as confusion, emotional reaction, tiredness, difficulty in remembering all the details). It is also worth pointing out he did not say anything about being *grabbed* in his evidence-in-chief, and thus his evidence in court was consistent. The 13-year-old witness is given no credit for what may well be his careful attention to avoiding exaggeration in court, following the magistrate's *warnings* about *telling the truth* in the court. It is also not at all clear whether Albert had used the word *grab* in his earlier report to mean *physically take hold of*, for example by taking his arm, or his shirt, or in the more colloquial sense of taking him aside. While *grab* in Australian English often implies the physical act of taking hold of, as in *he grabbed a handful of grapes*, it is sometimes used colloquially to refer to quickly taking an opportunity, as in *I'm going to grab some fresh air*. More importantly, it is also used to refer to quickly persuading a person to go somewhere with another person, as in *I was working in my office when the boss came and grabbed me for an urgent meeting*, where no physical contact is being reported.

In his following four turns (9, 11, 13, 15), DC1 repeatedly accuses the witness of lying, despite the prosecutor's unsuccessful attempt to point out to the court that *inconsistent answers don't necessarily imply lies* (Turn 10). These accusations take DC1 back to the proposition which the witness has already denied in Turn 6, and he uses shouted repeatings of the tag question *didn't you?*, until the witness gives in and answers °*Yes*°, in a barely audible voice, in turn 16. While of course we cannot know what is in the witness's mind, this extract has the hallmarks of classic gratuitous concurrence. The witness is in a powerless situation, and is given no choice but to comply with the harassment of the lawyer. This interaction should raise legal concerns about the strong suggestibility of the witness, especially given the research findings, reported in Section 1.2 above, about the likelihood of children changing their answer when asked the same question more than once in the same interview. Thus the Aboriginal tendency to use gratuitous concurrence compounds the strong suggestibility of a child witness in an exchange such as this. But these concerns are not addressed at all by the magistrate, either during the hearing or in his judgment. As we will see in Chapter 10, Albert's answers in Extract 4, which are highly likely to involve gratuitous concurrence, are interpreted literally as agreements to the propositions questioned. Further, these answers become highly consequential in the rejection by the justice system of Albert and his friends' assertion of their rights in relation to police practices.

In the next extract we see the presentation of the third witness, Barry, as an unreliable witness, as a result of his being easily and skilfully pressured into conflicting answers by DC1 on the central point of the whole hearing:

Extract 5. DC1 to Barry, Day 3, p170

1. DC1:	And you <u>knew</u> (1.4) when you spoke to these six police in the Valley that you didn't have to go anywhere with them if you didn't want to didn't you?
2. Barry:	(1.3) No.
3. DC1:	You <u>knew</u> that Mr (1.2) Coley I'd suggest to you- PLEASE DO NOT LIE YOU KNEW THAT YOU DIDN'T HAVE TO GO ANYWHERE if you didn't want to didn't you? (2.2) DIDN'T YOU? (2.2) DIDN'T YOU MR COLEY?
4. Barry:	(1.3) Yeh.
5. DC1:	WHY DID YOU JUST LIE TO ME? WHY DID YOU JUST SAY NO MR COLEY (4.4)? YOU WANT ME TO SUGGEST A REASON TO YOU MR COLEY? THE REASON WAS THIS- THAT YOU WANTED THIS COURT TO <u>BELIEVE</u> (2.1) THAT YOU THOUGHT YOU HAD TO <u>GO</u> WITH POLICE ISN'T THAT SO?

6. Barry:	(1.2) Yeh.
7. DC1:	AND YOU <u>LIED</u> TO THE COURT TRYING TO TO (1.2) YOU <u>LIED</u> TO THE COURT TRYING TO PUT ONE <u>OVER</u> THE COURT DIDN'T YOU?
8. Barry:	(1.8) °No°.
9. DC1:	THAT WAS YOUR REASON MR COLEY WASN'T IT? (3.1) WASN'T IT? (3.2) WASN'T IT MR COLEY?
10. Barry:	(1.9) Yeh=
11. DC1:	=YES. (2.9) BECAUSE YOU WANTED THE <u>COURT</u> TO <u>THINK</u> THAT <u>YOU</u> DIDN'T KNOW THAT YOU COULD TELL THESE POLICE YOU WEREN'T GOING <u>ANY</u>WHERE WITH THEM- THAT WAS THE REASON WASN'T IT? (1.5) WASN'T IT?
12. Barry:	(0.6) Yes=
13. DC1:	=Yes.

Turn 1 in this extract puts the proposition central to the defence argument: that the witness knew he did not have to go in the police car. The witness's answer of *No* (Turn 2) is not accepted, so he is harassed in Turn 3 until he does agree (in Turn 4). (In Turns 3, 5 and 9 DC1 addresses Barry as *Mr Coley*, highlighting that he is not a child, a point to be discussed in Section 6 of Chapter 6.) Of course, we cannot know what is in the witness's mind, but we can see the ideal situation for gratuitous concurrence, increased when defence counsel begins shouting angrily in Turn 3. The contradictory answers given by the witness in Turns 2 and 8 on the one hand, and Turns 4, 6, 10 and 12 on the other hand, are interpreted literally by defence counsel, to provide clear evidence that the witness is a liar (emphasised for the court with the refrain of *Why did you lie?*, to be discussed in Section 7 of Chapter 6).

However, an understanding of Aboriginal English background assumptions and ways of speaking, might well lead to a situated inference indicating that the answers of *Yeh* in Turns 4, 6, 10 and 12 are quite possibly answers of gratuitous concurrence – indicating the witness's realisation that he will be harassed until he gives the answer required by his interrogator. Thus, we cannot with confidence assume that Barry intends to agree with the proposition of the questions. It is also relevant that the question in Turn 11 contains four clauses embedded in the main clause, a sentence structure which would confuse many witnesses, regardless of age, sociolinguistic background, and experience with interviews.

What we have seen in Extracts 4 and 5 is a pattern which starts with the witness disagreeing with a pseudo-declarative proposition (Extract 4, Turn 6 and Extract 5, Turns 2 and 8). DC refuses to accept the witness's answer, and harasses him, with shouting and repeated questioning (Extract 4, Turns 9, 11, 15 and

Extract 5, Turns 3 and 9 – note that DC1 shouts consistently in this extract from Turns 3–9). This rejection of the witness's answer also includes accusations of lying (Extract 4, Turns 9, 11, 13, 15 and Extract 5, Turns 3, 5 and 7). This extreme harassment results in the witness giving in and agreeing with the proposition (Extract 4, Turn 16, in a barely audible voice; Extract 5, Turns 4, 6 and 10). Following this conceded agreement in Extract 5, the witness is further harassed, with accusations of lying and pressured questioning, (Extract 5, Turns 5 and 11). This follow-up harassing questioning succeeds in eliciting agreement (Extract 5, Turns 6 and 12), to a damaging explanation for the allegedly contradictory answers which have just been elicited.

Discussion of the extracts in this chapter has raised doubt about the validity of a literal interpretation of the *Ye#* answers given by the witnesses in cross-examination. But, as we will see in many of the extracts in the following chapters, a literal interpretation of the boys' *Ye#* answers appears to be central to this case. Legal concerns about gratuitous concurrence and the suggestibility of both child witnesses and Aboriginal witnesses (discussed in Sections 1.1 and 1.2 above) appear to have been ignored in this case. The CJC's report on Aboriginal witnesses expressed the general concern that if "a witness is suggestible ... there is an increased risk that judicial officers, lawyers and particularly jurors will misconstrue the significance of the answers given by the witness" (1996: 51). And this misconstrual is exactly what appears to have happened. As we will see in Chapter 10, the outcome of the case relied on a literal interpretation of the boys' *Ye#* answers in cross-examination. But, as the analysis in this book shows, it is impossible to exclude gratuitous concurrence from some of the boys' answers to questions about the central issue in the case, as well as to a wide range of other cross-examination questions. Indeed, as the analysis in the remaining chapters in this book will show, the shadow of gratuitous concurrence looms throughout the cross-examination of all three witnesses.

2.   Silence

2.1.   *Silence in Aboriginal interactions*

While gratuitous concurrence has been observed and commented on by a range of Aboriginal and non-Aboriginal people for many decades, the Aboriginal use of silence appears to be a more subtle pragmatic feature, which is generally below the level of conscious awareness. Ethnographic research with Aboriginal English speakers has found that silence is a positive and productive feature of many interactions (Eades 1988, 1991; Ngarritjin-Kessaris 1997; see also Kearins

1991). People often like to sit in silence with relatives, friends or acquaintances. This was explained to me many years ago as *one way of getting to know people better*. It can also signal that people want to take time to think about an important issue. Silence in conversations between relatives, friends, or even people who are not previously acquainted can be quite lengthy – many minutes is not seen as anything remarkable. Similarly silences can be an important part of Aboriginal "meeting talk" (Ngarritjin-Kessaris 1997). And when people are engaged in information seeking (not necessarily through direct questions, see Section 4 of Chapter 1, and Eades 1991), there are often considerable silences before requested information is provided. Similar ways of using silence are also reported among Aboriginal speakers of traditional languages (e.g. Stephen Harris 1984: 112–113; Liberman 1985: 137, 238; Walsh 1994: 220). And in a recent Conversation Analysis study in a remote commmunity with women speaking the Garrwa traditional language, the creole language Kriol, and English, Gardner and Mushin (2007: 35.3) found "large numbers of short to medium length inter-turn silences of up to about two to three seconds, at a higher rate than has been observed for Anglo-Australian conversations".

This use of silence contrasts with a common western reaction that silence in a conversation, whether formal or informal, is an indication that something is going wrong. Jaworski (1993: 46) points out that "a typical Western bias" means that people tend to treat "speech as normal and silence as a deviant mode of behavior". Conversation Analysis (CA) studies of English conversations in Western societies support Jefferson's (1989) finding that the "standard maximum tolerance for silence" is less than one second, and thus it is CA transcription convention to record conversational silences in tenths of seconds. By the time that there has been a silence of one second, or less, in many western conversations, participants are feeling uncomfortable, perhaps wondering if their interlocutor is offended, or socially awkward, or a snob. And many potential silences are filled before the one second time period has expired. This is particularly noticeable in interviews and meetings, and even if the person "filling the silence" is not ready to contribute anything of substance, people use verbal silence-fillers, such as *um, ah, let me see*, and so on.

It is not only Aboriginal Australians who have quite a different use and interpretation of silence compared to Western speakers of English. There are some parallels between Aboriginal Australians and Native Americans (see Basso 1970; Philips 1976, 1993; Gumperz 2001a). Other sociocultural groups whose different use of silence has been described include the Amish (Enninger 1987), Japanese (Lebra 1987) and Chinese (Young 1994).

The different uses and interpretations of silence have particular significance in interviews. The interview genre is typically a one-sided information exchange, where one party asks questions and the other provides answers. In intercultural communication workshops that I conducted throughout the 1990s, non-Aboriginal interviewers often reported that they experienced difficulty in eliciting information from Aboriginal interviewees, while Aboriginal interviewees often reported feeling rushed, pressured, and unable to take the time they need to answer questions properly. The lawyers' handbook, discussed in Chapter 2, gave this advice about silence (Eades 1992: 46):

> Do not interpret silence as an Aboriginal speaker's admission of guilt or ignorance, or even as evidence of a communication breakdown. Remember that silence is often used positively by Aboriginal people to think about things and to get comfortable with the social situation.

In my workshops for legal professionals, I am often asked how long they should wait for an Aboriginal witness's answer. My standard answer is that they should "wait until after the answer", explaining that while it may often be less than two or three seconds, it may sometimes be much longer. Research in a country town in New South Wales in the mid 1990s (Eades 2000) found that some lawyers were able to wait comfortably – at times for many seconds – for their clients to provide an answer, while others were not. And a particularly striking example of lawyers accommodating Aboriginal witnesses' silences and waiting for answers, in a 1992 Brisbane tribunal hearing, is discussed in Eades (2007).

2.2. Silence in the Pinkenba cross-examination

Turning to the Pinkenba cross-examination, there are a number of instances in which the two DCs allow little time between asking an initial question and following it up with pressured, often shouting, repetition of the verb phrase, as we saw above in Extract 2, Turn 1 and Extract 4, Turn 15. In such examples we can see that the witness is given little chance to think about the question, or to use the lengthy silence which characterises many Aboriginal conversations, as well as interviews with Aboriginal people.

But there are a considerable number of silences throughout the hearing. While the focus here is on witness silence in answer to a lawyer question, it is interesting to note the cross-examining lawyers' frequent use of silence <u>within</u> a clause, seemingly for emphasis (as we saw above in Extract 5, Turns 1, 7, and 11). The first lawyer silence in Turn 3 of this extract is quite possibly caused by a memory lapse, as he remembers the boy's surname for sarcastic effect. In Extract 54 in Chapter 8, we will see DC1's use of an 8.7 second silence to emphasise his shouted accusation that if Albert *THOUGHT* he *COULD GET AWAY WITH IT* he's *TOLD* him he'*D LIE* in court.

But it is silences which do not occur within a clause (or which occur at a turn relevance position, in CA terms) which are of most interest. Such silences can technically be filled by either the lawyer or the witness. Thus, some researchers transcribe such silences in courtroom interaction on a separate line (e.g. Matoesian 1993). For example, the two second silence in DC2's Turn 1 in Extract 2, or the three very long silences in DC1's Turn 5 in Extract 4, could have been followed with an answer from the witness. We will see many other examples of silences of up to about 7 seconds which are followed by witness answers. We will also see many examples where the DCs do not allow more than about two seconds silence in answer to a question, before they resume speaking. Consistent with the widespread Aboriginal use of silence at the beginning of an answer, many of the witness answers begin with some silence, as for example in most of David's answers in Extract 3, and all of Barry's answers in Extract 5. Given this Aboriginal tendency to begin answers to questions with a silence, and that the DC has the power to initiate turns in cross-examination, the practice adopted in this book is to transcribe silences between speakers at the start of the next speaker's turn, as for example in Extract 3, Turns 5 and 6 above.

The earliest sociolinguistic analysis of courtroom interaction pointed out that silences after a witness's answer in cross-examination "can be recognised as interactional strategies employed by counsel ... to display his disbelief or scepticism of the validity of an answer, to stress the particular significance of an answer, and so on" (Atkinson and Drew 1979: 68, see also Matoesian 1993: 144–146). This is arguably at least part of the reason for the 3.4 seconds silence in Turn 3 of Extract 2 above, and we will see other examples. Another reason, not mentioned in the literature, is that lawyers often take time looking through their notes, or whispering to their assistant, both of which I have often observed in courtroom hearings (but neither of which is ever recorded in offical transcripts). And such is the lawyer control over talk, that witnesses can be prohibited from speaking during such activities, as illustrated in the example cited in Eades (2000: 176).

The witness silences may perhaps be seen as the lawyer accommodating Aboriginal ways of speaking, but both DCs made sure that this is not how the long silences would be interpreted. The long silences, as well as many of the shorter ones, were followed by some form of harassment, often shouted in the case of DC1, as we saw above in Extract 4, Turns 5 and 9, and Extract 5, Turns 3 and 9. Further, on two occasions defence counsel got the witness to agree overtly to the proposition that his silence should be interpreted negatively, as we will see below.

Extract 6 takes place when 13-year-old Albert has been on the witness stand for more than 2 hours, most of it being cross-examination:

Extract 6.   DC2 to Albert, Day 2, p143

1. DC2:	And you told them <u>lies</u> to their faces didn't you? (3.7) didn't you Albert? (3.7) didn't you Albert? (2.2) you lied in their face didn't you? (3.6) Albert <u>an</u>swer my question please=
2. Albert:	=I don't wanna.
3. DC2:	Well I'm sorry but this isn't one that you can claim privilege on.
4. Albert:	I don't wanna.
5. DC2:	Pardon?
6. Albert:	I don't wanna.
7. DC2:	You don't want to answer?=
8. M:	=Well I'm telling you Albert- you have to answer this question okay? you can't get out of this [one.
9. Albert:	[(Inaudible).
10. DC2:	Now Albert (2.7) his worship's told you to answer the question will you or won't you? (6.5) **we have to take your silence as no** don't we? (2.5) Albert?
11. Albert:	(1.2) ˚Yes˚.

Here we see DC2, the less aggressive of the two DCs, constructing Albert as a liar, in relation to the way in which he had reported the Pinkenba incident to the lawyers at Aboriginal Legal Service (ALS). Most of the extract is a metapragmatic discussion of whether or not Albert will answer the question in Turn 1. Albert insists, in Turns 2, 4 and 6, that he does not want to answer the question asked in Turn 1, and defence counsel and the magistrate assert (in Turns 3 and 8 respectively) that this is not a question that he *can claim privilege on*. This refers to the ruling, (expressed to Albert 7 times by this stage) that "any person" does not have to answer any question that might incriminate him or her in relation to the commission of a criminal offence (Queensland *Evidence Act* 1977, Section 10, hereafter referred to as "the self-incrimination privilege" or "the privilege"). Much is made in the cross-examination of the three boys of their *criminal records* (mainly for minor thefts). So, as many of the questions ask about their *criminal activities*, the magistrate is obliged to inform the witness of this privilege. The invocation of this privilege by a witness is a tricky one, and it is hardly surprising that these young boys are unsure of how and when to use this right (as we will see in Section 1.2 of Chapter 5, and in Extract 34 in Chapter 7 and Extract 57 in Chapter 8). At this stage of his lengthy cross-examination, Albert appears to be trying to invoke it as a way to avoid answering questions.

Again, it is hardly surprising that this 13-year-old boy might see a question about lying to a legal officer as having the same legal status and possible consequences as a question about *throwing rocks at a street light* (although in fact, the former is not a criminal offence, unless it occurs in a courtroom).

However, he is told that he cannot avoid answering the question (about whether he *lied to* the *faces* of the ALS staff). But this is followed with a ridiculous question in Turn 10 – *Will you or won't you?*. It is hardly surprising that the witness uses a long silence at this point. The choice offered by this question seems to contradict the assertion by both DC2 and the magistrate that Albert does not have this choice. By this stage, it is clear that the cross-examination has moved beyond incrimination and harassment, to control and disciplining, which appears to be at the very least confusing, and much more likely, senseless. Having got the witness to this state of confused (and senseless?) subjugation, as well as exhaustion, defence counsel moves in with the powerful assertion *we have to take your silence as no*, presumably that he won't answer the question. From here it is very easy to get Albert to agree to this assertion (in Turn 11), in a context which strongly suggests that this is an answer of gratuitous concurrence. In his assertion that Albert's silence has to be interpreted as non-cooperation, defence counsel ignores widely available background knowledge which would suggest other (non-incriminating) interpretations of the Aboriginal witness's silence. For example, it would be quite reasonable to interpret an Aboriginal silence of 6.5 seconds to such a nonsensical question, as time being taken to try to understand the question referred to in Turn 10, which actually occurred nine turns previously, in Turn 1.

But instead, DC2 explicitly relies on a widespread Western culturally-based assumption that silence in answer to a question is "interpreted to the detriment of the silent person", for example as implying that the person asked the question has something to hide (Kurzon 1995: 56). Indeed, Walker's (1985: 65) study found that "hesitancy is the linguistic feature most often commented upon by attorneys who are asked their impressions of witnesses". The link between silence and negative inferences about veracity is encapsulated in the comment of one lawyer to Walker that if "a person is being honest, the time to respond is going to be shorter than it is if they are going to be dishonest" (ibid.: 66). While silence in answer to questions in a police interview, in many countries (although no longer in the UK), cannot be taken to imply guilt, adverse inferences may be drawn from silence in answer to questions in court. Perhaps, it might be considered to be hardly surprising that DC2 here relies on a widespread Western culturally-based assumption. But, it must be remembered that the DCs overtly display their access to the knowledge about the contrasting use of silence in Aboriginal English by their prominent positioning of the lawyers' handbook on the Bar

Table. And Aboriginal use and interpretation of silence was a feature widely publicised in media reports of the handbook and following Robyn Kina's case the previous year (as discussed in section 7.2 of Chapter 3).

Extract 7 occurs during DC1's cross-examination of David, the youngest witness. It occurs after several questions about where David had got the *Reebok* shoes he was wearing on the night of the Pinkenba incident. David has answered that he *swapped them off a fella* [i.e. swapped them with someone], a situation which would be quite consistent with Aboriginal use of clothing. But the point of DC1's questioning becomes clear – his implication is that David had stolen them:

Extract 7.   DC1 to David, Day 1, p32–33

1. DC1:	So without any other discussion you just swapped shoes? (1.3) you're [nodding your head again=
2. David:	[Yes.
3. DC1:	=please give us the courtesy of answering (2.9) (it) wasn't a situation that you stole them?
4. David:	(1.0) No.
5. DC1:	(1.8) I see well now you've- you agree that you've got these convictions back in nineteen ninety three don't you?
6. David:	(0.6) Yes.
7. DC1:	Are you going to commit more offences?
8. David:	(2.7) No.
9. DC1:	(0.6) **You paused a while before that-** what's the answer- probably you will?
10. David:	(2.2) I dunno.

In this extract, DC1 asks a question, in Turn 7, which may well be confusing for David. It is not clear whether the legal expression *commit more offences* would be one that David knows. His silence of 2.7 seconds before answering the question could well indicate his processing of the expression, or that he is thinking about the question before answering. But DC1 ignores either of these likely explanations for the pause here by a young Aboriginal speaker of English, instead apparently relying on the widespread Western presupposition, discussed above, that silence in answer to such a question implies guilt.

Extract 8 occurs later in the same day, after David has given the answer *I don't know* to DC1's question *I asked you- suggested to you- you've stolen lots of other things, remember? you have- haven't you?* (p47). This leads to a discussion about the *privilege*, followed by Extract 8:

Extract 8.   DC1 to David, Day 1, p47

1. DC1:   I'll ask you again- you've stolen lots of things- haven't you?
2. David: (1.8) Yes.

3. DC1:   (2.4) From lots of (1.3) shops other than just a pair of jeans haven't you?
4. David: (2.3) Yeh.

5. DC1:   (1.0) Well WHY DID YOU LIE to me and tell me you'd just stolen a pair of
             jeans from a shop? (8.8) well I'd suggest the reason to you because you
             DON'T WANT everyone to KNOW THE LITTLE CRIMINAL THAT YOU ARE do
             you? (2.5) that's the REASON ISN'T IT? (4.5) isn't it? (3.4) isn't it? (6.5)
             your silence probably answers it but I'll have an answer from you (1.0)
             that's the reason isn't it?

6. M: (25.6) David I am asking you (1.6) to answer the question- ask the question
             again please Mr Thorpe.

7. DC1:   (1.5) I'm suggesting to you that you don't want (1.0) the court to know
             the little criminal you are (0.7) isn't that right?
8. David: (4.4) Yes.

David's answer of *yes* in Turn 2 in this extract, contradicts his previous *I dunno*.
This gives DC1 the opportunity in Turn 5 to use pressured questioning with
the repeated question tag *isn't it?* to gain David's apparent agreement to his
construction of him as a lying *criminal*. Here again, DC1 overtly invokes the
Western interpretation that silence in answer to a question in court implies guilt.
As we have seen in this chapter there are other possible reasons for David's
silence here. This extract ends with DC1 enlisting the help of the magistrate in
getting David's agreement to his question which presupposes the construction of
David as a *little criminal*. While it is impossible to know if David's *Yes* answer
in Turn 8 is gratuitous concurrence, it is interesting to note it comes after a
considerable pause, and is followed by *Ye#* answers to the following 13 questions
(about being *great mates* with Albert, and with Barry, and about having *great
fun* with them *stealing people's things*).

3.   Eye contact

3.1.   *Eye contact in Aboriginal interactions*

The third feature of Aboriginal English communicative style to be discussed in
this chapter is a kinesic one, namely the avoidance of eye contact. While there is

little documented research on this topic, it is a widely observed and commented on difference between Aboriginal and non-Aboriginal ways of communicating, regardless of the language spoken. Thus, teachers throughout Australia are advised that Aboriginal students' avoidance of eye contact is not to be interpreted as lack of politeness (e.g. Groome 1995: 101; Nicholls 1994: 11).

More than two decades ago, Nash (1979: 106–107) observed that politeness and deference are behind the Aboriginal practices of "softness of speech, silence and averting the gaze", all of which have been interpreted in the courtroom as "sullenness or stupidity". Similar observations have been made by Kearins (1991: 4), and Walsh (1994: 221–222). As the lawyers' handbook (Eades 1992: 47) explains it:

> It is widely recognised throughout Australia that direct eye contact is frequently avoided in Aboriginal interactions where it is seen as threatening or rude. Conversely, in much non-Aboriginal interaction in Australia, the avoidance of eye contact, especially when asking or answering questions, is interpreted as rudeness, evasion, or dishonesty.

3.2.   Eye contact in the Pinkenba cross-examination

The second witness, 13-year-old Albert, is the most quietly spoken of the three witnesses, and he avoids eye contact on occasion, both with the prosecutor during examination-in-chief, and the DCs during cross-examination. The instance of the prosecutor asking Albert to look at him occurs at the beginning of his examination-in-chief. Immediately after the witness has answered the magistrate's initial questions about whether he knows *the difference between the truth and a lie*, the prosecutor's opening words to Albert are: *Albert can you tell me- can you look over here Albert- can you tell me your full name please?* (p103). It is most likely here that Albert is still facing towards the magistrate.

But on two occasions, DC1 harangues Albert for not looking at him while he is answering. Apart from the hostile and aggressive nature of the attacks, the first of these two instances is used by DC1 to get Albert to agree to a contextual presupposition which contradicts that widely commented on in relation to eye contact in Aboriginal society. Extract 9 occurs after a series of questions from DC1 about Albert's charge of breaking into a school and stealing pens almost two years before the hearing. In answer to DC1's repeated question *Why did you do it?*, Albert has replied *I don't know*. This leads to the following exchange in Extract 9:

Extract 9.   DC1 to Albert, Day 2, p116–117

1. DC1:	You're telling me a <u>lie</u> there aren't you?
2. Albert:	Nuh=.

3. DC1:   **=Look at me** for a minute- **can you <u>look</u> at me**? (1.7) **can you <u>look</u> at me**? you're TELLING LIES aren't you? (1.5) CAN YOU <u>LOOK</u> AT ME AND TELL ME THAT YOU'RE NOT TELLING LIES?

4. Albert: Nuh.

5. DC1:	**(0.5) CAN YOU <u>LOOK</u> AT ME?**
6. Albert:	(0.7) Nuh.

7. DC1:   (1.9) WHY NOT? (2.6) is it because **you think we'll see lies written all over your face**? (1.5) <u>well</u>? (2.0) <u>well</u>? (6.9) are you going to answer me? (7.3) you see you think this don't you that you can do anything you like and you'll (1.2) you won't get into much trouble isn't that so? (2.0) YOU <u>AN</u>SWER ME (3.1) will you direct him to answer me your worship.

In Turn 3, DC1 explicitly invokes the common western connection between avoidance of eye contact and *telling lies*. Albert's previous answer of *Nuh* in Turn 2, suggests that the same answer in Turn 4 is likely to be an answer to the first part of the double-proposition question *Can you look at me and tell me that you're not telling lies?*, (although it may of course, be an answer to both propositions). DC1's attack in Turn 7 further highlights his invocation of the interpretive connection between avoidance of eye contact and *telling lies*, with his suggestion that Albert can't look at him *because* he thinks they'*ll see lies written all over* his *face*. The same connection is made about 10 minutes later, during questions about whether Albert would *lie to get even with the police*. When Albert answers *Nuh* to this suggestion, DC1 says *Why can't you look at me? (2.6) I might not be the prettiest picture in the world but why can't you? (6.8) is it because you think that I'll see things on your face- that show you're lying? (1.8) well? (1.6) is it?* (p119). Albert's answer of *No* is followed by DC1's topic shift to *things* Albert *can tell* the court *about*, and he resumes haranguing on Albert's *criminal record*.

These examples show DC1 exploiting a widely-known feature of Aboriginal communicative style, making the explicit allegation that links avoidance of eye contact with *telling lies*, in the same way as with Aboriginal use of silence, discussed above.

4.   Secondary cultural differences?

It might be thought that the pragmatic features of Aboriginal English discussed in this chapter have arisen from what Ogbu (1995) terms an "oppositional frame of reference", and that the related cultural differences are secondary rather than primary cultural differences, in Ogbu's terms. That is, perhaps these are cultural differences that arise from opposition to another cultural group. If this is the case, then it would mean that Aboriginal people use gratuitous concurrence in answer to questions, and are comfortable with lengthy periods of silence, and often avert eye contact with their interlocutor, as patterns of opposition to members of the dominant Anglo culture. While there can be no definitive confirmation or rejection of this hypothesis, I am inclined to reject it for the following reasons.

Firstly, in regard to the use and interpretation of silence and the avoidance of eye contact, these are interaction patterns which I have observed over three decades <u>between</u> Aboriginal people <u>within</u> Aboriginal contexts in many parts of the country. That is, the use of these patterns is not limited to intercultural communication, and thus these patterns cannot be seen as part of an "oppositional frame of reference". The situation with gratuitous concurrence is somewhat different. As mentioned in Section 4 of Chapter 1, the use of repeated questions that characterises the interview genre is not typical of Aboriginal interactions, where much information is sought less directly, and in contexts of the exchange of information (see Eades 1991, 1992, 1994a, 2003b). Thus, interactions <u>between</u> Aboriginal people <u>within</u> Aboriginal contexts, do not provide nearly the same opportunities for gratuitous concurrence, which by definition comprises a response to certain questions, often in a context of repeated questioning. As discussed in Section 1.1 above, Liberman's (1980, 1981, 1985) work, which defines gratuitous concurrence, and focuses attention on its use in Australian Aboriginal interactions, sees it as a communicative pattern in intercultural communication, for which there are two explanatory elements – one which involves reaction to oppressive situations generally, and the other which involves continuities with traditionally-oriented Aboriginal ways of keeping immediate and surface harmony, while working on differences of opinion over time, and often indirectly. In relation to the first of these elements, the Aboriginal use of gratuitous concurrence in interviews can certainly be seen as part of an "oppositional frame of reference", while in relation to the second element it cannot be seen in this way.

It is for these reasons, that I see the three features of communicative style discussed in this chapter to be features of Aboriginal English. Further, the fact that these features are found in the traditionally-oriented languages (as discussed in Sections 1.1, 2.1 and 3.1 above) should not contradict my position that they are features of Aboriginal English (analogous to the sharing of grammatical features such as verbless equational/descriptive sentences).

5.   Conclusion

In this chapter we have seen the explicit invocation of culturally-specific presuppositions about the interpretation of silence and eye contact, which contradict Aboriginal English communicative style. We have also seen harassing questioning which has exploited the Aboriginal tendency to use gratuitous concurrence. This has succeeded in eliciting the boys' apparent agreement to interpretations which are at odds with Aboriginal communicative style, as well as to a range of damaging propositions about the central issue in the case. Perhaps these are subconscious strategies that form part of the DCs' general attacks on witnesses in cross-examination. But the fact that the lawyers' handbook about communicating with speakers of Aboriginal English (Eades 1992) is visible on the Bar table raises another possibility. It is conceivable that the defence team believes that, at some point, either during the hearing or after it, objections will be raised to the cultural insensitivity of some of their cross-examination techniques. For example, Justice Dean Mildren of the Northern Territory clearly would not have allowed some of these questions (Mildren 1999: 147). And the Kina case less than six months previously raised public and legal awareness on issues such as the Aboriginal use of silence in legal contexts (as discussed in Section 7.2 of Chapter 3). Thus, it is quite possible that the defence team are employing a deliberate strategy to prepare for objections about cultural issues, by getting agreement from the witnesses to propositions that contradict explanations in the lawyers' handbook about Aboriginal ways of using English.

Indeed, the expert report that the prosecutor asked me to present to the court on the final day of the hearing raised the three features of Aboriginal English communicative style discussed in this chapter. However, as explained in Section 6 of Chapter 1, the Director of Public Prosecutions ensured that my report would not be presented in court, and thus Aboriginal English communicative style was never raised during the case. But, it was not the only source for linguistic exploitation of the witnesses, as the following chapters will show. In Chapters 5–9 we will see that the cross-examination of the child witnesses in this case also involves the extreme use of a number of linguistic mechanisms which do not rely on the Aboriginality of the witnesses. I argue that this extreme use of these mechanisms is allowed because this case is a key struggle in the resistance of the Aboriginal community to the neocolonial control exercised by the criminal justice system.

Chapter 5
Lexical strategies[25]

Chapter 4 has examined the ways in which the cross-examination in the Pinkenba case exploits distinctively Aboriginal ways of using English. In this chapter, we will examine lexical strategies, which are widely used in cross-examinations, and which do not relate in any specific way to Aboriginal English. In examining lexical strategies used in this hearing, I focus mainly on lexical struggle, that is, struggle over the choice and meaning of words to name experiences and people involved in the Pinkenba event (Section 2). But first I briefly examine the lexical strategy popularly known as *using big words* and also popularly considered to be a major problem for witnesses in courtroom hearings, which we can separate into "apparently unfamiliar words" (Section 1.1), and "legal jargon" or "legalese" (Section 1.2).

1. "Big words"

Lawyers have a reputation for using what lay participants in the legal system often term *big words*, a term often used to refer to legal jargon and/or formal expressions. In the Pinkenba cross-examination, the witnesses appear to have recurrent problems with one formulaic expression which uses legalese (as we will see in Section 1.2). While there are not many instances of ordinary English words which clearly appear unfamiliar to them, it is impossible to know the extent to which the boys understand all of the words and phrases directed to them.

1.1. Apparently unfamiliar words

There appear to be a number of lexical items in the cross-examination which are unfamiliar to the boys, although they are not legal terms, and many adults would not have difficulty in understanding them. For example, the cross-examination of 15-year-old Barry begins with a question which he appears not to understand:

Extract 10. DC1 to Barry, Day 3, p157

1. DC1:   Where are you **residing** now Mr Coley?
2. Barry: (6.0) Could you say that again please?

3. DC1:   Where are you **residing** now Mr Coley?
4. Barry: **What does residing mean?**

5. DC1:   Where are you living now Mr Coley?
6. Barry: At my Aunty Helen's.

In this exchange, which will be discussed in Chapter 9, we see that Barry apparently does not understand the meaning of the word *reside*. Interestingly, this exchange shows parallels with part of my interview with Barry in June 2004. As we see in Extract 11 below, Barry appeared not to understand the meaning of the word *describe*, when I asked him about the youth refuge he had been staying in:

Extract 11.   Diana Eades (DE) interviewing Barry, May 2004

1. DE: Can you **describe** the street that it's in- Crest St?
2. Barry: (1.3) What street what it runs off?

3. DE: No- can you **describe** the street?
4. Barry: **What do you mean- describe?**

5. DE: Oh- sorry- can you tell me what the street's like?
6. Barry: (0.8) Quiet.

Another example which appears to indicate a witness's difficulty in understanding, involves the vague legal expression *the circumstances of that*, in Extract 12 below. However it occurs in one of the many exchanges where the actual question is both vague and comes after many harassing exchanges. Thus, it is unclear to what extent David's stated lack of understanding is because of the use of a lexical item which could be termed a *big word* (*circumstances*). This exchange occurs after 13-year-old David has been on the witness stand for more than 80 minutes, most of it cross-examination. DC1 has suggested that David and his friends are in the habit of taking a taxi and then running off without paying the fare, and that this had happened shortly before the police approached the three boys on the night in question. David maintains that it was a free ride (i.e. that the taxi driver agreed to take them the short distance for free). But DC1 persists with the theme that David and his friends are in the habit of taking taxis and *bolt*ing without paying. The exchange in Extract 12 below takes place after David's denial that this is what happened on the night of the Pinkenba incident. Interestingly, there was never any evidence produced in court, or even in newspaper reports, that the boys had been involved in fare evasion on that night. But DC1's allegation, in the cross-examination of both David and Barry, that the boys must have evaded payment for their taxi ride that night before the police approached them in the Valley, is one of the defence strategies used to support the common-sense view that the police were not doing anything wrong in removing the boys from the Valley area. Extract 12 follows the magistrate's delivery of the *warning* about the self-incrimination privilege, and David's admitting that he had once in the past taken a taxi and not paid the fare. DC1 asks him about this occasion:

Extract 12. DC1 to David, Day 1, p43

1. DC1:	What gives you the right to just- get into a cab and uh don't pay for it?
2. David:	(1.3) Nothing.
3. DC1:	(1.5) Come on now tell me the truth you've said you've done it once- that's not true is it?
4. David:	(0.5) <u>Yes</u>.
5. DC1:	**All right tell me the circumstances of <u>that</u>?**
6. David:	(1.4) **I don't know what you mean.**
7. DC1:	Well- where were you- when you got into this cab and decided not to pay?
8. David:	(2.0) Carina.
8. DC1:	Beg your pardon?
10. David:	Carina.
11. DC1:	Carina nd how far did you go in it?
12. David:	(0.9) Into the city.
13. DC1:	The city- how much was the fare?
14. David:	(2.0) (Mm) (1.6) Eight dollar something.

David's answer in Turn 6 is a clear and plausible expression of his lack of understanding of the phrase *circumstances of that*. Some other questions which are answered with a similar expression about comprehension difficulty include *regret* (Extract 61, Chapter 8), *overborne* (Extract 80, Chapter 9) and *roused* (Section 9, Chapter 7). But it is impossible to know how many other occasions arise where a witness does not express lack of understanding, or gives the impression that he understands, by agreeing to a question in situations that may involve gratuitous concurrence. It is not clear why the lawyers use such *big words*, although, following Tiersma (1999), we might suggest that legal "group cohesion" and in-group identity practices are involved. It is also quite likely that the DCs and magistrate are not experienced in talking to relatively uneducated young people, whether Aboriginal or not. The likely effect of these *big words* is to further contribute to the alienation and intimidation experienced by the boys in the formidable atmosphere of this courtroom.

1.2. Legalese

In terms of technical legal language (known as "legalese" or "legal jargon"), the most striking example is the *warning* about the self-incrimination *privilege*, which the magistrate is bound to deliver to witnesses in certain situations (as we saw in the discussion of Extract 6 in Section 2.2 of Chapter 4). The formulaic expression used most often by the magistrate to deliver the *warning* is *I warn you that you are not obliged to answer any question which will incriminate you in relation to the commission of a criminal offence*. He sometimes delivers it somewhat indirectly, by replacing the second person pronoun *you* with a third person form, such as *the witness*.

The magistrate does seem to have some concern that the boys might find this *warning* hard to understand, articulating it very slowly and carefully the first time he gives it (to David, p27), several times offering David (but not Albert or Barry) the option of going and talking to Aboriginal Legal Services about it, and once repeating it (to Albert p127). However, of the 18 times that the magistrate gives the *warning*, he makes only two attempts to explain or paraphrase it. On the first of these occasions he asks David if he knows *what the words claim privilege mean?* When David replies *No*, the magistrate says *It means you can refuse to answer questions which might incriminate you – you follow – all you have to say is- I refuse to answer because the answer might incriminate me* (p47). Although this comes after the magistrate has given David the *warning* for the 6th time, and David has been out of the courtroom to *speak to a legal representative* about it, it is arguably unlikely to help David's comprehension by explaining what *claim privilege* means, by defining it in terms of *questions which might incriminate you*, which is itself a very complex notion.

The magistrate's second attempted explanation comes on the following day to Albert, by way of a paraphrase, and it is also hardly clear. This paraphrase is *If you are asked a question about something for which you've been before the court and been found guilty or convicted you have to answer those questions* (p111). This attempted explanation includes an agentless passive in a subordinate clause (*if you are asked a question*), in which is embedded a relative clause containing another agentless passive (*for which you've . . . been found guilty or convicted*). To add to the confusion, in this embedded relative clause, *you* is the subject of an active clause (i.e. agent of the verb *to be*) in the first part (*'ve been before the court*), and of a passive clause (patient of the verbs *find guilty* and *convict* in the second part (*['ve] been found guilty and convicted*). Hardly surprisingly, there is evidence that the boys are quite confused about what this means and how to use this right, as we saw in the discussion of Extracts 6 and 8 in Chapter 4, and will see in Extract 34 in Chapter 7. We will also see in Extract 57 in

Chapter 8 that it can be confusing for legal practitioners. It is interesting to note that while this "right" is referred to legally as the self-incrimination "privilege", the performative speech act verb used in its delivery in this case is *I warn*, and the magistrate's solemn *warning* tone does not suggest that he is talking about a privilege. Further, it appears that the exercising of this right places the witness in a "Catch-22" situation: a witness can only refuse to answer a question, if doing so would be incriminating, thus refusing to answer a question amounts to admitting to a *criminal* act (although without giving any details).

Apart from the instances when a witness says he does not understand, we see little resistance from the witnesses to these first two lexical strategies: lawyers' use of "big words" and legal jargon. There are several consequences to the boys' lack of understanding of the self-incrimination privilege. Firstly, it is likely that confusion over what this means is at least partly behind attempts by the boys to refuse to answer certain questions, as for example in Extracts 8, 50 and 60. But, when the questions which they refuse to answer are not protected by the privilege, then this leads to exchanges which add to the presentation of the boys as uncooperative witnesses who are trying to hide something about their *criminal* past. Secondly, it is possible that on occasions they actually admit to *criminal activity* for which they could have used this privilege to refrain from disclosing, had they understood it (as for example in Extract 12 above, and Extract 32 in Chapter 7). And thirdly, the difficulty in understanding and invoking this privilege appears to add to the traumatic experience which they are suffering during the cross-examination.

As with the use of the unfamiliar lexical items, it is not clear whether the magistrate (or the lawyers) is aware of the comprehension difficulties involved in the ways in which the privilege *warning* is given. The magistrate appears to make attempts to make this *warning* clear to the witnesses. But it needs more than simple repetition or slowed articulation to make such complex legal language comprehensible to the child witnesses supposed to be protected by this privilege.

We will see a few other examples of legalese in extracts below, such as *entered a dwelling house with intent* in Extract 32, *convicted in respect of one*, also in Extract 32, and *breaking and entering a place with intent* in Extract 54. However, it should be pointed out that apart from the *warning* about self-incrimination, there are not many instances of legalese addressed to the witnesses in this case. This corresponds with my observation over many years in criminal courts in Queensland and New South Wales, that legal professionals generally do not use many terms of legal jargon or other unfamiliar lexical items in their questions to witnesses. Similarly, Heffer's (2005) study of more than 200 British criminal trials found that lawyers' talk to witnesses in court actually used very little specialised legal register.

2.   Lexical struggle

2.1.   Introduction

While the two lexical strategies discussed above are mostly uncontested, the most pervasive lexical strategy in the cross-examination involves struggle, between the two DCs and the three boys, over the choice of words to refer to central issues in the hearing. We will see that this lexical struggle – struggle over labels, descriptions, or lexical items – is part of the larger struggle over power between the state and Aboriginal people discussed in Chapter 3.

Lawyers are well aware of the power of words. For example, a much-used law textbook, Mauet's (2000) *Trial Techniques* tells lawyers: "Themes and labels are the trial vocabulary that become the psychological anchors you want the jurors to accept and adopt as their own during the trial. Once you have developed your theory of the case, you have to condense it into themes and labels" (ibid.: 25). It is these labels (which linguists term "lexical items") which are the specific focus of this section. Mauet defines the labels as "the ways you will refer to the people and events during the trial" (ibid.: 510). Mauet's textbook uses a psychological perspective to highlight the importance of labels, pointing out that they "convey meanings and values to the jury, since how we characterise things influences how others perceive them" (ibid.). Unsurprisingly, he appears to draw on the well-known psychological work of Loftus and her colleagues (e.g. Loftus 1979), for example contrasting the different images conveyed by calling "a death an event in which someone 'died'" vs "saying someone was 'slaughtered'".

A sociolinguistic perspective would take Mauet's point further, saying that not only does the way we talk about things influence how others perceive them, but it often actually constructs the "things" in a particular way, for instance defining the act of stabbing as murder rather than an accident. The groundbreaking sociolinguistic work in this area is Danet's (1980) analysis of the terms used by lawyers in a high-profile US abortion case to refer to the object of the abortion. No fewer than 40 lexical items are used with this reference in the case (ranging from "fetus" to "loved one", and including such terms as "baby boy", "the deceased" and "victim"). Danet examines the "remarkably fine-grained patterning" (ibid.: 210) in the use of terms by different parties, as they strove to define the opposing reality in this case.

A critical sociolinguistic perspective would go even further, asking what lexical means (including Mauet's term "labelling" tactics) are used by cross-examining counsel or magistrate to "control and constrain the contributions" (following Fairclough 1989: 46) of the witnesses. An excellent example of such critical sociolinguistic work is found in Ehrlich's work on rape trials (e.g. 1998, 2001, 2002a, 2002b), introduced in Section 2.4 of Chapter 2.

And going even further again, a critical sociolinguistic perspective would not stop with Mauet's one-sided description of lawyers' labels as "conveying meanings and feelings" in court. Two important CA studies of rape trials (Drew 1992; Matoesian 1993) show that the labelling is not limited to lawyers – witnesses sometimes resist lawyers' constructions by providing "alternative descriptions", either with or without overt markers of correction (Drew 1992: 486–491). As Matoesian (ibid.: 170) points out:

> although the resources with which to direct the course and outcome of interaction are asymmetrically distributed between the [Defence Attorney] and [Victim], both must struggle to negotiate meaning, to make their accounts count, and to reproduce their systematic courtroom relationship as a micro-mode of domination.

The major defence challenge – to show that the boys got into the police cars voluntarily – has striking similarities with the situation with rape cases, as mentioned in Chapter 2: victim-witnesses allege that they have been forced to engage in an activity, which would have been perfectly legal if they had given their consent. Hence the major legal strategy of the defence is to argue that such consent was given, there was no coercion, and thus no unlawful act. In rape trials, defence counsel work to "transform the [Victim's] experience of sexual violence into consensual sex" (Matoesian 1993: 170). And in the Pinkenba case, the DCs have to transform the boys' experience of being "abducted" into one of a consensual car ride. The work of four scholars who have analysed the language of rape trials is, therefore, relevant to the analysis of this case. Matoesian (1993, 2001) and Ehrlich (2001) have been introduced in Sections 2.3 and 2.4 of Chapter 2 respectively. While Matoesian (1993) focuses on the ways in which courtroom talk revictimises victim-witnesses in rape cases, Ehrlich (ibid.) shows the role of courtroom talk in "defining and delimiting the meanings that came to be attached to the events and subjects under scrutiny" in the rape cases she examined (ibid.:1). Both Drew (1992) and Cotterill (2004) analyse lexical strategies involved in this definition and delimitation of meanings, also in rape cases. Parallel to the linguistic treatment of rape victims in these studies, the lawyers in the Pinkenba hearing arguably redefine consent, using a number of sociolinguistic strategies, as analysed in this book.

The defence argument in this case is that the boys freely consented to going in the police cars, and that they are not only unreliable witnesses, but they are lying *criminals*. Following Mauet (2000), we will see how the labels chosen are a "condensation" of this defence theory, and we will also see the attempted struggle of the victim-witnesses against this labelling, or construction of the event and of themselves.

We have seen that lawyers are taught to control the way that people and events are perceived, with their choice of labels. We will see that it is not just the choice of key lexical items that is involved, but the <u>overt correction</u> of certain expressions used by witnesses, as well as the <u>covert substitution</u> of other expressions. The manipulative and sinister ways in which these lexical corrections and substitutions takes place, and in so doing, change the boys' story, lead me to refer to the DCs' practice in this case as "lexical perversion". We will see that while the lexical struggle in this hearing is decidedly asymmetrical, it is not entirely one-sided: there are instances of witnesses overtly correcting the lexical choice of the DCs.

2.2. Ideological struggle over the choice of words

In the lexical struggle between lawyers and witnesses we see the lexical realisation of the ideological struggle central to this case – over whether the boys consented to the ride in question – as well as the character portrayal of the boys. Following Fairclough (1989) and Gee (1990), I understand "ideological struggle" as a struggle over theories about how power and control (and other "goods") should be distributed. Underlying the Pinkenba case is an ideological struggle about whether Aboriginal young people have the right to complain about the way in which police treat them, and about whether it is acceptable for armed police officers to approach Aboriginal young people in the middle of the night, tell them to get into police cars, drive them to an industrial wasteland out of town and abandon them there. An important dimension of the ideological struggle in this case is lexical: having the power to determine word choice and word meanings is an important aspect of social and ideological power. In this chapter, I examine the courtroom struggle over:

1) the choice of words:
    friends vs *gang* vs *louts*; *walking* vs *wandering* vs *prowling*; *hop* vs *jump*; *told* vs *asked*;

2) the meaning of a key word in this case: *force*

In examining this lexical struggle in court, we see some small attempts at resistance, especially by Barry, the oldest witness, but it is clear that these Aboriginal boys have no chance of winning this ideological struggle.

My use of the term "lexical struggle" is similar to Cotterill's (2004: 521) term "lexical negotiation" to refer to the ways in which witnesses and lawyers in her study of cross-examination in rape and sexual assault cases, negotiate "about the particular representations of crime events and circumstances". I prefer to talk about "lexical struggle" however, as it is a central activity in the ongoing ideological struggle which comes to a climax in this case.[26]

What are the actual strategies involved in this lexical struggle? At the simplest level, the strategies involve word choice. Drew (1992) uses the term "alternative description" to refer to the common courtroom strategy of lawyers changing a witness's description or label for an event or state of affairs, or witnesses changing a lawyer's description. While at one level, this is what is involved in the lexical struggle in this case, I find the term "alternative description" unsuitable as it conveys a sense that either label is a possible alternative. But what we find here is a <u>process,</u> in which an interlocutor is overtly correcting a given lexical item to another, or more subtly substituting a given lexical item with another. The process of correction or substitution of the label for an event or person or state of affairs involves a (frequently subtle) change of meaning. Sometimes, this is as subtle as a change in connotative meaning, without changing the denotative meaning, as we will see in the *group of friends* vs *group of louts* example in Extract 13. Where this correction or substitution refers to the speaker's own experience, it seems appropriate to label it as "correction" or "substitution" (as we see with Barry in Extract 13). It is a different matter where this correction or substitution involves a speaker rejecting the interlocutor's labelling of the interlocutor's own experience (as we see with DC1, also in Extract 13), and in the process perverting the witness's story, resulting in a misrepresentation of their story. I view such correction or substitution (by a lawyer of a witness's account) to be instances of "lexical perversion".

Drew (1992: 472) points out that it is "common for [cross-examining] attorney and witness [to] offer alternative and competing descriptions or versions of events". Such lexical disputes, as we might call them, are not unlike practices involved in everyday arguing, as Drew further points out. An important aspect of both Drew's and Cotterill's (2004) studies is the analysis of how witnesses resist the cross-examining lawyer's version. Indeed many of the examples cited in both of these studies show strategic sophistication on the part of (adult) witnesses involved. In presenting an alternative description of some feature of the crime events and circumstances, the witness's answers often have no "overt markers of rejection or correction", although they may start with such an overt marker.

Drew's witness particularly uses more sophisticated and indirect disputing techniques in her answers than the Pinkenba boys: for example selecting to report a detail that does not support the DC's version (ibid.: 493) "in an implicit fashion and without using explicit markers of rejection or correction" (ibid.: 495). And further, in comparison to the Pinkenba cross-examination, the DC in Drew's study is much less overtly confrontational.

The witnesses in the Pinkenba hearing do try on several occasions to present competing versions, although generally with overt correction markers. However, as we will see in Extracts 13 and 14 below, the DCs' bullying tactics and the witnesses' susceptibility to gratuitous concurrence do not allow the competing description to stand. The central topics of these labelling disputes relate to the boys' activities that night and on similar occasions, as well as their social grouping.

A clear difference between Drew's study on the one hand, and the Pinkenba case and Cotterill's (2004) study on the other hand, is that the former does not discuss or exemplify the DC refusing outright to accept the witness's description, although this is common in the Pinkenba hearing, and there are examples in Cotterill's study. A more subtle defence strategy is operating in Drew's data than we find in the Pinkenba hearing, a strategy which Drew (1992: 472) terms a "contrast device": namely "a device for producing inconsistency in, and damaging implications for, a witness's evidence".

2.2.1.   Correction and perversion: from *gang* to *group of friends* to *group of louts*

The examination of lexical struggle in the Pinkenba case starts with an extract in which 15-year-old Barry uses lexical correction, which in turn is responded to by DC1 with lexical perversion. Barry's refusal to accept DC1's labelling of his social group as a *gang* is the first round in this important lexical struggle:

Extract 13.   DC1 to Barry, Day 3, p167

1. DC1:	Nd on <u>this</u> occasion the one I was talking to- to you about <u>yesterday</u>- what happened was this- that there was a **gang** walking down the street wasn't there? (2.8) there was wasn't there?
2. Barry:	°**Just a group of friends**°.
3. DC1:	Beg your pardon?
4. Barry:	**No gang just a group of friends**.
5. DC1:	**Just a group of louts** (2.2) is that the situation? (2.5) well?
6. Barry:	(2.8) Yes.

Barry starts this struggle over the labelling of his social group with a correction introduced by the relatively overt correction marker *just* (in Turn 2). This changes in Turn 4 to the most overt correction marker (the negative *no*) when he is asked to repeat the answer. (Turn 3 quite possibly is DC1's stalling for time as he plans his rebuttal of Barry's label.) DC1's refusal to accept Barry's correction is probably too subtle for the witness to apprehend. In Turn 5, he takes Barry's corrected term *a group of friends* and keeps the frame *a group of* —, substituting the neutral term *friends* with the negatively loaded *louts*. It is not clear whether Barry would have been familiar with the word *lout*, as it appears not to be used either in contemporary teenage talk or in Aboriginal English. It was a word frequently used by adults when I was a child in the 50s and 60s, to refer to what the *Macquarie Dictionary* of Australian English defines as "a rogue, uncouth, and sometimes violent young man".[27] Barry's apparent agreement to this term in Turn 6 comes after considerable silence on his part, as well as considerable pressure from DC1 in Turn 5, suggesting a strong likelihood of gratuitous concurrence. Also relevant is that this extract from Barry's cross-examination has been preceded by considerable shouting from DC1 (on the topic of Barry's theft convictions) on the morning of Barry's second day of cross-examination.

DC1 does not accept Barry's correction *group of friends* here, and he does not use it anywhere else in the hearing, using the negative term *louts* and the positive term *mates* instead.[28] He reserves the word *friend* to label the companion of a woman whose purse Barry had once stolen, and he once uses *friends* specifically to label Albert and David, the younger two boys of the three witnesses.[29]

2.2.2. Lawyers' lexical perversion: *walk around* to *wander around* to *prowl*

More prevalent in the Pinkenba hearing than lexical correction by a <u>witness</u>, is the <u>lawyers'</u> use of either correction or substitution (as we saw in Extract 13 above when DC1's substitution followed Barry's correction): that is, DC takes a witness description (of either an activity or a person/people) and <u>overtly corrects</u> it, or <u>covertly substitutes</u> it, with an alternative lexical item. As explained in Section 2.1 above, the way that this substituted or corrected lexical item then becomes adopted in the presuppositions of further questions, and even in the defence closing addresses, earns this linguistic strategy my term "lexical perversion".

The most noticeable use of lexical perversion relates to what the boys were doing in the Valley that night before the police came up to them and told them to get in the police vehicles. Let us look first at David, the first and youngest witness: in his evidence-in-chief, he says he was *walking around* the city and the Valley. This is a commonly used general Australian English, as well as Aboriginal English, description for a frequent and widespread youth activity in many cities throughout the world. The importance of *walking around* the city as an activity can be seen from my interview with David in June 1994. I asked him *what* he *did when* he was *down* in Brisbane, saying *don't talk about that night all the trouble is about- some other things you did while you were in Brisbane.* David's answer was *just walking around* (6.5) *nothing.* It is also interesting to note that recent research on the oral narratives told by Aboriginal English speaking school children in Western Australia finds that one of the four most frequently occurring schemas in these narratives is the "travel schema: experience of known participants organised in terms of alternating travelling (or moving) and nontravelling (or stopping) segments" (Malcolm and Sharifian 2005: 520; see also Malcolm and Rochecouste 2000). As *walking around* is not an activity commonly practiced by middle-class adults, it is possible that the lawyers simply do not understand it. Certainly, as with other areas of the boys' lives that are questioned by the lawyers, the notion of purpose is central to the line of questioning for each of the witnesses. Questioning <u>why</u> the boys were in the Valley and what they were intending to do, is an important part of both DCs' strategy of contructing the boys as *criminals*, who must have been in the Valley that night in order to carry out *criminal activity*.

Extract 14 below is part of David's cross-examination by DC1. We see that DC1 does not accept David's term *walking around* from his evidence-in-chief, and instead substitutes his own term *wander around*, a term David does not directly dispute, although he does not use it:

Extract 14.   DC1 to David, Day 2, p49

1. DC1:	You **wandered** around the streets of Brisbane- we know that you were in the mall up in the heart of the town we know you walked down towards North Quay- we can see you on- tapes- we know you were in the Valley.
2. David:	(2.7) Mm.
3. DC1:	And you were **just wandering around** (2.0) [weren't you?
4. David:	[Yes.
5. DC1:	For [what?
6. David:	[Yes.
7. DC1:	For what?
8. David:	(2.3) Lookin.
9. DC1:	Lookin (1.5) At what?
10. David:	(2.3) We was **just walking around for nothing**.

David's answer in Turn 8 to the *for what?* question is interesting: *lookin* or "observing the comings and goings of others around them" (Eades 1988: 104) is indeed an important Aboriginal social activity. And in Malcolm and Sharifian's (2005: 520) study of the narratives told by Aboriginal English speaking school children in Western Australia, one of the four most frequently-occurring schemas is what the authors term the "observing schema", in which experiences, usually shared, are recalled in narratives in terms of the details the narrator(s) observed.

After DC1's pressure with the question tag *weren't you* following 2 seconds silence in Turn 3, in Turn 4 David appears to accept the term *wandering around*, although this may well be an answer of gratuitous concurrence. In Turn 9, David substitutes *wandering around* with *just walking around for nothing*. He is explicit about the boys having no specific purpose <u>apart from</u> the general social activity common to Aboriginal people and to youth culture in Australia. It is not clear whether 13-year-old David is aware of the difference in meaning between *wandering around* and *walking around*. It seems that the difference between these two words in Australian English is exactly in terms of purpose: while *walk* has a destination implied, *walk around* does not imply a destination, but it does imply a purpose (e.g. "walking around window-shopping"). *Wander around* on the other hand seems to connote neither destination nor purpose, and it collocates easily with the adverb *aimlessly*. (The relevant definitions from the *Macquarie Dictionary* give *walk* as "1) to go or travel on foot at a moderate pace", and *wander* as "1) to ramble without any certain course or object on view, roam, rove, or stray; 2) to go aimlessly or casually".)

DC1 returns to his focus on the purpose of the boys' activity in the Valley that night some 40 minutes later (after much questioning about David's knowledge of Albert's and Barry's earlier *criminal activities*, and details of his train ride to the city on the day in question):

Extract 15.   DC1 to David, Day 1, p62

1. DC1:   Just **wandering around** for hour- after hour- after hour (1.7) cor<u>rect</u>?
2. David: Yeh.

3. DC1:   Why?
4. David: (1.5) I don't know.

5. DC1:   Why?
6. David: (2.0) Nothing else to do.

7. DC1:   Oh you- you could have gone home- gone to bed.
8. David: No.

9. DC1:   Like most <u>other</u> people your age (2.5) THERE'S NOTHING ELSE TO DO SO YOU **WANDERED around** the town- right?
10. David: Yeh.

11. DC1:   Did you <u>go</u> on any sort of a <u>pattern</u>- or did you **just wa:nder around**?
12. David: (1.7) **Wander around.**

In this extract DC1 continues with his substitution of David's earlier *walking around* with *wandering around*, and he ignores the boy's earlier answer about the purpose (*lookin*), which David does not try to offer again here. In this extract we see the verb *wander around* emphasised in Turns 1, 9 and 11, together with shouting in Turn 9 and lengthened vowel in Turn 11. In Turn 11, DC1 cleverly uses an *either/or* question to get David to admit that what they were involved in was aimless wandering. The lawyers' handbook, discussed in Section 1.2 of Chapter 2, advises against the use of *either/or* questions with Aboriginal witnesses, as it has been found that many Aboriginal English speakers opt for the second alternative, regardless of their belief about or understanding of the proposition (Eades 1992: 47–48).

Regardless of the extent to which the lawyers understand *walking around* without any express purpose as a youth activity, the cross-examinations of David by DC1, and Barry by both DC1 and DC2 make much of the implication that the boys did actually have a purpose, and that it was a *criminal* intention: that is, that the purpose of their activity in the Valley that night was to engage in the *criminal activity* of stealing, as we will see in Extract 16 below, as well as Section 10 of Chapter 9. This implication was central to the defence theory that the boys were lying *criminals* rather than victims of a police abduction (which will be investigated in the chapters in Part III).

Central to his construction of Barry as a *criminal*, who had *criminal* intentions on that night in the Valley, with him DC1 uses a powerful label to describe the boys' activities, namely *prowling*, as we see in Extract 16:

Extract 16.   DC1 to Barry, Day 2, p162

1. DC1:   I see- well what were you - what used you do around town the times when you were with these other two this uh Carter and- uh uh [Pender?

2. Barry: [Just **walk around.**

3. DC1:   Hey?

4. Barry: Just **walk around**.

5. DC1:   Just walk around (1.8) did you do that often?

6. Barry: (2.1) Yeh.

7. DC1:   Of a night? (1.2) [Well?

8. Barry: [°Yeh°.

9. DC1:   (2.0) You <u>did</u> didn't you? (3.6) well Mr Coley? (7.3) are you going to keep us here forever Mr Coley? you did it often didn't you?

10. Barry: Yeh often often.

11. DC1:	Beg your pardon? (1.8) what did you say?
12. Barry:	Often.
13. DC1:	Often (1.5) and did you **just <u>prowl</u> around** the town? (2.0) is that what happened?
14. Barry:	<u>Yes</u>.
15. DC1:	You and your mates?
16. Barry:	Yeh my mates.
17. DC1:	(3.2) And **just prowling around <u>look</u>ing for <u>mischief</u>** weren't you?
18. Barry:	(3.2) No- **just walking around**=
19. DC1:	=**Just walking around** (2.8) **admiring the sights of Brisbane?** is that what you were doing?
20. Barry:	(1.8) No.
21. DC1:	You were **<u>walk</u>ing around <u>look</u>ing to see if you could get into mischief** isn't that so?
22. Barry:	°No°.
23. DC1:	Beg your pardon?
24. Barry:	No.
25. DC1:	See if there was anything you could STEAL that was your WHOLE POINT WASN'T IT? (3.2) well?
26. Barry:	Yeh.

DC1's lexical perversion from Barry's *walking around* to *prowling around* involves a key shift in labels. Central to the meaning of *prowl* is that the agent is in search of something that is not legitimately theirs: *prey* or *plunder*, as the *Macquarie Dictionary* expresses it. Thus, this word *prowl* is a clever tool in the implication that the boys were intending to engage in *criminal activity*, and thus were "fair game" for law enforcement activity. It is also not clear if Barry understands the meaning of *prowl*: although he agrees to this label in Turn 14, it may be due to the pressure to respond with gratuitous concurrence. In Turn 18 he rejects the label *prowling around looking for mischief* and goes back to his earlier assertion that they had been *walking around*. But he is getting noticeably agitated and he is unable to sustain his version. This example illustrates a situation highly likely to involve gratuitous concurrence in Turn 26, following DC1's apparent determination to harass Barry until he agrees (for example in Turn 9) and culminating in his shouted harassment in Turn 25.

It is then an easy matter for DC1 just a few minutes later to move from what the boys were doing on that particular night to some of their past experiences in that area, while incorporating the presupposition that Barry was prowling around the streets, as we see in Extract 17 below:

Extract 17.   DC1 to Barry, Day 2, p163

1. DC1:	What **sort of things did you steal- when you were wan- prowling around the streets**?
2. Barry:	(3.5) Just purses.

DC1's repair from starting to say the word *wandering* (in Turn 1 of this extract) suggests the deliberateness of this lexical substitution strategy here.

Until the apparent gratuitous concurrence in Turn 26 of Extract 16 above, Barry appears to be presenting a consistent (and entirely plausible) line: that he had committed crimes on some of the occasions on which he had been walking around the Valley, prior to the night in question, but that he did not commit any crimes that night. Given that there were mall surveillance videos, and six police officers observing Barry and his two friends, and that they were never charged with any offence relating to that night, his story seems highly believable. It is important to remember that Barry is not on trial, he is a victim-witness, not an accused. However, this construction of Barry as a *criminal* is central to the defence theory, as we will see throughout Chapter 9.

The struggle over the label *prowl* has not been won, however. Barry's cross-examination continues the following day, and he again overtly corrects this term, as we see in Extract 18:

Extract 18.   DC1 to Barry, Day 3, p179

1. DC1:	And you had to be told several- or <u>ask</u>ed several times (2.0) to <u>wake</u> up didn't you?
2. Barry.	Yeh.
3. DC1:	Had **you'd been <u>out</u> prowling** the night before?
4. Barry:	(2.9) **Weren't prowling**.
5. DC1:	Beg your pardon?
6. Barry:	**Was on our way <u>home</u>** until we got picked up.

While *prowl* is used only by DC1, he uses it primarily with Barry, the oldest witness, whom he is most vigorously constructing as a *criminal*. In fact Extract 15 above, which shows DC1 constructing David's evidence on this point in terms of aimless wandering, is immediately preceded by DC1's use of the word *prowl*, in the question: *So you've used up all your money did you?- So then you went*

prowling *the town- is that correct?* After 2.2 seconds silence, David answers *Yeh*. However, DC1 does not pursue the implications of *prowling* with David with any overtness, leaving it to the cross-examination of Barry, as we have seen.

Barry's refusal to accept DC1's label *prowl* exemplifies the resistance found with this eldest witness (to be seen further in Chapter 9). Despite his susceptibility to gratuitous concurrence, and the extreme tactics of DC1, Barry has succeeded in resisting some of the labelling of DC1, through such correction (as we saw in Extract 16 Turns 18 and 22, and Extract 18 Turns 4 and 6), although it is not sufficient for him to succeed in his ideological struggle, and to have his version accepted.

The emphasis on *wandering* and *prowling* is evocative of vagrancy, which, although decriminalised in many other Australian jurisdictions, remained an offence in Queensland until its relabelling as an offence of public nuisance in 2005. The law of vagrancy (*Vagrancy, Gaming and Other Offences Act* 1931 Queensland – hereafter the *Vagrants Act*) covered a range of offences including "having no visible lawful means of support" (Section 4) and behaving "in a riotous, violent, disorderly, indecent, offensive, threatening or insulting manner" in any public place (Section 7). It has been evaluated by criminologists as a "source of grave injustice" (Walsh 2003: 76), and in a number of common law countries it has been found to be "a reflection of the society's perception of a continuing need to control some of its 'suspicious' or 'undesirable' members" (Chambliss 1964: 75), including homeless and indigenous people. While in Queensland, the *Vagrants Act* that was in force when the Pinkenba event occurred in 1994 did not include the verb *wander*, it did include prosecution for any person who "loiters or places himself in a public place to beg or gather alms". While the word *loiter* is not used by either of the DCs in this case, in some jurisdictions *wander* is also used in the legal definition of vagrancy. Thus the (American) *Black's Law Dictionary* (Garner 2004: 1584) defines vagrancy as "the state or condition of *wandering* from place to place without a home, job or means of support", pointing out that it is "generally considered a course of conduct or a manner of living rather than a single act" (emphasis added). The *Macquarie Dictionary* also defines the general (non-legal use of the) word *vagrant* in terms of a person who *wanders or roams*. While the three boys in this case were never charged with an offence on the night in question, it is apparent that in their cross-examination about this night and other occasions, they are effectively being "charged" with vagrancy.

2.2.3.   Lawyers' lexical perversion: *jump* to *hop*

The first two examples of lawyers' lexical perversion, discussed in Sections 2.2.1 and 2.2.2 above, concern the character portrayal of Barry and his friends, and what the three boys were doing in the Valley the night of the Pinkenba incident. We now move to lexical perversion over the central actions of the police that night: what did they say to the boys which led to the car ride? A rather subtle kind of lexical perversion occurs with the verb attributed by both DC1 and DC2 to the boys' reports of the action they were instructed to carry out by the police officers in getting into the police cars. Both David's and Barry's answer in examination-in-chief to the crucial question about what happened when the police came up to them in the mall is *They told us to jump in the car.* (Albert's answer was *Told us to get in.*)

This expression *jump in the car* is frequently repeated by each of the DCs, (especially by DC2 to Albert) but it is also changed a number of times in questions to both David and Albert, so that the DCs often instead substitute the expression *hop in the car*, and DC2 once uses it in addition to *jump in the car* as we see in Extract 19:

Extract 19.   DC2 to Albert, Day 2, p91

1. DC2:   Now am I right in thinking that what happened was (2.0) some- some police officer said to you **hop in the car** or **jump in the car**- is that right?

2. Albert: (1.1) °Yeh°=

3. DC2:   =And then you got then you got in the car? (1.0) is that right?

4. Albert: °Yeh°.

It is important to point out that none of the boys ever uses this expression *hop in the car* (or the word *hop* at all) in their evidence, but neither do they dispute or correct it in any way. While both *jump* and *hop* are used colloquially to refer to quick movement, there is a subtle difference in meaning in general Australian English – with *jump* able to include a connotation of urgency, while *hop* includes a connotation of briskness, rather than urgency. We see this difference in the *Macquarie Dictionary*, which gives as its second definition of *jump* "to move or go quickly", with the example "She jumped into a taxi". (The first meaning given is "to spring clear of the ground or other support by sudden muscular effort".) Its relevant definition of *hop* involves setting about something "energetically". As with the difference between *wander* and *prowl* discussed above, it appears likely that the young and intimidated witnesses are oblivious to the subtle difference in meaning.

In his frequent repetitions of these two expressions (*hop in the car* and *jump in the car*), it seems that DC2 is highlighting the colloquial and non-threatening tone of the word *jump* (as well as his substituted term *hop*). For example he says to Albert: *All that was said was hop in the car* (p148). During his concluding address, he says *what was actually said in all cases was neither more nor less than- hop in the police car or jump in the police car- or- hop in the back seat* by way of highlighting his claim that *it is a perfectly lawful thing to say*, as we will see in Extract 89 in Chapter 10.

The significance and effectiveness of the DCs' lexical perversion strategy with this term is seen in its adoption by the magistrate, as we will see in Section 2 of Chapter 10. In his decision the magistrate does not quote the boys' reports that they were *told to jump* in the police cars. Despite the fact that none of the boys ever used the word *hop* in their evidence, the magistrate accepts this label from the DCs, saying: *The three juveniles with one accord have conceded that the conversation at the scene was "hop in the police car".*

Certainly the verb *jump* (and the DCs' substituted term *hop*) taken in isolation in this expression connotes speed rather than force or duress. But given that meaning and interpretation is heavily dependent on context, the witness's answers in Extract 20 below make it very clear that he saw this expression *jump in the car* as involving compulsion. The forceful meaning of this expression was likely to have been conveyed by nonverbal means: structural (the inherent power of armed uniformed police in issuing commands to Aboriginal young people), historical (the known experiences of Aboriginal people when approached by police) and kinesic (posture and the way in which participants were standing in relation to each other). The forceful meaning of this expression may also have been conveyed by prosodic aspects of the utterance, such as intonation and volume, although we have no evidence of this.

2.2.4.   Lawyers' lexical perversion: *told* to *asked*

The fourth striking case of lexical perversion is the most troubling one. Referring to the central speech act of the police officers, both DCs substitute the boys' word *told*: that is, neither of the DCs accepts the boys' word *told*, but instead they both change it to *ask*, never using *told*. Each of the three witnesses says in their evidence-in-chief that the police *told* them to get into the police cars. After the first witness, David, says this, the prosecutor (using the neutral verb *say*) specifically checks whether they were *told* or *asked*, as we see in Turn 5 of Extract 20 below. David's unequivocal response in both Turn 6 and Turn 8 is *told us*:

Extract 20.   Pros to David, Day 1, p18

1. Pros:	When you got down to where the police were um- did anybody say any-thing to you?
2. David:	(3.6) No.
3. Pros.	(2.1) Did the police say anything to you?
4. David:	(2.6) Yes.
5. Pros:	Can you remember what they said to you?
6. David:	They **told us** to jump in the car.
7. Pros:	(2.1) Did they **tell you-** or **ask you**?
8. David:	**Told us**.

None of the witnesses uses the word *asked*, or any other word, such as *invited*, or *offered*, which could have suggested that they did not perceive it as a command. But both DC1 and DC2 explicitly reject this crucial word *told*, substituting this direct evidence erroneously with *asked* (and later with *said* as we will see in Extract 23 below). In each of the two instances the prosecutor objects, as we see in Extracts 21 and 22 below. Extract 21 occurs during DC1's cross-examination of David:

Extract 21.   DC1 to David, Day 1, p39[30]

1. DC1:	But you say you were **asked** to jump in the car- and you jumped in the car?
2. Pros:	He didn't say that- with respect.
3. David:	**They told us.**
4. DC1:	They **told you** to jump in the car did they?
5. David:	Yes.
6. DC1:	Who is they?
7. David:	The police officer.

This extract shows DC1 erroneously attributing the verb *asked* to David's preceding testimony during evidence-in-chief, saying *you say you were asked to jump in the car*, and the prosecutor corrects the error. Extract 22 below shows that DC2's attempt at the same lexical perversion is more intrusive. It occurs during examination-in-chief of Albert, when DC2 interjects, erroneously yet somewhat indignantly, insisting that the prosecutor has misquoted Albert on this crucial verb:

Extract 22.   Pros to Albert, Day 2, p106

1. Pros:	Nd what happened when the police cars came along?
2. Albert:	(1.3) **Told us** to get in.

3. Pros:	They **told you** to [get
4. DC2:	[They **asked us** to get in- is what he [said- and it was <u>ob</u>vious- with respect
5. Pros:	[I'm sorry - with respect ( )

6. Pros:	I heard something to [the contrary (xxxxxx)
6. DC2:	[It was obvious to me.

7. M:	(2.1) Yes ask the question again and we'll get the uh correct answer. (1.2) what did they say to you uh?
8. Albert:	**Told us** to get in.

(9.3) ((some whispering at the Bar table))

9. M:	It will appear in the transcript anyway as to [what was actually said.
10. DC2:	[Yes it will thank you Your Worship=

11. Pros:	=In fact Your Worship um- might the witness go outside and we replay that passage- just so there's no doubt about it=
12. M:	=Albert can you just go outside for a moment? we won't keep you long.

Note that the official transcript accurately gives *told*.

These unsuccessful attempts at lexical perversion during the witnesses' testimony, do not prevent DC2 from using his substituted term in his closing address (as we will see in Section 1 of Chapter 10). To describe and/or refer to the speech act, he uses the verb *say* several times, never uses *told* and explicitly says that the boys *didn't protest and got into the police vehicles when __asked__* (emphasis in original).

2.3.   Ideological struggle over the meaning of a key word: from forced *to* said

The lexical strategies discussed above involve lexical perversion, replacing a contested lexical item with another, whether by overt correction or covert substitution. The cross-examining lawyers insist on their labels being applied to people and events. In a central part of the lexical struggle, DC2 succeeds yet again in this outcome, correcting *forced* to *said*, as we see in Extract 23 below. But this example is more complex, as it involves a striking example of what

Fairclough (1989) terms the "naturalisation of word meaning" – using "common-sense" to deny contest over the meanings of words. A crucial dimension of this particular lexical struggle is the use of discourse strategies to elicit apparent gratuitous concurrence (discussed in Chapter 4), as well as the general syntactic strategy of using complex questions, in which more than one proposition is being questioned. Extract 23 starts towards the end of Extract 3, discussed in Chapter 4 above (with Turns 13–16 of Extract 3 numbered as Turns 1–4 of Extract 23):

Extract 23.   DC2 to David, Day 2, p97–98

1. DC2:	You got in the car without being forced David- didn't you?
2. David:	(1.5) No.
3. DC2:	You told us- you've told us a ((laughs)) number of times today you did.
4. David:	(1.3) **They forced me**.
5. DC2:	Eh?
6. David:	**They forced us.**
7. DC2:	Tell us- tell us how David come on?
8. David:	**They told us to jump in the car**.
9: DC2:	They told you to jump in the car?=
10. David:	=Yeh.
11. DC2:	That's <u>all</u> that was said?
12. David:	(1.0)Yeh.
13. DC2:	Nothing else was said to you apart from- jump in the car (2.2) that right?
14. David:	(1.2) Yeh.
15. DC2:	And you did get in the car?
16. David:	Yeh.
17. DC2:	You weren't <u>push</u>ed in the car- or held in the car?
18. David:	No.
19. DC2:	You never asked to get <u>out</u> of the car?
20. David:	(1.4) No.
21. DC2:	(4.6) And- all that happened because- <u>you</u> didn't <u>think</u> you were in any trouble- did you?
22. David:	(1.8) No.
23. DC2:	CORRECT?
24. David:	(1.9) °Yeh°.

25. DC2:   And that's why you had no trouble going <u>out</u> there getting in the car and travelling with the police- you <u>didn't</u> think you were in any <u>trouble</u>- did you?

26. David: We weren't.

[5 turns omitted here involved DC2's difficulty in hearing the answer]

27. DC2:   You weren't- that's right- that's right- what you're saying is I think- that if you'd just been walking along the street- you wouldn't have jumped in the car yourselves- **you got in the car because the police said to.**

28. David: Yeh.

29. DC2:   Ok- that's what you mean isn't it?

30. David: Yeh.

31. DC2:   **When you say <u>forced</u>- all <u>you</u> mean is- the police <u>said</u> so?**

32. David: Yeh.

33. DC2:   Mm?

34. David: Yeh.

In contrast to the monosyllabic utterances which were discussed in Chapter 4 as highly likely to be answers of gratuitous concurrence, David's disagreement with the simple proposition that he *got in the car without being forced* comes as a complete sentence (Turn 4, repeated Turn 6 and rephrased Turn 8): a relatively rare occurrence for this witness whose answers were overwhelmingly monosyllabic single words, primarily *yeh* and *no*.

In Turns 1–32, DC2 and David struggle over the meaning of the verb *force*. DC2 gets the witness to "agree" that no physical force or verbal threats were made by the police officers, and thus concludes that there was no force. In this way he has naturalised the meaning of the word *force*, clearly implying that it is common-sense that what happened cannot be described by the verb *force* (e.g. the lawyer's laughter in Turn 3, and his comment *nothing else was said* in Turn 13). It might well be argued that the power imbalance between the three Aboriginal boys and six armed police officers in the context of Aboriginal experiences of police violence, especially against young people (discussed in Chapter 3), in itself constituted a threat – although this is hardly the analysis which we can expect from a 13-year-old witness in cross-examination in an adult court, in answer to the question *tell us how* [the police forced you to get in the car]? His answer to this question (Turn 8) *They told us to jump in the car* is arguably the beginning of this explanation.

We have no way of knowing if the word *force* conveys exactly the same meaning to 13-year-old David, as it does to DC2. In its customary Australian

English usage, the verb *force* does not necessarily imply the <u>overt</u> use of physical force. The *Macquarie Dictionary* gives its first ("commonest") meaning as "to compel; constrain, or oblige (oneself or someone) to do something", with the notion of the use of overt force coming in only from its third commonest meaning, namely "to bring about or effect by force" (The second meaning given is "to drive or propel against resistance".) It would be quite plausible for the witness to be using the expression *They forced me* [to get in the car] in the same way as I might say *The police officer forced me to pull over to the side of the road* (where in the latter case no overt force was used, but I felt I had no choice because of the situation, and my understanding of police powers).

From both this cross-examination and DC2's concluding address (to be discussed in Section 1 of Chapter 10), it is clear that for him the word *force* includes the elements of overtly verbalised threat (Turns 11, 13) and physical force (Turn 17). His naturalisation of the meaning of *force* is so idiosyncratic that it does not even use the "fixed" dictionary definition (cf. Fairclough 1989: 108). Further, for DC2, David's non-consent would have had to be realised in a verbalised objection to the police officers (Turn 19). Issues such as the unequal power relations between the police and the boys, and the history of Aboriginal treatment of Aboriginal people, are ignored in this naturalisation of the meaning of the word *force*.

The lexical perversion through which the meaning of the word *force* has had its meaning naturalised, and then been substituted with *said* is reminiscent of what Ehrlich (2001) terms "selective (re)formulation". Ehrlich bases this term on the CA notion of "formulating" which refers to "summarizing, glossing or developing the gist of an informant's earlier statements" (Heritage 1985: 100, in Ehrlich 2001: 74). Heritage's analysis is of question-answer sequences in news interviews, but Ehrlich sees that cross-examining lawyers use the same strategy in order to "commit witnesses to descriptions that may be incompatible with previous versions of events" (Ehrlich 2001: 74). Ehrlich is particularly interested in the role of what she calls "controlling questions that are pseudo-declarative in nature" (ibid.), a linguistic mechanism which we will take up in Section 2 of Chapter 6. It is through such questions that the lawyer can "reshape and reconstruct the nature of witnesses' answers" (ibid.: 75). Thus, DC2 takes David's assertion that the police forced the boys to get in the police cars, and through pseudo-declarative questions in Turns 11, 13, 17, 19, reformulates the notion of police force to one of police saying something. Using Ehrlich's analysis of selective reformulation in this instance highlights the strategic significance of the discourse structure of courtroom interaction (see Eades 2000). Having such tight control over speaking turns and topics, provides the lawyers with a powerful tool to assist in the lexical perversion of the witness's account.

2.4. A labelling problem – what was the central speech act?

In naturalising the meaning of the word *forced*, in then correcting David's *forced* to *said*, and substituting the boys' *told* with *asked*, the DCs are cleverly distracting attention from the problematic nature of the act involved. The (uncontested) evidence is that the police approached the boys and told them to get in the cars, saying something like *jump in the car*. This clearly involved a speech act, and according to the defence, it did not involve force, and the boys were free to not get in the cars.

So what was the speech act? From the boys' point of view the speech act is clear: 13-year-old David says *They forced us*, and they all say *they told us*: thus they interpreted it as a command. In his closing address, DC2 argues that the boys should not have been allowed to give evidence as to whether they were *told* or *asked*, as that is *opinion evidence – being asked to characterise a form of words as an asking or a telling.*

The defence argument is that the crucial speech act that night could not have been a command, as their argument is that the boys were free to not get in the cars. So given that it was an utterance which led to the boys getting in the car, then was it an offer? or perhaps a suggestion? On the grounds of linguistic form, without even taking into account contextual factors such as relationships between speakers and hearers, it seems quite difficult to interpret the syntactic form *jump in the car* as either an offer or a suggestion. Indeed this imperative form is typically associated with the speech act of commanding. And such speech acts as offering or suggesting would need to include a phrase such as *Would you like to . . . ?* or *Why don't you . . .* respectively.

It is significant that throughout all the cross-examination, as well as the concluding addresses by both DCs, they almost never label the event in terms of its speech act, referring to it by such expressions as *this business* (p92, 142, 146), *that night* (p60, 63, 88), *this night* (p50, 88), and *when you got in the police car* (p191). The only times in which either of the DCs gives the speech act some label is when it is referred to in an adverbial clause with the agentless passive as *when it was said to jump in the car* (p191), and in vague terms (also as adverbial clauses, introduced with *when*) as *when these police spoke to you that night* (p94), and *when you spoke with these six police in the Valley* (p170). The only instance of the speech act referred to with a noun phrase, occurs in DC2's concluding address, when he twice refers to what the police said to the boys as a *statement*.

In Section 2.3 of Chapter 12, we will consider this labelling problem in terms of Solan and Tiersma's (2005) discussion of the "selective literalism" of American courts.

3. Conclusion

The six police officers in the Pinkenba case were charged that they had "unlaw-fully deprived" each of the three boys of "his personal liberty by carrying him away in a motor vehicle against his will". The data presented and analysed in the two chapters in Part II have shown how successful the two DCs were in gaining apparent agreement from each of the boys to the defence case that the boys had consented to the ride in question. As we will see in Section 5 of Chapter 10, the judge who reviewed the magistrate's decision in this case considered that the boys' evidence had been given in unequivocal terms. But, based on the analysis in this part of the book, I find this a problematic interpretation. We have seen some of the linguistic mechanisms by which the boys' apparent agreement to the defence has been elicited – including lexical perversion (as discussed in this chapter), and the exploitation of pragmatic differences between AE and SE, particularly related to gratuitous concurrence, silence and the avoidance of eye contact (Chapter 4).

Legally, the boys' agreement to the defence argument would have been enough for the charges against the police officers to be dropped. So, it might be thought that the cross-examination, and this book, could stop at this point. But, the defence in the Pinkenba case involved much more than this central issue over whether or not the boys consented to the ride. In Chapter 3, I have argued that this hearing played an important role in the ongoing struggle over power between the Aboriginal community and the state. The Aboriginal community, with the help of Aboriginal Legal Services and the Criminal Justice Commis-sion, was rejecting the two hundred year practice of police removal of Aboriginal young people. And the Queensland Police Service, through its engagement of two of the top barristers in the state, was arguing for its right to continue this practice. In order to naturalise this practice, much more work needed to be done in the cross-examination than simply to prove that the boys had consented to the ride. And it is this work which forms the bulk of the cross-examination of the three boys, and to which we will turn in Part III. By constructing the boys as lying *criminals*, who were making the streets unsafe, the two DCs invoke the moral panic which links Aboriginal young people with crime, and legitimises the actions of the police in removing the three boys from the Valley.

Part III

Constructing the identities of the witnesses

Chapter 6
Linguistic mechanisms for identity construction

The <u>central issue</u> in the Pinkenba hearing is whether the boys had got into the police cars willingly, while the <u>underlying issue</u> is whether police officers should have the right to remove Aboriginal young people as they did in the Pinkenba event. The immediate task of the DCs is to convince the magistrate that the answer to the central issue is *yes*. And it is my argument that they are also working to convince not just the magistrate, but also the wider society, that the answer to the underlying issue is also *yes*. It is this work being undertaken by cross-examination talk which is at the heart of how neocolonialism is reproduced.

In order to succeed in the immediate task, the DCs only need to show in their cross-examination that the boys *knew when* they *spoke to* the *six police in the Valley that* they *didn't have to go anywhere with them if* they *didn't want to*, and that they were not *forced* to go in the police cars. We have seen in Chapters 4 and 5 the linguistic mechanisms which are central to "proving" that the boys went willingly in the police cars. But much of the cross-examination goes far beyond this issue, dwelling at length on the *criminal records* of the boys, as well as on their characters generally. This is so extreme, that the judge who conducts the review of the magistrate's decision points out that "much of the evidence canvassed [in the cross-examination of the three boys] related to matters having only the most peripheral relevance to the elements of the offences charged" (*Purcell & Ors v. Quinlan & Anor* 1996: 2).

Thus, much of the questioning in cross-examination serves to build the identities of the witnesses. This identity work carried out by the two DCs covers much more than the boys' credibility and reliability as witnesses, and is best summarised in the words of the magistrate. He is decidely persuaded by the DCs' identity construction of these boys, finding that they *have no regard for members of the community, their property or even the justice system. They have no fear of the police.* Indeed, almost one-third of the magistrate's 447-word decision is concerned with the identities of the boys (as we will see in Section 2 of Chapter 10). The major identity struggle in the hearing involves the DCs establishing that these 13- and 15-year-old boys are not victims of a police abduction, but lying *criminal*s, who are a danger on the streets. This identity work by the DCs unmistakably relates to a moral panic about Aboriginal young people, which has pervaded Australian society for two hundred years, and which provides widespread support for police actions discussed in Chapter 3, and which, as we will see, includes the actions by the six police officers in the Pinkenba event.

If the DCs were only concerned to establish the *criminal* identity of the boys, they could assert or presuppose details of their *criminal records*. But questioning them about their *criminal record* provides many opportunities, particularly with the two younger witnesses, to expose them not just as *criminals*, but also as liars. Further, it provides many opportunities to fuel in very specific ways the general moral panic that constructs Aboriginal people as not *normal human beings*, but as a threat to public safety.

The chapters in this part of the book will examine linguistic mechanisms used by the two DCs in constructing the identities of the three boys, as well as the ways in which the boys at times comply with and at times resist these imposed identities. This chapter presents a description and example of each of the main linguistic mechanisms used by the DCs in presenting the elements of the boys' characters and reputations which constitute their imposed identities – who the DCs say that they are. This chapter does not aim to be comprehensive in its examination of these linguistic mechanisms, but rather to introduce and exemplify them. In Chapters 7–9 we will see many examples of these mechanisms, as we examine in detail how each of the boys' identities is constructed during their cross-examination, and the ways in which the boys deal with this identity construction.

1. Identity

In the simplest explanation, identity is "who and what you are" (Blommaert 2005: 203). From the beginning of modern sociolinguistics in the 1960s, sociolinguists have examined many dimensions of the central tenet that the way in which people speak is related to who they are. Early correlational studies linked sociolinguistic variables to social variables, such as speakers' social class, ethnicity and gender (best known in the work of Labov e.g. 1972). Anthropologically-influenced early sociolinguistic work examined the ways in which social identity is created and maintained in ways of speaking (best exemplified in the work of Gumperz e.g. 1982b). These early studies conceptualised social identity in terms of widely recognised social categories, such as gender and ethnicity, as well as specific roles and relationships, especially particular family relationships, such as that between a man and his brother-in-law (Haviland 1979).

With the impact of the social constructionist turn in sociolinguistics in the last two decades, perhaps most prominent in the work on language and gender, social identity is no longer conceived of in terms of static categories. The emphasis has shifted to the performativity of social identity, which, following West and

Zimmerman (1987), can be expressed in terms such as "doing being a woman" or "doing being gay" (see Holmes and Meyerhoff 2003). Thus, social identity is now conceived of as the "variety of culturally specific subject positions that speakers enact through language" (Bucholtz and Hall (2004: 369). While much work on social identity has looked at how speakers perform their own identity, Blackledge's (2005) research on the relationship between ethnic identity and power relations shows the need to distinguish between imposed identities – which are for one reason or another not negotiable; assumed identities – which are accepted and not negotiated; and negotiable identities – which are contested by groups and individuals (see also Blackledge and Pavlenko 2001). While it is ethnic identity that is at the centre of Blackledge's focus, his framework is relevant to the analysis of the identities of the three boys in this case, and the struggle between the identity they claim as victims on the one hand, and that of lying *criminals* imposed by the DCs on the other.

But, the identity struggle in this case involves more than a simple dichotomy between victim and lying *criminal*. Much current sociolinguistic work, informed by poststructuralist approaches, emphasises that social identity is multiple, complex and dynamic (e.g. Blackledge ibid.). As Bucholtz and Hall (2004: 376) point out, "identity inheres in actions, not in people". Thus, as we will see in Chapter 9, Barry does not contest the *criminal* aspect of his identity, but he does not accept all of the details which the DCs attribute to this identity. And he does not accept that it denies him the right to claim a victim identity in relation to what the police did to him in the Pinkenba event. And within the broader institutional and societal context of the Pinkenba hearing, the witnesses are widely described in the media as "Aboriginal boys", an identity label unlikely to be contested by anyone. But going further than simply investigating what identities are imposed, assumed, or negotiated, it is important to investigate what these identities mean, and how they are constituted and practised. What does it mean to be an Aboriginal boy, for example? What beliefs, attitudes and practices constitute this identity, both for Aboriginal boys and for others? We will see that much of the Pinkenba cross-examination is taken up with such identity questions.

The ways in which such questions are being answered by contemporary sociolinguists revolve around the detailed analysis of interaction (e.g. Antaki and Widdicombe 1998; Auer 2005; Bucholtz 1999; Holmes 1997; Ochs 1996). Thus, in showing how social identities are outcomes of social acts, Ochs (1996: 415) gives the example of English-speaking children learning from a young age about the use of linguistic forms which index social relationships such as teacher-student and parent-child. Ochs' (ibid.: 424) definition of "social identity" encompasses "participant roles, positions, relationships, reputations, and other dimensions of social personae". In the Pinkenba hearing, the participant roles and positions are indisputable, having such institutional labels as *witness, prosecutor, defence counsel* and *magistrate*. And these identities are indexed in many specific acts in the courtroom, ranging from the DCs asking leading questions, to the magistrate giving the *warning* about the self-incrimination privilege, and the witnesses being required to answer (almost) any question asked of them. But it is the relationships, reputations, and what may be termed in ordinary English the "characters" – all of which can be seen as encompassed in identity or subjectivity – which are the focus of struggle in the interaction. What is the power relationship between defence counsel and magistrate? Do any of the witnesses have any power over defence counsel? Are the witnesses really victims? Or are they *criminals*? Are the defendants the "real" victims in this case? What are the characters and reputations of the witnesses? To answer these and similar questions about social identities in this hearing, requires an analysis of the social acts, carried out mainly through talk. And we will see that the DCs use these identity questions and conflicts to address both the central and underlying issues in this case.

The central identity work in this hearing is the construction by the DCs of the identities of the boys (Blackledge's "imposed identities"), and it is this which will be the major preoccupation of the chapters in Part III. Ehrlich's (2005: 139) comment about gendered identities is relevant generally to sociolinguistic stud-ies of identity: she points out that not enough attention has been given to the "limits and constraints on speakers' agency in constructing ... identities" (see also Blackledge and Pavlenko 2001: 250). Her analysis shows how the identity that the victim in a Canadian rape case constructs for herself is "dramatically" different from that imposed on her by both the trial judge and the appeal judge in their decisions (Ehrlich 2005: 155). Ehrlich's work, like that of Matoesian (2001), highlights how the adversarial legal context is a prime site for the ex-ploration of limitations on speakers' agency in constructing their identities. The analysis of the Pinkenba cross-examination goes further, showing the power of cross-examining lawyers in not just limiting, but to a considerable extent determining the identities of witnesses.

We will see in Chapter 10 that this courtroom determination of the identities of the three boys is taken up by the magistrate in his decision and the judge in the judicial review. Thus the courtroom talk which provides details of how the boys are not *normal human beings*, and how they are a threat to public safety, takes up dominant themes in the media presentation of Aboriginal people, and plays a central role in legitimising and perpetuating neocolonial control over them. The chapters in this third part of the book are central to the critical sociolinguistic work of identifying some of the "processes and inferences" which enable the micro-event of the police actions that night in Pinkenba to become part of the macro-structure of neocolonialism (following Cicourel 1981: 67, discussed in Section 3 of Chapter 2). We will see that these processes and inferences centre around the detailed construction of the boys' identities.

But, do the boys play any role in the construction of their identities in the Pinkenba hearing? To what extent do they reject the imposed identities, perform their own assumed identities, or work to negotiate their identities in the courtroom? Do they comply with, or even assist in the imposed identity construction, or do they struggle against the characters and reputations being constructed by the DCs? What linguistic means do the boys have in the construction of their own identities, by themselves or the DCs? We will see, following Blackledge and Pavlenko (2001: 250), that in the Pinkenba cross-examination, "the power differential is such that resistance is [mostly] impossible". The boys use very little propositional content to this end, being successfully constrained and intimidated by question form and content. But, while they say very little, especially in comparison to the DCs, they do make some attempts to counter aspects of the identities being constructed for them.

2. Overt linguistic mechanisms used in identity construction

Central to the defence strategy in this case, are the linguistic mechanisms used to construct the boys' identities as lying *criminal*s who are a danger on the streets of Brisbane. As there is no legal restriction on bringing up a witness's *criminal record* in court, it is not at all difficult for the DCs to simply ask questions and make assertions about the boys' *criminal records*. There is nothing subtle about this. These questions and assertions provide the opportunity for the defence to tell the court, the media, and through them, the people of Queensland and the rest of Australia, details of the *criminal records* of these boys. Thus, much of the cross-examination of the three boys consists of overt and repetitive presentation of the witnesses as *criminal*s. But, as we will see, questioning the boys about their *criminal records* also provides the DCs with the opportunity of adding details to their construction of the boys' identities, while at the same time enabling them to rebuke, humiliate, threaten, harass and frighten them. The multifunctionality of questions in court is known from Sandra Harris' (1984) examination of the use of questions to make accusations in a British magistrates court.

2.1. Asserted propositions

The most overt mechanism for constructing the boys' identities does not even involve asking questions. On a number of occasions, one of the DCs simply makes an assertion about the *criminal record* of one of the boys, as for example in Extract 24:

Extract 24.   DC2 to Albert, Day 2, p147

1. DC2:	So **you've had- years of experience with the police before this** I'm indebted to my friend- so I'll just keep going through them then- sixteenth of February nineteen ninety three you appeared in court for breaking and entering the council chambers- that right?
2. Albert:	Yes yes.

This turn occurs after the prosecutor has corrected a miscalculation by DC2 about the time period between Albert's last conviction and the Pinkenba event. DC2 uses this mistake to highlight Albert's *criminal record*, saying *you've had years of experience with the police before this*. This allegation is not framed as a question, and Albert is given no chance to respond to it. We will see in Section 2 of Chapter 10, that the magistrate considers the boys' *years of experience* with the criminal justice system to be a relevant factor in dismissing the charges against the police officers.

2.2. Assertions in pseudo-declarative questions

Ehrlich (2001: 72–75) uses the term "pseudo-declarative" to describe the function or nature of Yes/No-questions which take the form of declarative statements with question intonation or questioning tag. These question types are often described as prosodic and tag questions respectively (e.g. Woodbury 1984). These pseudo-declarative questions, which have been found to constitute a considerable proportion of the questions in cross-examination, are generally considered in the literature on courtroom talk to be the most controlling questions (but see discussion in Section 2.1 of Chapter 2). Not surprisingly, a large number of the questions in the Pinkenba cross-examination are pseudo-declarative, as exemplified in the prosodic question from DC2 to Barry (p189) *Last year you were put on probation in July- end of July?*, and the tag question from DC1 to David (p48) *You're great mates with Coley are you?* Extract 24 above also provides a good example of the use of a pseudo-declarative question for asserting aspects of the boys' identities, in this example Albert's identity as a *criminal*, with *sixteenth of February nineteen ninety three you appeared in court for breaking and entering the council chambers- that right?* This particular linguistic strategy is perhaps the most pervasive of all the identity construction strategies used by the DCs, and we will see many examples throughout Chapters 7–9.

2.3. Presuppositions in pseudo-declarative questions

While sociolinguistics has focused on the control exercised by questions that can be termed pseudo-declarative, Ehrlich (2001: 74) points out that "presupposed propositions" may be even more powerful. This is because propositions that are presupposed are protected from interrogation, as well as negation. The witness is required to answer *yes* or *no*, while either answer preserves the truth of the presupposed proposition. (This is known in lay terms as the *have you stopped beating your wife?* question).

We see an example of this in DC2's question to Barry (p194) *It's not a bad place to steal some money- is it- from someone?* This question comes in a line of questions asking Barry what he was doing in the Valley on the night of the Pinkenba event. Barry has answered here, as he had to earlier similar questions, that he was *just walking* (see discussion in Section 2.2.2 of Chapter 5). DC2 then suggests that Barry was about to engage in *criminal activity* with the questions *Looking for some money Barry?* and *Looking for someone who might have been around in that lonely place?* Barry's answers of *Nuh* to both of these questions are not accepted by DC2, who then says *It's not a bad place to- steal some money is it from someone?* The presupposition here is clearly that Barry is a thief. Thus, it follows that the police action in removing Barry that night would result in making the streets safer. It doesn't matter whether Barry answers *yes* or *no* to this question: the presupposition is that Barry knows about good places for stealing money, and can evaluate the Valley Mall in terms of this knowledge. Thus, this question is a powerful tool in DC2's construction of Barry as an experienced *criminal*. In legal terms this question, like many other pseudo-declaratives, is a leading question (as discussed in Section 1.2 of Chapter 4).

2.4. Presuppositions in WH-questions

In the examination of lexical strategies in Chapter 5, we saw a good example of a presupposition in a WH-question in Extract 17, repeated here:

Extract 17. DC1 to Barry, Day 2, p163

1. DC1:   What sort of things did you steal- when you were wan- prowling around the streets?
2. Barry: (3.5) Just purses.

As we saw in Chapter 5, Barry has earlier rejected the verb *prowling* to describe what he and his friends used to do when they were *walking around*. But DC1 here incorporates this presupposition into the WH-question, and Barry's answer, which interestingly comes after a considerable pause, does not contest it. This is in contrast to the witness in Ehrlich and Sidnell's (2006) study, who openly challenges some presuppositions in cross-examination questions, with comments such as *I think that's not an assumption you ought to make*. This witness in Ehrlich and Sidnell's study has remarkable astuteness and ability to challenge presuppositions, and perhaps it is not unrelated to his experience as a leading politican. The witnesses in the Pinkenba hearing have no comparable experience, and, as we see exemplified in Extract 17, they do not try to challenge damaging presuppositions used in their identity construction.

2.5. Presuppositions in directives

As we will see in Section 5.1 below and throughout Chapters 7–9, DC1 uses a considerable number of abrupt commands. While these commands are not normally heard in cross-examination "questions", they are allowed without any restriction by the magistrate in this hearing. These directives are an important part of the affective stance of DC1 by which he indexes his authority over the witnesses, and particularly for David, his identity as a naughty child. Thus, DC1 introduces the presupposition that David is *telling lies* in his cross-examination in saying to him, in relation to breaking into houses (p48), *Listen to me and DON'T TELL ME LIES please- have you ever used that trick?* As with the asserted propositions discussed in Section 2.1 above, the witness has no obvious opportunity to counter such mechanisms which construct his identity, here as a liar. Similarly, on another occasion, DC1 says to David *tell me the truth- you must answer truthfully* (p42).

2.6. Lexical strategies

The lexical strategies examined in Chapter 5 are also part of the linguistic toolkit used by the DCs in the construction of the boys' identities. Unfamiliar lexical items and legal jargon are indirectly used in the ways in which the boys are presented as juvenile delinquents, vagrants and *criminals*. As we saw in Chapter 5, the most striking instances of lexical perversion relate to two issues: the central issue about the boys' alleged consent to going with the police, and the underlying issue which sought to justify the police removal of these young *criminals* who are a danger on the streets.

3. Culturally specific presuppositions

While the overt assertions and presuppositions concern the boys' identities as
criminals, liars and a danger on the streets, there are less overt assertions and
presuppositions which contribute to these identities. In Chapters 7–9, we will see
that these less overt strategies often rely on what we might call common-sense
knowledge about the world, which often involve culturally specific presuppositions. The role of culturally-specific presuppositions in interpreting utterances is
well known from the work of Gumperz (e.g. 2001b), and we have seen examples
of this in Chapters 4 and 5, as summarised in Section 3.1 below. This hearing
also shows the importance of culturally-specific presuppositions in interpreting
the actions, or inactions of others, as part of the evaluation of their character.

3.1. In interpreting courtroom talk

In Chapter 4, we have examined three features of Aboriginal English communicative style which are used by the DCs in addressing the central issue of the
hearing, that the boys knew that they did not have to go with the police, and
that they went willingly. We will see in Chapters 7–9 below that they are also
successful tools in constructing the identities of each of the boys. The Aboriginal
tendency to gratuitous concurrence is seemingly used in many questioning routines to elicit witnesses' apparent agreements to aspects of their identity, such as
their *criminal* nature. The ways in which the DCs overtly exploit the Aboriginal
English use of silence and avoidance of eye contact has been discussed and
exemplified in Section 2.2 and 3.2 of Chapter 4. Extracts 6–9 are examples of
how these features of Aboriginal English communicative style are interpreted
by the DCs as behaviours of liars and *criminals*.

3.2. In interpreting actions outside the courtroom

While Section 3.1 above has summarised the use of culturally specific presuppositions in interpreting courtroom talk, there are a number of such presuppositions used in interpreting the boys' actions outside the courtroom, including
their language practices. In Section 4 below, we will see DC1's common-sense
assumption that swearing in front of a *lady* indicates a lack of respect for her.
As the discussion in Section 4.2 of Chapter 3 has indicated, this assumption is
a culturally specific one, which is not generally found in Aboriginal societies.
But an unquestioning reliance on this mainstream Anglo norm is one of the

mechanisms used by DC1 in his construction of Albert's identity as a person who does not respect women (as we will see in Extract 25 below).

In the analysis of DCs' construction of the identities of the witnesses, we will see a number of differences in cultural norms, which are exploited by the DCs in an ethnocentric manner. We saw in Section 2.2.2 of Chapter 5 that the DCs appear not to understand that *walking around looking* is a practice common to youth culture around the world, and to Aboriginal culture around Australia. Each of the DCs makes much of the boys' seeming lack of future planning and purpose, linking it to their general delinquent lifestyle. But this also is a culturally specific presupposition: future planning is not a high priority in many Aboriginal societies, and neither are the overt and direct giving and seeking of reasons for actions or state of affairs (Eades 1988). Lack of short-term planning, for example for one's meals for the next 24 hours (see Extract 43 in Chapter 7) may be problematic for many middle-class Australians, but it would not be seen in this way for many Aboriginal people. Similarly long term planning, such as career plans, typify middle-class Australian society. To expect many other 13-year-old Australians to have an answer to the question *What are you going to be when you grow up?* (Extract 40 in Chapter 7) is both unrealistic and ethnocentric.

It is impossible to know if the DCs are aware of such cultural differences, although Aboriginal practices and expectations involving swearing are discussed in the lawyers' handbook (Eades 1992: 93), which, as indicated in Section 6 of Chapter 1, is visible on the Bar table throughout the hearing.

4.   Entextualisation

One of the important indirect strategies in the construction of the boys as liars is a common cross-examination strategy, which we can call "entextualisation", following Bauman and Briggs (1990) and Silverstein and Urban (1996). Entextualisation is defined by Bauman and Briggs (ibid.: 73) as "the process of rendering discourse extractable, of making a stretch of linguistic production into a unit – a *text* – that can be lifted out of its interactional setting" (emphasis in original). This process thus involves decontextualisation and recontextualisation. In this hearing, the DCs decontextualise earlier statements made by the boys about the Pinkenba event, and recontexualise them in cross-examination, by asking questions about selected aspects of them. This enables the DCs to elicit inconsistencies by the boys in their different tellings of the story. Inconsistencies elicited in this way are then labelled as *lies*. Entextualisation practices are of increasing interest in research on the ways in which talk and other kinds of text are repeated and recycled from one context to another, following widespread adoption of Bakhtin's work on intertextuality. Several scholars have studied the ways in which a story told in one legal context (e.g. a police interview) is transformed in some ways for a different legal context (e.g. courtroom evidence), most notably Matoesian (2001), Rock (2001), Cotterill (2002), Trinch (2003) and Ehrlich (2007).

Exposing inconsistencies between different tellings of an event in different legal contexts forms a central strategy in cross-examination. Textbooks on trial technique provide advice for trial lawyers on how to achieve and use this inconsistency. For example, Mauet (2000: 280) recommends "raising prior inconsistent statements" as the central strategy in "impeaching" a witness, that is, challenging their credibility. We will see that it is not difficult for the DCs to use the common cross-examination technique of entextualisation to support their construction of the boys' identities as liars.

The work of several sociolinguists is relevant to this use of entextualisation. For example, Trinch (2003) and Schiffrin (2006) highlight the different functions that can be fulfilled by telling stories. Trinch found that for Latina survivors of domestic violence, telling their story to lawyers or paralegals may fulfil many functions, including therapeutic ones. But the interviewers then have to produce a written version of the stories in affidavit form to present to the court in applications for protective orders. Here, the stories' main functions are legal: they must present the elements which fulfil the requirement for granting of a protective order, for example presenting the woman as a victim. Thus, any part of the original telling of the story in which the woman is also agentive is omitted or transformed. Trinch's study is a powerful reminder that the stories which victims tell to legal professionals fulfil many functions, and these are not restricted to legal functions. It also reminds us that legal retellings are selective, in presenting a particular identity of the storyteller. Schiffrin (2006: 328) makes the related general point that "although language serves several functions (often simultaneously), many linguists focus only on its referential function". Trinch's work highlights the fact that this limited focus is not restricted to linguists, as it is also a feature of legal approaches to storytelling.

Drawing on a wide range of research, Trinch (ibid.: 5) also shows that "narrative is an interactional achievment or a co-production". When the boys initially told their story to family members, as well as paralegals and lawyers at Aboriginal Legal Services, they would undoubtedly have been quite emotional, possibly traumatised, and most likely angry. It would be expected that their individual stories were co-constructed with each other, and with their interlocutors, especially as there was no legal constraint on co-narration. These early tellings of their story may well have fulfilled primarily emotional and social functions.

It would not be surprising if some exaggeration or inaccuracy occurred in some of these early tellings of the story. When the boys' stories became the subject of the CJC investigation they were required to give separate interviews, two each on two different days, for the purpose of legal investigation of their complaint. Following this investigation, they would have retold their stories to the prosecutor before the hearing, and then in the hearing they answer questions about it from the prosecutor in examination-in-chief, and from the two DCs in cross-examination. When they give evidence in court, the magistrate impresses on them the seriousness of the requirement to *tell the truth* in their evidence. The oldest witness, Barry, takes the affirmation corresponding to the oath, while the two younger boys answer four questions to the magistrate's satisfaction that they *know the difference between telling the truth and telling a lie* (p15, see also p103). Thus, we would expect the boys' courtroom evidence, which fulfils a legal evidentiary function, to be the entextualisations of their experiences to which they would give the greatest caution and attention to accuracy. But greater attention to accuracy provides just the "proof" needed by the defence to show that the boys are liars, as we will see in various extracts in Chapters 7–9.

Another consideration relevant to this use of entextualisation relates to memory and what Philips (1992: 249) reports from the psychological and legal literature as "perceptual failures" which lead to inconsistencies in evidence. The assumption made by the DCs, which is common in cross-examination, is that any discrepancy must relate to lying. However, in one of his few substantive objections, the prosecutor points out that *inconsistent answers don't necessarily imply lies* (p137). This fact is considered so important that in some jurisdictions it is part of standard (pattern) jury instructions. Thus, we read in Tiersma (1999: 253) that the jurors in the O. J. Simpson case were told to remember that "Failure of recollection is a common experience, and innocent misrecollection is not uncommon". (Tiersma (2006: 10) recommends that this example of a triple-negative legalese statement be revised to "People often forget things or they may honestly believe that something happened even though it turns out later that they were wrong".)

In addition to its purpose in constructing the boys as liars, entextualisation involving the boys' earlier statements to police provides another identity-construction function for DC1. That is, in reading the transcript from an earlier interview, questioning about an earlier conversation, and even playing an extract from the videorecording of an investigative interview, DC1 is able to bring as evidence into the hearing, earlier instances in which two of the boys had sworn at a police officer, or in front of a police officer. The decontextualisation of these utterances is particularly relevant to their interpretation, as we will see. The fact that teenage Aboriginal boys say the word *fuck* or *cunt* in a relaxed informal interview should index nothing more about their identity than that they are teenagers, or that they are Aboriginal, as we saw in Section 4.2 of Chapter 3. However, DC1 makes much of the three episodes of swearing to build his construction of the boys' *criminal* identities, as well as to harangue and humiliate them.

One of these episodes involves an utterance made by Albert during a car ride a few days after the Pinkenba event. He was being driven by a female police officer, who was working as a CJC investigative officer, back to Pinkenba to retell his story. At one point in the videotaped recording, which DC1 plays in court, Albert can be heard saying *Look at this Chinese cunt*, apparently referring to a man of Asian appearance crossing the road. It is unclear whether this man was delaying the traffic or in some other way earning Albert's annoyance with the term *cunt*. It is also impossible to tell if this was intended as a racist epithet. After playing this section of the CJC investigation tape to the court, DC1 makes Albert repeat the expression, in answer to his question *What did you say there?* (p118). Albert is clearly reluctant to comply, asking *When?* and *Who to?* This provides the opportunity for DC1 to impatiently admonish Albert, saying *Come on- come on- stop mucking around- tell me what you just said.* DC1 then has the tape played again, and when Albert finally does repeat the offensive expression, DC1 replies with *I can't hear you*, thereby ensuring that Albert has to say it in court yet again. In discussing this kind of defence strategy of playing part of an investigative interview tape in court, Matoesian (2001: 146) points out that the DC has the power to choose what extract to play, as well as how to contextualise it, and to "suggest how it should be interpreted and evaluated".[31]

This strategy of using recontextualisation to make Albert swear in the courtroom provides powerful evidence at several levels for DC1's construction of Albert as a juvenile delinquent, consistent with widespread police criminalisation practices of Aboriginal people who swear (discussed in Chapter 3). In going on to rebuke Albert for this expletive which he has been made to decontextualise and repeat in court, DC1 draws on a middle-class Anglo cultural value, which is not generally shared in Aboriginal cultures, that swearing indicates lack of respect for women, as we see in Extract 25:

Extract 25. DC1 to Albert, Day 2, p119

1. DC1:   Did you feel any respect for the lady present in the car? (3.2) did you? (4.2) DID YOU FEEL ANY RESPECT FOR THE LADY IN THE CAR?
2. Albert: Just slipped out of my mouth.

3. DC1:   Slipped out of your mouth eh?- did you know the Chinese gentleman?
4. Albert: Nuh.

5. DC1:	(2.8) Or were you deliberately trying to embarrass the policewoman?
6. Albert:	(1.7) Nuh.
7. DC1:	You see is your WHOLE- EVIDENCE HERE AN ATTEMPT AS A SQUARE UP with the police (2.0) is it? (5.2) is it? (3.1) ANSWER.
8. Albert:	I don't know what you mean.
9. DC1:	Are you trying to get <u>ev</u>en with the police?
10. Albert:	Nuh.
11. DC1:	You don't like the police do you? (2.3) do you?
12. Albert:	Nuh.
13. DC1:	Nd you'd lie wouldn't you- to get even with police- wouldn't you?
14. Albert:	Nuh.

This extract shows DC1's clever use of this episode of Albert's swearing. Not only does he have no respect for a *lady*, but he is a person *deliberately trying to embarrass the policewoman* and trying to *square up with* or *get even with police*, as we see in Turns 5, 7, and 9. Thus, in a cross-examination strategy which has parallels with the over-policing strategy known as the trifecta (see Sections 1.3 and 4.2 of Chapter 3), DC1 uses this episode of teenage swearing as a catalyst to suggest a *criminal* action designed to be an attack on police. This line of questioning enables DC1 to move to allegations that Albert would *lie* to police, and then to the questions discussed in Section 3.2 of Chapter 4, where DC1 exploits another difference between Aboriginal and mainstream Anglo language use, namely the avoidance of eye contact.

It is also relevant to mention that in the brief testimony of the CJC investigative officer to whom Albert had been speaking in the car, DC1 devotes most of his 16 minutes of cross-examination to questions about two incidents of swearing by Albert during these interviews (the other being at the Pinkenba scene when his voice is heard on tape to say to the investigator *oh fucking hell* p8). The CJC officer contextualises this language use saying *I simply wanted him to be himself in the journey*. In answer to the question *Did you try to reprimand him in any way when he used those words?* the officer replied *No ... I didn't see it was my role to correct him as far as his language went*. It is also relevant to point out that even in the punitive laws which criminalise offensive language in Queensland, swearing can only be a criminal offence in or near a public place. Thus, arguably the most that could be said about Albert's two episodes of swearing is that they were bad-mannered. However, many people would dismiss even this interpretation, including New South Wales magistrates Pat O'Shane and David Heilpern (based on their judgments discussed in Section 4.2 of Chapter 3 above). But we have seen that this recontextualisation of Albert's swearing in a private conversation provides DC1 with the opportunity to overtly present him as someone who has no *respect* for women, and is so determined to *get even with police* that he would swear in front of a female police officer (working as a CJC investigative officer).

Briggs (1993: 408) has shown that decontextualisation and recontextualisation "play a crucial role in infusing texts with power". We have seen how the everyday instance of Albert using a mild swear word, typical of Aboriginal people and young people, is given the power to construct Albert as a juvenile delinquent who is is trying to *get even with police*.

5. Lawyers' affective stance

In understanding some of the other less overt linguistic mechanisms involved in identity work, it is helpful to draw on Ochs' (1996) explanation of the central mediating role played by stance in linking linguistic form to social identity. Stance can be defined as a person's expression of their attitudes and beliefs with respect to a proposition, following Matoesian (2005a: 167). While stance is generally seen to comprise both evidentiality (or epistemics) and affect (following Biber and Finegan 1989), it is affective stance which plays a prominent role in identity construction in the Pinkenba cross-examination. Ochs (ibid.: 410) defines affective stance as referring to "a mood, attitude, feeling and disposition, as well as degrees of emotional intensity vis-à-vis some focus of concern".

Ochs (ibid.: 419–420) shows that the linguistic structures which index stance "are the basic linguistic resources for constructing/realizing social acts and social identities". Thus, for example a Japanese woman "may display hesitancy and delicacy to create a female gender identity" in some situations (ibid.: 424). While this example links stance to the speaker's identity, all identity is relational, and in the Pinkenba cross-examination, the stance of the two DCs is of considerable importance in their construction of the identities of their interlocutors, the three boys. Thus, as we will see, DC1's stance of impatience and anger serves to index both his identity as a tough barrister, and his construction of the boys' identities as uncooperative witnesses. While we will see a number of stance features used by the DCs which build their own identities, it is the identities of the boys which are much more important – it is their characters which are "on trial" in this hearing.

In a courtroom version of the well-recognised "good cop, bad cop" routine, DC1 frequently displays the stance of an impatient, aggressive questioner, and at times a stereotypically hostile schoolteacher disciplining a bad student. In contrast, DC2 displays the stance of a reasonable, mild-mannered questioner, who becomes impatient and incredulous with the boys' *lies* and *problems with* their *memory*. This contrast in their stances, between impatience and anger on the one hand, and reasonableness and mild manners on the other, can be highlighted in a comparison of their opening questions to David, the first and youngest witness:

Extract 26.   DC1 to David, Day 1, p26

1. DC1:	Why did you break into someone's home?	
2. David:	(2.0) (I dunno).	

3. DC1:	WHY DID YOU BREAK INTO SOMEONE'S HOME- IN NINETEEN NINETY THREE? (10.6) WELL WHY?
4. David:	(1.3) I dunno.

5. DC1:	(0.6) Beg your pardon?
6. David:	I dunno.

7. DC1:	I can't understand you speak up please.
8. David:	I don't know.

9. DC1:	Well you <u>did</u> break into someone's home didn't you?
10. David:	I dunno.

Extract 27.   DC2 to David, Day 1, p74

1. DC2:	David you're from Cherbourg are you?
2. David:	Yeh.

3. DC2:	Where do you live now? not your address but the place (you live) do you live at Cherbourg or here in Brisbane?
4. David:	(1.5) I'm living (at) Cherbourg.

In addition to the important difference in tone of voice, several lexical and grammatical differences are clear: In Turn 3 DC1 uses the insistent prompt *well* in an impatient manner (to be discussed in Section 5.2 below), in Turn 7 he uses the imperative form *speak up please*, he wastes no time in introducing the suggestion that David is a burglar, in Turns 1, 3 and 9. DC2 on the other hand begins with simple orientation questions about David's home town and current place of residence, with no obvious markers of affective stance. Thus, from the start we see a consistent difference between the two DCs in their affective stance: while DC2 often, but not always, displays no overt affect, DC1 frequently displays emotional intensity, expressing impatience, frustration and anger with pressured repeating of question tags, and frequently raised volume and emphatic intonation.

There are many linguistic mechanisms used to display stance, and this section will briefly introduce and exemplify the most obvious.

5.1. Metapragmatic directives

Perhaps the most overt mechanisms in DC1's display of affective stance are his many directives. It is not uncommon for cross-examining counsel to give metapragmatic directives about answering the question, but those of DC1 in this hearing are the most aggressive I have ever encountered in a courtroom. We have already seen some examples in Extracts 4, 5, and 9 in Chapter 4. Some others are:

Extract 28.   Selected metapragmatic directives: DC1

to David, p26, 28, 34, 49, 57, 68, 69:	*You must answer.*
to David, p52	YOU MUST ANSWER.
to David, p42:	*You must answer truthfully.*
to David, p27:	*Come on you'll ANSWER me boy.*
to David, p37:	*You will tell me*
to Albert, p110:	*When you are answering my questions you'll speak up do you understand that?*
to Albert, p114:	*Take your fingers out of your mouth will you.*
to Albert, p116:	SPEAK UP.
to Albert, p117:	YOU ANSWER ME.
to Albert, p117:	*Oh speak up for goodness sake will you.*
to Albert, p118 :	*Come on stop mucking around tell me what you said.*
to Albert, p119:	*Well answer my QUESTION* (4.8) *LOOK* (0.7) *YOU CAN BE HELD IN CONTEMPT OF THIS COURT LAD* (2.0) *AND THE WAY YOU'RE GOING I'M GOING TO ASK FOR IT VERY SHORTLY* (3.7) *now ANSWER MY QUESTION.*
to Albert, p127:	WILL YOU PLEASE- ANSWER IN A WAY THAT WE CAN HEAR WHAT YOU'RE SAYING- RATHER- THAN GRUNTING THERE.
to Albert, p140:	*Stop chewing your fingernails.*
to Barry, p159:	WILL YOU PLEASE OPEN YOUR MOUTH
to Barry, p161, 162:	ANSWER Coley.
to Barry, p178:	STOP PLAYING AROUND COLEY.
to Barry, p178:	*Come on Mr Coley don't play around.*
to Barry, p180:	I DON'T CARE HOW LONG YOU STAY THERE- YOU'LL ANSWER ME.

Clearly DC1's use of directives indexes his authority over the witnesses, and indeed many could be seen as what Jacquemet (1996: 222–226) calls "metapragmatic attacks". Many of these directives, or attacks, sound as if they could be used by an authoritarian teacher disciplining a delinquent child. The extent to which this might be a deliberate strategy is impossible to know, and it may be relevant to note that DC1 had been a schoolteacher before turning to law. Interestingly, DC1 does not use many overt directives with the oldest witness Barry, whom he constructs as a serious *criminal*. Indeed, his frequent use of the adult address form *Mr Coley* (to be discussed below) indexes his portrayal of Barry as an adult.

While most of the metapragmatic directives are about answering questions, they also function to control whatever limited actions the boys may take while in the witness box, such as chewing fingernails, and avoiding eye contact (as discussed in Section 3.2 of Chapter 4). Thus, these directives arguably work to give the witnesses the identity of naughty schoolboys, a theme echoed by particular questions about such topics as their school attendance and homework, as we will see in Extracts 40, 45 and 51.

Some of these directives appear to be related to DC1's difficulty in hearing some of the answers, as each of the boys is quite softly spoken, particularly Albert. However, DC2 deals with this problem in a much less aggressive manner, with requests such as:

Extract 29.   Selected metapragmatic requests: DC2

DC2 to Albert, p142:   *Albert just keep your voice up please.*
DC2 to Albert, p145:   *Albert answer my question please.*

DC2's polite directives are consistent with his general stance, and the indexing of his role as the DC equivalent of the "good cop". But the angry and impatient stance with which DC1 issues directives to the two younger witnesses also serves to admonish and threaten the boys, consistent with their portrayal as *criminals*.

DC1 uses two metapragmatic directives which convey extreme impatience, namely *well* and *come on*. Like the more explicit directives discussed above, these are also forms which I have not heard in any other courtroom, or seen any mention of in literature on courtroom talk. This use of *well* differs from other courtroom uses of *well* in several ways. Hale (2004: 71) describes the frequent use of the discourse marker *well* in cross-examination "as a sign of contradiction, marking disagreement". We see examples of this use of *well* in Extract 52, Turn 9, and Extract 70, Turn 11. In contrast to these turn-initial epistemic uses, the "insistent prompt" use of *well* usually occurs within a DC's turn or at the end of it, and often following a pause. It indexes DC1's affective stance of impatience and insistence, while at the same time also functioning as a command, equivalent to *answer me*. It is delivered in staccato tempo, and often emphatically and/or with raised volume, as we will see in Extract 35, Turn 7; Extract 55, Turn 5 and Extract 82, Turn 7. In this function, *well* is equivalent to the other insistent prompt *come on*, which we have seen in Extract 23 Turn 7, and will see in further examples, such as Extract 34 Turn 1, and Extract 52, Turn 9.

5.2. Sarcasm

One of the affective stances displayed on occasion by each of the DCs is that of sarcasm. Thus, for example, when presenting Albert with tape-recorded evidence of his use of a swear word (*cunt*) in front of a policewoman, DC1 says to him *Have a listen now to your delightful language* (p118, before the exchange in Extract 25 in Section 4 above). Sarcasm is characterised by Haiman (1998: 25) as a form of verbal aggression, in which the "speaker expresses hostility or ridicule of another speaker" with the "*intentional production of an overt and separate metamessage* 'I don't mean this' " (emphasis in original). In using this form of verbal aggression in cross-examination, the DCs highlight what they don't mean (Haiman's metamessage), simply by stating it overtly. Thus, in the example quoted, DC1's disdain of Albert's use of a four-letter word is highlighted by his sarcastic description of it as *delightful language*.

While the intended recipient of the verbal aggression is typically the addressee, sarcasm can be intended primarily for a third party, while being used against the addressee, who may be attending to the overt message while being unaware of the "I don't mean this" metamessage. We see an example of this use of sarcasm in DC1's questions to David about the boys' encounter with a security guard in the service station which they found after walking away from Pinkenba:

Extract 30.   DC1 to David, Day 1, p51

| 1. DC1: | And you- greeted him of course with some kindly wishes didn't you? |
| 2. David: | (1.1) Yeh. |

| 3. DC1: | Told him to get FUCKED didn't you? |
| 4. David: | <u>No</u> ((surprised tone)). |

David's compliant answer *Yeh* in Turn 2 suggests that he is unaware of DC1's sarcastic use of the expression *kindly wishes*. But DC1 doesn't mean that he thinks David *greeted* the security guard *with some kindly wishes*, as he goes on, in Turn 3 to allege that David swore at the guard. The exchange continues with David saying that he didn't swear at the security guard, although Barry did. In response to the question *What did he say?*, David reports that Barry *told him to get fucked*.

5.3.   *Prosodic features*

DC1 indexes his hostility towards the witnesses in a number of ways. As we have seen, this includes his propositions and presuppositions, as well as his metapragmatic directives. Throughout his questioning, DC1's tone variously expresses impatience, anger and/or resentment. Throughout much of his questioning his delivery is generally loud and forceful, and on many occasions he shouts at the witness, as we will see in a number of extracts (indicated by SMALL CAPITALS, as in Turn 3 of Extract 30 above). DC2's style is quite different, as I have indicated. However, his tone expresses sarcasm and/or disbelief on a number of occasions.

6.   Terms of address

The role of address terms in indexing social relationships is well known in more than four decades of sociolinguistic research, since Brown and Gilman's (1960) classic work. There can undoubtedly be considerable differences in local meanings which attach to specific choices in address terms. For example, titles are generally avoided in Australian English terms of address, and it would be very unusual to address a teenage boy with the form [Title + Last Name]. Nevertheless, one might imagine some formal contexts in which such usage could index respect and a recognition that the teenager is no longer a child. However, examining DC1's use of this address form to Barry, in comparison to his terms of address for David and Albert, and in the context of the rest of his talk to Barry, suggests that it is a part of DC1's construction of him as an adult *criminal* rather than a child victim, and that it is not a term of respect.

Table 1 shows all forms of address used in the hearing by the three lawyers to each of the three boys. The prosecutor uses only [First Name] when he uses a term of address. DC2, like the prosecutor, uses only [First Name] with each of the boys, even using the hypocoristic form *Davy* on one occasion. In marked contrast, DC1 never uses the [First Name] form with any of the boys. With the two younger boys, he mostly uses no term of address, although he uses *lad, boy* and *son* on a few occasions, such as *Come on- you'll answer me boy* to David

Table 1. Terms of address in examination-in-chief and cross-examination

		Prosecutor	DC1	DC2
David	lad		1	
	boy		3	
	Mr Pender		1	
	David	8		52
	Davy			1
	Albert			1*
Albert	lad		1	
	son		1	
	Mr Carter		4	
	Albert	10		53
	David			1*
Barry	Coley		8	
	Mr Coley		45	
	Barry	3		13

* Presumably an error

(p27), *Why did you lie about it son?* to Albert (p113), and *Look- you can be held in contempt of this court lad* to Albert (p119). But, he uses the form [Title + Last Name] to Barry 45 times, as well as 4 times to Albert and once to David. Given the other ways in which DC1 constructs Barry as an adult (as we will see in Chapter 9), we can assume that this is also the function of this term of address. The use on 8 occasions of the form [Last Name] is reminiscent of disciplinary address to high schoolboys in earlier generations.

Interestingly, it is not only DC1 who treats the oldest witness, Barry, differently from the other two witnesses in the way in which he addresses him. DC2 uses a personal address term considerably less with Barry than the other two witnesses. Also, his first question in Barry's cross-examination is the overt question, in a tone of polite request, *What do you want me to call you- Mr Coley or Barry? what's your preference?* Barry's unhesitating answer is *Barry* (p185). It is not clear whether DC2's deferential stance, which contrasts so much with the immediately preceding cross-examination by DC1, is simply a matter of personal style. It may well also involve the "good cop, bad cop" strategy, enabling him to use more subtle measures in his construction of Barry as a *criminal*.

7.   Repetition

A striking feature of the cross-examination is the repetition of questions, some examples of which have been seen in Turn 1 of Extract 25 in this chapter, and throughout Extract 5 in Chapter 4. Matoesian's (2001: 54) study of the "poetic features of courtroom talk" shows how lawyers can exploit repetition "to comment on or evaluate the testimony of a hostile witness in a strikingly marked fashion without overtly commenting on that evidence". Matoesian's study shows lawyers picking up on a witness's answer and variously repeating, expanding or elaborating it in succeeding questions. Much more common in the Pinkenba cross-examination are two other types of repetition: repeated questions or question tags, when DC1 refuses to wait for an answer, and the repeated "refrain" *Why did/do you lie?*

We have seen in Section 2 of Chapter 4 that the witnesses follow the typical Aboriginal pattern of often using silence as part of the answer to a question. We also saw there that DC1 in particular, frequently follows up witness silence with repetition of his question, or part of it, as in Extract 4, Turn 9 and Extract 8, Turn 5. We will see many other examples in extracts in Chapters 7–9. Clearly these repetitions index the DCs' impatience and frustration, while at the same time contributing to the portrayal of the witnesses as uncooperative. It will become apparent in the following chapters that repetition in the questions in the Pinkenba hearing also serves to "wear down" the witnesses, reducing them, through exhaustion and exasperation, to situations where it is easy for DC to get them to agree to damaging propositions.

The much used refrain *why did/do you lie?* is a an overt tool in the DCs' construction of the witnesses as liars, particularly by DC1. It is used 20 times, and the lexical item *lie* (in the form of *lie, lies, lied* or *lying*) occurs a total of 85 times. Both DCs use this label for the many inconsistencies they succeed in eliciting from the boys, despite possible other explanations that might account for at least some of these inconsistencies, as we have seen in Section 4 above. In addition, DC1 uses the word *fib* in the expressions *it was a fib* and *why did you tell a fib?* a total of 7 times. These occurrences are all within a 2 minute time period, fairly early in his cross-examination of the first and youngest witness, David (p37). After that, DC1 abandons the use of the word *fib* – presumably because of its connotation of trivial or childish *lies* – and persists with *lie* for the rest of his questioning.

A different kind of repetition which is also recurrent throughout is repetition by the boys, which is elicited by DCs' questions of *What? What did you say?, Beg your pardon?* and *Pardon?* It is possible that at times these questions are

DCs' responses to genuine mishearing or difficulty in hearing the witnesses, who are quite softly spoken at times. But at other times, this appears more likely to be a strategy designed to emphasise an answer, or to stall for time. We have seen an example of this in Extract 26, Turn 5 and will see many more in Chapters 7–9, for example in Extract 36, Turn 3 and Extract 70, Turns 13 and 17.

8.   The boys' answers

We have seen that the DCs use a number of strategies in their construction of the boys as lying *criminals* who make the streets of Brisbane unsafe. The following three chapters will show how the details of each boy's identity are constructed slightly differently, and the different ways in which each of them reacts to this identity construction. In this section, we will look in overview at the boy's answers.

Throughout Chapters 7–9, we will see that most of the boys' answers are very short, in contrast to the lawyers' turns, many of which are much more wordy. At least 60% of the boys' answers take the form of either *Ye#* or *No#* or *I don't know*. As explained in Section 1.3 of Chapter 4, I use the form *Ye#* to refer generically to the answers *yes*, *yeh* and *mm*, and the form *No#* to refer generically to the answers *no* and *nuh*. And as explained in Section 7 of Chapter 1, distinguishing between an answer of *I don't know* and *I dunno* can on occasion be impressionistic. Thus when I discuss *I don't know* answers in general terms, the discussion includes those answers transcribed as *I dunno*.

In this chapter and the three which follow, it will be helpful to provide a quantitative snap-shot of certain aspects of the cross-examination. However, it has not been possible to count the number of questions, as both DCs often ask several questions before there is an answer, as we have seen in many of the extracts above and we will see in many further extracts in Chapters 7–9. And the haranguing nature of many of the DCs' turns make it meaningless to count questions separately, as the following exchange exemplifies:

Extract 31.   DC1 to David, Day 1, p54

| 1. DC1: | Tell lies and you could be in big strife (0.8) any more? (6.1) any more- a sedan car? (6.9) well? |
| 2. David: | Not that I can't remember. |

8.1.   Minimal answers

Table 2 below provides a breakdown of the boys' minimal answers of *Ye#*, *No#* and *I don't know*, which combined make up for at least 60% of all of their answers. More than a third of all answers for each of the boys consists of the one-word answer of agreement, *Ye#* (that is, *yes*, *yeh* or *mm*). Section 1 of Chapter 4 has discussed the ways in which cross-examinations generally provide a situation in which it is easy to elicit gratuitous concurrence from Aboriginal people. It is, of course, impossible to know how many of these answers are gratuitous concurrence, and how many are genuine answers of agreement. A similar situation applies to *No#* answers to negative questions, which also have the possibility of being answers of gratuitous concurrence.

Table 2.   Minimal answers in cross-examination: *Ye#*, *No#* and *I don't know*

	David to DC1	David to DC2	David total	Albert to DC1	Albert to DC2	Albert total	Barry to DC1	Barry to DC2	Barry total
Answers	876	457	1333	416	128	544	456	146	602
Ye#[32]	291	180	471 35%	142	55	197 36%	171	54	225 38%
No#[33]	206	64	270 20%	108	25	133 24%	94	15	109 18%
I don't know[34]	95	35	130 10%	25	4	29 5%	20	5	25 4%
Total answers of *Ye#*, *No#* or *I don't know*			65%			65%			60%

Answers of *I don't know/I dunno* are similar to *Ye#* and *No#* answers, in that they also may not necessarily be intended to have a literal meaning. Drew (1992: 481) points out that *I don't know* and *I don't remember* answers in cross-examination can be used to avoid confirming or disconfirming damaging or discrediting information (see also Ehrlich 2001: 43). Researchers have also suggested that the high stress involved in answering questions in legal contexts can lead to answers of *I don't know* indicating "a reluctance to take a risk, rather than to a lack of knowledge" (Walker 1999: 69). Walker also cites other research which suggests that *I don't know* "can indicate a simple unwillingness to answer the questions ... or an inability to do so, particularly if the child feels intimidated by the questioning situation" (ibid.). In a non-legal interview context, Hutchby (2002) analyses a child's use of *I don't know* in a counselling interview, as a "strategic non-cognitive" way of trying to "close down an undesired line of counsellor questioning" (ibid.: 158). Thus, the considerable number of *I don't know answers* by the boys in this hearing may indicate their resistance to the DCs' questions. But it must be remembered that any of these answers may also be a literal comment on the boys' knowledge. It is interesting to note, as we see in Table 2, that it is the youngest boy, David, who uses the highest proportion of *I don't know* answers, with at least twice as many such answers as the other two boys. But unlike them, David gives almost no overt and unambiguous answers of resistance. It is impossible to know whether his greater use of *I don't know* indicates his relative lack of knowledge on the issues he is being questioned on, or a greater "reluctance to take a risk", or whether he is using this form more as an answer of resistance, in the absence of more direct forms of resistance.

8.2. Resistance to imposed identities

Chapter 2 has discussed the importance of seeing courtroom power in terms of relationships of struggle, rather than as a static one-sided situation. As Harris (1989: 135) points out, "even in contexts where participants are clearly *not* equals, the very notion of interaction presupposes some sort of linguistic reciprocation so that control of the discourse can never be absolute". While Harris' study was the first to describe defendant resistance in court, recent work by Drew (1992), Matoesian (1993, 2001), Ehrlich (2001), and Cotterill (2003) has provided more detailed examination. Drew (1992: 516) shows a rape victim's subtle attempts to "challenge" or "discredit" the defence lawyer's version of events, while Matoesian's (1993: 169) rape victim engages with the defence lawyer in a "delicate negotiation" of meaning. In another example which suggests witness subtlety, Matoesian (2001: 59) shows how a rape victim "is not the passive recipient of blame attributions by the defense attorney; she actively resists his linguistic formulations with considerable ingenuity and finesse during the course of a complex negotiation process". Cotterill (2003: 163) examines an expert witness "regaining or retaining some degree of control" from cross-examining counsel, and Ehrlich (2001: 108) shows how complainants and their witness in a rape trial and tribunal "implicitly and explicitly challenged and rebutted the characterization of events presupposed or 'asserted' by the cross-examining questioners and the tribunal members".

In contrast, there appears to be nothing subtle, delicate or ingenious in the way in which the witnesses in the Pinkenba hearing attempt to resist the DCs' control. This is no surprise, given that they are children in an adult court, and that the tactics of the DCs are so aggressive. However, as Harris (1989) has suggested, DCs' control of the discourse is not absolute. While it is impossible to know to what extent the boys' minimal answers might involve resistance to the identities being imposed by the DCs, there are a small number of answers in which the boys overtly reject DC's control over their behaviour and/or construction of their identity. We will see that the extent to which the boys perform this overt resistance is proportional to their ages, with Barry doing it the most, and David the least. There are so few of these examples, that each of them will be discussed in the relevant chapter for each boy in this part of the book.

Instead of the subtle and delicate negotiation engaged in by adult witnesses examined in other cases, the nature of the boys' overt resistance is more like typical teenage "answering back" to parents or teachers when being questioned or rebuked in a disciplinary context. Thus, while such answers as *You don't have to know my things what I do* (by Albert to DC2, p146), and *What's the matter with that?* (by Barry to DC2, p193) are clear examples of witnesses refusing to accept DC control, their defiant stance arguably serves DCs' aim of building the delinquent identity of the witnesses. Thus, rather than gaining the boys some control, these answers of overt resistance paradoxically support the defence strategy, as we will see in detail in Section 5 of Chapter 9.

The youngest witness, David, offers little unambiguous resistance, as we will see. However, as Table 2 indicates he has the highest proportion of *I don't know* answers, which, following the above discussion, may indicate resistance to questioning. It is also possible that his refusal to answer questions on the two occasions on which he has not been given that legal option, could be seen as resistance to questioning. But it is also possible that he genuinely believes that he has this option in those situations. The extent to which David rejects the identity imposed on him is difficult to assess, as we will see in Chapter 7.

9.   Aboriginal identity in the Pinkenba hearing

In the analysis of the identity constructions of the witnesses in this case, it is important to consider the relevance of the boys' Aboriginality. If this study adhered to the principles of Conversation Analysis, we may have to argue that the boys' Aboriginality is not relevant, given the strong claim in this approach that identities are only relevant to analysis when we can show that participants in an interaction are "demonstrably orientated to those aspects of who they are"

(Schegloff 1991: 52). In the cross-examinations, there is only one question (from DC1 to David) which makes overt reference to the Aboriginal identity of the boys. This is during DC1's questioning about David's possible involvement in a particular earlier assault (p48–49). He asks *I'll tell you about an incident where two young girls were walking along when a group of Aboriginal youths stole a purse belonging to one of them- and then assaulted a man who went to their help- do you know anything about that?* (David answers *No.*)

However, the word *Aboriginal* is used several times by the prosecutor, the DCs and the magistrate in referring to the *Aboriginal Legal Service*, which is also sometimes called *Aboriginal Legal Aid*. This occurs in questions about the boys' reports of the Pinkenba event, as well as questions about whether they want to speak to an *Aboriginal Legal Service* lawyer about the self-incrimination privilege. Thus, there is frequent indexing of the boys' membership in the Aboriginal community, although not in any direct way in the identity construction of the boys by the DCs. The only questions which directly ask the boys about being Aboriginal come from the prosecutor in his re-examination. He asks each of the three boys two or three questions about their socialisation in Aboriginal societies, for example *When you come to Brisbane or Riverview or Kingston- do you live with Aborigines or white people?* (to David p102), *Have you mostly lived with Aboriginal people or with Europeans?* (to Albert p149), and *As you've been growing up have your friends been Aborigines or white people?* (to Barry p195). These questions are undoubtedly related to his plan to call for a sociolinguistic report about Aboriginal ways of answering questions, which he intended to use in evidence following the conclusion of the boys' evidence (as discussed in Section 6 of Chapter 1).

But, the fact that the DCs do not directly refer to the boys' Aboriginality in their identity construction should not obscure the central role of this aspect of their identity to everything that happens in the hearing, as indeed in the whole case. Blommaert (2005: 206) points out that identity processes "need not be interpersonal", because identities "can be there long before the interaction starts and thus condition what can happen in such interaction" (see also Ehrlich 2002b). Further, the critical sociolinguistic approach taken in this book requires a reflexive examination of the micro-events of courtroom talk, not removed from the macro-structures within which it is situated, or other micro-events, outside the courtroom, which are also part of the construction of these macro-structures. Indeed, it is impossible to gain an adequate understanding of the courtroom interaction in this case, without understanding the wider institutional and societal struggles within which this situational struggle is located.

In fact, it is hard to argue that Aboriginal identity is ever irrelevant – or has ever been irrelevant – in interactions between Aboriginal young people and the criminal justice system in Brisbane (and most other cities and towns in Australia). Chapter 3 has outlined the social, historical and political context in which these interactions are embedded. It is also relevant to point out that the newspaper reporting of this hearing always referred to the witnesses as "Aboriginal boys", "Aboriginal children", "black children", and "Aboriginal complainants", and individually as an "Aboriginal boy". Arguably the most powerful overt indicator of the relevance of the boys' Aboriginal identity to this case is found in the response by the Criminal Justice Commission. As we will see in Section 6 of Chapter 10, the "public debate about aspects of the conduct of the committal proceedings in the Pinkenba case" (CJC 1996: 2) was one of the main catalysts for the CJC research project which resulted in its report titled *Aboriginal Witnesses in Queensland's Criminal Courts*.

10.   Identity in examination-in-chief

Before moving in the next three chapters to an examination of the identity work in the cross-examination of the three boys, this section will briefly consider their examinations-in-chief, which, as indicated in Chapter 1, are not the focus of analysis in this book.

Typical of many courtroom hearings, the examination-in-chief of each of the boys is characterised to a considerable extent by evidentiary harmony (Eades 2000: 170–171), in which "the lawyer is definitely in control of ... the witness's story, and it is being phrased in his words, and not the witness's, but the interaction between them is smooth and harmonious, characterized by contiguous utterances, and the apparent absence of misunderstanding". In taking the boys through the events of the Pinkenba night, the prosecutor asks short WH-questions, such as *Wherabouts did you see the police officers first?* (to Albert, p105), and factual Yes/No-questions about details of the event such as *Was it daylight or still night time?* (to David, p20). The witnesses have little trouble in providing answers, which are generally short. In a neutral, low-key and chronological way the prosecutor elicits the witnesses' accounts of *what happened* that night and asks them to point to locations on a photograph. This is in sharp contrast to the aggressive and hostile cross-examination, which takes five times as long as examination-in-chief. Arguably the prosecutor is presenting the boys' identities as that of experiencers of the action for which the police officers are charged, i.e. unlawful deprivation of liberty. Interestingly he does not ask any questions about the boys' emotional state during that night, such as whether they were frightened at any stage. His questions are limited to the elicitation of a descriptive account, plus one question about the voluntariness of their actions in getting in the police car to each of the two younger witnesses: *Did you want to be in the police car?* (to Albert, p110, and a similar question to David p25). It is possible that a more senior prosecutor might have worked within the constraints of examination-in-chief to present a fuller picture of the boys' victim identity. But as we have seen in Section 7.6 of Chapter 3, the prosecutor in this case is relatively inexperienced, and this, combined with his previous role as a suburban police officer, may have some bearing on what appears to be his relative disengagement from the courtroom struggle.

Studies of courtroom talk often characterise the central activity as being the portrayal of two competing versions of events (e.g. Cotterill 2003: 19; Gibbons 2003: 150). But this does not accurately account for what happens in this case, where competing versions of events (specifically, of *what happened* on the Pinkenba night) comprise only a small part of the difference between the examination-in-chief and cross-examination. While examination-in-chief builds the prosecution's version of the events of the Pinkenba night, this is a minor topic in the cross-examinations, where a major preoccupation is with the construction of the identities of the boys. As we will see in the following chapters in this section, much of the cross-examination does not deal with the topic of the examination-in-chief, namely *what happened* on the Pinkenba night (see Tables 3, 4 and 5 for a summary of the topics dealt with in the cross-examinations). Indeed, the number of questions which deal with that night are in the minority, with more questions relating to the boys' *criminal records* and *criminal activities*. And the questions which deal with the events surrounding the ride to Pinkenba are primarily about the boys' actions earlier in the day, as well as after the police left them at Pinkenba that night. There are very few questions about what took place when the boys were in the company of the police officers, and these questions almost all comprise pseudo-declaratives concerning the boys' mental state (e.g. *You knew … you didn't have to go anywhere with police if you didn't want to?*), rather than *what happened*.

Thus we can summarise the difference between the defence and prosecution approach by saying that the major focus of cross-examination is the construction of the identities of the boys, while examination-in-chief involves no overt identity work, focusing instead on a chronological account of *what happened*.

11. Conclusion

We saw in Section 9 above that the DCs never refer directly to the boys' Aboriginality, and thus they cannot be accused of overt racism. But the excessive identity work that they carry out in cross-examination is arguably all about their construction of what it means to be an Aboriginal young person. A sociolinguistic approach which is restricted to examining situational power struggles would analyse this cross-examination in terms of the struggle between the two DCs and the three boys over the characters and reputations of the boys: are they victims of a police abduction or are they lying *criminals* who are a danger on the streets of Brisbane? But this case is about much more than the ride to Pinkenba with police that night: it is an important event in the reproduction of neocolonialism. And as I have argued in Chapters 2 and 3, it is impossible to account for this situational power struggle, without seeing its place in the wider institutional and societal struggles between Aboriginal people and the police, with its more than 200 year history, and its attendant moral panics. Particularly coming so soon after the death of Daniel Yock while in police custody for a street offence (see Section 7 of Chapter 3), and the ensuing conflict between Aboriginal people and the state, the identity work in the Pinkenba cross-examination has much more at stake than simply the actions and characters of David, Albert and Barry. This cross-examination uses the propositions and assertions in questions, combined with the boys' answers and non-answers, to reinforce the widespread fear of Aboriginal people, and to legitimise police control over their movements. It is because these three boys are constructed in terms of difference (not *normal human beings*) and deviance (engaging in acts of delinquency and *crime*), that they are to be feared, controlled and denied the freedom to walk around the street. Thus the identity work in this cross-examination addresses much bigger societal issues, such as: Do police have the right to remove Aboriginal young people from the streets? Why do police need this power? What are Aboriginal young people like? What is it about Aboriginal young people that is so dangerous? Thus, we can see that the identity struggles in the Pinkenba cross-examination are addressing fundamental identity issues concerning what it means to be an Aboriginal young person, as well as constraints about how to perform or live this identity, and the rights to which Aboriginal young people can lay claim – all of which are central to the actions and justifications used in the perpetuation of neocolonialism.

The next three chapters follow the process of identity construction of each of the three boys in some detail, showing how the linguistic mechanisms outlined in this chapter are used in constructing slightly different identities for each boy, and how each of the boys reacts to this construction. It is only by a painstaking examination of exactly how cross-examination works in the construction of the boys' identities that we can see how it is that courtroom hearings work to perpetuate neocolonial control. We know from the sociolinguistic literature reviewed in Section 2.1 of Chapter 2 that talk is distributed in court in an asymmetrical way, with considerable restrictions on witnesses in terms of when they are allowed to talk, and on what topics. But the analysis in this book takes a much more microscopic focus on courtroom talk, for example showing how the entextualisation practices outlined in Section 4 above become tools in the construction of Albert as a lying *criminal*. If the courtroom rules of evidence were to place certain limitations on ways in which a witness's story could be entextualised, for example, it would arguably be much harder to present Albert's identity as it is in this case. But entextualisation practices are just one element in the toolkit of linguistic mechanisms which are used in this case to perpetuate neocolonialism. The interrelationship of these linguistic mechanisms is so complex that the best way in which to examine their workings is by means of a detailed analysis of the cross-examination of each of the three boys – Chapter 7 for David, Chapter 8 for Albert, and Chapter 9 for Barry.

Chapter 7
Absolutely no regard whatsoever for law and order: David

1. A *criminal*, a liar and a naughty boy

Although 13-year-old David is the youngest of the three witnesses, his cross-examination takes nearly twice as long as each of the other two witnesses. This is possibly because he is the first witness to take the stand, and the thoroughness with which he is cross-examined may be considered unnecessary for the other witnesses, once the damage is so extensively done with this first witness.

DC1's cross-examination wastes no time in getting to the presentation of this witness as a *criminal*. In Extract 26 in Chapter 6, we have seen his opening questions which aggressively presuppose David's identity as a *criminal*, asking twice *Why did you break into someone's home?* We saw that the second asking of this question was shouted, with DC1 wasting no time in presenting his stance of anger and impatience. David answers *I dunno* both times. This initial questioning about his *criminal record* reveals David as unwilling and/or unable to answer questions relating to his motive for this crime, and to the number of *break and enters* he has committed. Extract 32 below presents the interaction immediately following the opening attack in Extract 26:

Extract 32.   DC1 to David, Day 1, p26

1. DC1:	On the twenty eighth of November nineteen ninety three- you and a person named Albert Wess Carter (2.4) and others (2.2) entered a dwelling house with intent- and you broke entered and stole again on the same night didn't you? (8.0) don't you remember that? (1.7) please answer so it goes on the record.
2. David:	No.
3. DC1:	(2.3) Well have you ever broken into a house?
4. David:	(7.0) I don't know.
5. DC1:	You don't know- that's a lie lad isn't it?
6. David:	I don't know (I can't).
7. DC1:	You DON'T KNOW whether you've broken into someone's home- what has it been so frequent that you can't remember?
8. David:	Yeh.

9. DC1:	(3.8) You've broken into so many homes you can't remember a specific one is that what you're saying? (1.5) you <u>must</u> answer you nodded your head.
10. David:	Yes.
11. DC1:	How many have you broken into?
12. David:	I don't know.
13. DC1:	How many- more than ten?
14. David:	Nuh.
15. DC1:	More than five?
16. David:	No.
17. DC1:	(2.0) Well somewhere between (1.0) what (1.3) three and five?
18. David:	(2.1) No.
19. DC1:	How many?
20. David:	(6.2) Two.
21. DC1:	Two- and you've only been convicted in respect of one haven't you?
22. M:	(3.2) Witness says yes.
23. David:	Yes.

These and the immediately preceding opening questions of Extract 26 set the tone for DC1's presentation of David as a *criminal* (questioning about his *criminal* past in Turn 1), a liar (as we see in Turn 5), and a naughty schoolboy (as we see in the use of *lad* as a term of address, also in Turn 5). As Table 3, in Section 11 below, indicates, a significant amount of DC1's time is spent on David's *criminal* past. Indeed many of DC1's turns appear to function primarily as a strategy for presenting David's *criminal record* in court, and highlighting aspects of it. And the accusation that David is telling *a lie* or *tells lies* is repeated 22 times more by DC1 during his cross-examination of this witness.

In these early questions in Extract 32, we see DC1's use of several of the linguistic mechanisms for identity construction outlined in Chapter 6, including asserted proposition (Turn 1), assertion in pseudo-declarative (Turn 5), pre-supposition in WH-question (Turn 11), presupposition in pseudo-declarative question (Turn 9), choice of address term (Turn 5), and repetition (Turns 7 and 9). Further, DC1's hostile and aggressive stance is seen in his metapragmatic directive in Turn 9, shouting in Turn 7, and the generally impatient tone and tempo throughout. We see also some of the linguistic strategies which would make it difficult for young David to participate, including the use of legalese in Turns 1 and 21 (the former, presumably as he reads from David's *criminal record*), as well as a question asking two different propositions in Turn 1.

David speaks softly and hesitantly, and it seems likely that he is shocked at the topic and tone of these questions, given that he is not on trial, but giving prosecution evidence as a victim-witness. Typical of all of his cross-examination, his answers to these early cross-examination questions are predominantly *I don't know*, *No#* and *Ye#*. While *I don't know* is a common response indicating a child's unwillingness to respond to questioning (see Section 8.1 of Chapter 6), denials are generally seen as "preferred responses" to accusations, in Conversation Analysis terms (Garcia 1991: 821; see also Atkinson and Drew 1979: 59–60, 112–113). Preference here does not refer to a psychological predisposition, but to the systematic features of turns. Thus, in CA terms, if an accusation is not responded to with a denial (or a justification/excuse), the reply is structurally marked, for example with prefacing, repair, or delay. It should be noted, however, that the CA diagnosis of delay or silence as indicating a dispreferred turn takes no account of cultural differences in the use of silence, which are relevant here (as discussed in Section 2 of Chapter 4). Atkinson and Drew's (1979) study of blame sequences in a cross-examination shows a much more subtle cross-examination situation than in the Pinkenba case. Here DC1's outright accusations, using pseudo-declaratives, such as Turns 1 and 5 in Extract 32 above, are often responded to by David with outright denials or *I don't know*, as in the answers to these turns. In contrast, in Atkinson and Drew's (ibid.: 135–170) study, the lawyer uses complex blame sequences, many of which do not involve any outright accusation. In response, the police witness uses a number of strategies, such as descriptions of other parties' actions, as well as rebuttals and accounts, which aim to mitigate projected blamings.

But David's attempts to avoid DC1's accusations of his *criminal* identity are in vain. As we see at the end of Extract 32 above, within seconds of starting his questions, DC1 is successful in eliciting information about David's *criminal activity* which extends beyond his *criminal record*: David answers that he has broken into two houses (Turn 20), but he has only been convicted of one (Turn 23). This then requires the formal delivery by the magistrate of the *warning* against self-incrimination, discussed in Section 1.2 of Chapter 5 above. The magistrate gives the *warning* in standard legalese form, as we see in Extract 33:

Extract 33.   Magistrate to David, Day 1, p27

1. M: David I'm warning you at this stage that you are not obliged to answer
               any questions which might incriminate you in relation to the commission
               of a criminal offence- now do you want to speak to someone about that
               before we go any further? (3.8) Ok=

2. David: =°No°.

3. M: Do you understand what I'm telling you? (1.6) witness says yes.

David's answer in Turn 2 and his probable head nodding which lead to the magistrate saying *witness says yes*, are taken to mean that he has understood the privilege. But, although the magistrate *warns* him of this privilege or right with slow and clear articulation, this is arguably insufficient for making it intelligible. Neither this formal delivery of the *warning*, nor the magistrate's question about whether or not the witness understands it, provides any opportunity for checking witness comprehension. Attempting to check a witness's or suspect's comprehension by asking *do you understand* is a much-used strategy (as for example in police interviews, Gibbons 2001). But it clearly can invite an answer of gratuitous concurrence. This was recognised by Justice Forster in 1976 whose third Anunga Rule (in *R v Anunga*, introduced in Section 1.1 of Chapter 4) requires police officers to ask suspects to state, phrase by phrase, what the caution means, as a way of checking their comprehension of it.

DC1's cross-examination continues with an intensely aggressive set of questions about the second house which David has conceded that he has broken into, as we see in Extract 34:

Extract 34.   DC1 to David, Day 1, p27

1. DC1:	Come on where is the other house- the other place you broke and entered? (19.3) well what city we'll start firstly what city? (8.2) come on you'll ANSWER me boy- WHAT CITY? (11.7) will your worship direct him to [answer the question please?
2. M:	[Yes David do you know what city it was? was it Brisbane?
3. David:	I dunno=.
4. M:	=Was it Brisbane?- eh?
5. David:	I dunno.
6. M:	You don't know? okay well anyway- Mr Thorpe the gentleman there wants wants the question answered so I am directing you to answer it- that is if you have no objection to answering the question (3.9) so what city was it? again I warn you that you are not obliged to answer this question if it will incriminate you in relation to the commission of a criminal offence- again I ask you do you want to speak to someone about answering that question? do you want to speak to someone from Aboriginal Legal Aid?
7. David:	(2.7) Nuh=.
8. M:	=Witness says no- well ask the question again please Mr Thorpe.
9. DC1:	What city was it that you- committed this crime?
10. David:	(4.0) °Cherbourg°.

Extract 34 incorporates several of the linguistic mechanisms discussed in Chapter 6, and already exemplified in Extract 32 above. Turn 1 includes the insistent prompt *come on* twice, the insistent prompt *well*, repeated questions, and the metapragmatic directive *you'll* ANSWER *me boy*.

As we saw in Section 1.2 of Chapter 5, the *warning* against self-incrimination is not easy to understand in the best of circumstances. Turn 6 presents what must be, on any assessment, a contradictory directive to David: *directing* him to *answer* the question, *that is, if* he has *no objection to answering* it. The magistrate's careful enunciation of the *warning* which suggests the witness can choose whether or not to answer the question, comes as something of a contrast to DC1's impatient insistence that David must answer the question. Within 5 minutes of the start of cross-examination of the first witness in this hearing, it is clear that there are serious problems. But there is no mechanism for addressing these problems, apart from the prosecutor's right to object, a right which he rarely exercises.

The magistrate's contradictory directive is immediately followed by another invocation of the *warning*. This second *warning* is legally required, as the question about the city where the second break-and-enter took place is a new question. Each of the 6 times that the magistrate gives this *warning* to David, he reminds all present, and reinforces for himself, that David is quite a *criminal*. So effective is this reminder that on the 5th occasion on which he delivers the *warning* (p44), when he addresses David in the third person, he begins by saying *I warn the defendant- I'm sorry I warn the witness* ... This naturalisation of the prosecution witness as the accused in this hearing is so complete that by the 6th delivery of the *warning* (p46), the magistrate does not seem to notice that he begins by saying again *I warn the defendant* ....

2.   *Couldn't have cared less about going before the court*

DC1 proceeds to elicit details of other *criminal* activities from David's past, such as breaking into a school with some other boys, where he stole pens, and *made a mess*. DC1 constructs David as someone who has no reason to be worried about the consequences of such activities, because of the lenient way in which he would be treated by the legal process, as we see in Extract 35 below. Here, DC1 is drawing on widespread public discourse about the ways in which the courts "go soft" on juveniles, especially if they are Aboriginal (see Hil 1995: 51). There is no need for DC1 to overtly mention David's Aboriginality – the moral panic about Aboriginal young people is arguably so widespread, as discussed in Section 2 of Chapter 3, that it does not need to be overtly or directly invoked.

Extract 35.   DC1 to David, Day 1, p29–30

1. DC1:	Tell us about it tell us what you did.
2. David:	(5.4) Chucked chairs around.
3. DC1:	Why?
4. David:	(1.2) I dunno.
5. DC1:	WHAT GIVES YOU THE RIGHT TO DO THIS? (1.7) well?
6. David:	(1.3) I dunno=
7. DC1:	=WHAT DO YOU THINK GIVES YOU THE RIGHT TO GO AND DE<u>STROY</u> PEOPLE'S PROPERTY? (1.8) WELL?
8. David:	Nothing.
9. DC1:	NOTHING you just felt like doing it?(0.6) right? (1.5) did you?
10. David:	Yes=.
11. DC1:	=Nd you must have been <u>terribly</u> worried- if you got caught you'd come before the court- you must have been very worried about that were you? (2.2) what?
12. David:	Yes.
13. DC1:	You were? you wouldn't have given two hoots would you? (2.7) would you? (1.8) you couldn't have cared less could you about going before the court? (1.3) could you?
14. David:	(0.8) No.
15. DC1:	Because you knew that you- the most you'd get'd be a slap on the wrist isn't that so?
16. David:	(1.1) Yes.

In this extract, David provides some specific information about what he did when he broke into the school: he *chucked chairs around*. This is one of the many examples where one of the witness's answers supports what we might call their "juvenile delinquent" identity, although this particular term is never used in this hearing. But DC1 goes further in developing David's identity here, as in several other instances during the hearing. Asking *why* David engaged in this delinquent behaviour enables DC1 to presuppose another aspect of the witness's identity, as we saw in the opening questions in Extract 26, and as occurs frequently throughout DC1's cross-examination. David unwittingly co-operates in this identity-construction device with his frequent answers of *I dunno* to DC1's *why*-questions, as we see in Turns 4 and 6, and also in his first two cross-examination answers (seen in Extract 26). Using an aggressive and hostile stance, with the repeated tag questions ideally suited to the elicitation of gratuitous concurrence, DC1 uses pseudo-declaratives in Turns 13 and 15 to elicit David's agreement to the construction of him as someone who has no fear of the punishment he could receive for his juvenile delinquency. Following the sarcasm in Turn 11 (*you must have been te̲rribly worried . . .*), the pseudo-declarative in Turn 13 takes the form of a schoolteacher admonishment: *You wouldn't have given two hoots, would you?* The same admonishing tone is found in the shouted questions *WHAT GIVES YOU THE RIGHT TO DO THIS?* (1.7) *well?* (Turn 5) and *WHAT DO YOU THINK GIVES YOU THE RIGHT TO GO AND DES̲TROY PEOPLE'S PROPERTY?* (1.8) *WELL?* (Turn 7). Interestingly, David answers the second of these "questions" with what we might consider a "real" answer of *Nothing* (Turn 8), in contrast to his frequent *I dunno* answers.

Having succeeded fairly easily in securing David's apparent agreement to his construction of him, DC1 then uses pseudo-declaratives to fill out this guilty schoolboy *criminal* identity – getting David to accept that he was not at all concerned about the legal consequences of his actions because of his confidence that he had nothing to fear from being dealt with by the courts, knowing that *the most* he'd *get would be a slap on the wrist* (Turn 15). Interestingly, acceptance of this aspect of the identity construction is not straightforward, with DC1's initial question on this theme backfiring, as we see from the tone of surprise in the first part of DC1's response in Turn 13 (*You were?*) to David's answer in Turn 12. In a pattern which comes to typify DC1's cross-examination (which we have seen exemplified in Chapter 4), the answer in Turn 12 is not accepted – DC1 does not accept that David *must have been terribly worried* about getting *caught* and going *before the court*. So, he effectively asks the same question again in Turn 13, this time expressed as a negative question, using strategies discussed in Chapter 4, to elicit the desired answer of *No*, which may well be an answer of gratuitous concurrence.

3. *Swapping* **shoes** and *walking* **around the streets**

Having established David's identity as a *criminal lad* or *boy* with nothing to fear from the legal system, DC1 moves on to question him about the Pinkenba night, as we see in Extract 36 below. This extract follows immediately from Extract 35 above, with DC1's final question about the school break-and-enter:

Extract 36. DC1 to David, Day 1, p30

1. DC1:   Because you didn't give two hoots did you about other people's property (4.4) isn't that right?
2. David: Yeh.

3. DC1:   Beg your pardon?

4. David: Yes.

5. DC1:   Remember the night you say you saw these police officers- when you
              were down in the Valley you were wearing a nice pair of shoes weren't
              you? (1.9) weren't you?

6. M: (0.8) Witness says yes=.

7. DC1:   =Please answer?

8. David: Yes.

9. DC1:   Where did you get them?

10. David: I swapped (it) off a fella.

This appears to be a switch from the topic of David's *criminal* past, to the
circumstances of the police ride to Pinkenba. But, it involves a clever combining
of the two themes, with the development in the questions of the following 2–3
minutes of the insinuation that David was wearing stolen *Reebok* shoes that
night (p31–32). These questions involve such details as the name of *the fella*
involved in the shoe *swap*, details of David's shoes involved in the *swap*, and *why*
David wanted to *swap* them (to which he first answers *cause* he *didn't want them
no more*, and then *I dunno*). DC1's stance in the questions about the shoes is
hostile and accusatory, as indicated in Turn 5 in Extract 36 above, which includes
a repeated tag question. While it is impossible to know whether David's story
here is truthful, clothing is often shared among Aboriginal people. Rather than
being seen as individually and permanently owned by a single person, items
of clothing are widely seen as resources which circulate among people. Thus,
David's explanation that he *swapped* his shoes is consistent with Aboriginal
practice. However, DC1 closes this line of questions with the pseudo-declarative
It wasn't a situation that you stole them? (p32). Although David answers *No*,
DC1's accusatory stance and assertion present the strong suggestion that David
had stolen the shoes, reinforcing his identity as a thief.

DC1 then moves from presenting the idea that David is a thief, to questions
about whether or not it was *common* for him to *walk around the streets*. While this
could hardly be seen as *criminal*, it does however, evoke the crime of vagrancy,
discussed in Section 2.2.2 of Chapter 5. In this way, these questions suggest
another dimension of David's *criminal* nature, and help to build up the picture
of David as a threat to public safety, drawing on the moral panic about Aboriginal
young people in public places (discussed in Section 2 of Chapter 3). Thus, such
questions are part of the work done by the DCs in naturalising the need for police
to make the streets safe by removing young people like David. David's answer
to questions about whether it was *common* for him to *walk around the streets*,

provides the ideal opportunity for DC1 to assert David's identity as a liar, as we see in the presupposition in the WH-question in Turn 13 of Extract 37:

Extract 37.   DC1 to David, Day 1, p33–34

1. DC1:	The night that you say you were taken to Pinkenba- you were walking around the streets of Brisbane on <u>that</u> night?
2. David:	°Yeh°.
3. DC1:	And the early morning (1.6) weren't you?
4. David:	(1.1) °Yeh°.
5. DC1:	Was that common for you to do that?
6. David:	No.
7. DC1:	(1.7) Are you aware of th that there are cameras?
8. David:	(1.3) Yeh=.
9. DC1:	=that capture photos of people walking around the streets?
10. David:	Yeh.
11. DC1:	Now I'll ask you again- was it common for you to walk around the streets? (4.1) it was wasn't it? (3.3) WASN'T IT?
12. David:	Yes.
13. DC1:	WELL WHY DID YOU LIE TO ME? (4.9) WHY DID YOU LIE?
14. David:	I didn't know what you meant.
15. DC1:	You did so my boy you DID=.
16. David:	=Didn't.
17. DC1:	You didn't know what I meant when I said was it common for you?
18. David:	No.
19. DC1:	To walk around the streets you didn't know what I meant?
20. David:	No.

As we saw in Extract 36 above, and following the discussion of Extracts 4 and 5 in Chapter 4, in Extract 37 DC1 refuses to accept the witness's answer to a Yes/No-question (in Turn 6) and harasses him until he provides the opposite answer (Turn 12). This raises the possibility that David's agreement in Turn 12 is one of gratuitous concurrence. While it is impossible to know this, the likelihood is supported by DC1's use in the preceding turn of repeated tag questions and shouting. It is quite plausible that David might not understand what is meant by the decontextualised expression *common for you to do that* in Turn 5. It is also quite plausible that the inconsistency in David's two answers (Turns 6 and 12) is partly caused by confusion. But, consistent with DC1's typical pattern in such situations, discussed in Section 1.3 of Chapter 4, DC1 uses these contradictory answers to shout *WHY DID YOU LIE TO ME? WHY DID YOU LIE?* Thus, DC1 takes what appears to be a trivial matter, and one that is legal – whether it was *common* for David *to walk around the streets at night* – as an opportunity to present David as a liar, and to provide a schoolteacher-style rebuke *You did so my boy you DID [know what I meant]*. David's latched reply *Didn't* in Turn 16 is expressed in a defiant tone, and is one of this youngest witness's few answers which clearly indicate some resistance.

Walking around the streets at night is a legal activity. And it can hardly be argued that doing this pertains to David's reliability as a witness. But it could be argued that his contradictory answers in Turns 6 and 12 of this Extract 37 do, which is the reason for admitting evidence about a witness's *criminal record*. And it is directly relevant to the unspoken question being addressed by the cross-examination, and the underlying question of the whole case – do police have the right to remove Aboriginal children from public places as they did in the Pinkenba incident? David's identity as a street kid or a vagrant, which begins to be constructed here, is taken up at various other points by DC1, and then becomes a major focus of DC2's questions (although neither of the terms "street kid" or "vagrant" is ever used).

4.   *Upset to a considerable degree*

In the first 20 or so minutes of DC1's cross-examination of David, he has asserted, presupposed or suggested the following aspects of David's identity: he *tells lies*, is a *criminal*, with a history of *break-and-enter* offences, who *walks around the streets of Brisbane at night*, and is probably also a thief. He *couldn't care less about going before the court* because he knows that *the most* he'd *get would be a slap on the wrist*. While these aspects of David's identity have been overtly constructed, DC1 also uses several linguistic mechanisms to subtly construct David as a kid getting into trouble. We saw for example, DC1's choice of address terms such as *lad* and *boy*, metapragmatic directives such as *come on you'll ANSWER me boy*, as well as rebukes such as *You did so my boy YOU DID*.

David's voice is soft, and his answers are overwhelmingly monosyllabic, so it can be argued that it does not matter much what his actual answers are. It would need much more than monosyllabic answers to counter the force of DC1's impressive linguistic tool-kit. David's answers in Extracts 32–37 typify his answers throughout his cross-examination. He gives many *I dunno* answers, which, as discussed in Section 8.1 of Chapter 6, may indicate lack of knowledge, or may indicate unwillingness to answer, for any of a number of reasons. This answer can be construed as teenage defiance to adult authority, but it can also indicate other non-defiant responses, such as confusion. David also gives some answers which indicate compliance with DC1's construction of him as a kid getting into trouble, as we saw in Turn 2 in Extract 35 above. There are also occasional instances of David presenting a little self-defence, although these are rather isolated. Thus, we saw in Turn 14 of Extract 37 that he answers *I didn't know what you meant*, in answer to DC1's accusatory question *Why did you lie?* Further, he then answers back *Didn't* to DC1's argumentative follow up Turn 15 *You did so my boy you DID.*

Within 24 minutes of the beginning of his cross-examination, the prosecutor asks for an adjournment, so that David can *speak to someone from Aboriginal Legal Aid* about the self-incrimination privilege, pointing out that *the child is obviously only thirteen.* After this brief adjournment, the prosecutor asks for another 15 minutes adjournment, saying that *the witness is upset to a considerable degree- as a result of what's occurred it's difficult from what* he's *seen of him being spoken to outside the courtroom for him to give even articulate answers* (p36).

5.   *You feel nothing will happen to you*

After this adjournment, DC1's questions move between aspects of David's *criminal* past, and the events which took place on the night the boys were taken to Pinkenba by the police, as summarised in Table 3 in Section 11 below. Using the mechanisms outlined in Chapter 6, and exemplified there and in the preceding extracts in this chapter, DC1 takes up the theme we saw in Extract 35, asserting, presupposing or suggesting that David has *got absolutely no regard whatsoever for law and order*, and that he *thinks* he *can do whatever* he *likes and* he *can't be touched* (p37). In presenting more details of David's *criminal record*, DC1 reveals that David has:

- *stolen lots of things* (p47–48),

- broken *bottles on the road* (p50),

- once been involved in taxi fare evasion (p42–43),

- once ridden in a *stolen car* (p51–53),

- joined friends *throwing rocks* at *lights* at a *train station* (p54), and

- *thrown stones at a police car* (p64).

DC1 succeeds in gaining apparent agreement to these allegations in interactions similar to those we have seen. Considerations of space prevent an examination of each of them, but given the use of the mechanisms already summarised and exemplified, it is impossible to know to what extent David is freely agreeing with any or all of them. If all of these allegations are true, which is quite possible, does this provide legitimisation for the police in removing David from the Valley that night? This, of course, is not the question supposedly being addressed by the hearing, and it should be irrelevant to it, in the same way that if David were a defendant, any prior conviction would be legally irrelevant to that for which he was being tried.

However, such information is allowed to be presented in court for a witness (who is not the accused in this case), as it is deemed to be relevant to their character, and their credibility as a witness. And in the case of David and Albert, their *criminal record* provides DC1 with the opportunity to present them as liars. This is because for most of his *activities of a criminal type*, David first attempts to avoid "confessing", usually by answering *I dunno*, or with a denial, or by answering with only a part of the detail on the particular *criminal activity*, as discussed in Section 1 above. Thus, there are many opportunities for DC1 to construct David as a liar, who *lies deliberately* (p45), and to enrich the portrayal of this liar with such pseudo-declaratives as … *you're quite happy- to tell a lie if you think that I can't prove you wrong aren't you?* (p56). After DC1 angrily repeats the tag *aren't you?* twice more, David replies *I dunno*.

As David becomes more exhausted and overwhelmed, he seems more ready to answer *Yes*, and this enables DC1 to reiterate his earlier theme that David's *criminal activities* are unpunished by the legal system, as we see in Extracts 38 and 39:

Extract 38.   DC1 to David, Day 1, p46

1. DC1:	You can take and steal and uh- break into places and damage things just as- as you want to because you don't think anyone can do anything about it isn't that right? (1.7) I'm right aren't I? (1.2) you nodded you must say yes.
2. David:	Yes=.
3. DC1:	=Yes (1.8) you feel you can do whatever you want and uh nothing will happen to you (1.6) that's right isn't it?
4. David:	(1.1) Yes.
5. DC1:	(3.2) But let anyone else uh do something that might affect you and- goodness me- it's the end of the world isn't it?
6. David:	(1.7) Yes.

In Turn 3 of this extract DC1 makes strategic use of pauses, to emphasise his point that David feels a sense of immunity from the law. This goes to an important point in the defence argument on both the central issue, that he would not have got into the police car unwillingly, and the underlying issue, about whether it is acceptable for police to remove kids like David from public places. Extract 39 below addresses the same issue. While David's answer appears to indicate his agreement to DC1's construction of him, it is not clear if he actually understands the implicit decontextualised proposition being questioned – that David believed that *nothing could happen to him* if he broke the law.

Extract 39.   DC1 to David, Day 1, p52

1. DC1:	Because nothing could happen to you could it? (1.5) that was your belief wasn't it? (1.5) right?
2. David:	(1.6) Yeh.

Another aspect of David's identity which DC1 briefly presents, suggests that he is on track to become an adult *criminal*, as we see in Extract 40:

Extract 40.   DC1 to David, Day 1, p55

1. DC1	Do you ever do any homework (2.2) from school?
2. David:	(1.4) No.
3. DC1	What are you going to be when you grow up?
4. David:	(6.3) I dunno.
5. DC1	How do you intend to support yourself- [when you grow up?
6. David:	[I dunno.
7. David:	I dunno.
8. DC1	What <u>work</u> are you going to do to support yourself? (0.8) do you have any idea?
9. David:	No.
10. DC1	Or is it easier just to take what you want?- that's probably the easy way eh? (3.1) well- <u>isn't</u> it?
11. David:	(1.0) I dunno.
12. DC1	(1.7) Is <u>that</u> what you see yourself doing as you get older?
13. David:	(1.6) I dunno.

While it is impossible to know what David's *I dunno* answers mean, it is not surprising for a 13-year-old boy to have no idea of what they will *be* when they *grow up*. Further, such questions typify middle-class interactions between adults and teenagers, and are a type of planning talk which would not characterise conversational practice in many Aboriginal societies. But these questions arguably serve a useful purpose here in suggesting that David is heading for a *criminal* "career". Thus, these questions provide further support for the naturalisation of the police action against him that is the subject of the hearing.

DC1 also questions David about the central issue – whether he went in the police car willingly that night – on four different occasions. It is not difficult for DC1 with his impressive linguistic tool-kit to gain agreement from David to crucial questions, such as *So you knew that you didn't have to go anywhere with police officers if you didn't want to- didn't you? you knew that didn't you?* (p39). The discussion and examples provided in the previous three chapters should suffice to explain why it is my argument that David's answer of *Yeh* to this and similar questions should not be taken to indicate unequivocal agreement to the proposition being questioned.

6.   *Why did you lie?*

In his final 27 minutes of questions about the Pinkenba night, DC1 elicits inconsistencies about two elements from David's earlier tellings of what happened when the police took him to Pinkenba. David had claimed in his two interviews with the CJC, that when they were at Pinkenba one of the police officers *slapped Albert on the head*. Under cross-examination, DC1 reads out part of the transcript of David's initial interview with ALS, in which this incident is not mentioned. DC1 is unsuccessful in his attempts to get David to agree that it did not happen (that Albert was *slapped on the head*). It is impossible to know whether or not it did happen: Albert also mentions it himself in two interviews with the CJC, and in his cross-examination he insists that it happened. But Barry does not mention it at all, and none of the boys is given the opportunity to mention it in their examination-in-chief. Did Barry not see it? Did David forget to report it in his original ALS interview? Or did it not happen? DC1 is unsuccessful in his attempt to get David to agree to the asserted pseudo-declarative *Someone said to you- look- you'd better say one of you got hit over the ear that night- someone say that to you?* (p67). (David's answer is *No*.) But DC1 has worked so successfully to present David as a person whose answers are often inconsistent, and therefore as someone who *tells lies*, that David's answers are arguably not nearly as powerful as DC1's assertion: *someone* is behind David's complaint about being taken to Pinkenba. There is no suggestion here about who that *someone* is, but it is presumably either someone from the Aboriginal community or from ALS, a point to be taken up in DC2's closing questions, as we will see in Section 10 below.

The second inconsistency relates to another element of David's report to the CJC investigator concerning police abuse. David reported that the police had told the boys that when they were thrown into the river, they would be eaten by *piranha fish*. DC1 suggests that this was invented because David *wanted to give some degree of credibility to a claim that the police had threatened* him (p72). He asks several confusing questions about whether David had *ever heard the word before* (p72), as well as whether he had learned about it at school, *how you spell* the word (p67), and whether he *read the Encyclopaedia Britannica or something at some stage* (p73). The implication appears to be that David would not know the word *piranha*, something which would be impossible to verify or contradict. The lengthy questioning and harassment from DC1 on this point elicits David's longest utterance in that day's cross-examination: *I didn't hear it till they said it- they said it that night* (p72). It is not possible to be clear if there really is a discrepancy here, but even if there is, it is hard to see the relevance of this discrepancy to the central issue, as the police are only charged with deprivation of liberty, with no mention of any other abuse. Arguably it is relevant to the defence establishment of David as a liar. But it is troubling to realise that the truthfulness of the evidence of a child victim-witness has to be tested through such linguistic manipulation of memory, and complex entextualisation practices, which involve haranguing questions about isolated utterances from his earlier recounting of the event, (a point to be taken up in Section 2 of Chapter 12).

Even if the questions about *piranha fish* are considered to be problematic in establishing the witness's reliability or unreliability in this case, they do provide DC1 with yet another excellent opportunity to highlight his construction of David as a liar. The last 6 minutes of DC1's cross-examination (p72–73) present a powerful construction of David as a lying child or young person, which includes the following accusations:

Extract 41. Selected accusations of *lying*, DC1 to David, Day 1, p72–73

> YOU DID DENY IT BOY.
> WHY DID YOU LIE?
> *Rubbish lad.*
> *You're telling a fib there.*
> *Why did you lie to them?*
> *Why did you tell them that lie?*

7. An uncontrollable street kid

DC1 has spent only about half of his cross-examination time with David on the topic of the Pinkenba night, while the other half has been about his *criminal record* and related topics. In contrast, DC2 asks nothing about David's *criminal record*, devoting about half of his cross-examination to the Pinkenba night and David's reports of it, and about half to the construction of David as an unreliable street kid with a poor memory. His cross-examination starts with the portrayal of David's allegedly delinquent lifestyle at the time of the Pinkenba incident, having *run away from home* and not regularly attending school. DC2's focus on David's transitory residential pattern, resonates with a familiar institutional non-Aboriginal complaint about Aboriginal people (discussed in Section 3 of Chapter 1). While DC2 has some difficulty in establishing a neatly quantified sequence of David's time with different relatives and in different schools, and David is vague about time periods, he does give straightforward answers to DC2's questions such as *Where did you live before you were with your aunty?* (p75), to which he answers *Down at Nana's*.

In his factual cooperation with these questions, David assists DC2's middle-class construction of a young person moving from one relative to another with disrupted school attendance. An Aboriginal view of the same facts might well comment on the importance of spending time with different relatives, and the positive social benefits of such flexibility. Several of DC2's early WH-questions presuppose the "fact" that he has got David's apparent agreement to: that at the time of the Pinkenba incident David had *run away from* the *aunty's* home in the suburb of Riverview where he was living (approximately 30 kilometres from the Valley, where the police picked up the boys). These questions include:

Extract 42.   Selected DC2 questions about when David *ran away from his aunty*, Day 1, p74–77

> – *How long had you lived with your aunty David? how long had you lived with her before- before you ran away?* (p74), to which David answers *I dunno.*
>
> – *You'd been there about a week when you ran away- from your aunty- without telling anybody where you'd gone?* (p76) to which David answers *Yeh.*
>
> – *How long was it between when you ran away from Riverview from your aunty's place- to the time this business happened with the police?* (p77) to which David answers *I dunno.*

As with many of DC1's questions, it does not matter what answer David replies with. These questions serve to construct David as an uncontrollable child, although an understanding of Aboriginal social and cultural practices might suggest that this is an inappropriate and unfair interpretation. It is not clear that in David's family his actions that day would have been seen as *running away from home*, or that his aunty *would have been very worried about* him (p78). All three of the boys moved around between different households in their extended family, as well as a youth refuge, and at times they also lived on the street: as explained in Chapter 1, they could be seen as part-time street kids. In Section 3 of Chapter 1, we have seen that it is common for Aboriginal people to enjoy transitory residential patterns, and also that considerable autonomy is afforded to Aboriginal children and young people by their carers and extended family members. Thus, David's actions in leaving his *aunty's* house that day might not have counted as *running away from home*, although he does echo this term *ran away* in two of his answers (Turns 8 and 12 in Extract 43 below).

But DC2 makes much of David's *running away* – using the phrase *ran away* 9 times in the first day of his cross-examination of David. Further, he adds to the construction of David as an unreliable street kid, with his questions that go to the point of David's apparent lack of future planning when he *ran away from* his *aunty's* home, as we see in Extract 43:

Extract 43.   DC2 to David, Day 1, p77–78

| 1. DC2: | How did you plan to get by David when you left Riverview when you ran away from there without telling anybody? how did you plan to live- you know to eat- a place to stay? how [did you plan to do that? |
| 2. David: | [I dunno (um) (1.4) I met my friend Sheldon Grant in in the Valley. |

[10 turns omitted which confirm the friend's name, that he is a boy, and that David thinks he is 16-years-old]

3. DC2:	Did you plan to meet him did you?
4. David:	No.
5. DC2:	All right well back to my question- how did you intend to get <u>by</u> for that week?
6. David:	(2.7) But I met Sheldon then he took=
7. DC2:	=No no no be<u>fore</u> you met Sheldon how did you mean to live?
8. David:	I didn't I met him on the day I ran away.
9. DC2:	Be<u>fore</u> you met him- you only met him accidentally didn't you?
10. David:	Yeh.

11. DC2:	Right so before you met him- what idea did you have as to where you'd sleep and how you'd eat?
12. David:	(1.0) The day I ran away from Riverview- that's the day I met Sheldon.
13. DC2:	Oh- well the day you ran away before running into Sheldon- right- when ya when you're leaving Riverview you're getting on the train out there?
14. David:	Yeh.
15. DC2:	What then were you thinking about where you where you'd sleep- and how you'd get to eat? what were you thinking then?
16. David:	Nothing.
17. DC2:	Eh?
18. David:	Nothing.
19. DC2:	(1.5) Why did you ran away from your aunt?
20. David:	(1.4) I don't know.

This extract is insightful in relation to the discussion in Section 3.2 of Chapter 6 about the cultural presupposition of the lawyers relating to planning. David's answers (especially to the questions in Turns 1, 5, 7 and 11) make it clear that it is not just that he had no plans about where he would stay and how he would eat, but more fundamentally, he does not seem to understand the questions about this issue. His answers to the questions about how he planned to live and eat and get by are *I met (my friend) Sheldon (Grant)*. Had David been able to provide an intercultural analysis, his answer might have explained *I didn't need to make plans, because something always works out, and it did: I met my friend Sheldon Grant, and together we would have managed to take care of a place to live and food to eat.*

DC2 persists with building his picture of the irresponsible street kid with questions such as *Did you take any clothes with you- you know pack a bag?* and *You didn't get in touch with your aunty at all that week or with anybody?- with your mum or your dad or anyone?* (p78), to both of which David answers *No*.

8. *Problems with your memory*

Once DC2's picture of the irresponsible street kid is filled out, he turns (on p79) to questions about the event, focusing on what the police said to David in the car on the way to Pinkenba. These questions from DC2, who is much less aggressive and hostile than DC1, elicit David's longest utterances, which are:

Extract 44.   David's longest utterances: to DC2, Day 1, p81–82

> – *In the police car (1.0) the man who was in the passenger side- he asked me if I went to Southbank.*
> – *And I said no (0.6) and he said (0.6) he said don't bullshit.*
> – *Yeh- and then he said- then he said did you steal anything?- and I said no.*

Southbank is a tourist centre on the other side of the downtown area, about five kilometres from the Valley. It appears that the police were suggesting that David had committed a theft at Southbank earlier that day or evening. Thus it is possible that David could have thought that he was being <u>detained</u> for theft, which could support his claim of unfair treatment by police in the Pinkenba incident. But any such advantage for David is cleverly juxtaposed by DC2 returning to the issue of David's lack of reliability, by asking him several questions about where he *would have slept that night*, about how many days he had been staying in the Valley before the Pinkenba event, and on what day of the week it had happened. DC2 makes the most of David's three *I dunno* answers in a row (p81). Thus, as we see in Extract 45 below, DC2 presents David as someone who has *problems with* his *memory* (Turn 1), is not *going too well at school* (Turn 3) and who doesn't *go to school much* (Turns 5 and 8). DC2 then switches abruptly from gaining David's agreement to this portrayal of his unreliability, to the central issue in the case, as we see in Extract 45 below, beginning from Turn 14. (This extract finishes with the exchange we saw in Chapter 4 as Extract 2.)

Extract 45.   DC2 to David, Day 1, p81–82

1. DC2:	Do you have problems with your memory David?
2. David:	(5.9) I dunno.
3. DC2:	(1.4) Can't remember? (3.6) how have you been going at school? (4.1) not too well?
4. David:	(1.2) °Mm°.
5. DC2:	Don't go to school much do you? (1.1) eh?
6. David:	°Yeh°.
7. M:	Witness (says) yes.
8. DC2:	You stay away from school a bit don't you?
9. David:	Yeh.
10. DC2:	(4.0) So- you've told us everything you can of the conversation in the police car?
11. David:	Yeh.

12. DC2:	Out to Pinkenba?	
13. David:	Yeh.	

14. DC2:   (2.5) David if the police car- instead of dropping you off at Pinkenba- it just dropped you off back at the Valley- (2.2) understand what I mean?

15. David: Mm.

16. DC2:   If you'd driven out there and then back and just been dropped off in the same place where you'd been picked up?

17. David: Mm.

18. DC2:   You wouldn't have had any complaint would you?

19. David: No.

20. DC2:   Your complaint isn't about going out to Pinkenba it's the fact that you were left there isn't it?

21. David: Yeh.

22. DC2:   (3.4) It's not that you were <u>forced</u> to go in any police car- it's the fact that you were <u>left</u> out at Pinkenba- that's what you're complaining about- isn't it? (2.0) that's right- isn't it- David- cORRECT?

23. David: Yeh.

24. DC2:   (3.4) Your worship is that a convenient time? [i.e. to stop proceedings for the day]

25. M: Yes I was thinking about that Mr- uh- Hiller.

It is impossible to know whether David is actually agreeing to any of the propositions here. Certainly the situation is ideal for eliciting answers of gratuitous concurrence: David is exhausted from close to 2½ hours of cross-examination. A literal interpretation of the *Yeh* answer in Turn 23 arguably provides enough evidence to support the defence argument that he had gone willingly in the police car to Pinkenba. At this strategic high point in his cross-examination, DC2 asks for the court to adjourn for the day, the first of several strategically requested adjournments to be sought by DC2. It is interesting that Turn 25 indicates the magistrate's agreement that this is a *convenient time* for the end of day adjournment.

9.   Recurrent *I don't know* and *I don't remember*

David's second day on the witness stand begins with questions similar to some from the previous day, about *how long* he *had been around the Valley before this particular night* (p85) and the details of how much money he had at the time, and *where* he was *planning to sleep that night* (p86). David's recurrent *I dunno* answers make it easy for DC2 to construct in his questions the identity of an aimless street kid. This portrayal is amplified with a series of questions (p87–88) which elicit David's (minimal) account of how he and friends sometimes *jumped over a fence* to sleep underneath a vacant building in the Valley.

Then follows a series of questions (p89–90) related to one of the photographs, tendered as exhibits in the hearing, of the area in the Valley where the police approached the boys. The small number of the questions about the photograph are not accompanied by any challenge by DC2 about the answers, and the issue is not taken up in the closing addresses.

Much more fruitful for the defence challenge and identity construction is DC2's next questioning topic: about David's statement to ALS, and media reports of the Pinkenba event. DC2's strategy here is to find discrepancies between what DC2 alleges that David told the media within a few days of the event, and what he has told the court. DC2 relies unquestioningly on the newspaper account of what was said by David (identified in the paper as *the 12 year old- who comes from Cherbourg*, p92), as if it must have verbatim accuracy. To attribute this level of accuracy in evidentiary recontextualisation to a newspaper quotation is problematic, as we will see in Section 3 of Chapter 10.

In Section 4 of Chapter 6 we have seen the central role played by entextualisation practices in cross-examination in order to establish inconsistency in a witness's story. The key points that DC2 works to establish at this point of the cross-examination (p92–93), as he reads from a newpaper report, are that David had said to the journalists *They told us to jump in the car- they didn't say why*, and *When we got there they told me to take off my shoes- they were telling us stories- they said there were piranhas and fish in the water that would eat us*. The first of these two utterances presumably establishes that David could not have been under the mistaken impression that he was under arrest, while the second utterance relates to the issue raised by DC1 in his questioning of David the previous day about the contested point of the alleged police threat of *piranhas* (discussed in Section 6 above). Given that DC2 has the newspaper reports with these accounts of what David had allegedly told reporters, then there might appear to be little purpose to his questioning of David about them. But this particular recontextualisation serves the important legal purpose of getting the reports into the evidence in this hearing. Thus, DC2 is simply following standard evidential procedure, in asking the witness questions such as *Did you talk to some people from the TV and the papers and the radio?* (p92). These questions are to lead up to those that will elicit inconsistencies between David's different retellings of the event. But David does not seem to realise that these particular questions are not accusations, and he responds with answers of *I don't remember*, *I dunno*, and *I can't remember*, as well as a number of denials, which are his typical response to accusations (as we have seen in numerous extracts in this chapter). By this stage he is no doubt exhausted, if not also frustrated and/or angry with the lengthy cross-examination. It is also possible that these answers of *I don't remember*, *I dunno*, and *I can't remember* are answers of deliberate non-cooperation or resistance. The cumulative effect of these answers serves DC2's construction of him as an unreliable witness.

It is now clear that David's cross-examination is not working, which counts as success from the perspective of the defence. At this point, the role of the evidentiary process in identity construction is clear: the confused, exhausted, and probably scared and angry, 13-year-old boy in the witness box has been transformed by DC2 into a person who has problems with his memory, and can't stick to his story. While DC2 has not used the hostile and aggressive stance of DC1, or the disciplinary terms of abuse and metapragmatic directives, his quiet and calm use of recontextualisation with the confused and exhausted witness proves to be a powerful linguistic mechanism.

This is then a perfect time for DC2 to return to the central issue in the case, asking several pseudo-declarative questions, such as *You didn't think the police could harm you did you?* and *And you got in the car when they said to because- you didn't think you'd be in any trouble?* (p94). David's answers are straightforward answers of apparent agreement, with little of the hesitation and none of the disagreement which has characterised his earlier answers on this topic. It is impossible to know whether any or all of these answers are genuine agreement with the propositions questioned: the situation is certainly ripe for answers of gratuitous concurrence. DC2 brings these questions to a climax with a question which goes to the heart of the defence case on the central issue (Turn 1 in extract 46 below). Having secured David's apparent – though barely audible – answer to the question, it is now the perfect time for DC2 to ask for an adjournment. The magistrate's agreement, followed by his suggestion of *an early morning tea*, provides another opportunity for DC2 to highlight and reinforce David's supposed consent on the central issue:

Extract 46.   DC2 to David, Day 2, p94

1. DC2:   And you got in there of your <u>own</u> free will because you didn't think you'd be in any trouble for doing it?
2. David: (Yeh)=.
3. DC2:   =That's right isn't it? (1.4) correct?
4. David: (Yes).
5. DC2:   Yes.

6. DC2:   (2.9) Excuse me your worship (9.0) would your worship mind giving me
             a short break?

7. M: Yes we'll have a break ...

After the adjournment, DC2's questions return to David's talking to the media a few days after the Pinkenba event, focusing on allegations that he was *roused on for speaking to the press* (p96), presumably by people in ALS. After initially saying that he doesn't know what it means, David agrees to the accusation. DC2 then goes on to question him about allegations that he was involved in *putting graffiti around the* ALS building, and that he was present when one of his friends *was spraying a fire extinguisher* around the building (p96–97). With this clear picture of David as a juvenile delinquent, DC2 then switches abruptly back to the central issue in the case, with the questions discussed in Extract 3 in Chapter 4, followed by Extract 23 in Chapter 5. Here, as we have seen, DC2 uses a question with several propositions (Extract 3, Turn 9), and a number of pseudo-declarative questions (including Extract 3, Turns 1, 5, 9, 13, Extract 24, Turns 11, 13, 15, 17, 19, 27, 31), and likely gratuitous concurrence to gain David's apparent agreement to his definition of the word *force*. He then elicits apparent agreement that the police did not *force* him into the car, they just *said so*.

What follows are further questions on the same theme, such as *Did you know what your rights were- you don't have to talk to the police and don't have to go with them if you don't want to?* (p99), to which David answers *Mm*. This answer is clearly in contradiction to the earlier answer *They forced us* (p97). As we have seen in Chapter 5, David has no opportunity to explain how and why he felt forced to get in the police car. Arguably there is no inconsistency between knowing that you have the right to not go with police, and yet feeling forced to do so. But the possibility of this analysis – of the lack of inconsistency between these two mental states – is later negated in the defence closing addresses. As we will see in Section 1 of Chapter 10, DC2 argues that the boys could not possibly be afraid of the police, because they had had plenty of earlier dealings with police, and they had not been afraid to swear at (different) police officers on a different occasion.

10.   *Pushed around* and *used*

DC2 concludes his cross-examination of David with questions about his statements about the Pinkenba event made to ALS and CJC. Using a subdued and somewhat flat tone, he closes his questioning with the final feature of his identity construction of David. He has no trouble getting David to appear to agree that he's been *put under a lot of pressure by* [unnamed] *different people, . . . pushed around* and *used*, as we see in Extract 47:

Extract 47.   DC2 to David, Day 2, p100–101

1. DC2:	David- during <u>all</u> this episode (3.3) you've often said things- about it- because you thought it was what people wanted to hear- perhaps?
2. David:	(1.1) (wha) what=?
3. DC2:	=You've been <u>put</u> under a lot of pressure by different people haven't you?=
4. David:	=Yeh.
5. DC2:	Eh?
6. David:	Yeh.
7. DC2:	(2.0) And sometimes you've said things that weren't right (0.8) because of the pressure you've been put under? (1.0) that's right isn't it David?
8. David:	(1.5) Yeh.
9. DC2:	You've been pushed around a bit- you've been used haven't you?
10. David:	Yeh.
11. DC2:	Mm?
12. David:	Yeh.
13. DC2:	(3.3) Have you told me the truth today?
14. David:	(3.0) [Yeh.
15. DC2:	[(how nd) why you came to get in that police car and stayed?
16. David:	Yes.
17. DC2:	(4.2) If you've given a different version to other people (2.2) which one should we believe (okay)? the one you've given- to other people or what you've told me today? (3.4) who should we believe? (17.0) or don't you know anymore?
18. David:	(2.8) What?
19. DC2:	I mean has there just been so much pressure and so much talk about it that you can't be sure of what happened anymore?
20. David:	Mm.
21. DC2:	Is that true?
22. David:	Yeh.
23. DC2:	(4.6) Thank you David.

Who are the agents of this *pressure*, who has *pushed around* and *used* David, and why have they done this? While they are not named in these questions, they have been named several times in the immediately preceding questions – namely ALS and CJC. Thus at the close of cross-examination of the first witness, the defence moves beyond the situational struggle to the key institutional struggle at the heart of this case. As we saw in Section 5 of Chapter 3, the CJC was established as part of the reform of the police force which resulted from the Fitzgerald Inquiry into police corruption, and one of its major roles is to control the excesses of policing. And we saw in Section 4.1 of Chapter 3, that ALS was established by Aboriginal people in direct response to resentment about their experiences of police mistreatment. As DC2 completes his construction of David's identity, he is presented as a pressured victim of these institutions, whose work involves opposition to and some control over abusive police practices.

11. Conclusion

On the morning after his first day of evidence, David is accurately described in the major Brisbane newspaper as a "diminutive, softly spoken 13-year old" (Anon 1995a). On a number of occasions during his almost 4 hours on the witness stand over 2 days, he has been visibly upset. He has provided 1333 answers to cross-examination questions, but he has said very little, as the extracts in this chapter have indicated. The patterns of his answers suggest someone who finds it difficult to keep up with the pressure of cross-examination, but who is clear about why he got in the police car – *they forced us*.

But the propositions which have been put to David by both DCs contain many assertions and presuppositions which present a rather different character of this 13-year-old boy than his own (very few) substantive propositions do. DC1 has highlighted David's *criminal* past, and the evidence that he is a liar, combining terms of address and metapragmatic directives and attacks that index David's identity as a naughty schoolboy, with other stance features which index his own impatience in a disciplinary and punitive frame. He has also asserted that David *couldn't have cared less about going before the court* on the occasions on which his *criminal activities* have resulted in court proceedings. Using a less emotive stance, DC2 has focused mostly on presenting assertions and presuppositions constructing David's lifestyle as an uncontrollable street kid and his unreliability because of his poor memory. Thus, he has repeated the unquestioned ethnocentric presupposition that David had *run away from home* on the morning of the Pinkenba incident, as well as the assertions that he *had no plans* that day, that he has *problems with* his *memory*, and doesn't *go to school much*. DC2's final touch has presented David as a pressured victim of ALS and CJC, the major institutions which are engaged in the institutional struggle with the police force over the underlying issue in this case – namely whether police should have the right to remove Aboriginal people from public places.

All of the features of David's identity constructed by the DCs lay the groundwork for the justification of the way in which he has been treated by police on the Pinkenba occasion. DC1's masterful use of linguistic mechanisms which are allowed by the rules of evidence is an essential element in the micro-events which make up the cross-examination in this case, which in itself can be seen as a micro-event in the macro-structure of neocolonialism.

The identity work done by the two DCs is relentless, powerful and intense, while in contrast David provides little resistance or counter-identity work. In a number of instances he appears to resist the whole questioning process as well as individual propositions, answering *No* to allegations that he is then pressured to agree to, or answering *I dunno* to many other questions. Unlike the two older witnesses, David provides almost no direct resistance, for example by "answering back" or objecting to any of the questions. Table 3 provides a summary David's cross-examination.

Table 3.   Summary of David's cross-examination

DC1's questioning:	132 minutes, 876 answers, 47 transcript pages
DC2's questioning:	66 minutes, 457 answers, 24 transcript pages
answers of *yes*, *yeh*, or *mm*:	to DC1: 291 = 33% of his answers to DC1 to DC2: 180 = 39% of his answers to DC2
answers of *no* or *nuh*:	to DC1: 206 = 23% of his answers to DC1 to DC2: 64 = 14% of his answers to DC2
answers of *I don't know* or *I dunno*:	to DC1: 95 = 11% of his answers to DC1 to DC2: 35 = 8% of his answers to DC2
number of adjournments:	6
longest answer (20 words):	*In the police car- the man who was in the passenger side- he asked me if I went to Southbank* (to DC2, p79)

Main topic of questions:

DC1
pp26–30   David's *criminal record*
pp30–32   David's *nice* pair of Reeboks on Pinkenba night

pp33 on	David's habitual street kid activities
pp35	*criminal* past
[p36	legal discussion about adjournment]
p37	*criminal* past
p38–39	Pinkenba event, including central issue
p40–41	David's reports about Pinkenba night
p42	Pinkenba night to *criminal* past
p43–44	earlier taxi fare evasion to *criminal* past
p44–50	*criminal* past
p50–51	Pinkenba night (after police left them) to *criminal* past
p52–54	*criminal* past
p55–64	Pinkenba night, events earlier in that day
p64–66	*criminal* past
p66–74	Pinkenba night (including central issue), David's reports of Pinkenba night
DC2	
p74–76	David's transitory residential pattern and irregular school attendances
p76–78	David's plans on *running away from home* on morning of Pinkenba incident
p79	Pinkenba incident
p80	David's street kid behaviour
p81	Pinkenba incident (including central issue), and David's memory problems
[p82–84	END of DAY ONE court business, no evidence from David]
p85–88	START OF DAY TWO details of Pinkenba day, and street kid behaviour
p89–90	exhibits: photos of location in Valley where police approached boys
p91–94	David's reports of Pinkenba incident to ALS and media
p94	Pinkenba incident: central issue
p95	exhibits: photos of location in Valley where police approached boys
p96–97	David's delinquent activities
p97–99	Pinkenba incident: central issue
p100–101	David's statements about Pinkenba incident to ALS and CJC

We now move in Chapter 8 to a detailed analysis of Albert's cross-examination, in which we see further powerful use of a range of linguistic mechanisms in the construction of this second witness as someone who also deserved to be removed from the Valley by police that night. After the "success" of David's cross-examination, perhaps it might be thought that most of the work of the DCs has been done (and that most of the analysis of identity work for this book has also been done). But we will see that the power which the DCs have over the witnesses is not given, it has to be constantly worked for. And this critical sociolinguistic examination of the workings of neocolonialism necessitates attention to the details of talk. The patterns of Albert's answers will reveal some differences from David's, and the form and content of the DCs' identity work will also reveal subtle differences, as well as some similarities.

Chapter 8
More court appearances than some solicitors: Albert

1. A *big criminal*

DC1 begins his cross-examination of 13-year-old Albert by taking up and expanding a theme from David's cross-examination, namely the *criminal* identity of the witness. But DC1 contrasts the fact that Albert has come into the court positioned as a child (*protected by a friendly arm on his shoulders*), with his assertion that he is *in fact*, a _BIG_ criminal. Extract 48 below, which begins with DC1's opening questions to Albert, shows the hostile stance with which DC1 introduces Albert's *criminal* identity from the start:

Extract 48. DC1 to Albert, Day 2, p110–111

1. DC1:	°Do you want to be here°?
2. Albert:	(2.1) Beg your pardon?
3. DC1:	°Do you want to be <u>here</u>°?
4. Albert:	Where?
5. DC1:	°Here°?
6. Albert:	Nuh.
7. DC1:	°Eh°? (1.7) °What d'you say°?
8. M:	(2.2) He said [no.
9. Albert:	[No.
10. DC1:	(All right) (1.6) When you're answering my questions you'll speak up do you understand that?
11. Albert:	°Yes°.
12. DC1:	Speak up please.=
13. Albert:	=Yes.
14. DC1:	So we can hear you (3.2) we've seen you come into court- here- protected by a friendly arm on your shoulders haven't we? (3.1) haven't we?
15. Albert:	I dunno.
16. DC1:	You came into court and left court with an <u>arm</u> around your shoulders- didn't you- just a little while ago? (6.1) didn't you?
17. Albert:	Yeh.

18. DC1:	(2.4) You don't really need that do you- cause you're a little criminal aren't you?
19. Albert:	Nuh.
20. DC1:	You're a BIG criminal in fact aren't you?
21. Albert:	Nuh.
22. DC1:	Beside uh your mate- Pender uh or beside you Pender just doesn't exist really as a criminal does he? (2.3) compared to you does he? (2.1) DOES he?
23. Albert:	[Nuh.
24. Pros:	[With respect- the witness is being asked to comment on somebody else's uh=
25. DC1:	=Alright- okay I won't proceed with that- we'll let the facts talk for themselves- how many how many places have you broken and entered?
26. Albert:	None.

DC1's first 4 questions to Albert (Turns 1, 3, 5, 7) are delivered in a barely audible volume, presumably to highlight the need for Albert to *speak up* when *answering his questions*, as his quiet voice has become apparent during his examination-in-chief. In this opening extract, DC1 positions himself as a punitive schoolteacher disciplining a child with the tersely given directive *When you are answering my questions you'll speak up do you understand that?* (in Turn 10). It is hard to imagine such a directive being given to an adult witness. Although DC1 does not use this style as much with Albert as with David, he addresses him once as *lad* (p119), and he also refers to him being a *boy* in one question, expressed sarcastically as *You're going to be a good boy?* (p113). We also see in this opening extract, DC1 referring to the first witness David by his last name, Pender (Turn 22). This usage is consistent with DC1's use of dated school disciplining terms of address, as discussed in Section 6 of Chapter 6. (We also saw in Table 1 in Chapter 6 that DC1 never addresses any of the witnesses by his first name.)

But this opening extract also highlights the difference in DC1's construction of the first two witnesses, namely that compared to David's *criminal record*, Albert's is that of a *BIG criminal*. The prosecutor objects that DC1 is erring in asking the witness to comment on another person's (David's) *criminal record* (Turn 24). But, the impact of the question remains – DC1 has opened Albert's cross-examination by labelling him as a *BIG criminal*. The question in Turn 25 necessitates that the magistrate give the *warning* against self-incrimination, which he has given to David 6 times during DC1's questioning on the previous day (discussed in Section 1 of Chapter 7 above). Interestingly, this first time that

Albert is given the *warning*, the magistrate makes an attempt to explain it before pronouncing it, as we see in Turns 1 and 5 of Extract 49 below, which follows on immediately from Extract 48 above:

Extract 49. Magistrate to Albert, Day 2, p111

1. M:	Just hang on a moment- Albert I'm going to <u>warn</u> you at this stage- first of all if you're <u>asked</u> a question about something for which you've been before the court- and been found guilty or convicted you have to answer those questions.=
2. Albert:	=°Mm°.=
3. M.:	=Right?=
4. Albert:	=Yeh.
5. M:	But- if you're asked a question about something for which you haven't been before the court- you are not obliged to answer those questions- do you understand what I'm saying?
6. Albert:	Yeh.
7. M:	So I'm giving you the warning at this stage- you are not obliged to answer any question which might incriminate you- in relation- to a- criminal offence- do you understand that?
8. Albert:	Yeh.
9. M:	Okay now if you don't understand at any stage- tell me- okay?- Yes Mr Thorpe.

While Albert's answers of *Yeh* in Turns 6 and 8 are taken to mean that he has understood the *warnings*, it is impossible to know if he has indeed understood them, or if these are answers of gratuitous concurrence. Further, the explanation in Turn 5 is not accurate if taken literally. That is, if the witness *is asked a question about something for which* he hasn't *been before the court*, he is *not obliged to answer those questions*. But this is only true if those are questions which might *incriminate* him *in the commission of a criminal offence*. That is, witnesses do not have the right to refuse to answer questions such as Turn 5 in Extract 60 below, although a literal interpretation of the magistrate's explanation in Turns 1 and 5 above would indicate that they do have this right. This apparent assumption of a non-literal interpretation of the magistrate's explanation of the privilege appears to be accepted unquestioningly by the magistrate, the prosecutor and the DCs, a point to be taken up in Section 2.3 of Chapter 12.

2.   *I don't want to answer that question*

As the cross-examination develops, it is clear that Albert is aware of some right to refuse to answer questions, and unlike David who made only 3 attempts to exercise this right, Albert makes several attempts to do so. Extract 50 below, which follows immediately after Extract 49 above, shows DC1's expert circumvention of the self-incrimination privilege while pursuing his presentation of David as a BIG *criminal*:

Extract 50.   DC1 to Albert, Day 2, p111–112

1. DC1:	How many places have you broken and entered?
2. Albert:	(2.4) None.
3. DC1:	(1.1) What's your answer?
4. Albert:	No.
5. DC1:	(1.9) None?
6. Albert:	None.
7. DC1:	Is that right?
8. Albert:	Yeh.
9. DC1:	(1.1) Okay (1.7) how many things have you uh taken away from a shop?
10. Albert:	(4.1) I don't want to answer that question.
11. M:	°Okay°.
12. DC1:	Is it <u>lots</u> of things you've taken away from [shops?
13. Pros:	[With respect he said I don't want to answer that [question.
14. DC1:	[No he didn't- he said he didn't want to answer <u>that</u> question- I'm now asking <u>ano</u>ther question to which he can claim privilege if he wants to- but I'm perfectly entitled to an answer.=
15. M:	=Okay.=
16. DC1:	=Have you taken <u>lots</u> of things away from shops?
17. Albert:	(1.8) No.
18. DC1:	(3.6) All right (0.8) have you ever- damaged any property?
19. Albert:	(3.4) I don't want to answer any question.
20. M:	(2.0) Okay he's claiming privilege on that.=
21. DC1:	=Yes (3.0) have you (2.6) ever entered- someone's house with intent to commit an offence?
22. Albert:	(1.5) Nuh.

23. DC1:   (18.0) Have you ever (3.4) taken someone's motor vehicle?
24. Albert: (1.9) I don't want to answer any of your questions.

25. M: (1.3) You don't want to answer that question?
26. Albert: None of them.
27. M: Okay.

As we see in this extract, Albert shows more skilled resistance than David to DC1's construction of his *criminal* identity: in addition to answering, seemingly dishonestly as we will see, that he has not *broken into* any *places* (Turn 2) or stolen *lots of things* from *shops* (Turn 17), he attempts to invoke his right not to answer questions (Turns 10, 19, 24, 26). As we saw with David in Extract 37, on a number of occasions Albert responds initially to accusations with denial. But, unlike David, Albert then moves to attempt to invoke the privilege, saying *I don't want to answer that question*. It is quite likely that he has not understood that he can only use this right if it relates to a potentially *criminal* act for which he has not yet been charged. As we saw above, the magistrate's explanation of the *privilege* is unlikely to have helped Albert to understand it.

Finally, DC1 hands Albert a three page listing of his *criminal offences* (on p112). This apparently provides clear evidence of Albert's identity as a *criminal*, including for example, a charge of *stealing* from a shop. In addition to providing this evidence, which will enable DC1 to show that Albert has told *a lie*, DC1 extends the theme that he is a BIG *criminal* by projecting his future lifetime of *criminal activity* (in Turn 1 in Extract 51 below). This assertion is reinforced by DC1's use of the adult term of address *Mr Carter*, as we also see in Turn 1:

Extract 51. DC1 to Albert, Day 2, p112–113

1. DC1:   Well how are you going to spend your life uh Mr Carter- go on committing criminal offences will you? (2.0) will you?
2. Albert: (1.1) °Nuh°.=

3. DC1:   =Yes you will won't you?
4. Albert: Nuh.

5. DC1:   BEG YOUR PARDON?
6. Albert: No.

7. DC1:   (0.8) What are you going- you going to turn over a new leaf are you?
8. Albert: Yeh.

9. DC1:   You're <u>not</u> going to commit anything at all?
10. Albert: (0.9) No.

| 11. DC1: | All right- you're going to be a good boy? |
| 12. Albert: | Yeh. |

| 13. DC1: | (1.4) And er go to school? |
| 14. Albert: | (0.6) Mm. |

| 15. DC1: | Are you at school now? |
| 16. Albert: | (1.5) No. |

| 17. DC1: | Not going to school? |
| 18. Albert: | Not just yet. |

| 19. DC1: | Beg your pardon? |
| 20. Albert: | Not yet. |

| 21. DC1: | (1.2) Not yet you're thir how old are you fourteen? (0.5) when are you going to go? |
| 22. Albert: | After this finish. |

This extract also illustrates a constant theme in both DCs' identity construction of the three boys; as *criminals* (e.g. Turn 1), who are delinquent schoolboys (e.g. Turns 11, 13, 15, 17). The switch in Turn 11 to the schoolteacher style of questioning serves to rebuke Albert and highlight his irresponsible and delinquent behaviour. Albert's answers in Turns 18 and 22 seem to imply that he takes DC1's meaning of the time adverbial *now* to mean something like *during the period of this hearing*. DC1's angry shouting BEG YOUR PARDON? in Turn 5 becomes a recurrent feature of his cross-examination of Albert, who has a soft voice.

3.   *You are deliberately going to lie*

DC1 then switches abruptly back to Albert's *criminal record*, and moves in with aggressive presentation of him as a liar, with the refrain which we saw in his questioning of David on the previous day *Why did you lie?* Extract 52 below follows immediately from Extract 51 above:

Extract 52.   DC1 to Albert, Day 2, p113

| 1. DC1: | After here- all right- well let's have a look you told me you'd never broken and entered anything didn't you? (0.9) didn't you? |
| 2. Albert: | (0.7) °Mm°. |

| 3. DC1: | (1.0) Please answer me. |
| 4. Albert: | (1.1) °Yeh°. |

| 5. DC1: | (1.5) In fact that was a lie wasn't it? (1.7) that was a lie [wasn't it? |
| 6. Albert: | [°Yes°. |

| 7. DC1: | Beg your pardon? |
| 8. Albert: | Yes. |

| 9. DC1: | Well WHY DO YOU LIE? (2.7) WHY DID YOU LIE ABOUT IT SON? (2.8) COME ON I WANT YOU TO ANSWER WHY DID YOU LIE?= |
| 10. Albert: | =I dunno. |

| 11. DC1: | Beg your pardon? |
| 12. Albert: | I dunno. |

| 13. DC1: | Because you didn't think I knew about it isn't that right? (1.3) isn't that right? |
| 14. Albert: | Yes. |

| 15. DC1: | Yes (1.3) and that's what's going to happen here isn't it?- the whole time you're here if you think- you can get away with it you'll lie won't you? (2.1) won't you? |
| 16. Albert: | (0.6) °Mm°. |

| 17. DC1: | (0.6) Answer. |
| 18. Albert: | <u>Yes</u>. |

| 19. DC1: | Yes (2.3) and when you told his worship- the man up there before- that you know the difference between- telling a lie and telling the truth- and you said yes- you meant that didn't you? (1.3) you <u>know</u> the difference don't you? |
| 20. Albert: | (0.6) Yeh. |

| 21. DC1: | (0.6) And you ARE DELIBERATELY GOING TO LIE in your evidence if you think you can get away with it- AREN'T YOU? |
| 22. Albert: | (0.9) °Yeh°. |

After 10 minutes of questioning, DC1 has said nothing to Albert in connection with the Pinkenba event. His identity as a <u>*BIG*</u> *criminal* and someone who is *deliberately going to lie in* his *evidence* is secured before he has the chance to say anything in his cross-examination about the event which is the reason for his evidence. Turns 9 to 21 comprise extreme hostility and harassment by DC1, for example with his repeated questioning and shouting. As discussed in Chapter 4, such mechanisms create the likelihood of eliciting answers of gratuituous concurrence. Thus, it is impossible to know if Albert's very soft answers of °*Mm*° (Turn 16) and °*Yeh*° (Turn 22) are actually agreements to the extremely damaging propositions in Turns 15 and 21 respectively, that he is DELIBERATELY GOING TO LIE *in* his *evidence if* he *thinks he can get away with it.* Albert is visibly upset at this point of the cross-examination, and the magistrate agrees to the prosecutor's request for a short adjournment. The timing of this adjournment, while seemingly requested by the prosecutor as necessary for Albert's well-being, also serves to highlight the seriousness of the apparent admission in the final question-answer exchange (Turns 21–22).

After the adjournment, DC1's first three turns (seen in Extract 53 below) serve to highlight that Albert is a liar (Turn 1), to assert that he is under the questioner's physical control (Turn 3) and to ridicule his middle name (Turn 5). (The use of Albert's full name in these questions is presumably related to DC1 reading from a print-out of Albert's convictions.)

Extract 53.   DC1 to Albert, Day 2, p114

1. DC1:	Well we'll see if we can get a- truthful answer from you- what's your name?
2. Albert:	(1.3) Albert Wess °Carter°.
3. DC1:	Take your fingers out of your mouth will you- what's your name?
4. Albert:	Albert Wess Carter.
5. DC1:	Is that your real name°
6. Albert:	(1.4) Wess?
7. DC1:	Beg your pardon?
8. Albert:	Wess (1.6) W-E-S-S.

DC1's cross-examination continues with questions about Albert's *criminal record*, interspersed with repeated questions asserting that Albert will *lie if* he *thinks he can get away with it.* Albert's answers to such assertions are contradictory, sometimes agreeing, sometimes disagreeing, highlighting the problematic nature of the cross-examination in this case. There is clearly no accounting for the suggestibility of children when repeatedly asked the same question (as discussed in Section 1.2 of Chapter 4), or the tendency of Aboriginal people to give answers of gratuitous concurrence. It is impossible to know from p113–114 if Albert does intend to *lie*, or is simply telling DC1 what he wants to hear in order to speed up the painful cross-examination process. It is certainly likely that some of the presuppositions in DC1's questions are not understood by 13-year-old Albert, especially where they are sarcastic, such as in Extract 54.

4.   Experienced defendant and liar

Extract 54.   DC1 to Albert, Day 2, p114

1. DC1:	IF YOU THOUGHT YOU COULD GET AWAY WITH IT YOU'VE <u>TOLD</u> ME YOU'D LIE (8.7) YOU SEE WHAT YOU'VE DONE IS THIS- YOU'VE YOU'VE MADE MORE COURT APPEARANCES THAN SOME SOLICITORS IN THIS STATE- I'd suggest to you (1.1) THIRTEEN YEARS OF AGE- BREAKING AND ENTERING A PLACE WITH INTENT- YOU DON'T KNOW ANYTHING ABOUT THAT?
2. Albert:	(0.8) (That's a) long time.
3. DC1:	Beg your pardon?
4. Albert:	(0.6) I finished all that.

In Turn 1 of Extract 54, DC1 presents yet again his construction of Albert as a liar and a *criminal*, sarcastically asserting that Albert has *MADE MORE COURT APPEARANCES THAN SOME SOLICITORS IN THIS STATE*. Although this assertion is followed by the cross-examination tag *I'd suggest to you*, there is little interactional space for Albert to reply, before being challenged about a specific entry on his *criminal record*. DC1's sarcastic comment about the number of Albert's court appearances refers to *criminal* charges he has been to (Children's) court over, in his identity as an accused person or defendant. This identity of experienced defendant is taken up in DC1's closing submission, and eventually finds its way into the magistrate's decision, when he says that *the three complainant children ... know the court system well, having kept the court and legal representatives occupied on many occasions* (as we will see in Section 2 of Chapter 10).

As with his earlier questioning of David, and later questioning of Barry, DC1 also presents his construction of Albert as someone who doesn't *care two hoots about the property that* he damages *and who has to pay to repair it* (p115). The discourse structure of cross-examination provides the vehicle for DC1 to create this identity for the person who himself identifies as victim, while at the same time using his questioning to accuse and rebuke him, as we see in Extract 55:

Extract 55.   DC1 to Albert, Day 2, p115

1. DC1:	You laugh at the people whose property it is don't you? (2.0) don't you?
2. Albert:	°Nuh°.
3. DC1:	(0.6) Beg your pardon?
4. Albert:	Nuh.
5. DC1:	You don't- you feel sorry for them (4.9) well?
6. Albert:	(1.3) (°A bit°).

7. DC1:   Beg your pardon?
8. Albert: A bit.=

9. DC1:   =Oh don't tell lies (1.9) you've done too much of it to feel sorry for people
            I'd suggest to you (3.3) what do you say to that?
10. Albert: (2.9) Nothing.

This extract follows from Albert disagreeing with DC1's construction of him as someone who has *great fun* damaging property. There is no obvious contradiction between Albert's answers in Turns 2 and 6 here, but DC1 angrily rejects Albert's answers with the implication in his metapragmatic directive *don't tell lies* in Turn 9. The schoolteacher style of rebuke in this turn, combined with its occurrence after so many harassing questions, as seen in the preceding extracts, arguably mitigates against Albert providing any real reply to the complaint, which is disguised as an invitation to argue, *what do you say to that?* (Turn 9).

The portrait of the irresponsible young delinquent follows on from these allegations of not caring about the effects of his property damage, to questions relating to a charge of *breaking entering and stealing* (pens) from a school in mid-1993. During these questions (p116), DC1 uses the schoolteacher admonition style directive *speak up*. Intensifying the pressure on Albert, DC1 attacks him for not making eye contact while answering his questions, in an exchange discussed in Extract 9 in Chapter 4, which exploits cultural differences in communication. This harassment over eye contact provides the chance for DC1 to renew his attack on Albert for telling *lies*, a theme that was recurrent in David's cross-examination, as we saw in Chapter 7. In Albert's cross-examination DC1 uses the words *lie*, *lies*, *lied* or *lying* 30 times, while DC2 uses it 13 times.

Up to this point in his cross-examination of Albert, DC1 has been using the conventional courtroom question-answer discourse structure to make allegations, to construct Albert's identity and to harass and rebuke him. Following the exchange about eye contact, DC1 makes a remarkable attack on the witness, which is nothing short of a strong schoolteacher rebuke to a defiant school student, saying:

Extract 56.   DC1 to Albert, Day 2, p117

1. DC1:   I see you're not going to answer because you see- HERE YOU'RE CAUGHT
            AREN'T YOU? (0.9) in that witness box you can run but you can't hide
            (2.7) AND YOU'RE GOING TO SIT THERE AND YOU'RE GOING TO BE ASKED
            QUESTION AFTER QUESTION AFTER QUESTION (0.8) and you WON'T BE ABLE
            TO THUMB YOUR NOSE AT PEOPLE (1.0) AND COMMIT OFFENCES THERE DO
            YOU UNDERSTAND THAT?
2. Albert: (1.3) °Yes°.

Turn 1, most of which is shouted, highlights the abuse of cross-examination which is allowed unchecked in this case. Most of this turn is an extreme example of a pseudo-declarative, clearly serving no interrogative function. The final question *DO YOU UNDERSTAND THAT?* serves to transform DC1's turn into a question, maintaining the fiction of a question-answer discourse structure in this speech event. Perhaps more significantly, it also secures Albert's compliance in DC1's overt control over him.

After this rebuke, DC1 moves to the incident of Albert's use of "offensive language" from the tape-recording of the conversation in the car with the female investigating officer from the CJC, who was a policewoman. DC1's recontextualisation in court of this comment in a private conversation has been discussed in Section 4 of Chapter 6. As discussed there, DC1's questions to Albert about this comment, enable him to present an ethnocentric presupposition that Albert did not *FEEL ANY RESPECT FOR THE LADY IN THE CAR*, and that he was *deliberately trying to embarrass the policewoman* (Extract 25). Then, in a move which has parallels with the trifecta discussed in Sections 1.3 and 4.2 of Chapter 3, DC1 moves from this attack on Albert for swearing in the car *in front of a policewoman* to suggest that Albert's *WHOLE EVIDENCE HERE* is *AN ATTEMPT AS A SQUARE UP with the police* . . . , that he is *trying to get even with the police*, and that he would *lie . . . to get even with police*. Albert's denials of these suggestions are arguably of little consequence: DC1 has made them forcefully, using almost 6 times as many words as Albert. As we saw in the discussion of this extract (25) in Chapter 6, some of the linguistic mechanisms used by DC1 here include the use of culturally-specific presuppositions, as well as presuppositions in pseudo-declaratives, angry shouting and repetition.

DC1 then pursues his theme of Albert as a liar, by launching into his second attack on Albert's reluctance to make eye contact with him. He first asks *has someone told you not to look at me?* (p119), suggesting that Albert is not a sole agent in his presentation of evidence against the police. This was also a theme of DC2's closing questions to David earlier that day, as we saw in Section 10 of Chapter 7. As with the first attack on Albert's avoidance of eye contact, which was discussed in Section 3.2 of Chapter 4 (Extract 9), DC1 again alleges that this is a symptom of lying behaviour. This involves an overt exploitation of the cultural difference in communication, which is explained in the lawyers' handbook (Eades 1992), which is visible on the Bar table. Thus, as we saw in Section 3.2 of Chapter 4, he asks Albert two pseudo-declaratives, and finishes with the insistent prompt *well* and the tag question *is it?*, saying *Why can't you look at me?* (2.6) *I might not be the prettiest picture in the world but why can't you?* (6.8) *is it because you think that I'll see things on your face- that show you're lying?* (1.8) *well?* (1.6) *is it?* (p119). Albert answers *No*.

5.   *You can be held in contempt of this court lad*

DC1 then goes back to Albert's *criminal record*, and Extract 57 below shows him using questions to harass and threaten the teenager (with a *contempt of court* charge) in an exchange which is nothing short of ludicrous:

Extract 57.   DC1 to Albert, Day 2, p119–120

1. DC1:	This school now this Murgon School (3.4) did you destroy property at the school? (7.0) well <u>did</u> you?
2. Albert:	I dunno.
3. DC1:	(1.6) You <u>must</u> know (2.3) or is it the situation that you've committed so much- so many criminal offences in your short years that you don't remember- much about them at all? (1.9) is <u>that</u> the situation? (5.1) is that it?
4. M:	(57.1) Do you want to answer that question?
5. Albert:	(1.5) Nuh.
6. M:	(1.7) Anyway just proceed Mr uh.
7. DC1:	Well answer my QUESTION (4.8) LOOK (0.7) YOU CAN BE HELD IN CON-TEMPT OF THIS COURT LAD (2.0) AND THE WAY YOU'RE GOING I'M GOING TO <u>ASK</u> FOR IT VERY SHORTLY (3.7) now ANSWER MY QUESTION.
8. Albert:	I don't wanna.
9. DC1:	(0.5) Beg your pardon?
10. Albert:	(0.5) I don't wanna.
11. DC1:	Well you'll have to.=
12. M:	=Well I'm going to direct that you answer that question uh you can't claim uh privilege on that question.
13. DC1:	(6.6) °Well perhaps in retrospect he can claim privilege on the°
14. M:	(1.5) I suppose there is a suggestion=
15. DC1:	=cause I <u>asked</u> was it because he'd committed so many criminal offences uh- so maybe I
16. M:	(1.4) There may be a suggestion there of other offences for [which he hasn't been before the court.
17. DC1:	[Well more yes a statement perhaps.
18. M:	All right then what I'll say to you is this- don't you - I'm just telling you now that's a question you don't have to answer- so do you want to answer the question?
19. Albert:	Nuh.
20. M:	Ok- we'll leave it at that then.

This exchange in Extract 57 is one of several during DC1's cross-examination, in which the elicitive function of a question is so far subordinated to its functions of rebuking and harassing, as to seriously question the legal role of cross-examination in this case. In Turn 5, Albert attempts to invoke his right not to answer a non-specific question about his *criminal* past, namely whether he has *committed . . . so many criminal offences in* his *short years that* he doesn't *remember much about them at all*. In Turns 4 and 6 the magistrate accepts Albert's right to refuse to answer the question. DC1 completely ignores the magistrate's acceptance of Albert's decision here, as well as the magistrate's direction for DC1 to *proceed* (that is, with the next question). Instead of doing this, DC1 proceeds in Turn 7 to harangue the witness and shout his threat to have him charged with *CONTEMPT OF COURT*. This threat takes the intimidation of the child witnesses in this case to a new level, and is perhaps related to Albert's increasing attempts at resistance, by his attempts to invoke his right to refuse to answer certain questions. It is interesting to note that DC1's angry and abusive threat in Turn 7 appears to be a response to one of the longest silences following a question in this hearing – 57 seconds. (There are some longer silences after witness answers when the questioning lawyer can be heard going through papers, or whispering to someone at the Bar table).

The power of DC1 over the magistrate is clearly seen in this interaction, as the magistrate then changes his mind, and directs Albert (in Turn 12) that he has to answer the question. Somewhat surprisingly, DC1 then appears to consider that perhaps Albert might have had the right to refuse to answer the question. The ensuing brief discussion between him and the magistrate in Turns 13–17 results in the magistrate reverting to his original decision on this matter, and offering Albert the right to refuse to answer (in Turn 18). This exchange shows that even for adults with considerable legal training and expertise, it can be difficult to know when the self-incrimination privilege can be used. (This is also evident from a later exchange in DC1's cross-examination of Albert, which involves a complex dispute between the prosecutor and DC1 over the privilege, p132.)

Although it has now been effectively admitted by both the magistrate and DC1 that Albert's initial refusal (in Turn 5) to answer the question was unquestionably within his rights, the damage has been done. DC1 has made the strong allegation that Albert has *committed . . . so many criminal offences in* his *short years that* he doesn't *remember much about them at all*. He has further harangued and threatened Albert in an offensive manner, combining schoolteacher admonition style with the repeated imperative *ANSWER MY QUESTION* and the term of address *LAD*, shouting the serious legal threat of a charge of *CONTEMPT OF COURT*. Such is DC1's control over this hearing, that there is no revoking of this haranguing and threatening talk, let alone any apology to Albert, for either the procedural mistake which had resulted in the wrong insistence on an answer, or the offensive way in which this mistake was carried out.

6. *Why do you swear?*

DC1's cross-examination then continues with further questioning about Albert's *criminal record*, which gives rise to the magistrate issuing the *warning* against self-incrimination (p125, 127). This is interspersed with DC1's insults and attacks, including WILL YOU PLEASE- ANSWER IN A WAY THAT WE CAN HEAR WHAT YOU'RE SAYING- RATHER- THAN GRUNTING THERE (p127–128). When the prosecutor objects that *With respect this is just intimidation your worship*, the magistrate agrees, saying *Yes yes*. A discussion then ensues in which the prosecutor argues forcefully that *the witness naturally speaks quietly and is obviously intimidated by* DC1. The magistrate's acceptance of this point is *dispute*d by DC1. He seeks to disprove the assertion of Albert's quiet voice, by replaying in court a section from the tape-recording of Albert's conversation in the CJC investigation car-ride. Although the segment of tape played is not the one with the instance of the four-letter word above (Extract 25 discussed in Section 4 of Chapter 6), the recontextualisation of the same tape-recording arguably serves to reinvoke this episode. The prosecutor disputes any value that the tape has in disproving his assertion that Albert *naturally speaks quietly*, by pointing out that *there's . . . been evidence he had a microphone attached to his throat* (p128).

DC1 then moves the discussion of the audibility of Albert's voice to questions about whether he *yells abuse at people when* he sees *them in the streets from time to time* (p129). If interpreted with their literal meaning, Albert's answers of *Ye#, No#,* and *I don't know* indicate that he *swears very softly*, he doesn't *know why* he swears, and he *only swears at people he knows*. As already indicated in discussions above, and in Chapters 3 and 6, DC1's preoccupation with the very small amount of evidence that the boys sometimes swear is an overused and ethnocentric tool in the construction of the boys' *criminal* identity. But it powerfully evokes a major site of struggle between Aboriginal people and the police.

When the questioning then reverts to Albert's *criminal record*, the magistrate gives the self-incrimination *warning* for the third time for this witness, this time in the ritualised form used on the previous day for David, namely *Again- I warn you that you are not obliged to answer any question which will incriminate you in relation to the commission of a criminal offence* (p129). While this *warning* is usually given to defendants, it is the victim-witnesses in this hearing who are the addressees of this *warning* (a total of 18 times over the three days of evidence). So effective is DC1's construction of Albert as a *criminal* that the official transcript names Albert as "Defendant Carter" 11 turns after this instance of the self-incrimination *warning*.[35]

By this stage in his cross-examination, Albert is perceptibly tiring, and his voice is becoming quite soft. As DC1 is now constantly repeating questions such as *what did you say?* and *what was that?*, the magistrate has begun to repeat the witness's answers, which apparently are quite audible to him. This again leads to discussion between the magistrate, DC1, DC2 and the prosecutor about the speech volume/audibility problems, which results in an early lunch adjournment to enable a microphone to be arranged. Interestingly, during this discussion about the need for a microphone, the prosecutor mentions indirectly the fact that Albert is a child witness, saying that he has seen microphones used *before in courts with children in other sorts of matters* (p130). This is only the second time in the cross-examination in this hearing in which the vulnerability of the witnesses as children is referred to (the other occasion is discussed in Section 4 of Chapter 7). And this vulnerability is only considered here in relation to the technical aspect of speaking volume, and only by the prosecutor. There is no mention during the cross-examination of such language and communication issues as comprehension and suggestibility, or other factors such as fatigue and concentration for these child witnesses.

After the lunch adjournment, and the installation of a microphone for Albert, DC1 resumes questioning about Albert's *criminal record*, occasioning two more instances of the self-incrimination *warning* from the magistrate. It also provides the occasion for DC1 to engage in a complicated legal discussion with the prosecutor and the magistrate over whether an earlier answer of *No* to the question of whether Albert had *ever thrown rocks at a street light . . . would apparently be a lie*. The magistrate's direction to Albert is *if you don't incriminate yourself you have to answer the question* (p132). It is not necessary to quote and analyse the lengthy exchange here (p132–133) in which there are 501 words, of which 5 are spoken by Albert. It is primarily conducted between the legal professionals to the exclusion of the witness, as indexed in the legalese in such expressions as *my learned friend, I would respectfully ask*, and *the witness has claimed privilege*. DC1's attempted and complicated legal manipulation of the self-incrimination right is so plainly confusing that the prosecutor is moved to interrupt several times during this exchange. Apart from the harassment and confusion to which DC1 is prepared to subject the teenage witness, this part of Albert's cross-examination again highlights the fact that the self-incrimination right is very complex. But the legal system considers justice to be served by allowing DC1 to use this complexity, as well as Albert's lack of understanding of it, as tools in presenting the assertions which are central to his construction of Albert's identity as an experienced *criminal*, who has *thrown rocks at a street light* and *lie*d about it.

7.   *You lied to make things look bad for the police*

Following this, after exactly 60 minutes of cross-examination, DC1 finally turns to the Pinkenba event for the first time. It is significant that Albert has had no chance to position himself in the cross-examination as a victim of police actions on that night, until after DC1 has had ample opportunity to construct his identity as a *big criminal*, who *will tell lies if* he *thinks he can get away with it*, and who has a history of delinquent behaviour. Any credibility that Albert may have had in his asserted identity as a victim-witness, has by this stage been seriously challenged in the allegations made by DC1 in 60 minutes of aggressive questioning.

DC1's questioning of Albert about the Pinkenba night consists primarily of him exploiting inconsistencies between Albert's reports of the event at different times. The key discrepancy highlighted by DC1 is that in his initial telling of the story to the ALS, Albert reportedly used the verb *grab* to refer to the action of the police officers in relation to the boys, saying *they grabbed the three of us- two grabbed Barry- two grabbed me* (p136). Part of this section of Albert's cross-examination has been quoted as Extract 4 in Chapter 4, as it provides such a good example of strategies which appear to elicit gratuitous concurrence. Without repeating the analysis provided in Chapter 4, it will suffice here to summarise that DC1 uses a powerful combination of linguistic mechanisms, culminating in his shouted assertion YOU LIED TO MAKE THINGS LOOK BAD FOR THE POLICE DIDN'T YOU (1.2) DIDN'T YOU? (Turn 15 in Extract 4). These mechanisms include entextualisation, manipulation of the meaning of the lexical item *grab*, repetition, such as the refrain *why did you lie?*, and an impatient and angry stance as indicated in his repeated shouting. With such powerful linguistic mechanisms, it is impossible to know if Albert's agreements to DC1's repeated tag questions in Turns 1 and 15 of Extract 4 are gratuitous concurrence, or if Albert indeed agrees that he wasn't *grabbed*. Also as we saw in the discussion of this extract in Section 1.3 of Chapter 4, it is possible that Albert's use of *grab* in the first report did not intend to imply physical contact. As with discussion of the verb *force* in relation to David's evidence (Section 2.3 of Chapter 5), it is quite plausible to understand a young teenage boy's use of the verb *grab*, not to refer to physical contact, but in relation to the sense of urgency and powerlessness he felt in being told by armed police officers to get into a police car.

But regardless of the issue of whether or not Albert agrees that he hadn't been *grabbed* by the police, DC1 now has the perfect opportunity to construct his identity – as someone who *lied* in his earlier report in which he had used the word *grabbed* – *to make things look bad for the police*. So successful is DC1 in this assertion that the newspaper headline the next day pronounced: "'I lied to embarrass police': teen thief" (Anon 1995b), using quotation marks that gave the erroneous impression that Albert had said *I lied to embarrass police* (as we will see in Section 3 of Chapter 10).

This exchange in relation to Albert's reports of being *grabbed* by the police are then followed with further questioning about Albert's alleged report to ALS that *They forced me in* [to the car]- *pushed me*. In response to a field officer's reported question *Did they pick you up off the ground?*, Albert had reportedly replied *Yeh they were slinging David- slinging him along*. Then in answer to the field officer's reported question *Slinging- like pushing him around and dragging?* DC1 reports that Albert had replied *Threw him in the car*. The fact that these initial allegations were not given in Albert's examination-in-chief would tend to suggest that they may well have been an exaggeration in the first interview. Teenage exaggeration in recounting a story of police abuse might be understandable. But it should not form the basis of a *criminal* charge. And it did not. This likely exaggeration was not repeated and formed no part of the CJC recommendation or the charge against the police officers. But this legal reality is not mentioned in the hearing, either in the cross-examination, or in the prosecutor's closing address (where we might expect it), or in the magistrate's decision. But the rules of evidence allow DC1 to use the inconsistency between Albert's apparent initial exaggeration, and his later more careful attention to accuracy and truthfulness, as an opportunity to once again reiterate his identity as a liar, with forceful, repetitive, intense questioning that could well elicit gratuitous concurrence as we see in Extract 58:

Extract 58.   DC1 to Albert, Day 2, p138

1. DC1:   Now that <u>was a lie</u> wasn't it? (5.5) that was a lie wasn't it? (4.7) WASN'T
             IT?

2. Albert: °Yeh°.

3. DC1:   (0.8) Please answer.

4. Albert: [(I) <u>said</u> yes.

5. M: [He said yes.

Albert's answer in Turn 4 marks a new development in his answers, with an answer best described as "answering back", in a stance that perhaps indexes his identity as a defiant teenager, or at least as a witness with some agency. We saw an example of this kind of unambiguous resistance by David in Turn 16 in Extract 37 in Chapter 7. As we will see, Albert goes on to perform several other overt acts of resistance in answers to DC2, as does Barry, the last and oldest witness in answers to both DCs.

But DC1 continues with several pressured pseudo-declaratives which assert that Albert *made these things up, made them up to make the police look bad,* and was *prepared to tell any lies about what happened that night to make the police get into trouble* (p138). Again, it is impossible to know if Albert had the intention of making things look bad for the police, or whether his quiet answers of *Yes* to these pseudo-declaratives are answers of gratuitous concurrence.

8.   *You were wearing a nice pair of shoes that night*

The final 7 minutes of Albert's cross-examination by DC1 starts with questions about the circumstances of the police making him take off his shoes and throw them *in the bushes,* followed by questions about the boys' walk back from Pinkenba. This then leads to a series of questions similar to those asked of David the previous day about the *nice pair of shoes* he was *wearing ... that night* (discussed in Section 3 of Chapter 7). DC1's questions are delivered in a staccato tempo, indicating impatience. As with David's answers on this topic, Albert's answers are straightforward and brief. He says that the shoes were bought *in the Myers* [department store], *up Countrytown* [shopping centre], by his *mother* who paid *one hundred and twenty dollars* for them. These questions are asked at the end of DC1's cross-examination of Albert, in which more than half the questioning has been about his *criminal record.* And they follow DC1's suggestion to David the previous day on the same topic that it was *a situation that* he *stole* his *nice pair of shoes* (p32). Thus, it seems likely that this is the point of DC1's questions to Albert here. During this exchange, DC1 adds pressure to the witness by inserting a bald directive in impatient schoolteacher stance, which arguably should have no place in the cross-examination of a witness, saying *Stop chewing your fingernails.* Albert's answer demonstrates an element of resistance, by immediatedly replying, rather softly, °*I'm allowed*° (p140). DC1 makes no response to this, so it is possible that he did not hear it. The extent to which DC1's command is out of place in cross-examination discourse is signalled by its transcription in the official transcript with a question mark (see Eades 1996b). But this is one of the many instances in this case where it is impossible to sustain the legal fiction that the purpose of cross-examination is to ask questions of witnesses.

The detail on how Albert came to own a *nice pair* of *Nike* shoes concludes with a question about *where* David's *Mum* was *working at the time.* Albert answers *Down at the office ... in Cherbourg.* His account of his ownership of the *nice pair* of shoes presents his identity as a typical child in a typical family. But, DC1 recaptures the thief identity by following with three questions about whether Albert has *ever stolen any clothing*, and a brief discussion between DC1 and the magistrate about not needing the self-incrimination *warning at this stage*, because of Albert's *No* answer. This is immediately followed by the start of DC2's cross-examination.

The propositional content of Albert's answers at the end of DC1's cross-examination present him as a child who has not *stolen clothing*. But the minimalist and quiet presentation of this content pales in comparison to the aggressive and wordy assertions and presuppositions of DC1, who has already spent 98 minutes in powerfully presenting Albert as a <u>BIG</u> *criminal* who *tells lies*.

9. *You told them lies to their faces*

As with his opening questions of each of the other witnesses, DC2 starts with a pleasant and slightly deferential tone to Albert. He asks him such questions as *Albert if you don't understand anything I ask you would you tell me?* and *Could you just sit forward- would you mind doing that for me for a minute?* and *Is that okay- are you comfortable there?* (p141). After Albert's answers of *Ye#* to these questions, DC2 continues in his unthreatening tone, asking *Would you mind just putting your mouth closer to the microphone when you're answering the questions please Albert?* But Albert is apparently not ready to be compliant, answering *I don't talk on a mike*. This leads to saracastic comments from DC2 concluding with *let's see what you will do*.

DC2's questions begin with recontextualisation of Albert's earlier reports of the Pinkenba event. Albert answers a series of questions with *No#* about whether he saw *a lot of publicity about this business with* him in various media (*in the newspapers, on television, on the radio*) (p142). These negations appear to be then contradicted by his answer of *Yeh* to the pseudo-declarative question that he *went to a press conference at the legal service*. Asked to explain this contradiction, Albert effectively engages in an argument with DC2, the first sustained argument in the case, as we see in Extract 59:

Extract 59. DC2 to Albert, Day 2, p142–143

1. DC2: Albert- you went to a press conference didn't you?
2. Albert: (1.4) Nuh.=

3. DC2: =At the legal service (2.2) didn't you Albert?
4. Albert: Yeh.

5. DC2: (1.4) Why did you say no when I asked you [(that)?

| 6. Albert: | [I DUNNO WHAT YOU |
| | MEAN.= |

7. DC2:   =You don't know what I mean? (1.5) wh when I say- you went to a press conference you say no- when I asked you again you say yes (0.8) which [time don't you know what I mean?

8. Albert: [I dunno

9. DC2:   (1.4) Albert? (3.0) Albert?

10. Albert: What?

11. DC2:   You knew perfectly well what I meant didn't you?

12. Albert: Nuh.

13. DC2:   (3.3) Why did you answer my question differently- when I asked you a second time?=

14. Albert: =TOLD YOU I DON'T KNOW WHAT YOU MEAN.

15. DC2:   (1.7) So you said no and yes to the (simple) question but you still don't know what it meant (1.7) that right?

16. Albert: Yes.

It is impossible to know if Albert has genuinely not known what DC2's question in Turn 1 meant, or whether he only understands the meaning of *press conference* when it is contextualised with the location of the *legal service* in Turn 3. It is also possible that he is exhausted from the cross-examination, or that he is giving contradictory answers as a form of resistance. Certainly his answers in Turns 6 and 14 seem to be answers of resistance, with the aggressively shouted assertion *TOLD YOU I DON'T KNOW WHAT YOU MEAN* being one of Albert's longest utterances throughout his cross-examination. This defiance and contradictory stance of Albert's presents a developing aspect of his identity, which we saw towards the end of DC1's cross-examination. Albert is being pushed around by his questioners and he is getting sick of it. But his agentive self-identity work here is quickly overpowered by DC2's maximisation of the contradictory answers to a series of pseudo-declaratives which assert Albert's disdain for the truth, and which forcefully insist that Albert is someone who *tells lies*. Extract 60 below immediately follows Extract 59 above:

Extract 60.   DC2 to Albert, Day 2, p143

1. DC2:   Do you care what you say here?- do you care?

2. Albert: (1.0) Nuh.

3. DC2:   (2.4) You- don't care whether you tell us the truth or not (do you)? it just doesn't matter to you eh? does it?

4. Albert: Nuh.

5. DC2:   You couldn't <u>care</u> less whether you tell the court the truth or not could
           you? (2.0) Albert could you? (1.2) couldn't care less could you?=

6. Albert: =I don't want to answer that.

7. DC2:   Eh?

8. Albert: I don't want to answer that.

9. DC2:   (1.1) You don't want to answer? I ask you the question- you couldn't care
           less whether you tell this court the truth or not and you don't want to
           answer (1.8) having earlier said that- no you don't care- whether you tell
           the court the truth or not? (2.7) well Albert- are we right in thinking- that
           the police- didn't- <u>sling-</u> or <u>drag-</u> David into any police car? (2.4) is that
           right? (2.5) is that right?

10. Albert: Mm.

11. DC2:   Par[don?

12. Albert: [Yes.

13. DC2:   (1.5) You told people that they had- that they did that didn't you? (2.5)
           Albert?

14. Albert: (0.7) Yᴇꜱ.

15. DC2:   Now these people who were talking to you from the Legal Service- they
           were people you trusted weren't they? (2.3) Albert?

16. Albert: °Mm°.

17. DC2:   Albert were they people you trusted?

18. Albert: (0.7) Yes.

19. DC2:   That's right isn't it? (2.3) they were people who cared about you?

20. Albert: (1.1) Yeh.

21. DC2:   (3.2) And you told them <u>lies</u> to their faces didn't you? (3.7) didn't you
           Albert? (3.7) didn't you Albert? (2.2) you lied in their face didn't you?
           (3.6) Albert <u>answer</u> my question please=

22. Albert: =I don't wanna.

After agreeing with DC2's assertions with his answers in Turns 2 and 4, Albert
responds to the third accusation about his disdain for truth by attempting to
invoke the self-incrimination right to refuse to answer (Turns 6 and 8). DC2 ignores this attempt, persisting with the allegation that Albert had *lied* in his report
to ALS about the way in which the boys had been persuaded to get in the police
cars (following a similar line of questioning from DC1, in Extract 58 above).
This then leads to assertions that Albert *told lies* to the people he *trusted* ...

from the *legal service*. Again, Albert attempts to invoke the self-incrimination right to refuse to answer (Turn 22), which as we have seen in Section 1.2 of Chapter 5, and Extract 57 above, is quite a complicated right to understand. The last two turns in Extract 60 above, are the first two turns in Extract 6 in Chapter 4, where we saw DC2's interpretation of Albert's 6.5 seconds silence in answer to a question as indicating an answer of *no*. In the discussion in Chapter 4, we saw that confusion over just what was being questioned may also have been an important factor in this silence, especially given Aboriginal uses of silence in answer to questions.

In terms of the construction of Albert's identity, which is the main theme of this chapter, the magistrate's Turn 8 in Extract 6 is of particular interest. In answer to Albert's attempt to invoke the self-incrimination privilege, the magistrate tells him *you have to answer this question okay? you can't get out of this one*. The second part of this directive from the magistrate arguably presupposes an evasive and/or uncooperative witness, ignoring the difficulty which any 13-year-old would have in knowing when they can use this complicated legal right.

The following several questions, in Extract 61 below, pursue DC2's theme about Albert's disdain for *the truth*, and take up the *why did you lie* refrain, presumably still about the inconsistency in Albert's initial reports about being *grabbed* by the police:

Extract 61.   DC2 to Albert, Day 2, p144

1. DC2:	Well why did you lie to them? (1.8) why did you just sit there and lie °Albert°? why did you do that? (7.3) can you tell us why?
2. Albert:	(1.7) Nuh.
3. DC2:	(2.8) I think I might know (2.1) sometimes (1.0) sometimes we do things (2.9) that later we (0.7) wish we hadn't don't we? you ever done anything like that? (1.8) mm? done something later on you wished you hadn't? (2.1) mm? (2.7) is that right Albert? that ever happened to you? (2.6) Albert please listen to me.
4. Albert:	I never heard.
5. DC2:	Pardon?
6. Albert:	Can you say it again?
7. DC2:	(1.3) Surely you have occasionally done something that you've regretted doing- has that happened?
8. Albert:	I don't know (what that) means.
9. DC2:	All right you don't know what I mean when I use the word regret?- you don't know what that means?
10. Albert:	Nuh.

11. DC2:	Ok- ever done anything and later on wished you hadn't? do you know what that means? (2.0) eh?
12. Albert:	Nuh.
13. DC2:	You don't know what that means? (2.2-) y you telling me the truth are you?- you don't <u>know</u> what I <u>mean</u> when I <u>say</u> have you ever done something and later wished you hadn't?- y you don't know what I mean?=
14. Albert:	=Nuh.
15. DC2:	I see (4.7) Albert have you ever- acted in a way- which is less <u>brave</u> than you wished you'd been? (9.7) mm? (1.6) Albert? (7.5) °your worship I wonder if we might have a little break°.
16. M:	We (might) have a little break for ten minutes.

Much of this extract comprises DC2's attempts to present an image of Albert as someone who did something he later *regretted* – presumably reporting that he had been abducted by the police. Most of Albert's answers to these questions seem to indicate that he is unable to follow the questions, and DC2 asks for a short adjournment.

Following the adjournment, DC2 turns to the ultimate issue, with a series of questions culminating in a pseudo-declarative summary, seen in Extract 62 below, which is mostly consistent with Albert's evidence-in-chief, and appears to be agreed to by Albert. However, as discussed in Section 2.2.3 of Chapter 5, none of the boys has ever used the verb *hop* in their evidence, to report what the police told them to do. The directive they have consistently reported is *jump in the car*.

Extract 62.   DC2 to Albert, Day 2, p145

1. DC2:	So- <u>all</u> you can remember is this is it- some police officer said- hop in the back of the police cars- you did- the car went out to Pinkenba and you can't remember any conversation on the way?=
2. Albert:	=Nuh.
3. DC2:	(0.8) That right?
4. Albert:	Yes.

DC2 then goes back, yet again, to the inconsistency with Albert's earlier report on the topic of being *grabbed* by the police, securing Albert's apparent agreement to the suggestions that he *told that lie . . . to make things look worse for the police* (p145), which we have seen was also a theme from DC1's cross-examination (in Extract 4 in Chapter 4).

DC2 then moves to questions about Albert's *criminal record*, asserting that Albert *had plenty of contact with the police* [before the Pinkenba event], and asking, as he had with David, whether he had *ever seen one of those cards that the legal service used to distribute* (presumably about what to do when arrested) (p146). Albert's answers include *Can't remember, Can you say (that) again?* and *What cards?* While these answers might indicate exhaustion and/or confusion, there is one answer that unmistakably indicates resistance, and is Albert's longest cross-examination answer, given in Extract 63:

Extract 63.   DC2 to Albert, Day 2, p146

1. DC2:	Look Albert- I've got a criminal history of yours here and it tells me this- it tells me that in April of nineteen ninety one you went to court on a charge of unlawfully take shop goods away (1.4) (right) (3.0) Albert?
2. Albert:	You don't have to know my things what I do.

It is hard to know what the question is here, as DC2's turn consists of two asserted propositions, followed by Albert's name in rising intonation. But Albert's spirited and defiant answer in Turn 2 is clear: *You don't have to know my things what I do.* DC2 replies *Oh well- I'm sorry but I do,* and proceeds to ask more about Albert's *criminal record.* This series of questions establishes Albert as a *criminal,* who had *been represented by* ALS *when* he'd *gone to court,* and who repaid this *bunch of very dedicated, very committed people* who are *very concerned about* him by *telling them lies about what had happened with the police* (p147). In this series of questions we see some further evidence of Albert's resistance, with his answer *You heard* to one of the many times that DC2 responds to him with *Pardon?*

10.   Who *tells lies*?

Thus, Albert's identity as a deliberate liar is clearly asserted by DC1. There is, however, no room for the consideration of such factors, discussed in Section 4 of Chapter 6, as likely teenage exaggeration in the initial telling of the story to the ALS, which was when Albert reportedly had said that the police had *grabbed* him and his two friends. Neither is there any consideration of the colloquial use of *grab* which does not have to imply physical contact. Further, DC2 extends the theme of Albert as a liar, asserting that the whole story was *a lie,* as we see in Extract 64:

Extract 64. DC2 to Albert, Day 2, p147–148

1. DC2:	And you knew it was all a lie (3.4) didn't you Albert? (3.3) didn't you?
2. Albert:	I <u>told</u> you I said yes.
3. DC2:	The legal service here they were just- just acting on what you said (2.1) °y know° saying to the world that you that you kids had been forcibly abducted- and you <u>knew</u>- you <u>knew</u> that was untrue (3.8) wasn't fair to anybody was it Albert? (1.4) mm? (2.4) Albert?- just wasn't fair was it? (4.9) Albert please answer (8.6) see what happened was the police officers said hop in the car and you did didn't you?- that's what happened isn't it?
4. Albert:	(1.5) Yes.

Under pressure of the repeated questioning in Turn 1, Albert says with exasperation and defiance *I told you I said yes* (Turn 2). DC2's final questions to Albert summarise the central issue, and Albert says *Ye#* to three crucial pseudo-declaratives, as we see in Extract 65:

Extract 65. DC2 to Albert, Day 2, p148

1. DC2:	You knew perfectly well (1.1) what your rights were with the police didn't you David- Albert I'm sorry- you knew perfectly well didn't you? (4.0) <u>A</u>lbert?
2. Albert:	Yes.
3. DC2:	(4.4) You see (1.9) <u>all</u> that was said (2.0) was hop in the car (2.4) you knew you didn't have to (1.8) but you did (1.3) hop in the car- didn't you?
4. Albert:	(1.4) Yeh.
5. DC2:	(2.7) And <u>that's why</u> you <u>told</u> the people from the legal service and other people- that you'd been <u>dragged</u> and <u>man</u>handled into the car (2.9) isn't it? (4.4) you didn't want to tell the simple truth (1.5) that you'd just gone along and got in- knowing you didn't have to? (2.5) that's what happened isn't it Albert? °mm°? (2.3) mm?
6. Albert:	(0.7) Yeh.

These *Yes* and *Yeh* answers in Turns 2, 4 and 6 of Extract 65 are the 19th, 20th and 21st answers of *Ye#* in a string of 22 such consecutive answers. Albert is clearly defeated and compliant, so it is easy for DC2 to elicit these answers, in a situation which is likely to produce gratuitous concurrence. It is impossible to know whether Albert actually agrees with the propositions being questioned, but it is significant that just a few turns later, Albert answers three questions with a stance of defiance and impatience, and then accuses DC2 of *tell*ing *lies*, as we see in extract 66 below. This extract starts with DC2 asking Albert how many police were there *when this was said to* them *about hopping in the police car*:

Extract 66.   DC2 to Albert, Day 2, p148

1. DC2:	How many?
2. Albert:	(1.9) <u>Told</u> you there were six of them.
3. DC2:	(1.0) A all six standing around were they?
4. Albert:	Yes.
5. DC2:	Or were some in the police cars already?
6. Albert:	Nuh (0.6) (I'm) not [silly.
7. DC2:	[Eh?- Pardon?
8. Albert:	(1.0) They was all standing around.
9. DC2:	All standing around? (2.2) tell us exactly where then please °(Albert)°?- at the cars- were they?- a couple at each car or what?
10. Albert:	A<small>ROUND</small> us.
11. DC2:	Around where around you?
12. Albert:	Oh °where do you think°?
13. DC2:	Mm? (2.8) the only thing that was <u>said</u> was this one thing was it? (1.5) (by) one police officer- hop in the car (0.8) mm? (1.5) that's the only thing you can remember being said (1.2) right? (1.8) is that right Albert? (2.7) Albert?
14. Albert:	°Nuh you tell lies°.

In his construction of Albert as someone who has no consistent or reliable account of the Pinkenba event, DC2 goes too far for Albert. His answers in Turns 2, 6, 10 and 12 reveal defiance and impatience with the questioner, something which we have glimpsed on a few earlier occasions (in Extracts 59 and 63). But it is Albert's answer in Turn 14 which is most defiant, accusing DC2 *°you tell lies°*. With this answer, we have the first direct attempt by one of the witnesses to engage in his own counter identity work. While there is no detail of which of DC2's propositions Albert sees as *lies*, this bold and substantive accusation may well relate to DC2's distortion of what had happened when the police told the boys to get in the car. However, Albert's *°you tell lies°* is uttered quietly, and it is not clear if DC2 hears it. He does not respond to it.

Unlike DC1, DC2 does not express overt commands or threats. He has the damaging admissions he needs, and his cross-examination ends with the final questions in Extract 67 below, which immediately follow Extract 66 above:

Extract 67.   DC2 to Albert, Day 2, p148–149

1. DC2:   So you've told us that you didn't say anything to the police while you were in the car on the way to Pinkenba- that right? (2.0) is that right Albert? (3.5) Albert?

2. Albert: Can you say it again?

3. DC2:   Didn't say anything when you were in the police car? (1.7) hh? (2.2) Albert?

4. Albert: Yeh.

5. DC2:   (11.9) Didn't ask- to stop to be let out- did you? (0.8) never said anything like that did you Albert?

6. Albert: (0.7) Nuh.

7. DC2:   No.

11.   Conclusion

When Albert leaves the witness stand after just over 2 hours of cross-examination, his identity has been created as a _BIG_ *criminal*, who *tells lies*. There have been some instances of DC1 treating him as a naughty schoolboy, for example calling him *lad*, and ordering him *Stop chewing your nails*. But this is much less prevalent than in the cross-examination of David, the youngest witness. Indeed, there have been several examples of DC1 treating 13-year old Albert as an adult, or _BIG_ *criminal*, including the term of address *Mr Carter*, and threatening him with *contempt of court*. While DC2's construction of David includes the portrayal of him as easily confused and manipulated, both DCs have presented Albert as someone with an agenda of *making things look bad for the police*, for example by *telling lies* and *swearing*.

As indicated on Table 4 which summarises Albert's cross-examination, his *criminal record* has been a major focus of DC1's questioning (as it was with David), and also of DC2's questioning (in contrast to David's questioning by DC2). The *why did you lie* refrain has been important in Albert's questioning, as it has been with David. But with this older witness, much has been made of the inconsistency between aspects of his earlier reporting of the Pinkenba event and his answers to cross-examination questions. In this, entextualisation has been a key linguistic mechanism. While the prosecutor has pointed out that *inconsistent answers don't necessarily imply lies*, and both DCs have used clever lexical manipulation with the word *grab*, there has been no opportunity for Albert to explain his answers. But, unlike the first and youngest witness, Albert has made several attempts to resist the questioning, including a few shouted replies, such

Table 4.   Summary of Albert's cross-examination

DC1's questioning:	98 minutes, 416 answers, 31 transcript pages
DC2's questioning:	25 minutes, 128 answers, 8 transcript pages
answers of *yes*, *yeh*, or *mm*:	to DC1: 142 = 34% of his answers to DC1 to DC2: 55 = 43% of his answers to DC2
answers of *no* or *nuh*:	to DC1: 108 = 26% of his answers to DC1 to DC2: 25 = 20% of his answers to DC2
answers of *I don't know* or *I dunno*:	to DC1: 25 = 6% of his answers to DC1 to DC2: 4 = 3% of his answers to DC2
number of adjournments:	3
longest answer (10 words):	*You don't have to know my things what I do.* (to DC2, p146)

Main topic of questions:

DC1

p110–112	Albert's *criminal record*
p113	Albert *telling lies*
p114–116	Albert's *criminal record*
p117–119	Albert's four-letter word to investigator
p120–127	Albert's *criminal record*
p128–129	Albert's speech style
p129–130	Albert's *criminal record*; Albert's speech volume
p131–133	Albert's *criminal record*
p133–140	Pinkenba event and Albert's reports of it

DC2

p141	Albert's speech volume
p142 on	Albert's reports of Pinkenba event
p143–145	Albert's *lies* about Pinkenba event
p146–147	Albert's *criminal record*
p147–148	Albert's reports and *lies* about Pinkenba event

as *TOLD YOU I DON'T KNOW WHAT YOU MEAN*, and the defiant replies *I told you I said no* and *You don't have to know my things what I do*. Most significant is his single and bold attempt at constructing the identity of his questioner, saying to DC2 °*you tell lies*°. We will see in Section 1 of Chapter 10, that his defiance is used to support the defence theory that he would not have gone unwillingly with police.

As with Chapter 7 above, and Chapter 9 below, the detailed examination in this chapter of the struggle between the DCs and Albert over his identity has revealed some of the workings of neocolonialism. Albert's evidence in this case has come about as a result of Aboriginal resistance to an act of over-policing, namely the police removal of him and his two friends from the Valley that night. The refusal by the three boys and their families, as well as the Aboriginal Legal Service, to accept such police control has been seen in Chapter 3 to be part of an ongoing struggle between the police and the Aboriginal community. But this police control is part of a wider societal structure of neocolonialism, which includes moral panic about Aboriginal people as a threat to public safety, and legislation and police practices which criminalise them. Thus the intricate presentation of Albert as a lying *criminal* who is a threat to public safety is an important component in the actions which comprise the workings of inequality. We now turn, in Chapter 9, to the analysis of the way in which the courtroom struggle over this neocolonial inequality is enacted in the cross-examination of the oldest witness.

Chapter 9
Not a person to be overborne: Barry

1. A *criminal* but *not a dog*

DC1's opening questions to Barry present him as a *criminal*, while at the same time (possibly unintentionally) asking questions that are unclear to the witness. Compared to the opening attacks on David (*Why did you break into someone's home in 1993?*), and Albert (*Do you want to be here?*), DC1 begins more subtly, as we see in Extract 68 below, which starts with DC1's first question. (The first 6 turns of this were given as Extract 10 in Chapter 5 in the discussion of the use of apparently unfamiliar words in cross-examination questions.)

Extract 68. DC1 to Barry, Day 2, p157

1. DC1:	Where are you residing now Mr Coley?
2. Barry:	(6.0) Could you say that again please?
3. DC1:	Where are you residing now Mr Coley?
4. Barry:	What does residing mean?
5. DC1:	Where are you living now Mr Coley?
6. Barry:	At my Aunty Helen's.
7. DC1:	At?
8. Barry:	My Aunty Helen.
9. DC1:	Your Aunty Helen's (1.5) where's that?
10. Barry:	(1.7) Kedron.
11. DC1:	And were you there- did you sleep there last night?
12. Barry:	(2.8) No.
13. DC1:	I can't hear you- perhaps if you took your chewing gum out it might- be easier to hear you- would you mind doing that?- put it in your pocket (inaudible)- thank you (1.8) did you sleep at your Aunty Helen's last night?
14. Barry:	No.
15. DC1:	(2.4) Where did you sleep last night?
16. Barry:	(5.3) At Wilson.
17. DC1:	Eh?
18. Barry:	At Wilson.

19. DC1:	At Wilson nd where did you sleep the night before?
20. Barry:	(5.4) At the bus stop.

21. DC1:	And where did you spend Christmas?
22. Barry:	(1.9) In Wilson.

23. DC1:	Where are you living now Mr- Coley?
24. Barry:	(2.6) At my Aunty Helen's.

25. DC1:	Beg your pardon?
26. Barry:	At my Aunty Helen's.

27. DC1:	Aren't you- does your Aunty Helen have a community corrections officer at her place?
28. Barry:	(4.0) I don't know.

29. DC1:	See this man sitting beside you here?
30. Barry:	Yeh.

31. DC1:	D'you know him?
32. Barry:	Nuh.

33. DC1:	Aren't you in custody right now?
34. Barry:	Yeh.

35. DC1:	Haven't you been in custody since November last year?
36. Barry:	Yeh.

37. DC1:	And have you been living at Wilson since November last year?
38. Barry:	Yeh.

39. DC1:	Does your Aunty Helen live there also?
40. Barry:	Nuh.

41. DC1:	(2.3) So you're living at Wilson now that's the- truthful answer isn't that so?
42. Barry:	Yeh.

43. DC1:	(1.9) And you're living there- because you were charged among other things with robbery in company with violence isn't that so?
44. Barry:	(0.8) Yeh.

As discussed in Section 3 of Chapter 1, it is common for Aboriginal people to move between various relatives. In my interviews with these witnesses in June 1994, it was clear that this residential pattern was a part of their lives. Thus it would not be unexpected to use the address of one of these relatives as a current address. Barry may have thought this was involved in the meaning of *residing*. So, this may have been the sense in which Barry answered that he was *living now* with his Aunty Helen (Turns 6 and 24). DC1 has presumably chosen to open his cross-examination of Barry by highlighting that he is currently *in custody*, for a serious offence *robbery in company with violence . . . among other things*. It is impossible to know whether DC1 is also attempting with these introductory questions to portray Barry as lying (about the fact that he is currently *residing* in a juvenile detention centre, known as 'Wilston', referred to by both Barry and DC1 as *Wilson*). Whatever DC1's intentions with this opening questioning strategy, it is clear from the outset that Barry's seemingly straightforward answers can cause him trouble.

In DC1's directive about Barry's *chewing gum* (Turn 13), we see an interesting contrast to similar directives to Albert. In Chapter 8, we saw the bald directives *Take your fingers out of your mouth will you* (in Extract 53) and *Stop chewing your fingernails* (in Section 8, uttered in the same hour as the polite request to Barry about his *chewing gum*). It is impossible to know if the more polite request in Turn 13 of Extract 68 is part of DC1's approach of treating Barry as an adult, consistent with the theme that he is an adult *criminal*. It is also possible that it is considered strategically advisable to address this witness with more respect than he has done with the previous two witnesses. For example, DC1 may be concerned that the level of abuse which he has directed at the younger two witnesses may backfire, and that this oldest witness may have sufficient skills in the witness box to enlist the magistrate's help in constraining DC1's aggressive style. However, we will see that although Barry is more active in resistance than the two younger witnesses, DC1's agression is not challenged or restrained in any way by the magistrate.

DC1 continues with questions about the incident which had led to this charge of *robbery in company with violence*. Unlike many of the answers of the first two witnesses, Barry agrees in a straightforward manner with the questions about this crime, as we see in Extract 69:

Extract 69.   DC1 to Barry, Day 2, p158

1. DC1:   Did you steal her purse yourself?
2. Barry: (3.9)[(Yeh).

3. DC1:   [Did you yourself steal her purse?
4. Barry: Yeh.

5. DC1:   (1.7) She had a young friend with her didn't she?
6. Barry: (1.9) Yeh.

7. DC1:   And of course you didn't run away once you did this did you?
8. Barry: (1.8) Nuh.

9. DC1:   You just walked <u>bra</u>zenly on didn't you?
10. Barry: (0.9) Yeh.

While the younger two witnesses have denied many accusations relating to their *criminal record*, or answered *I don't know*, Barry's apparent agreement to the questions in Extract 69 may be due to many possible reasons. It is possible that he could be more honest, and/or more experienced in interviews and courtroom cross-examination. Or he may be more susceptible to gratuitous concurrence, a less likely explanation if he is more experienced in courtroom talk. On the other hand, we will see throughout his cross-examination that Barry does not seem to contest the DCs' construction of him as a *criminal*. By the age of 15, many Aboriginal young people have a *criminal record*, and Barry's experience with the criminal justice system may mean that he does not care about what aspects of his past are brought up. Thus, it is interesting to notice the questions to which Barry does not agree, some of which are in Extract 70:

Extract 70.   DC1 to Barry, Day 2, p159

1. DC1:   And then you just grabbed the bag as you went past- is that so?
2. Barry: (0.9) °Yeh°.

3. DC1:   And (2.0) the girl kept saying give me back my bag (1.8) correct?
4. Barry: (1.0) Yeh.

5. DC1:   And you just walked away (1.4) right? (1.4) laughing at her were you?
6. Barry: (1.3) Nuh.

7. DC1:   Laughing at these- the plight of these two young women- was this about
            two thirty in the morning?
8. Barry: (1.0) Yeh.

9. DC1:   (1.2) And you thought it was a great joke didn't you?
10. Barry: (1.2) Nuh.

11. DC1:   Well you were laughing about it weren't you?
12. Barry: Nuh.

13. DC1:   Beg your pardon?
14. Barry: Nuh.

15. DC1:   Didn't you tell me just before you were laughing?
16. Barry: Nuh.

17. DC1:   Beg yours?
18. Barry: (1.0) Nuh.

19. DC1:   You weren't laughing? (2.1) well you didn't try to escape did you?
20. Barry: °Nuh°.

21. DC1:   Because you <u>knew</u> that if those girls had- tried to stop you physically-
            you'd have bashed them up wouldn't you?
22. Barry: (1.4) Nuh.

23. DC1:   Course you would have wouldn't you Coley?
24. Barry: Nuh.

25. DC1:   What would you have done then Mr Coley?
26. Barry: (1.6) Nothing.

While Barry's *criminal record* makes it easy for DC1 to present him to the court as a *criminal*, DC1 fills out this identity, adding assertions that present an image of Barry *laughing* at his victims, similar to the pseudo-declarative we saw to Albert in Turn 1 of Extract 55. Although Barry denies this pseudo-declarative in Turn 6, as Albert had, DC1 uses it as an asserted presupposition in Turn 7, before asking a pseudo-declarative question about the time of the *robbery*. Although Barry never agrees to the assertion that he was *laughing* about the *robbery*, DC1 persists with it, saying it 3 more times (in Turns 9, 11 and 15). Barry also rejects the portrayal of him as a thief who would assault his victims (in Turns 21 and 23). In the last two questions of this extract, DC1 uses two different terms of address: while *Mr Coley* signifies that this witness is no child, *Coley* is a term of address formerly used by teachers to schoolboys.

As DC1's momentum builds, so does Barry's resistance. Within 10 minutes of the start of his cross-examination, Barry counters DC1 with his own identity counter-construction, while at the same time rebuking DC1 with his own metapragmatic directive, the first to be used by a witness in this hearing, as we see in Extract 71:

Extract 71. DC1 to Barry, Day 2, p160

1. DC1:   Oh look look (1.8) can you under<u>STAND THE DISTINCTION BETWEEN A
           GUTTURAL YES AND GUTTURAL NO? WILL YOU PLEASE ANSWER SO WE
           CAN UNDER<u>STAND</u> YOU.
2. Barry: (0.9) No (1.9) No need to <u>yell</u> at me I'm not a <u>dog</u>.

3. DC1:   (0.6) I'm sorry?
4. Barry: No need to yell at me I'm not a dog.

5. DC1:   Oh I wouldn't add that insult.
6. Barry: (1.5) Yeh (well no need bust) yourself at me.

7. DC1:	I wouldn't add that insult (3.4) well now you will speak up to me will you in the same tone? (1.5) you'll keep your voice up please.
8. Barry:	°Yeh°=
9. DC1:	=How many uh break and enters have you done Mr Coley?
10. Barry:	(2.5) (I) don't want to answer that question.
11. DC1:	Why is that? (2.4) why won't you answer it? (3.9) why won't you answer it?
12. Barry:	Because- I don't want to.

After only 10 minutes of cross-examination, DC1's prosodics are projecting an aggressive stance, shouting loudly in Turn 1. Barry is not contesting DC1's construction of him as a *criminal*, but he explicitly rejects what he interprets as the construction of him as a *dog* (Turn 2). It is possible that DC1's phonetically inaccurate labelling of Barry's *yes* and *no* answers being *guttural* has been analysed by Barry as *gutter-al*, thus suggesting a *dog* in the *gutter*. Barry's attempt to assert some control over his questioning is also seen in his answer to the question in Turn 9. While this question should have triggered the *warning* about self-incrimination from the magistrate, it seems that he has accepted the presentation of Barry as an adult, as he does not give the *warning*. After a 2.5 second pause, Barry appears to invoke this right in his answer (Turn 10).

2.   *Normal human beings don't act without a reason*

DC1 then goes on to ask Barry about his *criminal record*, with questions about the number of *break and enter* offences for which he has *been before the court*. Barry has no problem in answering that the number is *nine*, an answer which appears to tally with the version of his record from which DC1 is reading, although DC1 initially falsely accuses him of *seventeen* such offences, due to his difficulty in reading the record. On this matter, contrary to DC1's attempt to expose him as *lying*, Barry appears to be truthful. DC1 accepts the correction with the sarcastically asserted proposition that *nine break and enter* offences is *not very many at all*, and then switches to questions about Barry's motivations for these crimes, as we see in Extract 72:

Extract 72.   DC1 to Barry, Day 2, p161

1. DC1:	Well it's not very many at all it's only nine- times that you broke and entered dwelling houses (2.4) or eight- a dwelling house and one maybe a dwelling house is that correct?
2. Barry:	(1.0) Yeh.

3. DC1:	Why did you do that?
4. Barry:	(6.5) I dunno.

5. DC1:	Beg your pardon?
6. Barry:	I dunno.

7. DC1:	Must be a reason (2.7) what's the reason Mr Coley? (4.0) well Mr Coley?
8. Barry:	No reason.

9. DC1:	Yes there has to be a reason (1.0) normal human beings don't act without a reason what was your reason?
10. Barry:	(6.7) Wanted money.

11. DC1:	Beg your pardon?
12. Barry:	Wanted money.

13. DC1:	Wanted money (0.7) well- do you get any government hand-out or did you at the time?
14. Barry:	Nuh.

15. DC1:	(2.2) Did you think of trying to get a job or anything like that?
16. Barry:	(1.2) Nuh.

17. DC1:	You wanted money eh so you broke into people's houses (1.5) is that what happened?
18. Barry:	(2.1) Yes.

This exchange provides DC1 with the opportunity of showing that Barry is not a *normal human being*, suggesting that his livelihood amounts to a choice between a *government handout* and *breaking into people's houses*, connecting to widespread general complaints about Aboriginal people (Augoustinos et al. 1999: 367–368; Jakubowicz et al. 1994: 38–39). Section 3.2 of Chapter 6 has discussed possible cultural difficulties in expecting Aboriginal people to be able to give reasons for their actions. While Barry's answers in Turns 14, 16 and 18 may be genuine answers of agreement, the questions which follow immediately (in Extract 73 below) show a pattern which is quite likely to involve gratuitous concurrence, as discussed in Section 1 of Chapter 4. Extract 73 below follows immediately from Extract 72 above:

Extract 73.   DC1 to Barry, Day 2, p161

1. DC1:	Did it concern you that the houses might belong to elderly people with virtually no money?
2. Barry:	(0.7) [Yeh.

3. DC1:	[Did that worry you?

4. Barry:	(1.3) Nuh.
5. DC1:	(1.8) Wouldn't have mattered two hoots would it- if they'd been poor old pensioners down on their uh- down to their last few dollars wouldn't have worried you would it? (2.2) would it? (2.1) would it Coley?
6. Barry:	°No°.
7. DC1:	Eh? (1.3) would it? (2.7) ANSWER Coley(1.8) would it?
8. Barry:	(3.0) No.
9. DC1:	(2.1) What gives you the right to break the law like this Mr Coley? (3.1) Can you advance any reason that you might have for any legitimate (1.6) claim or grouch or anything like that as to why you couldn't break into people's houses?
10. Barry:	(2.9) No.

In his first two answers here we see Barry continuing with straightforward *Yeh* and *Nuh* answers. It is not clear if he is indeed changing his mind, as the two answers are contradictory. But the question form in Turns 5 and 7, which typifies much of DC1's questioning of the two younger witnesses (comprising repeated tag questions and shouting), suggests a likelihood that the answer will be gratuitous concurrence. Having gained Barry's apparent agreement that it *wouldn't have mattered two hoots* to him, if the victims of his *break and enters* had been *poor old pensioners down ... to their last few dollars*, DC1 again asks for a reason (in Turn 9). This turn provides DC1 with the chance to fill out the identity of Barry as a danger to society. DC1 then goes on to project Barry's adult identity as a serious *criminal*, as we see in Extract 74:

Extract 74.   DC1 to Barry, Day 2, p161

1. DC1:	What are you going to do when you grow up- go on to bigger and better criminal activity?
2. Barry:	(1.1) Nuh.
3. DC1:	Is that your intention?
4. Barry:	(1.0) Nuh.
5. DC1:	Are you going to turn over a new leaf?
6. Barry:	Yeh.
7. DC1:	You're going to become a good little Mr Coley are you?
8. Barry:	°Yeh°.
9. DC1:	Be respectful to people and their property are you?
10. Barry:	Yeh.

11. DC1:   (0.8) I see- when did you decide to do this? (4.5) When did you decide
             you were going to do this?

12. Barry: When I get out.

13. DC1:   When you get out you're going to go straight are you?

14. Barry: Yeh.

15. DC1:   I see- well what were you- what used you do around town the times when
             you were with these other two- this er Carter and uh uh [Pender?

16. Barry: [Just walk
             around.

Barry's answers, which project his adult identity as that of a law abiding citizen, are ridiculed by DC1 with the sarcastic juxtaposition of *bigger and better
criminal activity* (in Turn 1) with *good little Mr Coley* (in Turn 7). DC1 then
switches to fill in the picture of Barry and the *other two* in town, habitually
looking for potential *criminal activity* (with the questions discussed as Extract
16 in Chapter 5 which involve DC1's lexical perversion, substituting Barry's
walking around with *prowling around*, consistent with his portrayal of Barry
as a *criminal*). Barry cooperates with this construction of his *criminal* identity,
which is so successful, that even the magistrate forgets that he is not on trial in
this hearing, as we see in Extract 75, which overlaps with Extract 16 in Chapter 5
(Turn 21 of Extract 16 is Turn 1 of Extract 75).

Extract 75.   DC1 to Barry, Day 2, p162

1. DC1:   You were <u>walk</u>ing around <u>look</u>ing to see if you could get into mischief
             isn't that so?

2. Barry: °No°=

3. DC1:   =Beg your pardon?

4. Barry: No.

5. DC1:   See if there was anything you could STEAL- that was your WHOLE- POINT
             WASN'T IT? (3.1) well?=

6. Barry: =Yeh.

7. DC1:   (3.6) And looking to see what you could <u>dam</u>age- isn't that so?

8. Barry: (2.9) °Yeh°.

9. DC1:   And you threw- we know you threw some rocks at street lights didn't
             you?=

10. M: =Yes I warn the defendant at this stage that he is not required to give any
             evidence which might tend to incriminate him in relation to the commis-
             sion of a criminal offence- do you understand that?

11. Barry: (0.6) °Yeh°.

DC1's questions here, overlapping and then following from those cited in Extract 16 appear to refer to the habitual activities of the boys, given that there is no specific time reference. Barry starts (Turn 2) by rejecting DC1's pseudo-declarative suggesting that he was looking for delinquent activity. His agreement to the more specific suggestion in Turn 5 of intended theft may be an answer of gratuitous concurrence, coming as it does after the insistent prompt *well*. Turn 10 in Extract 75 is the first time that the magistrate has delivered the self-incrimination *warning* to Barry, and he does not even realise that he has addressed him with the (third person) address term *the defendant* instead of *the witness* (used twice in addressing David on Day 1, as we saw in Section 1 of Chapter 7). Barry then says *I don't want to answer* in reply to several questions. This leads DC1 to explain that invoking the right is in effect an admission of guilt, without giving the particular details of the illegal act. His explanation is that *you can only refuse to answer if the answer might incriminate you in a criminal offence*, and *If you're innocent of any criminal offence you can't claim privilege- that's what it means- thus- if you in fact had never ... done any damage or never stolen anything you couldn't claim privilege* (p163).

This leads to DC1's question discussed in Chapter 5 (as Extract 17): *What sort of things did you steal- when you were wan- prowling around the streets?* When Barry replies with *just purses*, DC1 wants to know *how many*, as we see in Extract 76:

Extract 76.   DC1 to Barry, Day 2, p163

1. DC1:   How many times did you do that- how many did you steal?
2. Barry: (1.5) I dunno.

3. DC1:   (0.9) Heaps?
4. Barry: I don't count how much purses I steal.

5. DC1:   Eh?
6. Barry: I don't <u>count</u> how much purses I steal.

7. DC1:   Well maybe you can't <u>count</u> that high how many did you steal?
8. Barry: (0.8) I dunno.

9. DC1:   Lots?
10. Barry: Nuh.

In answer to the question about how many purses he has stolen, Barry answers *I dunno*, the expression which typifies answers found to such questions with David and Albert. But under pressure from DC1 in Turns 1 and 3, Barry's reply is agentive and has a confident stance: *I don't <u>count</u> how much purses*

I steal (Turn 6). In order to suppress this agentive Barry, DC1 counters with the accusation of the seriousness of his stealing combined with his lack of intelligence, resulting in *maybe you can't <u>count</u> that high* (Turn 7). As DC1 then returns to a question about Barry's *criminal* habits, incorporating his identity as one of a *group of louts* (see Section 2.2.1 of Chapter 5), the prosecutor intervenes to ask that Barry have the opportunity to talk to ALS about his self-incrimination right. This results in the end of day adjournment.

3.   You believed *you could do whatever you wanted*

The second day of Barry's cross-examination continues with questioning about his *criminal record*, presupposing the phrase *totally brazen* in a question about his purse theft (p168). DC1 also suggests that Barry feels a sense of immunity from the law, a theme which we saw in his cross-examination of David in Section 2 of Chapter 7. Thus, he suggests that Barry believed that he *could do whatever he wanted and he wouldn't be in strife* (p169). Barry denies both of these suggestions. DC1 then continues with general questions about Barry's knowledge of his rights and the *little card*, presumably the ALS card reminding people of their rights when approached by police officers, and when arrested (see also Section 9 of Chapter 8). It is significant that the particular rights of which Barry was allegedly knowledgeable, as well as the details on the *little card*, are never explicitly discussed, although Barry agrees that he had seen the *little card*.

DC1 then turns for the first time with Barry, to the central issue of the case, with the pressured questions which have been presented in Extract 5 in Chapter 4. This crucial part of Barry's cross-examination, it has been argued there, relies on gratuitous concurrence to gain Barry's apparent agreement to the defence central claim that Barry *knew when he spoke to these six police in the Valley that* he *didn't have to go anywhere with them if* he *didn't want to* (p170).

DC1 then tries to establish that there was no *threat* from the police officers, and that Barry went willingly with them. Interestingly, the mention of *threat* by the police leads Barry to mention a point raised by each of the three boys at different times, namely that when they were at Pinkenba, the police *threatened to chop off* the boys' *fingers* (as we see in Extract 77 below). Although the boys all talked about this threat in investigative interviews before the hearing, and in their examination-in-chief, it is not a part of the charge against the police officers, who are charged only with deprivation of liberty.

Extract 77.   DC1 to Barry, Day 3, p170–171

1. DC1:	Yes (5.1) and the reason is- you see Mr Coley you don't suggest any threats made by any of these police do you? (2.4) do you?
2. Barry:	(1.2) Beg your pardon.
3. DC1:	You don't suggest that any of these police threatened you do you?
4. Barry:	(0.8) Yes they did threaten (me).
5. DC1:	Well tell me when- <u>when</u> Mr Coley?
6. Barry:	They threatened to chop our fingers off [out
7. DC1:	[Chop your fingers off- out at Pinkenba?
8. Barry:	Yeh.
9. DC1:	°I see°- who threatened that Mr Coley?
10. Barry:	(2.6) A couple of them.
11. DC1:	°I see°- you wouldn't know who?
12. Barry:	Nuh.
13. DC1:	°Mm° (2.4) All right- well Mr Coley you certainly knew this (0.7) that morning when you were in the Valley you knew these things I'd suggest to you (1.3) that you didn't have to talk to police correct?
14. Barry:	(0.8) Yeh.
15. DC1:	(0.8) That you didn't have to go anywhere with police if you didn't want to correct?
16. Barry:	(0.8) Nuh not unless I was charged.
17. DC1:	Beg your pardon?
18. Barry:	If I was charged I would have went with them=
19. DC1:	=Yes but you knew you didn't have to go with them unless you were- arrested isn't that so?
20. Barry:	Yeh.
21. DC1:	(2.0) You knew uh (2.8) that you- uh could have de<u>man</u>ded- legal advice at that very time (2.7) you knew you could've said to the police I want someone from the Aboriginal Service here didn't- couldn't you?
22. Barry:	(2.6) Forgot all about it.
23. DC1:	But you <u>knew</u> that you- I mean you ((laughs)) maybe weren't interested but you knew you could do that didn't you? (1.6) didn't you?
24. Barry:	(1.4) Wasn't thinking about it.

In this extract, we see Barry's apparent agreement to propositions that he knew that he didn't have to *talk to police* (Turn 14) or *go with them* (Turn 16). However, these apparent agreements come only after pressured questioning, including the tag *correct* in Turns 13 and 15. This suggests the possibility that these answers are not genuine agreement, but answers of gratuitous concurrence. The only statements that occur as Barry's own propositions, rather than agreements to propositions put by DC1, are that he *forgot all about it* (Turn 22) and *wasn't thinking about it* (Turn 24).

4. *You expect us all to believe that?*

Having secured apparent agreements to crucial questions on the central issue of the case, DC1 returns to Barry's *criminal record*, highlighting a *robbery* incident when Barry *declined to be interviewed* and *gave a false name* (p171–172). A brief set of questions follows, relating to the identification of the hair colour of the policewoman involved in the Pinkenba event (presumably to provide a possible opportunity to expose inconsistency on this point, an opportunity which is not pursued). The questioning then returns once again to Barry's *criminal record*. It is not as easy for DC1 to catch Barry out, as it was with the younger witnesses. Barry's answers are straightforward, accepting the evidence that is used to construct his *criminal* identity. Thus for example, he answers *Yeh* to the question *you've been before the court on a lot of break and enters haven't you?* (p173). DC1 proceeds to ask twice *How many more have you done that you haven't been caught on?* (p173), which leads to the magistrate's delivery of the self-incrimination *warning*. Barry answers both times *That was all of them.* When DC1 replies, somewhat incredulously, *That's all- you've been caught every single time?*, Barry replies *No I did a clean up*, meaning that he has admitted to everything he has done. This leads to DC1's sarcastic questions in Extract 78:

Extract 78. DC1 to Barry, Day 3, p174

1. DC1:	And is that because you are going to change over a new leaf?
2. Barry:	(1.0) Yeh.
3. DC1:	Young people will be safe young women will be safe to walk the streets will they now?
4. Barry:	Yeh.
5. DC1:	As far as you're concerned?
6. Barry:	Yeh.

7. DC1:	(3.8) And you expect us all to believe that I suppose- do you?
8. Barry:	(1.0) You don't have to [believe me.
9. DC1:	[Do you expect to be believed?
10. Barry:	(1.2) You don't have to believe me- (no)=
11. DC1:	=Beg your pardon?
12. Barry:	You don't have to believe [me.
13. DC1:	[No I certainly don't- but do you expect to be believed?
14. Barry:	(4.5) I don't care what youse think.

DC1's question ... *you expect us all to believe that?* (Turn 7) provides a more subtle presupposition about the witness as a liar than he has used with the two younger witnesses. Barry does not accept DC1's sarcasm and disbelief, answering with agentive repartee *You don't have to believe me* (Turn 8). Barry seems happy to repeat his defiant answer (in Turns 10 and 12), and to add his agency to this defiant stance with *I don't care what youse think* (in Turn 14). (This answer uses a common Aboriginal English second person plural pronoun form *youse*, indicating Barry's sensitivity to DC1's use of the plural first person pronominal phrase *us all* in Turn 7). DC1's turns in this extract highlight one part of the process of criminalising Aboriginal young people: a legal process which makes much of refusing to accept that delinquent teenagers can turn away from *criminal activity*.

As we have seen earlier, Barry is much more active in identity work than the two younger witnesses, standing up to DC1's sarcasm and bullying to some extent. And in some small ways, these defiant and resistant answers succeed in having DC1 retreat a little in his aggressive style. Thus, immediately following Barry's answer *I don't care what youse think* in Turn 14 above, DC1 returns to factual elicitation of features of Barry's *criminal record*, asking *What about stealing charges?- now have you stolen anything that you haven't been before the court on?* (p174). This ongoing elicitation of matters relating to *stealing clothes from shops*, and *breaking bottles in town* requires the magistrate to deliver the self-incrimination *warning* again. Seemingly accepting DC1's establishment of Barry as a serious *criminal*, the magistrate in these three instances does not actually give the *warning*, as he did with the two younger witnesses, but simply says *Again I give you the same warning* (p174, 177) and *I give you the same warning* (p176).

5. *Not the sort of person who can be forced into things*

Within seconds Barry again tries to take some control over the questioning, answering this time with irritation and shouting, as we see in Extract 79:

Extract 79. DC1 to Barry, Day 3, p176

1. DC1:	Have you ever gone for a ride in a stolen car? (2.5) again you can claim privilege if you want to.
2. Barry:	(9.6) °I don't remember in a stolen- being in a stolen car°.
3. DC1:	I can't understand you could you please speak up.
4. Barry:	I don't remember being in a stolen car.
5. DC1:	Well a car that someone uh- borrowed without the consent of the owner have you ever been in a car like that?
6. Barry:	(3.0) Can't remember.
7. DC1:	Oh you'd remember Mr Coley if you'd ever been in a car that had been borrowed without the consent of the owner you'd remember that (1.0) wouldn't you?
8. Barry:	Nuh.
9. DC1:	It might have happened it might not have happened is that so?
10. Barry:	(3.0) Probably.
11. DC1:	(1.4) What does probably mean you probably have been?=
12. Barry:	=I DON'T KNOW I SAID I DON'T REMEMBER.

Barry is clearly getting exasperated with DC1's questioning, and indeed this set of questions seems particularly relentless. Barry says that he doesn't *remember being in a stolen car*. His answer of *Probably* in Turn 10 is not specific enough for DC1 who pursues this in Turn 11 further than Barry is prepared to tolerate, leading him to shout *I DON'T KNOW I SAID I DON'T REMEMBER*. The fact that DC1 does not pursue the topic suggests that he does not have evidence of Barry riding in a stolen car. But while Barry's earlier resistant answers appear to provide some temporary success in countering DC1's aggression, on this occasion DC1 cleverly turns Barry's outburst against him, as we see in Extract 80 below, which immediately follows Extract 79 above:

Extract 80. DC1 to Barry, Day 3, p176

1. DC1:	I notice Mr Coley that you're not a person to be er- uh- overborne- are you? (2.6) are you?
2. Barry:	I don't know what it means.

3. DC1:   What it means is that you've been quite prepared to snap back at me
             haven't you? (1.4) haven't you? (4.5) you accept that don't you Mr Coley?
4. Barry: (1.1) °Yeh°.

5. DC1:   (1.8) Don't you?
6. Barry: Yeh.

7. DC1:   (4.1) You're not the sort of person who can be forced into things are you?
             (5.5) are you?
8. Barry: (4.9) Nuh.

Adding a key element to Barry's identity, DC1 succeeds in gaining Barry's
apparent agreement to the pseudo-declarative assertions that he is *not a person
to be overborne*, that he *has been quite prepared to snap back* and that he is
not the sort of person who can be forced into things. The last of these apparent
agreements comes after two pauses of about five seconds each (Turns 7 and 8).
These apparent admissions are of course directly relevant to the central issue
in the case in relation to Barry, namely whether he went with the police to
Pinkenba *of his own free will*, or whether he *was forced*. It is also significant that
while Barry's official identity in this hearing is that of a victim-witness, in this
exchange on the crucial issue, DC1 constructs him not only as someone who is
not likely to yield to victimisation, but also as an adult, through the use of the
address term *Mr Coley*.

   As DC1 continues with questions about Barry's *criminal record*, Barry makes
another attempt at resistance, answering *Maybe I haven't got a good memory, eh*
(p176) to the repeated pseudo-declarative *You'd know very well whether you've
been involved in riding in stolen cars wouldn't you?*

6.   *Absolutely no respect for this court*

DC1 then switches to questions about the car ride which Barry took to Pinkenba
with a CJC investigator and an ALS officer. This is presumably part of the
investigation of the boys' complaint carried out a few days after the Pinkenba
event, although DC1's questions give no time reference. Barry seems confused
by the questions, answering with questions such as *Which car was I in?* and *Was
this in a police car?* (p178). It is quite likely that Barry's confusion is genuine,
especially as the CJC investigative officer was a police officer. On the other hand,
it is also possible that he is trying to use confusion as a way of subverting the
cross-examination process. This latter explanation is the one adopted by DC1,

whose volume begins to increase, culminating with the shouted metapragmatic directive *STOP PLAYING AROUND COLEY*, as we see in Extract 81:

Extract 81.   DC1 to Barry, Day 3, p178

1. DC1:	STOP PLAYING AROUND COLEY.=
2. Barry:	=I'm not playing around.=
3. DC1:	= JUST STOP PLAYING AROUND.
4. Pros:	Your worship that's just abuse I object [(xxx)
5. DC1:	[No it's not [it's
6. Pros:	[With respect it is abuse- I object to that- if the witness is having trouble and needs a prompt to recall it's legitimate for him to ask that- and for my learned friend just simply to abuse him is objectionable.=
7. DC1:	=I submit it's not objectionable because the witness is playing around with me by not answering a question when he obviously knows the answer.
8. M:	Yes it is obvious to me that he knows the answer so I'll ask- allow the cross-examination to continue.

DC1's abusive metapragmatic directives in Turn 1 and 3 spur the prosecutor to object, with a strongly worded complaint (in Turn 6). The exchange between prosecutor and DC1 results in the magistrate siding with DC1 in Turn 8. It is clear that the magistrate has accepted DC1's construction of Barry's identity as a troublesome witness.

Having gained this advantage, DC1 maximises his opportunity to harass the witness, and to add to his identity the important assertion that Barry has *ABSOLUTELY NO RESPECT for this court* as we see in Extract 82:

Extract 82.   DC1 to Barry, Day 3, p178–179

1. DC1:	Come on Mr Coley don't play around (1.5) you've been down once with an inspector of police haven't you?
2. Barry:	(0.6) Yes.
3. DC1:	(1.0) And you knew that when you were asking me those questions before didn't you? (1.0) DIDN'T YOU?
4. Barry:	(1.3) (Okay then yes).
5. DC1:	Beg your pardon? (2.6) what did you say?
6. Barry:	(2.0) YES.
7. DC1:	Why did you play games Mr Coley? (4.8) I'd suggest an answer to you- you have ABSOLUTELY NO RESPECT for this court have you? (4.1) have you? (5.9) well Mr Coley?

8. Barry: (0.8) I dunno.

9. DC1:   You don't know- see you've come in with your mouth full of chewing
               gum again today haven't you? (2.8) haven't you? (1.8) or [don't you
               know- don't you know?

10. Barry: [My
               mouth's not full my mouth's not full of it but.

In repeating his presupposition that Barry (addressed again as an adult, *Mr
Coley*) has been *play*ing *around* (in Turn 1), DC1 has little difficulty in securing
Barry's apparent agreement to the allegation that he had not been confused about
the earlier questions about the ride to Pinkenba with an inspector of police (Turns
4 and 6). Given that this question had no time reference, or contrast to the ride
which is the subject of the hearing, it is also confusing. But the significance
of the question is now lost, except for the opportunity it provides for DC1 to
harass the witness, presupposing that he was *play*ing *games*, and amplifying
his construction of Barry's identity as someone with ABSOLUTELY NO RESPECT
for the *court*, with the pseudo-declarative in Turn 7. This phrase parallels DC1's
suggestion to David that he has *absolutely no regard whatsoever for law and
order* (see Section 5 of Chapter 7). Both suggestions are to be echoed in the
magistrate's finding that the boys *have no regard for* ... *the justice system*, as
we will see in Section 2 of Chapter 10.

DC1 provides further evidence of Barry's lack of *respect for* the *court* in Turn
9, with the pseudo-declarative alleging that Barry has come into court with his
mouth full of chewing gum. This is a less direct attack than the metapragmatic
directives he has used with the younger two witnesses over their soft voices,
and Albert having his fingers in his mouth and *chewing* his *fingernails*. Barry's
answer in Turn 10 is both straightforward and resistant, revealing a level of pre-
cision suited to legal proceedings (*my mouth's not full of it but*),[36] and continuing
with his identity work as someone who does not accept being pushed around.

DC1 then returns to the ride that Barry made in a police car with a CJC
investigating police officer and an ALS officer (again with no time reference).
The point of the questioning appears to be to harass Barry for the fact that,
as recorded on the video camera in that police car, he had to be *asked several
times to wake up*, although it was *at half past eleven in the morning*. Evoking
Barry's identity as a vagrant (discussed in Section 2.2.2 of Chapter 5), DC1
suggests that this was because Barry had *been out prowling the night before*.
Barry counters that he *was tired* because he *was trying to find a way to get home*
from Pinkenba. DC1 becomes increasingly agitated, but makes no attempt to
explain his questioning, for example with clarifying time reference. Finally the
magistrate does this, explaining *Mr Coley- it's alleged that you were taken out*

to Pinkenba by the police on the tenth of May, and then *What Mr Thorpe is asking you- he's asking you about an event on the nineteenth of May- which is nine days afterwards- Okay?* (p180).

The questioning that immediately follows the magistrate's clarification is nothing less than rebuke, as we see in Extract 83:

Extract 83.   DC1 to Barry, Day 3, p180–181

1. DC1:	That was the day that you went with Mr Dan Weston- Inspector Grainger and a Mr Nixon and a video camera in a police car to Pinkenba- you got that fixed in your mind?
2. Barry:	Yeh.
3. DC1:	(5.3) You're going to answer me [Coley.
4. Barry:	[Yeh I said [Yes.
5. DC1:	[I DON'T CARE HOW LONG YOU STAY THERE- YOU'LL ANSWER ME.=
6. Barry:	=Yes I said yes.
7. DC1:	No you didn't you sat there and said NOTHING.
8. Pros:	I heard him say yes your worship with respect.
9. DC1:	Oh after after [(xxxxxxx).
10. Pros:	[No before my friend's before my friend's tirade he said Yes- I heard it.

DC1 is clearly on the offensive with this witness. Although he claims not to have heard the witness's answer in Turn 2 it is audible to the prosecutor, who is sitting at the Bar table where DC1 is standing. It also seems on the audio-recording to be of the same volume as Barry's other answers. But DC1's asserted inability to hear this answer precipitates a command *You're going to answer me Coley*, which takes both the syntactic form of a schoolteacher directive and uses a form of address (last name only) which also typifies such talk. It is interesting that after Barry's several defiant and resistant answers seen above, DC1 has now reverted to the style of directive more typical of his talk to the two younger witnesses. Barry's annoyed *Yeh I said yes* (in Turn 4), initially results in another school teacher style directive (which is shouted) *I DON'T CARE HOW LONG YOU STAY THERE YOU'LL ANSWER ME* (in Turn 5). The easy substitutability of a form such as *eat your vegetables* for *answer me*, shows how this turn also takes the form of a parental directive well recognised in the establishment of control over young children.

But Barry retains his ground, repeating his answer of Turn 4 in Turn 6. DC1 then transforms the questioning into an argument in Turn 7, leading to the prosecutor's objection in Turn 8. This exchange in Turns 8 to 10 arguably has little to do with the initial question about whether Barry has a certain day *fixed in* his *mind*. It is a clear example of the disciplinary function of cross-examination questioning, which is at the same time controlling, rebuking and harassing. It also shows that DC1 has *absolutely no respect for* the witness. The magistrate then intervenes, changing the frame of the exchange, by establishing a straightforward explanation of the initial question, and several low-key questions and answers follow about Barry's *walking* from *the City* to *Kedron*, where he was staying at the time.

7. *You have deliberately told lies*

The cross-examination then switches to a series of turns in which DC1 refers to the magistrate's statement about perjury to Barry before he started his evidence on the previous day. He then alleges that Barry has *deliberately told lies* in court (p182), although he does not specify what Barry has *lied* about. While he has earlier asserted that Barry *told lies* about knowing that he didn't *have to go with police* (in Extract 5, in Chapter 4) the presentation of the witness as a liar has been much less predominant for Barry up till now, than it was throughout the cross-examination of the two younger witnesses. DC1 then engages Barry in a hypothetical metapragmatic exchange, as we see in Extract 84:

Extract 84.   DC1 to Barry, Day 3, p182

1. DC1:	If you did tell lies- we can look at the transcript- if you did tell lies- you told them knowing that you shouldn't tell lies- correct?
2. Barry:	Yeh.
3. DC1:	And you told them knowing that it's a serious offence to tell lies- correct?
4. Barry:	Yeh.
5. DC1:	But it wouldn't worry you very much would it if you told a lie? (1.7) would it?
6. Barry:	Yes [it would.
7. DC1:	[If you told a lie there in the witness box that wouldn't worry you would it?
8. Barry:	Yes it would.
9. DC1:	Beg your pardon?
10. Barry:	It would.
11. DC1:	Why?
12. Barry:	(3.6) Because it just would.

13. DC1:   Beg your pardon?
14. Barry: Because it would.

15. DC1:   Well why would it?
16. Barry: Because it just would.

17. DC1:   Because it just would- well that's a good answer I suppose (1.9) because
             it just would- well you knew that you shouldn't tell lies didn't you?
18. Barry: Yeh.

19. DC1:   Beg your pardon?
20. Barry: Yes.

21. DC1:   (1.8) And you've known that right throughout your evidence that you had
             to tell the truth- correct?
22. Barry: Yeh.

23. DC1:   (77.0 secs [includes sound of pages turning]) (Tell me) this now- you went
             down to Pinkenba with Mr Weston and these two other young gentlemen-
             Carter and- Pender didn't you?
24. Barry: Yes.

Barry's answer of *Yeh* to the complex hypothetical question in Turn 1, combined
with his answer to the following question, might indicate that he has *told lies* in
court. DC1 has slipped from the hypothetical possibility of Barry *tell*ing *lies* in
court in Turn 1, to the presupposition that he did, in Turn 3. But the possibility
that Barry's *Yeh* answers in Turn 2 and 4 are answers of gratuitous concurrence,
and not genuine agreement, is supported by the answers which Barry then gives
in his Turns 6 and 8, which might appear to contradict his first two answers.
In Extract 5, we have seen DC1's use of repetition as the main mechanism to
present Barry as a liar. With the two younger witnesses, it has been much easier,
as they have given many contradictory and non-compliant answers, that have led
to the *why do/did you lie* refrain. Barry's much more straightforward answering
has produced much less inconsistency, and the main mechanisms used in the
construction of him as a liar are the hypothetical questions and repetition we
see in this extract, and the strategies to elicit what appears to be gratuitous
concurrence in Extract 5 in Chapter 4.

Following the exchange which serves to invoke DC1's earlier construction of
Barry as a liar (discussed as Extract 5), DC1 returns to questioning about Barry's
report of the Pinkenba event to the ALS officers. These questions contrast to the
hostile and aggressive stance, and argumentative structure of the immediately
preceding questioning, which was asking about little other than whether Barry

remembered this reporting event (some 10 days after the Pinkenba event), and why he was falling asleep in a police car at eleven in the morning. The stance of these substantive questions about the reporting event is relatively neutral. But included in the propositions of the questions is the accusation that the three boys *put* their *heads together* to come to an *agreement* about how to report the hair colour of the policewoman involved (p183), an accusation which Barry repeatedly denies.

DC1's cross-examination closes with 37 questions about the details of the taxi ride that the three boys took from the city to the Valley, before they were approached by the six police officers on the night of the Pinkenba event (p183–184). The tone and pacing of these questions and answers is relatively neutral, with questions such as *There's a pub nearby- isn't there?*, and answers such as *Yeh- on the corner.* Following several questions about the cost of the taxi ride, who paid it, whether the *exact* amount was paid, and what the *change* was, DC1 asks his final cross-examination question:

Extract 85.   DC1 to Barry, Day 3, p185

1. DC1:	Or is this the situation Mr Coley- that the three of you got into that cab- when the cab pulled up- you all got out without paying for the cab fare?
2. Barry:	(2.5) No I paid him.

With this question, addressed to the witness as an adult (*Mr Coley*), DC1 uses a pseudo-declarative to suggest that Barry had engaged in a *criminal offence* (taxi fare evasion) shortly before being approached by the police officers. Given his explicit and lengthy construction of Barry as a *criminal* and a liar over the preceding 78 minutes, no elaboration is required, or argument is engaged in, and Barry's denial is arguably inconsequential.

8. *You've lied on oath*

DC2 immediately starts his cross-examination with a softer approach, as we saw in Section 6 of Chapter 6, asking Barry *What do you want me to call you- Mr Coley- or Barry? what's your preference?* Somewhat unsurprisingly, given DC1's frequent use of *Mr Coley* in harassing and hostile turns, the witness answers *Barry.* DC2 then launches into questioning about the details of payment for the taxi ride which has been the subject of DC1's final questions. DC2 tells Barry that *both David and Albert say that that was a free cab ride… arranged… with the driver.* While Barry insists he remembers *getting the change off* the driver, he says *Yeh* to the suggestion that he doesn't *remember actually paying.* DC2's final question on this topic is *So it may well have had the appearance that when you arrived- the three of you got out and if I was standing there watching I wouldn't have seen you pay- that could easily have happened right?* This pseudo-declarative addresses the underlying issue in the case, suggesting a possible reason why the police approached the boys. Barry's answer is *Probably-I dunno* (p186).

The questions then move to the false name that Barry gave police that night, and Barry readily answers with that name. This is followed by a series of questions in which DC2 sets out to show that Barry was inconsistent in his earlier statements *made on oath* about the name which he had given the police. This is the first and only time in Barry's cross-examination in which his earlier report of the Pinkenba event is directly entextualised. This mechanism was used much more with the two younger witnesses, with whom, as we have seen, it was not difficult to use entextualisation to show inconsistency. According to DC2's reading from the earlier statements, Barry had told the ALS *The police wanted to know the names first* and *all three of us told them our names*, and he had told the CJC *a young blonde policeman asked me my name- I told them my name* (p187). DC2 uses an apparent inconsistency (explained below) to repeat DC1's earlier accusations that Barry had *lied on oath*. However, Barry appears quite confused by this accusation and alleged inconsistency, and he and DC2 appear to be talking at cross-purposes. DC2 constructs as *a lie*, the fact that Barry told both the ALS and the CJC investigators that he gave the police his name. It is noteworthy, however, that neither of those reports appears to indicate that any distinction was made about whether he gave his real name or a false name. Arguably there is no significant inconsistency between these two statements (to ALS and CJC) on the one hand, and his cross-examination admission (on p186) that he had given the police a false name, on the other hand. Barry does once give the answer of *Yeh* to DC2's repeated insistence that *those statements tell a lie about that* (p188). But his own explanations, combined with DC2's use of repeated question tags to elicit that answer, might suggest that this answer is one of gratuitous concurrence, rather than genuine agreement with the proposition that he had *lied on oath in those statements*. Barry's explanation, repeated several times, is *I thought I had to use my real name for the statement* and *I didn't know I had to tell them my false name* (ibid.). In the longest answer of his cross-examination, Barry says *I thought I had to- give my real name in the statement- I didn't know I had to tell them of my false name- write down the false name what I gave to the police* (ibid.).

Barry's explanation seems to be this: he had given the police his false name in the Valley that night, but he thought he had to use his real name for the statement. But DC2's allegation is that having given his false name to the police in the Valley that night, it was *a lie* to say in his statements *I told* the police *my name*. But DC2 feels no need to pursue the misunderstanding, having clearly made his point that Barry had *lied on oath* in the two statements. At this point, after Barry has spent 64 minutes in cross-examination that day, the magistrate calls for a morning break.

9.   *Contempt for law and for the courts*

DC2's cross-examination continues with questions about Barry's *criminal record*, leading to the observation that the stealing offence for which he was serving a custodial sentence since the previous November had taken place *in the street* at *three o'clock in the morning*. DC2 immediately follows with the construction of Barry as *a sort of a nocturnal person* ... doing *most of* his *waking hours at night* (p189). The juxtaposition of these two features of Barry's identity are important context for the underlying issue in this case, namely the rights of police to remove Aboriginal young people like Barry from the streets at night. Strengthening the unspoken defence argument on this underlying issue, DC2 goes on with questions about Barry's *breach* of a *curfew order* which occurred in connection with the November 1994 stealing offence (committed some months after the Pinkenba incident). In asking questions about this *curfew order*, DC2 makes another general statement about Barry's identity as a *criminal* with the pseudo-declarative ... *at night time you committed offences such as breaking and entering and stealing things from people in the street*. Barry answers *Yeh* (p191).

Further questions about Barry's *breach* of *curfew* provide the opportunity for DC2 to further construct Barry's identity as a person with *contempt for law and for the courts- for magistrates*, as we see in Extract 86:

Extract 86.   DC2 to Barry, Day 3, p191

1. DC2:	And yet the magistrate <u>still</u>- still gave you another chance (1.8) trusted you?
2. Barry:	Yeh.
3. DC2:	(2.7) You threw that trust back in his face didn't you?
4. Barry:	(1.6) Yeh.
5. DC2:	(4.0) Nd d'you- do you just have contempt for law and for the courts for magistrates- is that- just have contempt for them just don't <u>care</u> about- don't care what they say? (5.9) is that it?
6. Barry:	(6.7) Yeh.

DC2 has little trouble in getting Barry's apparent agreement to the damaging propositions in Turns 1, 3 and 5 about his *contempt for the law and the courts*, a theme which is to become important in DC2's closing submission, as well as the magistrate's decision, as we will see in Chapter 10. DC2's question in Turn 5 uses the mechanism of partial repetition of the question, a much-used mechanism in DC1's questioning, and one that increases the likelihood of an answer of gratuitous concurrence.

10. *It's not a bad place to steal some money*

DC2 then attempts to fill out another aspect of Barry's identity, namely that he has problems with his memory, which, as we saw in Chapter 7 was also important in his construction of David's identity. However, this proves a little more difficult as Barry persists in giving increasingly specific answers to the questions about where they were when the police approached them, even answering *About a metre and a half* to the question *How far way from you was David?* (p192).

DC2 then asks a number of questions about the route taken by the taxi, in which the boys had travelled from the city to the Valley earlier that night. These questions are similar to those at the end of DC1's cross-examination of Barry the previous day. As with those questions, Barry answers DC2's questions on this topic in a straightforward and clear manner. DC2 does however succeed in finding a locational inaccuracy in Barry's account, in terms of whether one of the turns taken by the taxi was a *left* turn or a *right* turn (p192–193). This is followed by several questions about *why in particular* Barry had wanted to *go to the top of the mall*. As we see from Extract 87 below, Barry has no particular answer to this *why* question, and begins to get impatient with DC2:

Extract 87.   DC2 to Barry, Day 3, p193

1. DC2:	Why in particular did you want to go to the top of the mall?
2. Barry:	(3.0) I dunno.
3. DC2:	(1.8) Was it something the oth- one of the other two wanted to go to? (4.1) eh? [(did they want to go)?
4. Barry:	[Top of the mall is still in the Valley.
5. DC2:	Eh?
6. Barry:	Still in the Valley what's the difference?=
7. DC2:	((laughs)) =I'm just asking you why that particular part of the [(mall)?=
8. Barry:	=[I dunno.

9. DC2:   Eh?
10. Barry: I dunno.

Remembering the discussion in Section 2.2.2 of Chapter 5 about the common youth culture activity of *walking around* the city and the Valley, it is easy to see why Barry might not know why he asked the taxi driver to take him to a particular location. We have also seen that the assumption of planned activity implied in such a reason-seeking question is an ethnocentric one. But DC2 apparently has a strategic reason for the line of questioning: his final questions to Barry suggest that he was about to commit a crime, as we see in Extract 88 below, which follows almost immediately from Extract 87 above:

Extract 88.   DC2 to Barry, Day 3, p194

1. DC2:   What were you doing?
2. Barry: (4.8) I dunno just walk (1.8) walk around.

3. DC2:   (What were you doing David?) I'm sorry Barry what were you doing?
4. Barry: (1.5) Just <u>walk</u>ing.

5. DC2:   Looking for some money Barry?
6. Barry: Nuh (1.8) no-one was around anyway.

7. DC2:   (1.8) (<u>aha</u>) Looking for someone who <u>might</u> have been around in that lonely place?
8. Barry: Nuh.

9. DC2:   (2.1) It's not a bad place to- steal some money is it from someone?
10. Barry: Nuh.=

11. DC2:   =Deserted sort of area?
12. Barry: Nuh.

13. DC2:   Is that why you went to the top of the mall?
14. Barry: Nuh.

15. DC2:   (4.4) Same time of day as when you were stealing the wallet wasn't it?
16. Barry: (4.2) °Nuh°.

In Turn 9, DC2's presupposes Barry's evaluation of the Valley in his identity as a habitual thief in his pseudo-declarative that it was *not a bad place to- steal some money*. As discussed in Section 2.3 of Chapter 6, either a *yes* or a *no* answer to this question accepts the presupposition. But in all of his answers in this extract apart from this question, Barry gives no ground on the allegation that he was looking for an opportunity to commit a crime. However, given DC2's earlier establishment of Barry's identity as a *nocturnal sort of person*, who *committed offences such as breaking and entering and stealing things from people in the street ... at night time*, then it is arguably inconsequential what Barry's answers are to these final questions.

11. Conclusion

Table 5 on the next page summarises Barry's cross-examination. While it is shorter than that of the two younger witnesses, the construction of his identity by the two DCs is powerful. The establishment of Barry's identity as a *criminal* is easy on two grounds. Firstly, he was serving a custodial sentence at the time of the hearing, and as DC1 makes explicit, he arrives at court each day accompanied by a *community corrections officer*. And secondly, as we have seen, Barry's answers to the pseudo-declaratives about his *criminal record* mostly cooperate with this presentation of his identity as a *criminal*.

While more than half of Barry's cross-examination relates to his *criminal record*, it is the seriousness of his *criminal activity* that is highlighted by the DCs. On this point, DC1's lexical choice, as well as the propositional content of questions, work to establish Barry as an adult, despite the fact that he is 15 years old at the time of the hearing (and 14 at the time of the Pinkenba event). In Chapter 5, we examined DC1's lexical perversion which substitutes the term *louts* to refer to Barry and his *friends*, as well as the verb *prowl* to describe what they were doing in the streets. DC1's choice of address terms for Barry also work to establish him as an adult, as summarised in Table 1 in Chapter 6, and as seen throughout the extracts above.

But further than this, Barry is presented in the content of DC1's questions and pseudo-declaratives as *totally brazen*, someone who is not a *normal human being*, whose livelihood amounts to a choice between *government handout* and breaking *into people's houses*. He thus juxtaposes his denial of Barry's identity as a *normal human being*, with two of the most widespread negative identities attributed to Aboriginal people generally: being reliant on *government handouts* and being *criminals*. While DC1 emphasises Barry's *prowling around the streets* as one of a *group of louts* looking for crime, DC2's version is that he is *a sort of a nocturnal person ...* doing *most of* his *waking hours at night*, when he *committed offences such as breaking and entering and stealing things from people in the street*. Further, DC1 suggests that he is going to *grow up* to *go on to bigger and better criminal activity*.

Table 5.   Summary of Barry's cross-examination

DC1's questioning:	78 minutes, 456 answers, 26 transcript pages
DC2's questioning	31 minutes, 146 answers, 8 transcript pages
answers of *yes*, *yeh*, or *mm*:	to DC1: 171 = 37% of his answers to DC1
	to DC2: 54 = 37% of his answers to DC2
answers of *no* or *nuh*:	to DC1: 94 = 21% of his answers to DC1
	to DC2: 15 = 10% of his answers to DC2
answers of *I don't know* or *I dunno*:	to DC1: 20 = 4% of his answers to DC1
	to DC2: 5 = 3% of his answers to DC2
number of adjournments:	2
Barry's longest answer (35 words):	*I thought I had to- give my real name in the statement- I didn't know I had to tell them of my false name- write down the false name what I gave to the police* (to DC2, p188)

Main topic of questions:

DC1

p157–163   Barry's *criminal record* END of DAY TWO

[p164–165   bail extended for defendants, cover sheet for DAY THREE]

p166–169   START OF DAY TWO: Barry's *criminal record*

p170–171   Pinkenba event, including central issue

p171–172   Barry's *criminal record*

p173   hair colour of policewoman from Pinkenba event

p173–177   Barry's *criminal record*

p178–185   Barry's reports of Pinkenba event

DC2

p185–188   Pinkenba night and Barry's reports of it

p189–191   Barry's *criminal record*

p191–194   Pinkenba night

We saw in Chapters 7 and 8 that much is made in the cross-examination of the two younger witnesses of their *lies* in the court and in the inconsistencies between their reports of the Pinkenba event. The entextualisation which is so effective with the two younger witnesses is hardly used with Barry, as we have seen. The DCs have found little opportunity to expose Barry in acts of inconsistency. But this does not stop DC1 from using hostile prosodics, and repeated tag questions in Extract 5 in an exchange in which gratuitous concurrence seems most likely to be involved, in Barry's apparent agreement to the presupposed assertion that he *lie*d on the central issue. This, combined with DC2's brief and confusing set of questions which recontextualise Barry's reports over the name he gave to police, discussed in Section 8 above, are used to establish that Barry too is a liar. Thus, he is presented as someone who *lied on oath*, has *deliberately told lies ... on oath*, and *wouldn't worry ...* if he *told a lie ... in the witness box*. Just as both DCs present this view of Barry, they also both explicitly talk about his *contempt for law and for the courts- for* magistrates and having *absolutely no respect for this court*. We will see in the next chapter, that this is an important theme in the magistrate's decision.

But Barry does not accept the DCs' construction of his identity without protest. In this, he differs considerably from David, the youngest witness, who makes little overt attempt to resist or alter the identity constructed for him, apart from simply denying accusations. Barry also differs somewhat from Albert, the middle of the three witnesses, who makes some defiant replies and one bold statement to construct the identity of DC2 as someone who *tell*s *lies*. Barry, on the other hand, gives some clear indications that he does not accept being pushed around, arguing with DC1 particularly, and raising his voice in some replies. In his argumentative reply to an accusation about coming to court with his *mouth full of chewing gum*, Barry shows legal attention to accuracy and detail, saying *My mouth's not full my mouth's not full of it but*.

As with Albert's construction of DC2 as a liar, Barry constructs DC1 as someone who is *yell*ing at him as if he is *a dog*. He further articulates his own identity as someone who is not intimidated by the hostility of his interrogators saying *You don't have to believe me, I don't care what you think*, and *I don't count how much purses I steal*. But, Barry's resistance and his attempts to retain some self-respect in the face of the demeaning and aggressive cross-examination are counter-productive. They are used as evidence that he is *not a person to be overborne*, that he *has been quite prepared to snap back* and that he is *not the sort of person who can be forced into things*. All of these characteristics support the central issue being addressed by the defence. That is, Barry's behaviour in cross-examination indicates a person who would not have got into the police car unwillingly.

Taken together, these aspects of Barry's identity work powerfully to address the underlying issue in the case: that police are keeping the streets safe by removing Aboriginal young people as they did in the Pinkenba event. To further support this unspoken assertion, both DCs add a (different) finishing touch to their construction of Barry's *criminal* identity: DC1 implies that he had already committed a crime that night – evading taxi fare –, while DC2 suggests that he was about to commit an offence on the night in question – stealing money from someone in the street. The fact that there was no evidence for either of these suggestions, and that no charge was made in relation to any of the activities of Barry (or the other two boys) on that night, is apparently inconsequential.

When the evidence of the complainant witnesses is complete, a major achievement has been made in the reproduction of neocolonialism. The linguistic mechanisms allowed by courtroom rules of evidence have provided the opportunity for the DCs to provide a great deal of detail about what Aboriginal young people are like. In their presentation of these three boys in terms of difference (not *normal human beings*) and deviance (both delinquent and *criminal*), the DCs have argued the need for police to remove them from the streets. To achieve this outcome, the DCs have both drawn on and contributed to widespread ideologies about Aboriginal people, which have circulated since the earliest colonial times, and which remain strong. And we have seen that the construction of Aboriginality which has taken place in this cross-examination has been interactional. The DCs have cleverly co-opted the three boys in this identity work, with varying degrees of ease.

This critical sociolinguistic analysis of the courtroom struggle does not end when the cross-examination ends. We now move to an examination of how the case concluded, in the first of the three chapters which make up the Conclusions part of the book. In Chapter 10, we examine the effects of both the identity work (which addresses the underlying issue) and the apparent agreement which the DCs have elicited to the central issue, about whether the boys had got into the police cars willingly. We see that while police are at the front line of neocolonial control, and the Pinkenba cross-examination has been the site for major contestation over this control, there are other important agents, who work both for and against it. It is this work of these agents which is examined in Chapter 10.

Part IV

Conclusions

Chapter 10
No fear of the police: closing the Pinkenba case

We have seen in chapters 7–9 the thorough work done by the two DCs in present-ing the three witnesses as liars and *criminal*s, who are a danger on the streets of Brisbane, and who knew that they did not have to get into the police cars on the night of the Pinkenba event. This work is recapitulated in the closing addresses of each of the two DCs, as we will see in Section 1 below. For the defence, the boys' identities as *criminal*s and liars necessarily eliminates any claim to identity as victims of police abuse. In Section 2, we examine how this defence theory is taken up unquestioningly by the magistrate in his 447-word decision to dismiss the charges against the police officers. But this case involved much more than the immediate courtroom participants. In Section 3, we briefly glimpse labelling and recontextualisation practices used by the print media, in the more widespread adoption and promulgation of the defence construction of the boys' identities and their consent to the ride to Pinkenba. From the media, we move in Section 4 to examine the next phase in the struggle over the po-lice control over these Aboriginal boys. This involved the ALS supporting the application of the boys' "next friends" for a judicial review of the magistrate's decision, which is discussed in Section 5. Just as the ALS did not stop with the magistrate's decision, the CJC continued to act on concerns raised by the Pinkenba event and hearing, as we will see in Section 6. In Section 7 we move to official police reactions to the Pinkenba case, which include those of the Police Commissioner, the Police Minister, and the President of the Queensland Police Union. At this highest level of policing, we will see the adoption of the identity of the boys who were taken for a ride by the police as that of *juvenile offenders* and *thugs*.

1. Closing addresses

The fourth morning of the hearing starts with 9 minutes of evidence from a monitor operator about the surveillance videos used in the Valley Mall. Fol-lowing his evidence, there are two consecutive adjournments. The afternoon begins with the prosecutor's closing address of 15 minutes. Presented in a rather low-key and understated style, he refers to the witnesses as *the boys* and *the children*. The first 4 minutes of his address presents details relating police log books to the named defendants, which is relevant to the identification of the officers involved. He then focuses on the boys' evidence-in-chief, in which they have said *they were told to get into the police cars, . . . they didn't want to be there, . . . they were not told where they were going, nor did they have any relatives, friends, what-have-you . . . at Pinkenba.* Acknowledging that *the answers given by the children in cross-examination . . . are inconsistent with their evidence in chief,* the prosecutor says that this would give rise to *the most taxing question* for the magistrate, namely *what to make* of these answers. Referring to *the aggression of some of the cross-examination,* the prosecutor suggests, with some prolixity, that the magistrate *and any subsequent jury might be entitled to conclude that whatever answers were given in cross-examination that contradict their evidence-in-chief . . . were derived simply by being overborne, and to that extent- should be attributed little weight.*

In contrast to the prosecutor's brief address, the first defence closing address is 47 minutes long. While it is DC1 who has opened the cross-examination of each witness, and asked the most questions, in the defence closing addresses it is DC2 who speaks first and for the longest time. This is undoubtedly related to his claim that his cross-examination of each of the witnesses *was measured, restrained and at all times polite.* Like both the prosecutor before him and DC1 after him, DC2's tone is somewhat subdued in his closing address. This contrasts to what Cotterill (2003: 199) has described as the "undeniably theatrical quality" of this speech event in trials, where it is a performance for the jury.[37] But the Pinkenba committal hearing has no jury. Instead it is the magistrate who is the primary audience, while the public gallery and the media are also intended audiences (in Cotterill's 2003: 106 terms, they are "secondary addressees"). And through both the public gallery and the media, it is arguably the wider Queensland and Australian society generally who are also intended audiences for this closing address performance. These secondary addressees and wider audiences are arguably being catered to with questions such as *could anyone say that I was aggressive?,* which have the form of a rhetorical question.

DC2 first addresses the legal offence of *deprivation of liberty,* arguing that *to deprive a person of their liberty is not by itself an offence- what must be established is that such deprivation was unlawful.* He then presents his summary of what happened in the Pinkenba event, saying:

Extract 89.   DC2 Closing address[38]

> *what was actually said in all cases was neither more nor less than- hop in the police car or jump in the police car- or- hop in the back seat- the evidence is positive that that statement was not followed by any threat . . .*

> *it's not in official language- it's not in threatening language- it is a perfectly*
> *lawful thing to say- and the fact that it is said by a police officer makes no*
> *difference*
> *it can hardly <u>be</u> that a <u>crime</u> is made out by somebody saying to somebody*
> *else hop in the police car*

In this summary of the central interaction of the Pinkenba event, DC2 removes agency from the police officers, using passive (as in *what was said*), and impersonal constructions (as in *it's not in official language*). Also removing any trace of roles or relationships between the participants in the interaction, he presents it as a situation of equal participants: *somebody saying to somebody else hop in the police car*. (In Section 2.2.3 of Chapter 5, we saw that none of the boys used the verb *hop* in reporting in the courtroom what the police had said to them.)

Unsurprisingly, DC2 then draws on the propositions to which he has elicited apparent agreement from the witnesses, to assert:

Extract 90.   DC2 Closing address continued

> *each of the persons who heard this statement and acted by getting in the*
> *police car- <u>knew</u> that they had no obligation so to do …*
> *they <u>knew</u> that they <u>didn't</u> need to do it …*
> *(we have a) statement not couched in official or threatening language-*
> *not followed up in threatening language- made to three individuals- all of*
> *whom <u>knew</u> their rights in point of law- who <u>did</u> what was said- next- we*
> *have this as well- that each of those three get <u>in</u> the police vehicle <u>but</u> then*
> *make- no- protest …*
> *the evidence is <u>po</u>sitively to the effect that <u>there- was- no- protest</u>*

The detailed examination of the cross-examination interaction presented in Chapters 4–9 has made it clear that these assertions by DC2 can only be made by taking a decontextualised and literal interpretation of the mostly minimal answers given by the boys, an issue to be taken up in Section 2.1 of Chapter 12. Misrepresenting what Albert has said, he asserts:

Extract 91.   DC2 Closing address continued

> *[Albert] told Mr Thorpe in cross-examination that the <u>reason</u> that he'd*
> *said the police had grabbed him and forced him into the car <u>was to</u>*
> *make- things- look- worse- for- the- police*

In Extract 4 in Chapter 4, we have seen that Albert has not told Mr Thorpe (DC1) that. He has answered °*No*° to this shouted suggestion (Turn 6, Extract 4). DC1 has refused to accept this answer, and continued to shout, and use repeated tag questions until Albert finally says °*Yes*° in Turn 16. This is one of many instances in which DC2 switches authorship attribution. In this instance, he uses the verb *told* to attribute propositions from the questions of either himself or DC1 to one of the boys.

Having dealt with the legal point of deprivation of liberty, and presented his version of what happened, DC2 moves on to his summary of the witnesses' characters and identities. Up to this point, he has used the terms *persons, individuals, somebody, people* and *witnesses* to refer to the boys, masking the fact that the witnesses are children. In contrast to these neutral terms, he now specifically addresses their youth:

Extract 92.　DC2 Closing address continued

> *it is just not real to treat these youths as children ignorant of the ways of the world ... who have a ... learned response of compliance with authority ... imagine a twelve thirteen fourteen fifteen year old- your average one ... can you imagine the average ordinary child behaving as defiantly to you- your worship? in court re<u>fus</u>ing to answer questions- inventing <u>lies</u> to make things look worse for the police- for that is what we are <u>told</u> by Albert Carter he did- he did it- he invented a lie- to blacken the police ...*

He then refers to the evidence that one of the boys has sworn at a police officer, using poetic alliteration in the rhetorical question: *this is an example is it- of craven <u>cow</u>ering to the coppers- hm?- reflexively [sic] going along with authority? ... telling the police false names- never protesting?* Having argued against their identity as *children*, DC2 goes back to evidence elicited by DC1 from David about Barry having sworn at one of the two police officers the boys had met while walking back to the Valley (p51, discussed in Section 5.2 of Chapter 6). In response to considerable questioning, David had finally told DC1 that Barry *told him to get fucked.* DC2 now reports this incident in his denial of the boys' victim identity, sarcastically labelling them as *shrinking violets,* saying *get fucked- that's what was said to two police by these shrinking violets- get fucked.*

Combining the presentation of people who are not afraid to swear at the police, with a misrepresentation of their evidence, he says *these are the very same- who- didn't protest and got in the police vehicles when <u>asked</u>.* As we have seen in Section 2.2.4 of Chapter 5, none of the boys ever said in examination-in-chief, or accepted in cross-examination, that they were *asked* to get in the police cars. They consistently said they were *told* and *forced,* and they rejected *asked.* In a somewhat striking contradiction, DC2 misquotes the witnesses on what is arguably the central word in the whole case. Yet he has allowed a teenage exaggeration and colloquial use of the verb *grab* to be recontextualised as a wrongful claim of physical violence (as we saw in Section 1.3 of Chapter 4 and Section 7 of Chapter 8). DC2's wrong and misleading misquotation of the boys' evidence on the central issue goes unchecked, and is reproduced in the decision of the judicial review, as we will see in Section 5.

As well as the strategic use of lexical perversion on the central issue, DC2 also recontextualises extracts from the cross-examination, by reading selected questions and answers from the official transcript. Official transcripts are made for the purpose of recording <u>what</u> was said, and not <u>how</u> it was said. For this reason, they record only the propositional content of courtroom talk, and pay virtually no attention to the interaction (Eades 1996b). Thus, in his evenly-paced monotone reading of decontextualised questions and answers from the official transcript, DC2 has no trouble in significantly distorting what has happened in cross-examination. The main impact of this distortion is that as he reads questions followed by answers in the same volume and with no pauses, there is no indication of the haranguing and coercion of the questioners, or the reluctance with which the boys have conceded damaging propositions (DC1 later does the same with some transcript reading during his closing address.)

Having presented the boys as juvenile delinquents who are *perfectly capable of disobeying authority*, DC2 moves to a summary of their status as *criminals*, whose experience with the criminal justice system must mean that they *knew their legal rights*. Contrasting them with *the great majority of the population*, he argues that *these three probably are more aware of their rights as against the police than most of the people paying their taxes and working*.

DC2's closing address ends with a forceful and dramatic comment addressing his rhetorical questions *why are we here? why all this furore?* He argues that the criminal justice system is not the place to deal with *bad manners* which are *being elevated into criminal offences*. In a statement which suggests that he sees the struggle between police and Aboriginal people as a *social problem*, he argues that *we're not here to solve social problems or to condemn social ills . . . .* But further than this, he refers to the political nature of this struggle, saying *social and political issues (ought to remain) exactly where they are*, and complains about the fact that *battles are fought here* (i.e. in the courtroom). In his view, *so much pressure is created for our criminal justice system . . . that it's starting to creak under the weight*.

DC1's closing address is brief and is presented in a mostly understated tone, as *there is very little that* he *wants to add* to that of DC2. Speaking for only 20 minutes, most of his attention addresses the *aggressive* nature of his cross-examination, which we have seen is one of the few issues raised by the prosecutor in his earlier closing address. DC1 argues that his *aggressive cross-examination* has been essential to arriving at *the truth* in this case (an issue to be taken up in Chapter 12), saying:

Extract 93.   DC1 Closing address

> there are times in court when there has to be- aggressive cross-
> examination- it's <u>not</u> very often that one has to resort to that- but if
> the cross-examination on my part was not aggressive ... we wouldn't
> have obtained the truth of the situation ... there's nothing wrong with
> aggressive cross-examination ...

DC1 then cleverly co-opts what we might argue is the magistrate's lack of judicial independence in this case. As we have seen in Section 1.2 of Chapter 4, the magistrate had the power to stop any of DC1's questions. DC1 points out that he has chosen not to exercise this legal right, saying:

Extract 94.   DC1 Closing address continued

> had I've been out of order your worship would have done something about
> it- your worship would have stopped me- you have the <u>power</u> under the
> Evidence Act- to stop questions if you feel I'm badgering a witness or-
> insulting or am scandalous or browbeating a witness- you have a duty and
> a power in relation to your running of the court to stop me.

The magistrate's power referred to here is in Section 21 of the *Evidence Act 1977* titled "Scandalous and insulting questions", which, as we saw in Section 1.2 of Chapter 4 specifies:

21.(1)   A court may disallow a question which, in the opinion of the court, is indecent or scandalous unless the question relates to a fact in issue in the proceeding or to matters necessary to be known in order to determine whether or not the facts in issue existed.

(2)   A court may disallow a question which, in the opinion of the court, is intended only to insult or annoy or is needlessly offensive in form.

DC1 also briefly addresses the characters of the boys, whom he describes as *people who have no respect for authority.* In an extreme and unchecked act of distorted recontextualisation, he says *you've got to give a <u>lot</u> of weight to a statement I'll <u>lie</u> if I think I can get away with it- and you won't know when I'm telling the truth and when I'm not.* As we have seen in the preceding chapters, none of the witnesses has made such a *statement*. The closest to which any of the witnesses has come to anything resembling this *statement* has been examined in Extract 52 of Chapter 8. Here we have seen Albert's minimal answers to DC1's pressured pseudo-declaratives on these points. Albert has given no propositional content. There can be no doubt that transforming a literal interpretation of Albert's *Ye#* answers, and attributing DC1's propositions to him, can lead to such a recontextualisation. In Chapter 12, we will consider the role of such distorted recontextualisation in the delivery of justice.

DC1 concludes by briefly addressing the central issue. Here again, he recontextualises the boys' minimal answers, extracted as we have seen through highly pressured questioning, to argue that:

Extract 95. DC1 Closing address continued

> *any suggestion that these young people were in a position of inferiority really is not borne out by the fact that all of them knew their rights- all of them could say in the most forceful terms to police officers what they could go and do with themselves- they were in a position where they well knew what the situation was ...*
>
> *there's not only no protest- but no-one on the evidence ever <u>asked</u> for the car to be stopped for them to be let out- and this all from people who knew their rights ...*

DC1's closing address is followed by a brief response from the prosecutor in which he makes three points. In a rather indirect suggestion that the boys were not able to protest about going with police, he says that *they are in a position to assess the context in which they are being driven- the evidence suggests there was one occasion where there was a protest- that's by Albert Carter- and for his trouble he was given a clip over the ear.* When the magistrate points out that this was *out at the scene*, not before getting in the car, the prosecutor replies that it *speaks volumes about the context in which the police were travelling with these children.* His second point is that DC2 *asserted that there was no evidence of <u>unlawful</u> conduct*, that *clearly these police had arranged to do what they were going to do- took the children out to Pinkenba- dropped them there- and made-threats to them there-* and that *there's nothing <u>lawful</u>- about doing that.* His summary point on the central issue is *the question is not whether they knew their rights but whether in the whole context of the case it was clear that their rights were not going to be recognised- and the picture painted is that they were not.* The prosecutor's concluding point concerns the issue of recontextualisation of the boys' answers, saying that *as far as I can ascertain without exception-<u>all</u> of the answers upon which* the DCs *rely were brought about as a result of leading questions.* For this reason he argues *that differential weight is to be given* to these answers.

2. The magistrate's decision

On Friday 24 February, one day after the Pinkenba hearing has concluded, the magistrate reads his decision to a packed courtroom. His reading of the prepared statement of 447 words takes almost 5 minutes. His oral presentation conveys written punctuation with clarity, with breath groups clearly indicating commas, full stops and new paragraphs, as indicated in Extract 96:

Extract 96.   Magistrate's decision[39]

[1]   The defendants are six police officers. They are facing charges under Section 355 of the Criminal Code of unlawfully depriving three juveniles of their personal liberty in carrying them away in a motor vehicle against their will.

[2]   It is the submission of the defence that the deprivation of liberty was <u>not</u> unlawful. The prosecution points to the fact that they were <u>told</u>, that is the juveniles were told, to get into the motor vehicles, they didn't want to be there, there's no relatives or friends at Pinkenba. The prosecution has also alluded to events which occurred at Pinkenba.

[3]   The three juveniles with one accord have conceded that the conversation at the scene was *hop in the police car*. Albert Carter admitted that he told the Aboriginal Legal Service that he had been grabbed and forced into the car. This is contrary to what he said in his evidence-in-chief. Each child has admitted that there were no threats to get in, no threats on the way, there is no evidence that they even <u>asked</u> to get out of the motor vehicle. Pender admitted that the main complaint was the fact that they had been <u>dumped</u> at Pinkenba.

[4]   The three complainant children have more knowledge as to their rights in relation to the police than the ordinary child in the street, and in many respects they have more knowledge than many of our adult community members. They have admitted knowing the contents of the card issued by the Aboriginal Legal Service. As well as that, they know the court system well, having kept the court and legal representatives occupied on many occasions. In fact Pender has three pages of previous history and he was the youngest of the trio.

[5]   All three of them, by their <u>history</u> and their own testimony have no regard for members of the community, their property or even the justice system. They have no fear of the police. You only have to look at what they said to the police officers who came upon them at the bus shelter. They <u>all</u> knew that they had the <u>right</u> to re<u>fuse</u> to get in the police motor vehicle, but despite of [sic] this knowledge they proceeded and got in.

[6]   The pertinent words of the section are, and I quote, "against their will". Their evidence suggests that they <u>knew</u> they didn't have to get into the motor vehicle, there were no threats for them to get in, they didn't ask to get <u>out</u> on the way. It is <u>my</u> opinion that there is insufficient evidence to place <u>any</u> of the defendants upon

their trial for the offence as charged or in fact any indictable offence. The defendants are discharged.

As the summary in Table 6 below shows, one-third of the magistrate's decision concerns the character and identity of the witnesses. Consistent with the rights of defendants who are "innocent until proven guilty" in the adversarial system, the characters of the accused police officers are not relevant to the decision. As the evidence against the police officers has come from the three boys, it is their evidence which must be addressed by the magistrate. While adopting the DCs' interpretation of the boys' minimal answers, the magistrate's recontextualisation of their answers is more accurate, as he says that they *admitted* and *conceded* to the allegations made in cross-examination questions (paragraphs 3 and 4). Unlike the DCs he does not switch authorship attribution. But he pays no attention to the interactional context in which they *admitted* and *conceded* to these allegations, focusing only on decontextualised propositions.

Table 6.   Structure of magistrate's decision

Topic	Paragraph Number	Number of words	Number of sentences
Charge	1	37	2
Defence submission	2	15	1
Summary of examination-in-chief	2	46	2
Summary of cross-examination	3	98	5
Identity and character of boys	4–5	145	7
Central issue	5	27	1
Point of law and decision	6	79	4
Total		447	22

In writing his decision, the magistrate has clearly followed the defence construction of the boys' identities as *criminal*s who knew *their rights* and *have no fear of the police*. The magistrate has taken up key points raised by DC2, rather than the actual evidence of the boys. Thus, he reports that the boys *conceded* that the police said *hop in the car*. As we have seen in Section 2.2.3 of Chapter 5, while they did concede this under pressure, none of the boys ever actually used the verb *hop* in reporting what the police said. They used the verbs *jump* and *get*. Similarly, the magistrate echoes a point raised by DC2, in saying *the three complainant children have more knowledge as to their rights in relation to the police than the ordinary child in the street, and in many respects they have more knowledge than many of our adult community members* (paragraph 4). The only way in which this conclusion could be drawn is by a literal interpretation of the *Ye#* answers to questions such as we have seen in preceding chapters. None of the witnesses has given any other indication of their knowledge of legal rights. Of course, this claim, by the magistrate, echoing that of DC2, is also drawn, by inference, from the examination of the *criminal records* of the boys, which are thus effectively highlighted in the decision, by the assertions in paragraphs 4 and 5. The magistrate even goes so far in his presentation of the boys' identities as *criminals* and juvenile delinquents to say *All three of them, by their history and their own testimony have no regard for members of the community, their property or even the justice system* (paragraph 5). To draw this conclusion from their testimony is only possible by the farcically literal interpretation of the boys' *Ye#* answers to pressured and harassing questions, such as those we have seen in earlier chapters.

Paragraph 5 presents the magistrate's conclusion that the boys *have no fear of the police*, which is combined with his assertion that they got in to the cars, in the knowledge that they knew they had *the right to refuse to get in*. The third sentence in paragraph 5 reveals an interesting contrast from the rest of the decision. Until this point, the decision is presented as a depersonalised report on the charge and aspects of the case, including the evidence and character of the boys. The assertion (in paragraph 5) that they *have no fear of the police* is crucial to the central issue, and the magistrate now switches to a persuasive stance, supporting this assertion by directly addressing a personal audience, arguing *You only have to look at what they said . . . .* Following Fairclough (1989: 128) it could be argued that this use of second person pronoun also implies a "relationship of solidarity" between the magistrate and his addressees, namely the courtroom audience, and the wider Queensland community. This personal persuasive stance provides further support to a notion that the magistrate lacked judicial independence.

In Chapter 12, we will consider the individualised mental concept of consent which underlies the magistrate's interpretation of the boys' evidence. It is sufficient at this point to reiterate that the cross-examination linguistic mechanisms which enable the magistrate to draw this conclusion have included:

– assertions and presuppositions which the boys have been unable to challenge

– the exploitation of different cultural norms and communicative practices

– lexical perversion of the boys' claims about the central event

– recontextualisations which have transformed inconsistencies into *lies*

– hostile and aggressive directives and prosodics

While the magistrate has adopted the DCs' presentation of the boys as *criminal*s and juvenile delinquents who have *no fear of the police*, and who knew they could have refused to go with police, he has not taken up in any overt way the vigorous construction of them as liars. His statement in paragraph 3 that part of Albert's cross-examination is *contrary to what he said in his evidence-in-chief* is the only comment which indirectly addresses the issue of *lying*, which we have seen has been a major theme in the cross-examination of all three boys. Thus, in coming to his decision to drop the charges against the police officers, the magistrate has focused on the ways in which the boys' identities and experiences as *criminal*s support the defence argument on the central issue: that the boys must have gone willingly with the police. In making this determination, it is clear that he has focused on the propositional content of the lawyers' questions, to which the boys' minimal agreement has been wrought, by the array of linguistic mechanisms discussed in Parts II and III of this book. It is not surprising that the magistrate has accepted the *criminal* identity of the boys as the central issue: we have seen in Chapters 7 and 9, that he had already internalised this during the cross-examination, addressing two of the boys as *the defendant* on three separate occasions.

At the conclusion of the magistrate's reading of his decision, there is a spontaneous loud applause from the family and friends of the police officers, a rather unusual occurrence in a courtroom.

3. The print media

While the defence construction of the identities of the three boys in this case had a powerful impact on the magistrate's assessment of their characters, it was also having a similar impact on newspaper reporting of the case.

In Section 2 of Chapter 3, we saw how the case resonated with widespread moral panic about a perceived "breakdown in law and order" especially in relation to Aboriginal juveniles (see also Hil 1995; Mickler and McHoul 1998; Trigger 1995; Sercombe 1995). We also saw that the media plays an important role in the generation of moral panic. Decades of research in a number of countries have also shown that the media plays a central role in the reproduction of racism, and that minorities are widely defined in much media coverage as a "problem", even as a "threat" (Van Dijk 1991: 245). It is beyond the scope of this book to undertake an analysis of the media reporting of the Pinkenba event and hearing. However, in this section, we will have a brief glance at some aspects of the newspaper reporting of the hearing. We will see an example of how the linguistic mechanisms which "worked" in the courtroom impacted on the ways in which most Queenslanders and other Australians were "informed" about who these boys were, and about how their claims of being mistreated by the police were assessed by the justice system.

Daily reports in the largest Queensland newspaper (*The Brisbane Courier Mail*, hereafter *CM*) and the largest national newspaper (*The Australian*, hereafter *AN*) unsurprisingly highlighted the identity aspects of the boys emphasised by the DCs during cross-examination. Thus, the *CM* headline for the report of David's first day of evidence proclaimed "Police dumped us: teen thief" (Anon 1995a). The verb *dump* was pervasive in almost all of the *CM* reports on the hearing, with its most consistently used phrase to refer to the Pinkenba event being *the alleged dumping*. David did not say the *police dumped us*, but the headline does not use quotation marks, so perhaps it is intended as a paraphrase. The verb *dump* was only once used by one of the boys in examination-in-chief or cross-examination. This was the oldest witness Barry, who said at the end of his examination-in-chief on the day after this headline, *On the way to that BP service thing two police in one car asked us what was we doing out this late at night- and we said we got dumped out around the corner and that- next to the creek* (p156). The legal charge was "unlawful deprivation of liberty", which would have been quite a mouthful for a daily newspaper. But in ordinary English, it would most readily be described as *abducting*, a lexical item which rarely occurs in the *CM* reports, although it was often used in *AN* reports. The most striking feature which distinguishes *dump* from *abduct* is the expected object of the verb – in the case of *abduct* we would most typically expect the object to be a person, while with *dump* the object would most typically be garbage. In using *dump*, it is possible that the *CM* was expanding the defence line that the boys in this case were not victims – they could be seen as garbage to be *dumped*. On the other hand, it is possible that the *CM* use of *dump* can be seen as a criticism of the police actions in treating the boys in this way.

But the most striking aspect of the newspaper reporting of the Pinkenba hearing was its recontextualisation of the boys' evidence. Just as the DCs in their closing addresses, and the magistrate in his decision, took propositions from cross-examination questions and recast them as propositions uttered by the boys, so too did the newspaper reports. Once again, the misleading impression of verbatim accuracy is used in recontextualisation of evidence on issues central to the case. In Extract 4 in Chapter 4, we saw the extreme harassment used by DC1 to gain Albert's minimal answers of agreement to the shouted pseudo-assertion YOU LIED TO MAKE THINGS LOOK BAD FOR THE POLICE. On the day after

Albert's evidence, the *CM* newspaper carried the headline "'I lied to embarrass police'" with the sub-headline "Boy, 13, tells 'dumping' trial" (Anon 1995b). The statement "I lied to embarrass police" was enclosed in quotation marks, which together with the verb "tells" gives the clear, but completely false, impression that these are the exact words used by the witness. As we have seen, the most that the witness ever said on this point was a very soft °*Yes*° after repeated harassment, and DC1's rejection of his earlier answer of °*No*°. The story below the headline gives some transcript excerpts, which are edited in a misleading way. This is how the newspaper quoted the questions and answers on this point (ibid.):

> "You lied to make things look bad for the police?" Mr Thorpe asked.
> The boy replied: "Yes."
> "You made these things up- made things up to make the police look bad?" Mr Thorpe repeated.
> The boy replied: "Yes"

The way that the second question is quoted in the newspaper gives the impression that it is a fairly close transcription, seeming to record the lawyer's false start (although after repeated listening to the tape recording I am unable to find any utterance which matches this). However, "journalistic licence" has been used to omit repeated tag questions, and there is no mention of the shouting, which we saw in the transcript given as Extract 4 in Chapter 4. Further, there is no mention that the boy denied this proposition (as we saw in Turns 6 and 8 in Extract 4) until he was harassed into agreeing with it. In fact as we have seen in Extract 4 (of which Turns 15 and 16 are repeated below), a more accurate transcription of the first exchange quoted from the newspaper above would find a way of indicating DC1's shouting, his repeated tag questions, the long delay before Albert's response, and the noticeable softness in this response.

from *Extract 4*, DC1 to Albert, Day 2, p136–137

15. DC1:   YOU LIED TO MAKE THINGS LOOK BAD FOR THE POLICE- DIDN'T YOU?
           (1.2) DIDN'T YOU?
16. Albert: (3.5) °Yes°.

The second exchange given in the paper as if it immediately followed the first, actually occurred several minutes later. A closer transcription of this exchange reveals similar harassment as the first (but with less shouting):

Extract 97.   DC1 to Albert, Day 2, p138

1. DC1:   And again- you said those things to- make things look bad for the police
          didn't you? (4.3) <u>didn</u>'t you? (3.4) didn't you?
2. Albert: °Yeh°.

3. M: He said yes.

[brief discussion omitted between DC1 and magistrate about need to get witness to repeat the answer for the record (as it was so hard to hear)]

4. DC1:   Well you said- you MADE these things UP didn't you?
5. Albert: Yes.

6. DC1:   You made them up to make the police look bad didn't you?
7. Albert: °Mm°.

8. DC1:   WHAT?
9. Albert: Yes.

A few days after this newspaper headline, I discussed its misleading nature with one of the journalists involved. He told me that it is "journalistic licence" for newspapers to use quotation marks for utterances attributed to speakers, but not actually uttered by them. He saw no problem with it, and refused to correct the misleading impression it had caused. The newspaper completely ignored my criticism of this headline in a press release which I issued a few days later, although they did accurately report other issues I raised in this press release. Thus, on 28 February, the *CM* report headlined "Public inquiry call on Pinkenba case" (Anon 1995d) and the *AN* report headlined "Aboriginal youths abduction verdict 'a travesty of justice'" (Scott 1995) both reported issues from my press release, as did the reports following these headlines.

While the immediate newspaper reporting of this case unquestioningly took up the defence construction of the boys as *a criminal* threat as its major focus, radio and television presented a more critical view. In several radio and television current affairs broadcasts immediately following the hearing, and the leading television documentary series a year later (ABC 1996), a number of aspects of this case were problematised. These included the actions of the police officers, the response of the Police Commissioner and the Police Minister, as well as the conduct of the hearing, particularly the way in which the boys were cross-examined. In the struggle over police control over Aboriginal young people, investigative journalists play an significant role, as they have in a number of other important Australian power struggles (see Masters 1992).

4.   The struggle continues: ALS vs DPP

Despite the magistrate's decision to discharge the police officers, the ALS was not ready to concede defeat in the struggle over police control of the movements of Aboriginal young people. A few days after the magistrate's decision had been handed down, ALS sent a letter to the Director of Public Prosecutions "formally request[ing]" him to take the police officers to trial by way of "ex officio indictment" (an indictment which would put the officers on trial despite the charges having been dismissed by the magistrate). This letter also "complained that a statement from Dr Diana Eades 'in relation to the socio-linguistic issues in the case' had not been put before the magistrate who discharged the [six police officers] and requested that the director give reasons for the decision not to use that statement" (*Purcell & Ors v. Quinlan & Anor* 1996: 3). (This statement has been briefly discussed in Section 6 of Chapter 1.) The ALS letter concluded:

> We are unconvinced that the boys possessed sophisticated knowledge of their legal rights at the material time, given their youth and the social context from which they come. The evidence supporting the opposite conclusion was only adduced by the defence through a series of "yes" answers which amounted to a classical example of gratuitous concurrence.
> We feel that evidence led at trial in a culturally sensitive manner is capable of leading a properly instructed jury to decide upon a guilty verdict ...

According to the ensuing judicial review (*Purcell & Ors v. Quinlan & Anor* 1996: 3), the Director of Public Prosecutions had replied to the ALS that he did not "propose to present an ex officio indictment", saying that:

> Dr Eades' evidence in my view was arguably inadmissible. Furthermore, having regard to the evidence that had unfolded, I was of the view that any further prosecution of the police six would not have had reasonable prospects of success.

A few weeks later, in March, in a rare legal occurrence, the magistrate's refusal to commit the police officers for trial was appealed against by the three boys (through a close relative of each of them), who sought a judicial review of the decision. In May, the police officers applied to dismiss the application for review. The judge who heard this application at the end of May dismissed this attempt to prevent the review of the magistrate's decision.

5. The judicial review

The resulting judicial review of the magistrate's decision involved the review judge considering "extensive and very detailed arguments in writing" submitted by the applicants (the boys through their close relatives) and the respondents (both the magistrate and the six police officers) (*Purcell & Ors v. Quinlan & Anor* 1996: 4). In the words of the review judge (ibid.: 5), the strong contention of the applicants was "that the stipendiary magistrate had wrongly considered their credibility and/or reliability (which had been severely tested in the course of cross-examination) in reaching his conclusion" that there was insufficient evidence for taking the police officers to trial. The review judge did not accept this contention, citing (ibid.: 6) "a very long line of authority to support the proposition that indeed in determining whether the prosecution has adduced sufficient evidence to put a defendant on trial, a committing magistrate should have regard to the reliability of the evidence not for the purpose of determining whether he personally is persuaded of guilt but for the purpose of determining whether any reasonable jury properly instructed could return a verdict of guilty upon it".

The review judge then went on to evaluate the boys' evidence which he found to be "evidence given in unequivocal terms" (ibid.: 9), using the word "unequivocal" about their evidence 5 times in his 13 page report. As with the DCs in their closing addresses, as well as the magistrate in his decision and the newspaper in its reporting, the review judge counted the boys' minimal agreement to propositions put in questions as being equivalent to propositions uttered by the boys. Thus, for example he says (ibid.: 9) that David "said they were not in any trouble, did not object to getting in the cars and did not ask to get out". We have seen that David did not say this. He did however, provide minimal answers of apparent agreement to these and similar propositions put under hostile and aggressive questioning, using the linguistic mechanisms outlined in Chapter 6.

The review judge also accepted the lexical perversion which was central to the DCs' argument on the central issue in the case, saying (ibid.: 8–9) that David "said that the applicants got into police cars because they were asked to do so". As we have seen in Section 2.2.4 of Chapter 5, neither David nor either of the other two boys used the word *asked* in reporting the police speech act which led to the boys getting in the police cars. They said they were *told* and *forced*. Further, as with DC2 in his closing address, and the magistrate in his decision, the review judge also used Albert's early use of the word *grab* to refer to the police actions as evidence of his unreliability (see discussion in Section 1.3 of Chapter 4 and Section 7 of Chapter 8).

The review judge also dismissed the "socio-linguistic" considerations put by the applicants, which had drawn on my report, and particularly on the problem caused by gratuitous concurrence for taking a literal interpretation of many of the boys' minimal answers. In the judge's view, such arguments "really seem to involve rejecting evidence given in unequivocal terms by the applicants and concluding that by reason of 'socio-linguistic' factors or 'obvious cross-cultural communication difficulties' experienced by them when giving evidence, their evidence which on its face would seem to negative expressly one of the essential elements in the offence alleged against [the six police officers] should be disregarded and it ought to be assumed that they intended to give evidence to the contrary of that which they did in fact give" (ibid.: 9). Thus, we see, from the judge's perspective, interpreting the boys' answers is limited to a farcically literal interpretation in which any *Ye#* answer by a witness is taken to be equivalent to the witness's expression of the proposition put in the question. The analysis in chapters 4–9 above shows that this is a seriously flawed perspective, one which will be taken up in Chapter 12. The review judge's focus on propositional content, and apparent exclusion of any interactional dimensions of the evidence, suggest that he did not listen to the audio-recordings of the evidence, but based his examination of the evidence on the official written transcript.

Unlike the magistrate in his decision, the review judge did not deal with the boys' identities, noting that "much of the evidence canvassed related to matters having only the most peripheral relevance to the elements of the offences charged" (ibid.: 2). He concluded by dismissing the application, thus upholding the magistrate's decision.

6. *Not the end of the matter:* CJC re-enters

Following the magistrate's decision, and while the boys' families were applying for the judicial review, the CJC was making its own response to the outcome of the committal hearing. In the words of the CJC Chairman the acquittal was "not the end of the matter" (CJC 1995). The CJC media release on 3 March went on to say:

> There remains a considerable body of evidence that the boys were abandoned at Pinkenba, some 14 kilometres from the Valley, at an early hour of the morning. They were taken there in three police vehicles, without authorisation, leaving the Valley area virtually unstaffed by uniformed police for a considerable time.
> These matters raise serious issues about the conduct of the police and their supervisor in allowing the incident to occur.

The CJC therefore referred the matter to the Police Commissioner "to institute departmental disciplinary proceedings", emphasising that "it regards these matters very seriously" (ibid.). But it was not only the conduct of the police in the Pinkenba event which was of concern to the CJC. The CJC Chairman, in his 3 March media release, went on to comment on the committal hearing, saying:

> The general manner in which the case appears to have been conducted raises serious questions about the adequacy of the protections offered to vulnerable witnesses in court proceedings. These issues will be addressed in a report to be prepared by the Commission's Research and Co-ordination Division.

As a result, the CJC instituted a wide-ranging and comprehensive research project which produced a 125-page report some twelve months later titled *Aboriginal Witnesses in Queensland's Criminal Courts* (CJC 1996). In the report's introduction, the CJC attributes its decision to carry out this research to "public debate about aspects of the conduct of the committal proceedings in the Pinkenba case", as well as issues that "had also arisen, to varying degrees, in other prominent cases involving Aboriginal people" (ibid.: 2). Two of the three cases named here have been discussed earlier in this book, namely the Condren case (see Section 1.1 of Chapter 2), and the Kina case (see Section 7.2 of Chapter 3). The CJC's assessment was that "these cases highlighted possible systemic problems in the way in which the court system has dealt with Aboriginal witnesses" (ibid.). Further, it expressed concern over the fact that "many Aboriginal people lack confidence in the legal system".

The CJC researchers carried out a thorough review of relevant Australian literature, received submissions from 17 individuals and organisations, and carried out interviews by phone or in person with 150 individuals and groups. Addressing "the barriers that face Aboriginal people who are called to give evidence as witnesses in criminal proceedings" (CJC 1996: xi), it examined language and cultural issues, as well as issues involving interpreters, the court environment, and Aboriginal women specifically. Its 38 recommendations range from the provision of cross-cultural awareness training for lawyers, as well as new judges and magistrates, to the consideration of the needs of hearing impaired persons in the design of future court facilities, given the high incidence of hearing impairment among Aboriginal people. Several of its recommendations were specifically focused on linguistic issues in courtroom interaction, and are thus of particular relevance to this book. Three of these particular recommendations suggested changes to the *Evidence Act*, so that (ibid.: xix–xx)

- a witness has the possibility of giving evidence-in-chief wholly or partly in narrative form
- a court has the power to disallow a particular leading question in cross-examination, and in using this power should take into account "among other things the extent to which the witness's cultural background or use of language may affect his or her answers"
- in deciding whether a question is indecent, scandalous, insulting, annoying or offensive (under section 21, see discussion in Section 1.2 of Chapter 4), the court is required to take account of the witness's cultural background

These recommended changes to the *Evidence Act* became part of the comprehensive review of the act which the Department of Justice undertook (CJC 1997b: 14–15). In the discussion of the 2003 amendments to the *Evidence Act* in Section 3 of Chapter 11, we will see that the third of these recommendations was adopted in this form. While the first two were not adopted in exactly this form, some of the changes to the act addressed these issues.

A related recommendation, which did not require any change to the rules of evidence, was that prosecutors should be instructed to "object to questions asked of an Aboriginal witness which, because of the witness's linguistic and cultural background, are inappropriate". The report pointed out that the rules of evidence already provided for such objections with "the court's discretionary power to control cross-examination or sections 20 or 21 of the *Evidence Act 1977*". We have seen in Section 1 above that this part of the *Evidence Act* gives power to the court to disallow any question which is "intended only to insult or annoy or which is needlessly offensive in form". This suggests that the existing legislation did provide safeguards which could have effectively prevented much of the questioning in the Pinkenba case, if it had been used, an issue to be taken up in Section 3 of Chapter 11.

7.   The Police Commissioner, the Minister and the Union

Although the CJC had asked the Police Commissioner to institute departmental disciplinary proceedings against the six police officers for their misconduct involved in taking the boys to Pinkenba, there appeared to be little support from the commissioner to take any action against the officers. An internal police department inquiry into the actions of the six police officers involved placed them on probation, effectively deciding not to punish them in any way (Anon 1995f) and they reportedly returned to normal duties (Amnesty International 1997: 7).

Information about reactions from within the police service, the government and the union are available from the investigative television documentary about relationships between Aboriginal people and the Queensland police, which was screened one year after the Pinkenba hearing (ABC 1996). Three key people interviewed in this documentary provided views on the Pinkenba incident and hearing from police perspectives.

The President of the Queensland Police Union (hereafter, the union president) defended the actions of the police officers involved, emphasising their difficulties in *dealing with juvenile offenders*. For the union president, it was the police officers who were the victims in the Pinkenba hearing, who were *put through hell- what they've gone through ... is more than any police officer would go through had he been charged with a criminal offence*. Interestingly this statement ignores the fact that the police officers in the Pinkenba case were *charged with a criminal offence*, unlawful deprivation of liberty.

The Police Commissioner, who is the administrative head of the police force, also argued against disciplinary action being taken against the police officers involved. However, he told the television interviewer that what the police did in the Pinkenba event was *not the type of conduct I will tolerate ... these people will pay a price as well as those who should have been supervising them.* It has never been clear what he expected this price to be.

The government leader in police matters is the Police Minister, who spoke of the Pinkenba incident in neutral terms as *an unfortunate incident.* When pressed by the television interviewer, he conceded that it was *an extremely unfortunate incident- to play on words* [sic]. He did not see any need for disciplinary action against the police officers, arguing that *they should be free to go about their duties.* He had earlier been reported in the newspaper as saying that they should not have to face a misconduct hearing because they had been "cleared by a court" (Anon 1995c).

The television interviews with these diverse official representatives of the police reproduced the general identity of the three boys which had been established by the defence during the Pinkenba hearing. The union president referred to the boys as *juvenile offenders*, while the Police Commissioner rejected the interviewer's concerns about the pressures placed on these kids in an adult court. Echoing the construction of DC2, which we have already found echoed above in the magistrate's decision, the commissioner said (ABC 1996):

> *I don't believe the boys were in any way intimidated by the process- they might have been young in terms of age and years- but very old and wise in terms of the world ... they were not your everyday Sunday school children- they were committing many many serious offences and had committed them for some time ... [they] were very skilled in the ways of the world*

An earlier newspaper report had reported the criticism by the ALS senior solicitor of the term which this police commissioner had used to refer to the three boys, immediately after the magistrate's decision had been made. This ALS lawyer "said that [the Police Commissioner] had used a press conference to denigrate the three Aboriginal complainants as 'thugs'" (Anon 1995e).

8.   Conclusion

In this chapter we have seen the results of the array of linguistic mechanisms used by the DCs in cross-examination to gain minimal answers to their damaging allegations about the boys and the Pinkenba event. At all the stages of the criminal justice process which followed their cross-examination, the boys' evidence was decontextualised and recontextualised, as it also was in print media reports which provided the main source of information to the wider community about what "had happened" in the Pinkenba event and the courtroom hearing. These entextualisations resulted in a powerful presentation of the boys in terms of the widespread construction of Aboriginal people as a criminal threat to society, and of the legitimisation of the police actions that night in taking the boys for a ride. This ride to Pinkenba and the courtroom cross-examination were micro-events in the exercise of neocolonial power over Aboriginal people. It is in just such agency of individuals in the criminal justice system that this power is perpetuated – these are key events in the reproduction of inequality in contemporary Australian society,

But power is not static or uncontested. The agency of the boys and their families, together with ALS and CJC, had resulted in the courtroom contest over the police exercise of power in that ride to Pinkenba. And for the ALS and the CJC, the outcome of this contest – in which the magistrate decided to drop the charges against the police officers – was *not the end of the matter*. In taking the Pinkenba case to judicial review, and in the review of Aboriginal witnesses in criminal courts, the ALS and CJC respectively exercised their power in productive ways in the struggle over police control over Aboriginal people. In the ten years since the Pinkenba case was closed, there have been a number of developments in the participation of Aboriginal people in the criminal justice system. It is to some of these developments that we turn in Chapter 11.

Chapter 11
Developments since the Pinkenba case

The Pinkenba case has highlighted two aspects of the participation of Aboriginal people in the criminal justice system: police control and courtroom cross-examination. I have argued that the ways in which the witnesses were cross-examined in the Pinkenba case led to the legal system legitimising the police control over them, which involved taking them out of town and abandoning them, an act of over-policing involving harassment and abuse. Central to the cross-examination in this case was the denial of the boys' claimed identities as victims of police abuse, and the construction of them as lying *criminal*s, who are a danger on the streets of Brisbane. We have also seen that this case is not an isolated incident of police mistreatment of Aboriginal young people: it is part of an ongoing struggle over societal control of Aboriginal people, in which the criminal justice system plays a central role.

It is now more than a decade since the Pinkenba case, which was extreme, both in terms of the criminal charges being laid against six police officers, and the language practices in the courtroom. It is impossible in this book to adequately address the question: what has been the impact of the Pinkenba case on the policing of Aboriginal Queenslanders? It has been a decade of change in many ways in the criminal justice system in Queensland, and it would be naïve to attempt to attribute direct causes for this change. Instead this chapter will present selected events and developments in the criminal justice system which relate to the ongoing struggle between Aboriginal people and the police since this case. While the focus of this chapter is Queensland, we will glimpse a few incidents at the end of the chapter which indicate that the current struggle between Aboriginal people and the police is not limited to Queensland, and that Australia is not the only country where there is a struggle over neocolonial control exercised by the police over Aboriginal people.

1.   Policing of Aboriginal people

The "success" of the Pinkenba case can perhaps be seen in the fact that there has been no conviction of a police officer for abuse of an Aboriginal person since this case. Further, until January 2007 there have been no criminal proceedings against a police officer for abuse of an Aboriginal person (see Section 5 below for a recent development). Given the way in which the Pinkenba case legitimised police abuse of Aboriginal people, it is perhaps hardly surprising that Amnesty International found support for "the allegation that police use of excessive force [on Aboriginal and Torres Strait Islander people] often occurs in the context of alleged street offences" (1997: 5). While raising concerns about the extent of police violence reported by Aboriginal people, the Amnesty International report focused on one particular incident. This occurred in a shopping mall in Ipswich, a city contiguous with Brisbane, just two years after the Pinkenba hearing, in March 1997. The incident, which began with an altercation between two Aboriginal young people, was filmed on security video cameras. Several local police attended the altercation, assisted by visiting US military police, who had apparently been asked to be available should any trouble occur between Aboriginal people and visiting US servicemen. According to the videorecording and accounts from bystanders there were a number of violent attacks by the local police on several Aboriginal people. To my knowledge, there were no criminal proceedings against any police officer involved in these attacks. While the Amnesty Report is nearly a decade old, we will see in Section 5 below that police violence against Aboriginal people has not ceased.

But it is important not to essentialise the Queensland police. While there is evidence of abuse against Aboriginal people, there have also been institutional attempts within the Queensland Police Service to improve its dealings with Indigenous (as well as "ethnic" or immigrant) communities, driven to some extent by the need to address "the 'problem' of Indigenous people *for* police" (Cunneen 2001: 228, emphasis in original). Many of these initiatives are also driven by community and government insistence that the police service address the many recommendations of the Royal Commission into Aboriginal Deaths in Custody (discussed in Section 6 of Chapter 3).

One of these initiatives is in the area of community policing, such as reported by CJC (1998) for Brisbane policing divisions. One example comes from a division which had been experiencing an increase in the number of complaint calls about the behaviour of young Aboriginal and Torres Strait Islander people. A "problem" was identified as "more young [Indigenous] people walking the streets late hours of the night" (ibid.: 45). We have seen that the legal activity of walking the streets late at night makes Indigenous young people particularly vulnerable to police abuse, so this might be expected to be a situation in which the community is particularly cautious in accepting police support. However, in this area a number of Aboriginal community members worked with police and Neighbourhood Watch (a community organisation). One of the outcomes was the organisation of a camp for local young people which aimed to encourage the education of the young people in Aboriginal and Torres Strait Islander customs.

The CJC (ibid.) reported that there had been a decline both in crime and in complaints since the implementation of this strategy.

Other initiatives (with similarities to developments in other states) include the introduction of cultural awareness training for police officers, the appointment of cross-cultural liaison officers to improve relations between police and the Indigenous (and ethnic communities), and the recruitment of increasing numbers of Indigenous people to the police force (Queensland Police Service 2005). It remains to be seen what the effect of these measures will be. The experiences of Queensland's highest ranking Aboriginal police officer, Inspector Col Dillon, who retired in 2000, are disappointing. Reportedly (Balogh 2000), in his 35 years of service as a police officer, he had "never once been asked how he believes racism can be countered. He brands his previous appointment in the service's cross-cultural advisory office as a political 'showpiece' position which failed to make inroads". Further, he felt that Queensland was not an isolated state, saying that "the taint of racism still exists within the nation's police ranks" (ibid.).

Dillon's complaints provide support for Cunneen's (2001: 227–228) suggestion that most of the developments such as those discussed above, are basically limited to indigenisation of existing police structures, which "reflect the power relations of neocolonialism". As Cunneen explains (ibid.: 228) it is "a form of control which essentially relies on Indigenous people carrying out particular functions at the interpersonal edge of policing where the priorities and goals of that system of control are being determined largely outside of Indigenous political mechanisms".

But, while the changes within the Queensland police may be open to criticism for not going far enough, others complain they have gone too far. Evidence which suggests some changes in the policing of Aboriginal people since the Pinkenba case comes from the complaints of a retiring police officer in a 2005 letter to the editor of *The Queensland Police Union Journal* (Ellis 2005). In the opening paragraph of this 600-word letter, the officer self-identifies as one of those charged in the "infamous 'Pinkenba 6' incident", saying "I hate to think where we might have ended up without the best legal team" (Ellis 2005: 19). The main complaint in the letter is that changes to the police service have resulted in "the loss of brotherhood" for Queensland police. The officer attributes much of the blame for this to Tony Fitzgerald, who had conducted the inquiry into police corruption, discussed in Section 5 of Chapter 3. (Interestingly, the report of this inquiry was released in 1989, some five years before the Pinkenba incident, and there were already significant changes within the Queensland Police Service by the mid-1990s, as reported in CJC 1997a). Ellis is also critical of the premier at the time of Fitzgerald's report, and the "upper management" of the police service. Sixteen years after Fitzgerald's report and the establishment of the CJC, and ten years after the Pinkenba hearing exonerated this officer and his five colleagues, this officer explains what has gone wrong with policing in Queensland in his view (Ellis 2005: 19):

> Mr Fitzgerald may have been a brilliant QC – but he was definitely no copper! He simply never understood that to have an effective Police Force, you need to be able to trust your colleagues implicitly. He set out to break down the code of silence and the brotherhood, and have a more transparent Police Force. As far as I'm concerned the Police Force should be like a Rugby League side ... all trying to move in the same direction. If you have individuals trying to break that up – the harmony is lost, and the other side wins.

This letter suggests that the Fitzgerald Inquiry may have had what many would regard as a positive effect in changing the "code of silence" in the police force. This retiring officer complains that "there is simply no place in this job for a guy who can't trust anyone under the rank of Senior Constable – and has no respect for anyone over the rank of Sergeant" (ibid.). This may be evidence that post-Fitzgerald police recruitment, training and changes would make it harder for police to treat Aboriginal people in the way that the three boys were treated in the Pinkenba event. The letter does not specifically refer to Aboriginal people. But, the "us" versus "them" discourse which we saw in the police-Aboriginal struggle leading up to the Pinkenba event (in Section 7 of Chapter 3), is taken up in Ellis' point that one of the consequences in the "loss of brotherhood" in the police force is that "the other side wins".

2.   Sentencing of Aboriginal people

Potentially the most significant change to the participation of Aboriginal Queenslanders in the criminal justice system has been not at the level of policing, but at the level of sentencing. In 2002, the Murri Court was introduced as a sentencing court for Indigenous people who plead guilty to criminal cases which are normally dealt with in the lower courts. This is consistent with the introduction of Indigenous courts in other states, and it represents a major development in addressing the over-representation of Indigenous people in prison. There are different models in each state, with the Indigenous court in Queensland called the "Murri Court", after the word for Aboriginal person widely used throughout the state.[40] Unless otherwise specified, information here about the Murri Court comes from the Queensland Department of Justice and Attorney-General (QJAG 2005, 2006).

The most significant difference between the Murri Court on the one hand, and the Magistrates and Children's Courts, on the other, is in the participation of

Indigenous Elders or respected persons who sit with the magistrate. Their role is four-fold (QJAG 2005: 1), to:

- tell the Magistrate about cultural issues
- help the offender to understand what is being said and what is happening in court
- help the Magistrate decide on a sentence that is most appropriate (but just like any other Magistrates Court, the Magistrate makes the sentencing decision)
- act as a connection between the court and the local Indigenous communities

The participation of the Elders and respected persons represents a significant change from other courts, where Indigenous people often feel alienated, and where, as we have seen in this book, aspects of Aboriginal lifestyle and culture can be misunderstood or ignored (see also Eades 2000). Another significant change is that the Murri Court is less adversarial than other courts, as an important priority is for participants to talk to each other about diverse aspects related to the offender's situation, in order to constructively work out "a plan for the offender which targets those issues that have led to the illegal behaviour" (QJAG 2005: 2). The review of the Murri Court (Parker and Pathé 2006: 17–18) found that it is characterised by relatively informal language, and that offenders and victims are encouraged to talk freely. While there has been no study of language use in the court, it would be expected that, given the key role of Elders and respected persons, there would be comfortable use of Aboriginal English by many of the participants. This would presumably include a move away from the dominance of question-answer format, which characterises all other court proceedings. The style of the hearing involves discussion among all parties about the offender, the offence and the sentence, in a way which should remove the need for cross-examination. While this might seem like a significant innovation, it should be remembered that the Murri Court effectively only conducts sentencing hearings. Such hearings in regular courts do not generally involve intensive cross-examination, as the guilt or innocence of the defendant is not at issue. Eades' (2000) study of thirteen sentencing hearings in New South Wales found that of the nineteen Aboriginal witnesses who gave evidence, seven had no cross-examination, and the remaining witnesses had only short cross-examinations.

One of the main aims of the Murri Court is to "reduce the over-representation of Indigenous offenders in prison" (QJAG 2005: 1). Thus the court follows the recommendation of the Royal Commission into Aboriginal Deaths in Custody that prison should be the sanction of last resort (Johnston 1991a: 52). Considerable attention is paid to the possibilities for drug and alcohol treatment programs, as well as "psychological and violence treatment agencies" (QJAG 2005: 4). The fact that in its first three years, the Murri Court dealt with only about 0.2% of adult Indigenous court matters, and about 1.5% of juvenile Indigenous matters (Cunneen et al. 2005: xvi), suggests that its impact to date cannot be significant. Cunneen et al. (ibid.: 150) point out that the Murri Court is an initiative of the magistrates, and in its first four years of operation it received no government support. The Elders and respected persons participate on a voluntary basis, and until a government commitment to adopt recommendations in the review of the court, there was no administrative support for the many tasks associated with successful running of the court (Parker and Pathé 2006).

Being sentencing courts, the Murri Court cannot hear pleas of not guilty, which continue to go through the regular courts. Further, they are not used in cases where the witnesses are Aboriginal, but the defendant is not, such as the Pinkenba case (which was also a case involving pleas of not guilty, by the charged police officers). The Murri Court, like the Indigenous courts in other states, represents a serious and innovative approach within the criminal justice system to address the criminalisation of Indigenous people at the level of sentencing. But, it can have no direct impact on over-policing, found to be a central issue in the criminalisation of Aboriginal people (as discussed in Section 1.3 of Chapter 3). It may be found to have some indirect impact on over-policing, as some police officers may gain more understanding of Aboriginal culture and lifestyles, and more respect for Aboriginal people, through working cooperatively with Elders and respected persons in Murri Court. But it may not work quite like that, following White's (1994) concerns about some of the features of early models of alternative juvenile sentencing courts, which share a number of features with the Indigenous courts. White argues that these juvenile alternative sentencing processes were effectively extending the power of police by giving them a role in sentencing, and that they were "extending the degree of state intervention into the lives of young people (ibid.: 195, but see Braithwaite 1994).

3.   Changes to the Evidence Act

In 2003, the Queensland government legislated changes to the *Evidence Act*, many of which related to the evidence of children. These new rules of evidence should reduce the likelihood for any future cross-examination of children in committal hearings as extreme as we saw in the Pinkenba case. These 2003 amendments recognise that a child "tends to be vulnerable in dealings with a person in authority" and the new rules are intended to give a child witness "the benefit of special measures" when giving evidence. The act now sets out the following general principles for child witnesses (Section 9E):

a) the child is to be treated with dignity, respect and compassion
b) measures should be taken to limit, to the greatest practical extent, the distress or trauma suffered by the child when giving evidence
c) the child should not be intimidated in cross-examination
d) the proceeding should be resolved as quickly as possible

Amendments to Section 21 of the act make a number of specific provisions for child witnesses consistent with these general principles. These include a requirement for children who give evidence-in-chief in committal hearings, to do so not in court, but in the form of a statement (Section 21AF). Most relevant to the conduct of the Pinkenba case are the two new lengthy sections on cross-examination of children in committal proceedings (Sections 21AG and 21AH). While these sections place a number of limits on the cross-examination of a child witness, this depends ultimately on the magistrate's discretion. The rules of evidence now stipulate that a child cannot be cross-examined at all in a committal hearing, unless a magistrate requires this. A party who wishes to cross-examine a child must convince the magistrate of the relevance of the child's evidence, as well as "the purpose and general nature of the questions to be put to the child" (Section 21AG3). Thus, while the new rules of evidence can provide considerable protection for child witnesses in committal hearings, a magistrate could accept defence arguments that could arguably still result in the type of cross-examination which we have seen in this book. The evidence of a child in a preliminary hearing, such as a committal hearing, must be videotaped, and it is this videotape which is presented to court if the matter proceeds to trial. But child witnesses can still be cross-examined in a <u>trial</u>, although there is now provision for them to have a support person sitting close by while they are giving evidence.

In addition to these amendments which protect the vulnerability of child witnesses, particularly in committal hearings, Section 21A also considerably extends the protections of special witnesses. We saw in Section 5 of Chapter 1 that, at the time of the Pinkenba hearing, witnesses considered to be "special witnesses" could give evidence-in-chief behind a screen, or by videotape. The 2003 amendment to the rules of evidence extend this protection. Special witnesses (often also referred to as "vulnerable witnesses") are defined in Section 21A primarily in terms of their "age, education, level of understanding, cultural background or relationship to any party to the proceeding". As before, special witnesses can be protected to some extent by a court (i.e. the ruling judge or magistrate) ordering that the defendant be excluded from the witness's view, or that other people be excluded from the court, or that the special witness can give their evidence-in-chief by videotaped recording. But the court now also has the power to order that questions be kept simple, and/or limited by time, and/or limited in number on a particular issue. While these provisions may be able to minimise the likelihood of gratuitous concurrence with Aboriginal witnesses, the power still rests with the court to decide whether a witness is a special witness, and is thus entitled to these protections. Similarly, the decisions about placing restrictions on specific questions, also rests with the court. The Pinkenba magistrate's apparent view of the witnesses in that case as defendants, suggests that vulnerable witnesses may not always receive this new protection in high stakes cases, such as Aboriginal complainants in cases in which police officers are charged.

Another important amendment to the *Evidence Act* considerably extends the earlier powers of the court (i.e. the presiding magistrate or judge) to disallow certain questions in cross-examination. This power is not restricted to child witnesses, or to special witnesses, as in the provisions discussed above. The new Section 21 is more general than the one it replaces, which, as we saw in Section 1.2 of Chapter 4, gave the court the power to disallow any question which is "intended only to insult or annoy or is needlessly offensive in form". This power now extends to any question which the "court considers is an improper question". An "improper question" is defined as "a question that uses inappropriate language or is misleading, confusing, annoying, harassing, intimidating, offensive, oppressive or repetitive". Section 21 also specifies characteristics of witnesses which "the court must take into account" when "deciding whether a question is an improper question". These include the characteristics which are involved in the definition of a special witness (see above). Most relevant for our consideration here is that the characteristics to be taken into account include age and cultural background (the latter being one of the CJC 1996 recommendations, as we saw in Section 6 of Chapter 10). As with the other new provisions, the ultimate decision over when to use this power rests with the judge or magistrate. It is hard to imagine that many of the questions addressed to the Aboriginal children in the Pinkenba cross-examination could have still been allowed if this new legislation had been in place at the time. However, in such a politically charged case as a police officer charged with abuse of an Aboriginal person, the discretion of the judge or magistrate may still permit such questions.

Changes to the *Evidence Act* did not make any provision for leading questions to be disallowed in certain situations, thus not taking up the CJC (1996: 53) recommendation which would have provided some protection against gratuitous concurrence (as discussed in Section 1.2 of Chapter 4). Further, there was no change which could allow a witness to give evidence wholly or partly in narrative form (as the CJC 1996 report had also recommended).

It is to be hoped that magistrates and judges are better informed now about issues affecting Aboriginal witnesses, and would thus be ready to use their powers under the new rules of evidence. Cultural awareness training and effective communication is now considered to be important for the judiciary, as well as for police, lawyers and detention centre staff (Cunneen et al. 2005). Two recent publications for judiciary and others who work in the Queensland criminal justice system deal with issues involved in communicating with Aboriginal witnesses. The Queensland Department of Justice (2000) *Handbook on Aboriginal English* is based primarily on my lawyers' handbook (Eades 1992). The Queensland Supreme Court's (2005) *Equal Treatment Benchbook* was prepared by judges for judges, to address the need for an understanding of differences in order to provide equal treatment. Primarily related to ethnicity, religion, disability, age, sexuality and gender, this benchbook devotes one chapter to "Indigenous language and communication" (which also draws heavily on my work).

4.   The Justice Agreement

The 2002 introduction of the Murri Court and the 2003 changes to the rules of evidence, which have the possibility of being used for Aboriginal witnesses, need to be seen in the light of more wide-ranging developments in Queensland which relate to the participation of Indigenous people in the criminal justice system. This issue is most frequently discussed in terms of the high over-representation of Aboriginal people in police custody and prisons, discussed in Chapter 3. This over-representation has provided the focus for national summit meetings of Indigenous leaders and government ministers, and for ongoing public attention to the many ways in which the criminal justice system continues to fail Indigenous people. In 2000, the Queensland government undertook a major policy initiative directly aimed at "reducing Indigenous contact with the criminal justice system to parity with the non-Indigenous rate" (Queensland Government 2001: 11). In partnership with the Aboriginal and Torres Strait Islander Advisory Board the government signed a 10-year "Aboriginal and Torres Strait Islander Justice Agreement". The Agreement document outlines a range of initiatives in the area of criminal justice as part of a wider Ten Year Partnership which also addresses issues of family violence, reconciliation, economic development, community governance, service delivery and human services, as well as land, heritage and natural resources. Central to the Justice Agreement are principles of Indigenous participation, acknowledgement of the past and respect for Indigenous cultural values.

While it is impossible in this book to provide even an overview of the initiatives involved, it is important to make the point that the Queensland government is taking the participation of Indigenous people in the criminal justice system seriously, and implementing a considerable number of initiatives in a range of ways. In their evaluation of the agreement after the first five years, Cunneen et al. (2005: xiv-xv) found "progress in some areas", such as youth justice conferencing and police cautioning, cross-cultural training, and the Murri Courts. They were however, critical of the level of support provided and the ways in which this limited the impact of these developments. We saw in Section 2 above the evaluation report's (Cuneen et al. 2005: 150) criticism of lack of government funds to enable the Murri Court to hear more than a tiny fraction of relevant cases. The government was responsive to this criticism, and related recommendations of the review of the Murri Court (Parker and Pathé 2006), and allocated some funding for the court in the 2006–2007 budget.

Perhaps the most important aspect of the justice agreement is that it involves partnership between the government and Indigenous organisations. Thus there are Indigenous representatives on all the committees, and the agreement is intended to work in such a way that "the community has its say" (Queensland Government 2001: 16). But the over-representation of Indigenous Queenslanders in prison continues: while they comprise 3.5% of the state's population, they comprise 27% of adult prisoners and 60% of juveniles in detention (Parker and Pathé 2006: 4).

5.   The struggle continues

Despite recent positive developments related to the participation of Indigenous people in the criminal justice system, the struggle with police is far from resolved, as we will see in a few recent Queensland cases.

Legislation which criminalises so-called "offensive language" continues to be used against Aboriginal people. Late one night in September 2000, a police officer confronted a drunk Aboriginal woman in a Brisbane street less than two kilometres from the area where the police had picked up the boys before taking them to Pinkenba. Details of this case come from the applicant's submission in her 2001 appeal (*Del Vecchio v Couchy* 2001 Applicant's submission). The woman was an alcoholic who was "usually itinerant", and was well known to police. This particular police officer and the woman knew each other, and she said to him *I'm lost. Where am I?* The police officer went away and returned a few minutes later with two more officers. The female police officer then asked the woman for her full name and address. The woman replied with "words to the effect of *fuck you cunt* or *you fucking cunt* or *fucking cunt*". There was no one else in the vicinity apart from the woman and the police officers. She was then arrested for using insulting words (and there was no other charge). She was found guilty and sentenced to three weeks imprisonment. Her appeal to the District Court resulted in the sentence being reduced to seven days. Further appeals to the Supreme Court and the High Court were unsuccessful (*Del Vecchio v Couchy* 2002; *Couchy vs Del Vecchio* 2004). The fact that an Aboriginal person, who was not charged with any other offence, can go to prison for a week for swearing at a police officer, shows clearly that the legal system continues to support the neocolonial control of the police over Aboriginal Queenslanders in the 21st century.

While it is unclear how often Aboriginal people are arrested for swearing, the above incident was not an isolated one. Just six months after the episode discussed above, the same woman was found guilty of swearing in a house in Brisbane. On this occasion police were called to a house where the woman was involved in an argument. During the course of their visit, police threatened to arrest her if she did not *calm down* and *keep* her *voice down*. This prompted the woman to say to the police officer "words to the effect of *I'm not talking to you cunts. You can go and get fucked.*" (*Couchy v Guthrie* 2005). Her appeal against this conviction was unsuccessful (ibid.).

And in December 2004, the same woman was convicted in the Brisbane Magistrates Court of committing a public nuisance – namely, swearing at a security guard in a shopping mall, as well as obstructing the arresting police officer in the performance of the officer's duties. The magistrate found that the accused woman had verbally abused the security guard, saying *You can't kick me out of this place because you are a fucking racist.* She appealed and the appeal court judge agreed with the magistrate's decision about the "offensive language". However, he overturned the conviction, finding that the woman's arrest without a warrant was unlawful, as the offence of which she was suspected and then charged, was not an indictable offence (*Couchy v Birchley* 2005).

These swearing cases give some indication of the ongoing struggle between Aboriginal people and police. A much more serious event occurred in Palm Island (in North Queensland) in November 2004, when an Aboriginal man, Mulrunji, died in a police cell from injuries he received in the police station. Following his death there was a hasty police investigation which did not follow the "standards" set by the state coroner and the Royal Commission into Aboriginal Deaths in Custody (Clements 2006: 9). Angered by the death and this investigation, 300 Palm Islanders gathered at the courthouse one week after Mulrunji's death. In their protest, some people set fire to the courthouse and police station, leading police to declare a state of emergency (Hollinsworth 2005: 16). In response to widespread outrage over the conduct of the initial investigation, a coronial inquest was held which took 22 months. The coroner's report (Clements 2006) provides a damning account of the actions of the police officer involved. In summary, the coroner found that Mulrunji was a fit, healthy man, who was not a trouble maker, and had never previously been arrested on Palm Island. He was arrested while intoxicated for the offence of "public nuisance" (ibid.: 3), after swearing at police officers in the street. This is typical of the over-policing of Aboriginal people, which was decried by the Royal Commission into Aboriginal Deaths in Custody (No 87, Johnston 1991a: 50), which recommended "the principle of arrest being the sanction of last resort", as well as the decriminalisation of both public drunkenness and offensive language. The coroner found that the senior sergeant's decision to arrest Mulrunji was "completely unjustified" (Clements 2006: 3), pointing to alternatives such as giving a caution, issuing a direction or commencing proceedings by way of notice to appear or summons (ibid.: 28). She pointed out that the detailed recommendations from the Royal Commission into Aboriginal Deaths in Custody (discussed in Section 6 of Chapter 3) are "still apt and still ignored" (p28). Mulrunji's arrest was also in contravention of one of the specific ways of "building capacities" given in the state Justice Agreement document signed just a few years earlier (Queensland Government 2001: 14). This agreement gave as an example of ways of addressing the over-representation of Aboriginal people in custody: "not charging people who are drunk but taking them to a diversionary centre and offering them rehabilitation".

While resisting being taken to the police cell, Mulrunji punched the senior sergeant in the jaw. The coroner found that the senior sergeant's response resulted in both men falling to the floor where the police officer hit Mulrunji "a number of times". Over the next hour, cell surveillance video filmed Mulrunji "writhing in pain as he lay dying on the cell floor" (Clements 2006: 32). Cursory cell inspections did not lead to any action, apart from the senior sergeant "nudging Mulrunji with his foot". Mulrunji was dead when an ambulance came, one hour after he had arrived at the police station. Two autopsies found that he died from blood loss caused by his liver being "virtually completely ruptured" (ibid.: 7). He also had four broken ribs and a ruptured spleen. In her finding about how Mulrunji received the injuries which caused his death, the coroner rejected some of the senior sergeant's evidence as "untruthful" (ibid.: 25), and found that Mulrunji's death was the result of being hit by him.

As he did with the police officers involved in the Pinkenba case a decade earlier, the Queensland Police Union President defended the senior sergeant found to have caused Mulrunji's death, saying *He's done nothing wrong and he has the full support of the union* (ABC radio news 27 September 2006). In his criticism of the coroner, the union president described the inquest as a *witch-hunt* and said *she's cherry-picked the evidence to support her anti-police agenda* (ABC television news 27 September 2006). These and similar comments resulted in the president being charged with contempt in November 2006, which could have resulted in imprisonment (ABC radio news 29 November 2006). Just before his appearance in the Supreme Court four months later, the president made a public statement, in which he admitted to contempt and apologised, saying *It was wrong and insulting for me to accuse [the coroner] of bias and prejudgment and I now realise that I should not have done so*. The court then decided not to record a conviction against him (ABC radio news 19 March 2007).

The union president's construction of an *anti-police agenda* on the part of the coroner in this case suggests that the "us versus them" mentality which pervaded police-Aboriginal relations at the time of the Pinkenba incident and hearing is still current more than a decade later. An even clearer statement of the ongoing struggle came from an unnamed Palm Island Aboriginal woman featured on national television news on the day the coroner's report was released (ABC television news 27 September 2006). This demonstrably triumphant woman used a war metaphor in expressing her reaction to the coroner's finding, saying *Yes! Yes- you beauty! Victory finally! Yes! They found- they found that he got hit three times by the officer on the way down.*

The coroner's finding represented a highly significant first occurrence in the history of Aboriginal deaths in custody – *a landmark case*, in the words of lawyer Andrew Boe (who represented the Palm Island community in the inquest). As Boe explained: *for the first time a coroner has made findings that a police officer may have been involved in a criminal offence in relation to an Aboriginal death in custody* (ABC radio news 28 September 2006).

Twelve weeks after the coroner's finding, the Director of Public Prosecutions announced her decision not to lay charges against this police officer. There was widespread condemnation of this decision, and the Queensland government appointed a former chief justice of neighbour state, New South Wales, to review it. Following this review's recommendation, the Attorney-General instructed the Crown Solicitor to issue proceedings to charge the police officer with manslaughter and assault. This decision resulted in large protest meetings by members of the police union in both Brisbane and Townsville.

The trial of the police officer took place in Townsville over seven days in June 2007. In his evidence, the accused police officer said that he *must have accidentally caused the injuries* which killed Mulrunji when they both fell during the struggle while he was taking Mulrunji to the cell (ABC radio news 15 June 2007). The main issue for the prosecution related to these events in the police station, for which there was only one Aboriginal witness to give evidence. Lawyers present at the trial found that the cross-examination of this witness and the four other Aboriginal witnesses was "surprisingly vigorous" (reported to me "off the record"). This is not the place for an analysis of this case. However, readers of this book would not be so surprised to hear of vigorous cross-examination of Aboriginal Queenslanders who are prosecution witnesses in criminal proceedings against a member of the police force. Given the evidence, analysis and argument presented here, perhaps it is also unsurprising that the jury took only four hours to return a verdict of not guilty on both counts.

In this case of the police officer accused of assault and manslaughter of the Aboriginal man he had arrested for swearing, the struggles over power between police and Aboriginal people were clearly visible. In his closing address, defence counsel told the jury that *you would have to have eyes political to conclude [the senior sergeant] did what he is accused of* (ABC radio news 19 June 2007). (That is, he was arguing that a guilty verdict would be a political conclusion, not a legal one.) And on the day following the acquittal of the senior sergeant in this case, the Queensland Police Union launched a state-wide advertising campaign accusing the government of political interference in the case – namely the Attorney-General's actions in going against the original decision of the Director of Public Prosecutions not to charge the police officer. A major theme of the advertisements was that the charges against the senior-sergeant had been an injustice to him. In an ironic twist of the race relations issue, these advertisements included the statement *Martin Luther King once said injustice anywhere is a threat to justice everywhere* (ABC radio news 21 June 2007). At the same time Aboriginal leaders were making their own response, and organised a national day of action to call for justice for all Aboriginal people affected by a death in custody. Brisbane Aboriginal activist and former ALS administrator Sam Watson was reported as saying that the verdict had *brought race relations in this country to an all time low*, but that *the battle does not end here* (ABC radio news 20 June 2007).

At the time of writing at the end of 2007, Mulrunji's family have launched a civil case against the Queensland government and the police officer involved in his death. The Ethical Standards Command of the Queensland Police Service is still to complete its internal investigation into the mishandling of the original investigation into Mulrunji's death.

6.   Only in Queensland?

6.1.   New South Wales

While the focus in this book has been on the state of Queensland, the struggle over the policing of Aboriginal people continues in other parts of Australia. One particularly conflicted area is in the inner Sydney suburb of Redfern. "Deep resentment" (Eggleston 1977: 353) over police treatment of Aboriginal people in Redfern was the catalyst for the establishment of the first Aboriginal Legal Service in 1970 (see Section 4.1 of Chapter 3). For decades, concerns have continued to be raised about police abuse of Aboriginal people in the Redfern area, one of which has been discussed in Section 4.2 of Chapter 3.

These concerns erupted into violent conflict in February 2004, in response to the death of a 17 year-old Aboriginal boy, TJ Hickey, from injuries he received "during police operations". While riding his bicycle away from police officers in Redfern, Hickey was catapulted over the handlebars, and became impaled on a metal picket fence. The Redfern Aboriginal community reacted angrily to his death, believing that it was a result of being pursued or chased by police. The day after his death Redfern was the scene of a nine-hour riot, reported as "probably the worst street violence in Sydney for decades as young Aborigines attacked police with Molotov cocktails and rocks, setting alight Redfern railway station" (Cornford and Jacobsen 2004).

The incident which had led to Hickey's death had occurred when police were looking for an Aboriginal man who had allegedly earlier carried out a "bagsnatch" robbery at the Redfern railway station. Although Hickey was not the suspect, a police car followed Hickey, who was in the habit of riding fast, and whose bicycle had defective brakes. The coronial inquest found that Hickey, who had a criminal record, had good reason "for not wishing to be spoken to by police" as there was a warrant for his arrest from the Children's Court (Abernethy 2004: 3). There was conflicting evidence on the details, but the coronial inquest found that the police car followed Hickey, but did not pursue him (ibid.: 23–24). However, one of the two key police witnesses refused to give evidence, and the other, in the coroner's words, was "quite a poor witness with an extraordinary lack of memory of what [the coroner] would have thought were significant events" (ibid.: 21).

Hickey's family and others in the local Aboriginal community were outraged at the coroner's finding that his death was a "freak accident", and not the result of a police pursuit, although technically occurring during "police operations" (ibid.: 1). Hickey's aunt expressed the feeling of many Aboriginal people, when she said "If you're black and you see a police car you just run" (Dick et al. 2004). Further, many people felt that the coroner's finding would have been different if the two key police witnesses had been compelled to give a truthful account of the event. A highly respected Aboriginal leader and former federal senator, Aden Ridgeway, was reported as saying that an "oppressive cloud of silence still hangs over the events of that day ... The sense of unfinished business, or worse, business as usual is overwhelming" (Stevenson 2005).

6.2. *"Drop-offs" in Saskatchewan, Canada*

But the struggle over police control of Aboriginal people is not limited to Australia. In the last decade, several Canadian inquiries have investigated allegations of police officers abusing Aboriginal people in the same way as occurred in the Pinkenba event: that is, removing them from a public place and abandoning them in an isolated area. The fact that there is a single lexical item "drop-off" (e.g. Wright 2004: 17) used to refer to this practice in Canada, suggests that it is not an unusual occurrence. In 2000, the Royal Canadian Mounted Police established a task force "Project Ferric", to investigate allegations by a Cree Aboriginal man, Darrell Night, that police had abandoned him on the outskirts of the city in freezing weather in the city of Saskatoon, in the province of Saskatchewan. This investigation resulted in criminal charges against two Saskatoon constables, who, in contrast to the police in the Pinkenba case, were later convicted on the charge of unlawful confinement and fired from the department (Adam 2005).

In a much more serious case in the same city, a six-month judicial inquiry (Wright 2004) investigated the death of 17-year-old Neil Stonechild some 14 years earlier, in 1990.[41] Stonechild, an Aboriginal teenager who had been in trouble with the law on previous occasions, was approached by police late at night, when allegedly making a nuisance in a suburban area. This typifies one of the main situations in which Australian Aboriginal young people are over-policed and mistreated, as we have seen. But Stonechild's fate was much worse than that of the boys in the Pinkenba case. He was taken into police custody (unlike the boys in the Pinkenba case, who were never in custody on that night), and was last seen alive in the back of a police vehicle. This arrest took place in mid-winter when the overnight temperature was minus 18 degrees celsius. Stonechild's frozen body was found five days later in a remote industrial area, with injuries and marks that were "likely caused by handcuffs" (Wright 2004: 212). The inquiry into this case found that the initial police investigation into Stonechild's death was "superficial at best and was concluded prematurely" (ibid.: 198). Justice Wright further found that "the deficiencies in the investigation go beyond incompetence or neglect" (ibid.: 199). The Stonechild inquiry also heard evidence of "other situations where SPS [Saskatoon Police Service] officers decided to transport prisoners to remote locations rather than to a recognized detention facility" (ibid.: 196).

The Stonechild inquiry brings up an issue relevant to our discussion of the Pinkenba case: namely the limitations of a criminal trial in dealing with police abuse of the rights of Indigenous youth. In a criminal trial in such a case, the outcome depends on what the Aboriginal young person says in court. We have seen an extreme example of how such evidence can be manipulated. Pointing out that the rules of evidence and the procedures followed by a judicial inquiry are very different from those of the courts, Justice Wright concluded that "the findings of fact in an inquiry may not necessarily be the same as those that would be reached in a court" (ibid.: 191). However, a few weeks after Justice Wright's report was released, the two police officers involved in Stonechild's ride were dismissed from the police force, having remained there for 14 years since the event. While this is far from the justice that should be expected in such a case, it did at least indicate that the police service did not condone the actions of the officers. In the Pinkenba case, on the other hand, there was no inquiry, and the judicial investigation of the incident was restricted to the committal hearing and the judicial review, which proved to be inadequate in hearing the complaints of the victim-witnesses.

7. Conclusion

These examples from New South Wales and Saskatchewan remind us that struggles over neocolonial control exercised by police over Aboriginal people are not restricted to the "deep north" of Australia. And the Palm Island case shows us that despite a number of steps forward since the Pinkenba case, the over-policing of Aboriginal people still occurs for trivial reasons, and that Aboriginal people still have good reason to fear police harassment and violence. As lawyer Boe pointed out, the Palm Island case, which resulted in a tragic death, started in the same way as many Aboriginal dealings with the law, with *a resort to criminalisation when Aboriginal people are suspected of being a ... "public nuisance"* (ABC radio news 27 November 2006).

So, the struggle over police control of Australian Aboriginal people in public places continues. It is a complex struggle, taking place at every level of engagement: on the streets, as well as in police stations, courts, parliaments, inquiries, public meetings, summits and the media. Neocolonial control of the police over Aboriginal people is not static, and it is not inherent in the structure of the police service. It is carried out through the actions of individuals and groups of people, and it is constantly challenged by the actions of other individuals and groups of people. While the state continues to exercise oppressive power in a number of ways, in other ways it has used its power to create positive changes, as we saw for example in this chapter with some changes to the sentencing of Aboriginal people (Section 2), to the Evidence Act (Section 3), and with the Justice Agreement (Section 4). In addition to policy changes, there have been some personnel changes. Aboriginal people need no longer fear being cross-examined by either of the DCs who appeared in the Pinkenba case, as they are both now deceased. DC2's death six months after the Pinkenba hearing resulted from an apparent stroke, four weeks after a car accident in which he had "a cocktail of seven different drugs including ... high levels of morphine ... and cannabis in his blood" (Whittaker 1995). Four months before his death, a police raid on his home had found marijuana, heroin and methadone and syringes. While his wife pleaded guilty to possession of the drugs, and was fined $900, the barrister has been referred to in media reports as "suspected heroin-addicted Queens Counsel" (e.g. Callinan 2004).

But the Palm Island case shows us that despite these changes to personnel and policy, it is still possible for a police officer to be completely exonerated in relation to abusive actions towards Aboriginal people. However, the point must be made here that this instance of excessive police interference over the freedom of movement of an Aboriginal person did result in a damning and detailed coroner's report which attributed Mulrunji's death to the actions of the police officer. But coroners have no legal right to make findings of guilt. And the right of the accused to be innocent until proven guilty beyond reasonable doubt is so strongly protected in the criminal justice system, that once again the courtroom process has managed to legitimise the actions of the police officer. Given the central role of talk to everything that happens in courtrooms, this Palm Island case reminds us of the central role of courtroom talk in the perpetuation of neocolonial control. The words of criminologist Cunneen (1996: 13) more than a decade ago, remain apt today: "the neocolonial state is asserting power over Indigenous peoples through the use of naked force, clothed in the legitimacy of justice".

From the examination in this chapter of developments since the Pinkenba case, I turn in the concluding chapter to the consideration of what the critical sociolinguistic analysis of the Pinkenba case has revealed about courtroom talk and neocolonial control.

Chapter 12
The power of courtroom talk

This concluding chapter brings together the arguments and analysis from the book to examine the power of courtroom talk in the struggle between Aboriginal people and the police, which is at the heart of neocolonialism in Australia. Section 1 looks at the two main ways in which justice failed in the Pinkenba case. Firstly, we examine the effect of courtroom talk in legitimising the actions of the police in taking the boys to Pinkenba, and in constructing their identities, not as victims of police abuse, but as lying *criminals*, who are a danger on the streets. Secondly, we turn to the effects of courtroom talk in punishing the boys and the Aboriginal community for getting the police into trouble. The linguistic mechanisms involved in the courtroom talk in this case have been analysed in some detail in the chapters in Parts II and III above. Underlying these linguistic mechanisms are assumptions about how language works, which are examined in Section 2. Section 3 provides a short summary of these assumptions in ordinary English (written primarily for readers with no background in sociolinguistics). Section 4 considers the relevance of the analysis in this book for Aboriginal witnesses in other cases. Finally, Section 5 brings my sociolinguistic analysis of the Pinkenba case to a conclusion by raising two related questions: the first concerning the ability of the criminal justice system to deliver justice to Aboriginal people in cases of police abuse, and the second about whether we can expect an end to neocolonialism without far-reaching changes to courtroom rules of evidence.

1.   The justice system fails to deliver justice

Aboriginal people have good reason to fear the police, as we have seen. In Chapter 3, we glimpsed some of the nearly 200 year history of police control over the lives of Aboriginal people, which has been characterised by victimisation, excessive surveillance, over-policing, harassment and violence. Less than 6 months before David, Albert and Barry were taken from the Valley by the six armed police officers, another Cherbourg teenager, Daniel Yock, was arrested for a public order offence, only a few kilometres away. His arrest resulted in his death in a police vehicle. And only one month before the Pinkenba incident, the inquiry into Yock's death found that there was not sufficient evidence to charge any of the police officers involved with any offence. It seems likely that this finding gave a boost to police confidence in "dealing with" Aboriginal young people on Brisbane streets, while at the same time it increased the fear of these young people when approached by police officers, as well as the determination of the Aboriginal community not to let police *get away* with further such abuses.

At the time of the Pinkenba incident, the Queensland *Juvenile Justice Act* included several provisions for how police should deal with a young person who commits an offence, recommending diversion (away from the courts) by cautioning in the presence of either a parent, or an adult chosen by the child or parent. Section 17 made specific provision for the cautioning of an Aboriginal or Torres Strait Islander child: the police officer "must consider whether there is a respected person of the community who is available and willing to administer the caution", and if so, "must request the person to administer the caution". Thus, the criminal justice system had legislated guidelines about dealing with young troublemakers, and these guidelines took account particularly of the situation of Indigenous children (consistent with recommendations from the Royal Commission into Aboriginal Deaths in Custody, discussed in Section 6 of Chapter 3, and the United Nations Convention on the Rights of the Child[42]). But these recommendations, legislated guidelines and international conventions were ignored that night in Pinkenba, when the boys were not even charged with an offence. It is hardly surprising then, that a formal complaint was made by the families of David, Albert and Barry, assisted by the legal service which works to represent and advocate for Aboriginal people in the justice system. And given the details of the event, it is also hardly surprising that the Criminal Justice Commission recommended that the police officers be charged with "unlawful deprivation of liberty".

While members of the police force can operate without public scrutiny, it is quite different when a matter goes to court. Here the workings of the criminal justice system are (usually) open to the public, including the media. Citizens can have the expertise and representation of a qualified legal practitioner. The ultimate issue is decided by a supposedly impartial decision-maker, either a magistrate or judge, or a jury. Almost everything that is said is recorded, and can be subject to scrutiny. What more could a society want in the workings of its criminal justice system? The detailed analysis in this book has shown that the way in which the criminal justice system worked in the Pinkenba case was not enough to enable justice to be delivered. And while it is an extreme case, it needs to be seen in the wider context, some of which we have seen in Chapter 3 and Chapter 11. This case has shown how the criminal justice system works in perpetuating neocolonial control over Aboriginal Australians.

And the Australian situation needs to be seen in the international context. Conley and O'Barr (1998: 13) have concluded that a wealth of sociolegal research has documented ways in which the law has failed "to deliver on its biggest promises, especially the equal treatment of all citizens". In this book, we have seen the details of how this failure works in the reproduction of inequality based on the division between coloniser and colonised in Australia, particularly in the state of Queensland. In Section 5 below, I will suggest that this is also relevant to other Indigenous colonised people.

There are two different ways in which justice failed in the Pinkenba hearing: firstly in legitimising the actions of the police in taking the boys to Pinkenba, and secondly in the way in which the boys were abused and punished in court. The following two sub-sections will summarise these two failures of justice, in which the linguistic mechanisms discussed in this book played a central role.

1.1.   The naturalising effects of courtroom talk

The successful defence argument was that the boys had willingly got into the police cars despite knowing that *they had the right to refuse*. It was through arguing that they had gained the boys' agreement to this proposition, that the DCs were successful in gaining the consent of the justice system to this style of policing of Aboriginal young people. In Gramscian terms, the coercive power of the police to remove Aboriginal young people from the streets, was legitimised by the hegemonic power – power by consent – exercised in the courtroom (see Section 2.2 of Chapter 2). This case revolves around what we may term a "consent loop": the magistrate's decision, which was upheld by the review judge, provided the consent of the criminal justice process to the police removal of Aboriginal children, whose consent to this removal was "proven" by linguistic mechanisms, particularly gratuitous concurrence, in answer to pseudo-declaratives in cross-examination. Consent is also central to the other main issue in the cross-examination, namely the construction of the boys' identities, not as victims of police abuse, but as lying *criminals* who are a danger on the streets. We have seen in Parts II and III the array of linguistic mechanisms used by the DCs to gain the boys' consent to the many presuppositions and pseudo-declaratives which constituted these identities for the boys. Thus, the cross-examination process which succeeded in legitimising and naturalising the actions of the police officers revolved around layers of consent.

On the notion of consent, we can again learn from research in rape cases (cf. Sections 2.3 and 2.4 of Chapter 2). Drawing on work by Lacey (1998), Ehrlich (2001: 92) points out that the legal notion of consent used in rape cases is that of an individualised mental construct which excludes such issues as power relationships and the details of the material circumstances involved. In the same way, in the Pinkenba case, consent was defined in terms of the boys knowing that they *had the right to refuse to get in the police motor vehicle* when they did. The particular situation in which six armed (adult) police officers confronted three young Aboriginal boys was not considered. It is only possible to accept the argument that the boys consented to the ride, by accepting the encounter between the police and the boys as one between equal participants, and by denying the social, historical and political context in which this encounter was embedded. As with rape cases, conditions such as the victims' fear and unequal power relations were not considered. Neither was the nearly 200 year history of police treatment of Aboriginal people (outlined in Chapter 3).

In dealing with the issue of consent, very little attention was paid in the hearing, the magistrate's decision and the judicial review, to what the accused police officers said and did: it was the boys' actions or inactions that were questioned, discussed and considered. It is relevant to point out that Estrich (1987: 86) talks about the need to shift the focus in rape prosecutions from what the victim did or did not do (consent or resist) to what the defendant did. And Ehrlich (1998: 164) observes that in the rape case she examined "it was the complainants' behaviour that was generally interrogated as to its appropriateness, not the defendant's", taking up a similar point made by Sanday (1996).

Another parallel with rape cases lies in the conceptualisation of consent not in terms of "mutuality" (Lacey 1998: 114), but as the "absence of resistance" (Ehrlich 2001: 25). Ehrlich's examination leads her to the view that "'real' resistance is [seen to be] expressed aggressively and directly" (1998: 163). This notion is entirely consistent with that found in the cross-examination in the Pinkenba case, as we saw in Extract 23 in Chapter 5, where DC2 uses lexical perversion to change David's allegation of being *forced* to go in the police car, to one in which *the police said so*. This notion of consent is also reflected in the magistrate's decision, as we saw in Section 2 of Chapter 10. Ehrlich (2005) discusses a Canadian case in which an appeal court judge upheld the acquittal of a defendant charged with sexual assault, relying on the defence of "implied consent". "Implied consent" was defined by the judge as "consent by conduct" (ibid.: 154). With likely parallels to the boys in the Pinkenba case, the victim-witness in this Canadian case was "frozen by a fear of force" (ibid.) and did not communicate her fear to the accused. The appeal court's decision that this lack of action constituted implied consent was not accepted by the Supreme Court of Canada, which overturned the acquittal and returned a conviction of sexual assault. Although the term "implied consent" is not used in the Pinkenba case, this is undeniably what is involved in the successful acquittal of the police officers: apparent absence of resistance is taken to imply consent, although the situation makes it unbelievable that the boys would have been able to exercise "free will".

In interpreting the boys' responses in court and when approached by the police in the Valley as consent, the legal system legitimised the actions of the police officers in removing the boys from the Valley. The magistrate made no comment about policing practices or the legislated provisions for dealing with young troublemakers (discussed in Section 1 above). His decision effectively justified the actions of the police officers that night, on the basis of his finding that the boys have *no regard for members of the community, their property, or even the justice system*. But further than being justified, the police actions that night, and indeed the general practice of police removal of Aboriginal young people, were naturalised, that is taken to be common-sense. In his closing address, DC2 argued that it was legitimate and natural for the police to act as they did in the Pinkenba incident, saying:

Extract 98.   DC2 closing address

> *What are people supposed to do? I mean- what are the police supposed to do if- if they say to someone- fully cognisant of his legal rights- look- hop in the police car- he de<u>cides</u>- in accordance with his legal rights- to do so- and then they're <u>accused of CRIME</u>- now this is just re<u>mark</u>able . . .*

This common-sense nature of the police actions that night was reinforced by the police union president who said (ABC 1996) that the six police officers:

> *felt hamstrung in what they could do- it's very difficult dealing with juvenile offenders ... and it was an act of frustration that saw them take this action to remove what they saw as the problem from the area just for the short term- for some- to give it a little bit of respite*

We have seen the unsubstantiated suggestions during cross-examination that when the police approached the boys in the Valley they had committed a crime (taxi fare evasion), or were likely to commit a crime (theft), or could possibly have been charged with vagrancy. Despite these suggestions, the police officers clearly acted outside the legal provisions for dealing with young troublemakers. But the conclusion of the committal hearing and subsequent judicial review was not only that their actions that night were not illegal, but that they were acceptable. For DC2 (in his closing address), the worst that could be said about the police actions that night, is that they were an example of *bad manners*, which through the committal hearing were unfairly *being elevated into criminal offences*, as we saw in Section 1 of Chapter 10. Thus, the Pinkenba case played an important role in legitimising the control of the police over Aboriginal people, which, as we saw in Chapter 3, has been entrenched for nearly two hundred years in Queensland.

But, as we have seen in Chapter 10, the naturalisation of the police actions in the Pinkenba case were not accepted without question: the neocolonial
control over Aboriginal people is subject to ongoing struggle. The Aboriginal
Legal Service was tenacious in its refusal to accept that it is permissible for
police to remove Aboriginal young people in this way. And the Criminal Justice
Commission (1995) also resisted this naturalisation, calling for "departmental
disciplinary proceedings" against the police officers, and conducting research
on the "serious questions which the case had raised" about "the adequacy of
the protections offered to vulnerable witnesses in court proceedings" (ibid.).
Given that the CJC was a state organisation, and that many of its staff were
seconded police officers, it is clear that the power relations involved in this
struggle over police control of Aboriginal young people were more complex
than a simple division between Aboriginal people and the state. The Pinkenba
hearing therefore, played a pivotal role in testing the claims of a significant part
of the criminal justice system over the "common-sense way" for police to deal
with young Aboriginal people.

It was not only the actions of police officers in their dealings with Aboriginal
people that were naturalised in the Pinkenba hearing. This case also served to
naturalise the widespread view of Aboriginal young people as a threat on the
streets, through its forceful presentation of the three boys, not as the victims
of police abuse, but as lying *criminals* who were a problem on the streets of
Brisbane, as we saw in detail in the chapters in Part III. Not only were they
constructed in this way throughout the cross-examination, but this construction was taken up by the magistrate, the review judge and the media, as we
saw in Chapter 10. Aboriginal young people have been seen as a legitimate
target of police intervention for decades, and criminologists such as Cunneen
(1994: 145) have shown that the policing of Aboriginal young people in public
spaces has been a "critical component in the interaction between Aboriginal
youth and police". And in the media since the 1960s there has been an "increasing portrayal of Aboriginal people in a criminal frame" (Sercombe 1995: 77),
which has fed widespread moral panic. We have seen that much of the Pinkenba
cross-examination revolved around specific instantiations of this moral panic,
in relation to each of the three boys. The DCs constantly drew on this public
image of Aboriginal young people in their construction of David, Albert and
Barry, using an array of linguistic mechanisms. The prior convictions of these
three boys for theft and *robbery* served to convict them of intention to *commit a
crime*, and to deny them their basic rights as citizens – to *walk around* a shopping mall *lookin'* – while at the same time legitimising the actions of the police
officers who were "keeping the streets safe". Interestingly, the particular area
which they were removed from was one being upgraded for tourism, exactly

the kind of public space in which Aboriginal people are often over-policed (see Section 1.3 of Chapter 3).

In Chapter 10, we saw how the DCs' construction of the boys as lying *criminals* was adopted by the magistrate in his decision, the judge who carried out the judicial review and the newspaper reporting of the hearing. In its trajectory from assertions, questions and pseudo-declaratives in cross-examination, to judicial decisions and mainstream print media, the notion that young Aboriginal people are a menace on the streets has become a cyclical "truth", consistent with the wider theme of Aboriginal people as a criminal threat (Jakubowicz et al. 1994: 39). The continuing naturalisation of this view of Aboriginal people is a central element in the vicious circle (which we saw in Section 1.3 of Chapter 3) in which over-policing leads to resistant behaviours, such as swearing, which leads to criminalisation, which perpetuates over-policing. Thus, this case has played an important role in reinforcing and naturalising the identity of young Aboriginal people as constituting a threat to public safety, and in the continuing cycle of their criminalisation. At the same time, this case has worked to remove any suggestion that police officers may at times pose a threat to public safety.

1.2. The punitive effects of courtroom talk

The second way in which there was a failure of justice in the Pinkenba hearing concerns the ways in which the boys were abused and punished by the DCs. It is hard to remember that the boys were not on trial, and in fact, the magistrate publicly forgot this on three occasions, as we have seen. The due process of the legal system has provision for charging, taking to trial, convicting and punishing juvenile delinquents. And each of the three boys had been subject to this system in relation to various *criminal activities*. As they were legally children, their treatment as accused persons had rightly taken place in the Children's Court. But in the Pinkenba hearing, they were effectively on trial again, for a range of *criminal offences*, for most of which they had already been through the court. But this time they were arguably tried as adults, without the protection of Children's Court.

Sandra Harris (1984) has argued that many cross-examination questions are used to make accusations against witnesses, and this is certainly well-exemplified in this case. A number of the DCs' utterances did not serve an interrogative function, despite being consistently transcribed with a question mark in the official transcript. Many of them were speech acts typical of the disciplining and punishment of children, namely accusations, admonishments, rebukes, attacks, and threats, as we have seen throughout the chapters in Part III. The levels of abuse, aggression and humiliation to which the boys were subject in these rebukes made it clear that they were being punished. In this, we see a parallel with Lees' (1997) view of the rape trial as "a mechanism of 'disciplinary' power" (as expressed by Ehrlich 2001: 21–22.) We also see some similarity with Chang's (2004) analysis of Chinese criminal courtrooms, where questioning serves to persuade defendants of their guilt and to publicly shame them. But, like rape victims, the boys in this case were not defendants but victims. In the Pinkenba hearing, the boys were punished both for getting the police into trouble, and for their *criminal records*, as we saw in DC1's overt invocation of the widespread view that the courts had not punished them sufficiently in the past (for example in Extract 35).

Extract 56 in Chapter 8 (repeated here) exemplifies the abuse of cross-examination which was allowed unchecked in this case:

Extract 56.   DC1 to Albert, Day 2, p117

1. DC1:	I see you're not going to answer because you see- HERE YOU'RE CAUGHT AREN'T YOU? (0.9) in that witness box you can run but you can't hide (2.7) AND YOU'RE GOING TO SIT THERE AND YOU'RE GOING TO BE ASKED QUESTION AFTER QUESTION AFTER QUESTION (0.8) and you WON'T BE ABLE TO THUMB YOUR NOSE AT PEOPLE (1.0) AND COMMIT OFFENCES THERE DO YOU UNDERSTAND THAT?
2. Albert:	(1.3) °Yes°.

Most of DC1's turn is an extreme example of a pseudo-declarative, clearly serving no interrogative function. Indeed the extent to which the DCs' turns were harassing rebukes and metapragmatic attacks and directives highlights the extent to which it is a legal fiction that the purpose of cross-examination is to ask questions (a fiction that is upheld orthographically in the official transcript). The final utterance in this harangue is a routinised disciplinary rebuke *Do you understand that?* The interrogative syntax of this rebuke served to transform DC1's turn into a question, maintaining the fiction of a Q/A discourse structure in this speech event. Perhaps more significantly, it also secured Albert's compliance in DC1's overt control over him. In his closing address, DC1 naturalised the punitive and hostile nature of his cross-examination, saying *there's nothing wrong with aggressive cross-examination*, as we saw in Extract 93 of Chapter 10.

Why did the magistrate remain silent during this and other rebukes? Why did he not use his power under Section 21 of the *Evidence Act 1977* to stop cross-examination that is "intended only to insult or annoy or in needlessly offensive in form"? It seems that the magistrate shared DC1's "common-sense" view that the *aggressive cross-examination* was necessary in order to obtain *the truth of the situation*. And it is hard to avoid the conclusion that the magistrate was providing the support of the court and the legal system generally in punishing the boys for getting the police into trouble. Given that the magistrate could not avoid seeing the boys as *defendants*, as we have seen, he may also have been using their appearance in court as an opportunity for punishment. This would be consistent with how some analysts have seen the treatment of juvenile offenders, with Cunneen (2001: 133), for example, suggesting that the "real" punishment for juvenile offenders may be in the policing and court appearance rather than the final sentence. Of course in the Pinkenba case, there was no opportunity to punish the boys at all with a final sentence, as they were not accused of any crime.

But the punitive effects of the talk in the Pinkenba hearing were not limited to the boys. While they were the victims of the police abuse, and then the victims of courtroom abuse, the complaint against the police came not just from them. As they were children, the complaint was made by their relatives with the assistance of ALS. We saw in Section 10 of Chapter 7, that DC2 suggested that David had been *pushed around* and *used*, with the implication that this was being done by the ALS and the CJC. Arguably, the wider Aboriginal community, including the ALS, as well as the CJC, were also being punished in this hearing for getting the police into trouble.

Further, the message which rings clear from this hearing is that if you have a criminal history, you do not deserve protection from police abuse. In many jurisdictions, it is no longer allowed for a rape victim's previous sexual history to be overtly brought up in court (Henning and Bronitt 1998).[43] The successful argument behind the "rape shield" laws which make this provision, is that what is at issue is whether a person was raped, not whether their previous sexual experiences mean that they are more likely to consent to sex. Any amount of previous sexual experience is irrelevant to the issue of whether in a specific situation a person was forced to engage in sexual activity. In a similar way, a victim who alleges police abuse should not have to have their previous history with the police brought up in court. Any amount of previous experience with the police is irrelevant to the issue of whether in a specific situation a person was forced by police to go with them.

2.   Language ideologies and the failure of justice

The above section has outlined how justice failed in the Pinkenba case, facilitating the reproduction of neocolonial control over Aboriginal people. The linguistic mechanisms which have provided the tools for this achievement have been analysed in Chapters 4–9. Many of the uses of these linguistic mechanisms appear to be unreasonable or extreme, as we have seen with metapragmatic attacks, lexical perversion and the elicitation of gratuitous concurrence, for example. Many legal professionals have expressed the view that the cross-examination in this case is the most extreme they have encountered.[44] But, as Jacquemet (1996: 12) has pointed out, extreme circumstances "are the best windows to the normal because they highlight basic mechanisms which would otherwise be ignored". The detailed examination of this hearing has exposed just how far the adversarial justice system can go in its use of these linguistic mechanisms. But to what extent can we attribute the extreme use of linguistic mechanisms in the Pinkenba hearing to the particular individuals involved?

Throughout the book, I have avoided personalisation of the legal professionals involved in this case, referring to them by role rather than personal name (personal pseudonyms have been used for the boys because of the repeated use of their names throughout the hearing). But, of course, the legal professionals were all individual agents who made choices about which mechanisms to use in which ways and for which purposes. Another prosecutor may have made many more objections, another barrister may have used less haranguing and angry coercion, another magistrate may have disallowed many of the harassing and aggressive questions, and another review judge may not have found that the boys' evidence was *given in unequivocal terms*. But the common law adversarial system allows the extreme practices used in this hearing as part of the way in which justice is delivered. Thus, this case serves to expose the language practices which are allowed in hearing the evidence of witnesses, and which can play a crucial role not only in the determination of justice, but also in the reproduction of neocolonial control over Aboriginal people.

The prosecutor made few objections to these language practices, and neither the magistrate nor the review judge found any problem with their use. Thus, we see that they are accepted as "normal" ways of talking in cross-examination. This acceptance means that these ways of talking are "naturalised", in the same way as the police actions in taking the boys were naturalised in this case. Using the term "discourse type" in a similar way to my use of "ways of talking", Fairclough (1989: 91) explains naturalisation as occurring when a discourse type "so dominates an institution that dominated types are more or less entirely suppressed or contained". This dominating discourse type is seen not as arbitrary, but "as *natural*, and legitimate because it is simply *the* way of conducting oneself" (emphasis in original). Underpinning the naturalisation of these ways of talking are a number of "common-sense" assumptions about how language works. In contemporary linguistic anthropology and sociolinguistics, such assumptions are termed "language ideologies" (e.g. Schieffelin et al. 1998). Blommaert (2005: 253) defines "language ideology" as "ideas, images and perceptions about language and communication" which are "socially, culturally and historically conditioned".

The term "language ideology" has the potential for alienating readers not famil-iar with this scholarly tradition, for whom the term "ideology" may persistently evoke a Marxist-oriented interpretation. Given that potential, and my hope that this concluding chapter can be particularly accessible to readers from diverse backgrounds, I will use the term "assumptions" as well as "language ideologies".

2.1.   In entextualisation

Entextualisation is central to the legal process, and its use has been introduced and exemplified in Section 4 of Chapter 6. There have been several other exam-ples of entextualisation in Chapters 7–9. The focus in this section is on some of the assumptions which underlie its use in the legal process.

2.1.1.   Inconsistency

In Section 4 of Chapter 6, we have seen that exposing inconsistencies between different tellings of an event in different legal contexts forms a central strategy in challenging the credibility of a witness in cross-examination. While it may appear that inconsistency can be a reliable symptom of untruthfulness, the anal-ysis in the chapters in Part III has pointed to a number of other factors which may give rise to inconsistency in aspects of a witness's account, such as memory problems and perceptual failures. Thus, as we saw in Section 4 of Chapter 6, the jurors in the O. J. Simpson case were reminded that "innocent misrecollection is not uncommon" (Tiersma 1999: 253). Further, using entextualisation to deter-mine witness credibility relies on a number of problematic assumptions about storytelling. For example, it assumes that people always tell the same story in the same way. Recent sociolinguistic work on narratives shows that this is a naïve assumption. Schiffrin's (2006) analysis of individuals retelling a particular story over a period of time (not in a legal context) shows that no two tellings are the same: there are shifts in perspective and different details are included or omit-ted, highlighted or backgrounded. It also denies the possibility of co-constructed versions of stories, as for example, would have been likely when the boys first told the story about what happened when they were taken to Pinkenba.

But these perceptual and social dimensions of inconsistency in storytelling are ignored by the legal system, which, as Matoesian (2001: 37–38) points out, conceives of inconsistency as "logical" incongruity. Matoesian argues, on the contrary, that inconsistency is not necessarily an attribute or failing of an in-dividual, it is interactively constituted and sustained. That is, inconsistency is achieved through the interactional work which is done during the hearing. We have seen many examples of the interactional achievement of inconsistency in this hearing, and the central role of linguistic mechanisms such as gratuitous concurrence and lexical perversion in this achievement. This interactionally achieved inconsistency between two or more tellings of a story, whether by different witnesses, or the same witnesses in different contexts, is used by lawyers to guide "finders of fact" to "the truth". Thus, in the way in which "the truth" is determined in a legal matter, there is an underlying "linguistic ideology of inconsistency" (Matoesian ibid.: 68). As Matoesian (ibid.: 133) summarises it, "trial discourse rests on a theory of intertextuality, decontextualizing speech from one speech event and recontextualizing it in a new one, to consitute its evidentiary and epistemological field". In the linguistic ideology underpinning the adversarial cross-examination process, the interactional nature of inconsistency is not considered: it is the failing of individual witnesses, who can be therefore deemed to be lacking reliability and truthfulness. The example of DC1's assertions about Albert's use of the verb *grab* in his early (pre-courtroom) narration of the event provides a good example (as discussed in Section 1.3 of Chapter 4 and Section 7 of Chapter 8).

2.1.2.   Accuracy

But, while witness inconsistency is taken as evidence of lying and/or lack of credibility, lawyer inconsistency is accepted. Further, the distortions of a witness's evidence which result from lawyer inconsistency can become an essential ingredient in a judicial decision. Thus, we saw in Chapter 5 that the evidence of each of the boys was that the police *told* them to *jump in the car*. Lexical perversion by both DCs resulted in this being changed to *asked*, in a pseudo-declarative by DC1 (Extract 21) and an erroneous correction by DC2 (Extract 22). It is this distorted, inaccurate or exaggerated characterisation of the crucial speech act which became central to DC2's closing address, when he said that the boys *didn't protest and got into the police vehicles when asked* (as we saw in Section 1 in Chapter 10, emphasis in original). And in a remarkable reproduction of this erroneous report of the boys' evidence, the review judge wrote in his "Reasons for Judgment" (*Purcell & Ors v. Quinlan & Anor* 1996: 8–9) "Pender said that the applicants got into police cars because they were asked to do so" (as we saw in Section 5 of Chapter 10). Thus, while accuracy is central for witnesses, it is flexible for legal professionals, including judicial decision makers.

2.1.3.   Decontextualised propositions

In the entextualisation process, the isolation of particular words and phrases from earlier versions can be particularly powerful. This often combines with the presentation of inconsistencies in two or more decontextualised pieces of text (discussed in Section 2.1.1 above). The example of *grab*, which was discussed in Section 1.3 of Chapter 4 and Section 7 of Chapter 8 illustrates both aspects of the assumptions about language use. The decontextualisation of evidence from its interactional production is important to the legal process in other ways, as found in a study which compared official courtroom transcripts with recordings of hearings (Eades 1996b). Put simply, legal decision-making attends to "what is said" rather than "how it is said". The study of official transcripts concluded (ibid.: 251) that the assumption behind such transcription "is that the evidence given is valid out of context, for example with the legal argument removed, and also with counsel's feedback removed. In addition, the emotive/affective context is removed, as there is no transcription of prosodic or paralinguistic features". The study further showed "that the production of the verbatim courtroom transcript takes for granted certain changes and omissions not considered to have any legal consequence" (ibid.). This process of decontextualising situated interaction is undoubtedly involved in the review judge's conclusion that the boys' evidence had been *given in unequivocal terms*. It is hard to imagine how a careful listening to the audio-recorded courtroom interaction, rather than a reading of the official transcript, could have led to such a conclusion about the boys' evidence.

But this book shows a much more consequential type of decontextualisation, in which key propositional content is selectively and successively decontextualised and recontextualised. We have seen how parts of the boys' stories of what happened in the Pinkenba event were taken from the initial reports to the ALS and interviews with the CJC investigative officer, and repackaged into a number of pseudo-declaratives in cross-examination questions. These transformed assertions were then further repackaged into claims made by the DCs in their closing addresses, and eventually they formed the basis of the magistrate's "factual" finding that the three boys *all knew that they had the right to refuse to get in the police motor vehicle*. In Parts II and III, we have seen the complex interactional process which stripped the boys' claims of being *forced* and transformed the event from an abduction to a consensual ride. Central to this stripping process have been the linguistic mechanisms, examined in Chapters 4–9, which include lexical perversion, gratuitous concurrence, metapragmatic directives, and hostile, aggressive and sarcastic pseudo-declaratives and repeated tag questions. Also central to this process are the language ideologies or assumptions discussed in this section.

The decontextualising of propositions from their interactional context is part of a wider reliance in the legal process on the written version of spoken language (see Tiersma 2001; Komter 2006a). A written record of courtroom interaction, or of an earlier investigative interview, effectively "freezes" certain propositional content and elevates its status, so that it can be quoted in a decontextualised manner in order to transform selected assertions or to show inconsistency (as discussed in Section 2.1.1 above).

2.1.4. Authorship

But it is not just that entextualisation in the criminal justice process takes utterances out of their interactional context and transforms them in this way. This decontextualisation also conceals the <u>process</u> by which stories are generated, and the role of the interviewer in the ways in which stories are told, including what is left out, what is included, and what is emphasised. The ways in which such interactional processes involve collaboration between interlocutors in everyday storytelling have been studied by researchers such as Norrick (1997).

In the legal context, several scholars have found that while written witness or suspect statements result from an interactional process, namely an interview, they are presented as the product of a single person, that is the person being interviewed (e.g. Trinch 2003; Rock 2001; Komter 2006b; Jönsson and Linell 1991). Further, in such written statements there is often what Jönsson and Linell (p434) term "the blurring of source distinctions". They explain that "one cannot know from reading the reports under what conditions a given piece of information has been introduced". For example, has it been introduced "more or less spontaneously by the suspect in a narrative turn", or is it introduced in the proposition of the interviewer's question and only then "confirmed (or sometimes, modified or denied) by the suspect"? (This blurring of source distinctions has also been investigated by Shuy in his work on undercover FBI recordings, e.g. 2005). In the Pinkenba case, source distinctions were frequently blurred in the closing addresses, the magistrate's decision and the judicial review. As we saw in Sections 1, 2, 3 and 5 of Chapter 10, in all of these contexts in which the boys' stories were summarised and evaluated, the boys were treated as the sole authors of these stories. With the exception of the statements in paragraph 3 of the magistrate's decision (given as Extract 96 in Section 2 of Chapter 10) where his use of the words *admitted* and *conceded* indicates co-authorship, there was no recognition of the role of cross-examination questions, with all the coercive pressure they contained.

While this may seem remarkable, it is nevertheless consistent with what Trinch (2003: 49–50) refers to as the "ideology of narrator authorship", which she says is found not just in the culture of the law, but more generally in Western culture. This ideology relies on the "prevalent" and "tenacious" cultural notion of the "true story", but ignores the collaborative nature of storytelling, as well as its situated interactional nature. As Trinch points out, one of the problematic consequences of this ideology comes in the form of challenges to the credibility of the narrator, in ways that link this ideology of narrator authorship with the ideology of inconsistency, discussed in Section 2.1.1 above.

Some of the serious consequences which can arise from the linking of these two language ideologies are found in Maryns' (2006) examination of the ways in which the stories of asylum seekers are repackaged, retold and evaluated as they go through the bureaucratic, and sometimes also legal, steps in verifying their claims to refugee status. The studies referred to here demonstrate that it is problematic to view the stories which emerge from interviews as the sole product of the interviewee, although this is exactly the way in which such stories are typically received and assessed within the legal process.

In addition to concealing the ways in which the boys' stories are co-constructed, and to blurring source distinctions for information attributed to them, there is a more blatant authorship problem about some of the key issues in this case, namely the switching of authorship attribution. Thus, in Extract 4 in Chapter 4, we saw the pressured exchange in which DC1 extracted a softly spoken °*Yes*° from Albert, 3.5 seconds after shouting at him YOU LIED TO MAKE THINGS LOOK BAD FOR THE POLICE- DIDN'T YOU? (1.2) DIDN'T YOU? DC2's recontextualisation of this exchange in his closing argument significantly switched authorship, using the speech act verb *told*. Thus he said that Albert *told [DC1] in cross-examination that the rea̲son that he'd said the police had grabbed him and forced him into the car wa̲s to make- things- look- worse- for- the- police* (as we saw in Extract 91). But, as we have seen, Albert did not *tell* DC1 this: the most that can be attributed to Albert in relation to this assertion, is that he *conceded* or *admitted* it, if, following the magistrate and the review judge, we accept a literal interpretation of his °*Yes*° answer (which was only elicited after the shouted and pressured rejection of his °*No*° answer). The switching of authorship attribution is routine in cross-examination, but it is not limited to courtroom practices: as we saw in Section 3 of Chapter 10, it is also an acceptable media practice, found in the newspaper headline: "'I lied to embarrass police': Boy, 13, tells 'dumping' trial".

2.2.   In repeated questioning

One of the most important language ideologies underpinning the cross-examination process is that repeated questioning provides the opportunity to properly test a witness's truthfulness. Correspondingly, one of the most powerful conclusions from the analysis of the Pinkenba cross-examination is that this is a seriously flawed assumption. We have seen numerous extracts from this hearing in which each of the witnesses has given contradictory answers to the same question. But, given the extreme harassment and linguistic trickery being used in the questioning, it is impossible to be sure which of these contradictions reveal dishonesty, and which can be attributed to other dimensions of the interaction, including intimidation and gratuitous concurrence, and the strong tendency of children to change their answers when they are asked the same question more than once in the same interview.

The analysis of this hearing calls into question the probative value of repeated questioning. The challenge for the justice system is to allow cross-examination, which is the right of all defendants, while protecting "suggestible" witnesses. As we have seen in Section 1.2 of Chapter 4, there are already legal provisions in Australia to protect suggestible witnesses, which are taken up by some courts (e.g. Mildren 1999: 147). Section 21 of the *Evidence Act 1977* gave the magistrate in the Pinkenba hearing the power to stop any questions "intended only to insult or annoy" or "needlessly offensive in form". That he did not use this power in a single instance in this hearing highlights the problem of trying to understand courtroom talk in the absence of an understanding of its social and political context, specifically in this case in terms of the work it undertook in the reproduction of neocolonialism.

2.3. *In selective literalism*

Central to the successful defence argument was the non-literal interpretation of the utterance by the police officers to the boys which resulted in the ride to Pinkenba: *Jump in the car*. DC2 said in his closing address that the boys should not have been allowed to *characterise* this *form of words as an asking or a telling*, as that amounted to *opinion evidence*. But the defence argument relied on the interpretation of this utterance as a suggestion or an offer, and not a command (as discussed in Section 2.4 of Chapter 5). The issue of literal and non-literal interpretations of speech acts has been discussed by Solan and Tiersma (2005) who find a situation of "selective literalism" in the American legal system: courts sometimes interpret speech acts literally, as direct speech acts, while at other times interpreting them non-literally, as indirect speech acts.

An example of the former is the US Supreme Court case of *Bustamonte*. This case revolved around a police officer who stopped a motorist late at night, and searched the trunk of the car, despite not having a search warrant, and not having grounds to search without a warrant. The officer's question *does the trunk open?* was interpreted by the court as a question, and not as a command to open the trunk. Solan and Tiersma point out that the motorist in the case interpreted the question as a request or command to open the trunk. This was consistent with the fact, ignored by the court, that indirect commands often take the form of a question. But such literal interpretations are selective: the authors point to the case of an "impetuous youth" who sent a letter to President Regan which contained the sentence: "resign or you'll get your brains blown out". The letter writer was convicted of threatening the life of the president: what is literally a prediction was given its indirect speech act interpretation as a threat. In the Pinkenba case we see another example of a court choosing a non-literal and indirect speech act reading of an utterance – the utterance *Jump in the car* was interpreted non-literally, seemingly as the indirect speech act of an offer or suggestion.

In considering the Bustamonte case, Solan and Tiersma argue that the contextual factors, particularly the power that the officer has over the driver in this situation, make it most likely that the officer's utterance *does the trunk open?* was functioning as a command, and that the driver felt he had no choice, and thus did not "freely and voluntarily" consent to open the trunk. The authors' (ibid.: 41) discussion of the way in which police utterances are interpreted by the public has poignant relevance to the Pinkenba case:

> People who are stopped by the police alongside the road in the middle of the night quite logically assume that if the police "ask" them to do something, the police have both the power and the right to force them to comply.

A comparison of these two cases (Bustamonte and Pinkenba) on the issue of consent is also enlightening. Solan and Tiersma (ibid.: 37) report that:

> To decide whether a suspect's will had been overborne, the Court held in *Bustamonte* that judges should examine the totality of the surrounding circumstances, such as the suspect's age, education, intelligence, and whether he had been advised of his rights. Knowledge of the right to refuse consent was one of the factors that should be considered, according to the opinion, but it was not a dispositive issue.

Interestingly, the Pinkenba case suggests the opposite legal reasoning: issues such as the ages of the three boys and their education, were ignored, as we have seen. The only issue bearing on whether or not the boys had been taken for a ride against their will, was the repeated assertion that they knew their legal rights. Ironically, there was no legal requirement for the boys to be advised of their rights in this situation, as they were not under arrest, and thus they were not legally in custody.

Another example of non-literal interpretation comes from one of the instances in which the magistrate explained the self-incrimination privilege to

Albert, in Extract 49 in Chapter 8. We saw in the discussion of this example that the magistrate told Albert that if he is *asked a question about something for which [he hasn't] been before the court [he is] not obliged to answer* .... But the magistrate did not explain that this right applies only to questions about a criminal act. There were many questions which Albert said he did not want to answer, but not all of them related to *criminal offences*. For example, in Extract 60 in Chapter 8, Albert does not want to answer the question *You lied in their face, didn't you?* (about his interview with ALS). A literal interpretation of the magistrate's explanation in Turn 5 of Extract 49 would mean that Albert did not have to answer this question. But such questions are not protected by the privilege. It is interesting to observe that the magistrate's inaccurate explanation of the privilege – which is a fundamental right of witnesses in the criminal process – appeared to be accepted unquestioningly by the magistrate, prosecutor and DCs.

This acceptance of a non-literal interpretation of the magistrate's explanation, combined with the court's acceptance of the defence argument about the non-literal interpretation of *Jump in the car*, presented a stark contrast to the literal interpretation of the boys' *Ye#* answers to crucial questions on the central issue in this case. The analysis throughout this book has highlighted the problematic nature of such a literal interpretation, owing to the extreme harassment in many of the questions which elicited such answers, together with the suggestibility of the boys, and the well-known Aboriginal tendency to use gratuitous concurrence.

Solan and Tiersma's (2005) discussion of the selective literalism of the US courts may also be relevant to these contrasting examples in the Pinkenba case. Solan and Tiersma believe that "it is hard to avoid the impression that courts have somewhat of a double standard when it comes to considering pragmatic information. They are significantly more likely to take it into account when it benefits the government, and less so when it helps the accused" (ibid.: 47–48).

2.4. *About* normal human beings

Witness credibility is central to legal decision-making, as are more general evaluations of a witness's character. As I have earlier pointed out, understanding a person's character "is inherently a process of cultural interpretation" (Eades 2000: 188). In Section 3 of Chapter 6, we saw some of the culturally specific presuppositions, which are not shared between Aboriginal and Anglo-Australian societies, but which nevertheless played a significant role in the

DCs' construction of the boys' identities. Thus, *swearing* in front of *a lady* was assumed to indicate lack of respect for her, in DC1's presuppositions in Extract 25. And avoidance of eye contact with the interviewer was assumed to indicate dishonest behaviour in Extract 9. These and other culturally specific presuppositions, discussed in Section 3 of Chapter 6, and in specific examples in the chapters on Parts II and III, were used in the DCs' portrayal of the boys as irresponsible and unreliable (see for example Extracts 6, 7, 8, 40 and 43). But, as we saw in the discussion in Section 3 of Chapter 1 and Section 4 of Chapter 6, the gender issues which surround the relative seriousness with which swearing is assessed, are often not found in Aboriginal societies. And neither is the interpretation of the avoidance of eye contact as indicating dishonesty (as we saw in Section 3 of Chapter 4). Further, the evaluation of responsible residential arrangements for children is not the same in Aboriginal and middle-class non-Aboriginal Australian societies. The expected movement of Aboriginal children between the homes of various relatives might look like *running away from home* to a non-Aboriginal observer. And similarly, judgments about a witness's reliability are partly based on the interpretation of conversational features such as silence and minimal *Ye#* answers, which can be used and interpreted quite differently by Aboriginal and non-Aboriginal people. Following Matoesian (2001: 37–38), we can see these as examples in which the DCs used "cultural logic" to generate inconsistency. Further, these actions, such as *swearing* in front of *a lady* and *running away from home* contribute to the ways in which the behaviour of the boys is defined as "deviant". As we saw in Section 2 of Chapter 3, this is part of the process of creating moral panic. And the police actions in taking the boys for a ride typify what happens in situations of moral panic, where the social group defined as "deviant" receives a "disproportionate and punitive reponse, usually by the criminal justice system" (Cunneen and White 2002: 90).

Underlying the culturally-specific assumptions in the Pinkenba case is a more pervasive general one, namely that cultural difference is irrelevant to understanding behaviour, and that the values of middle-class Anglo-Australians provide a fair basis for evaluation of a witness's credibility, and character generally. In a study of examination-in-chief in sentencing hearings in New South Wales (Eades 2000), I discuss examples of the lack of recognition of Aboriginal lifestyles and culture.

DC1 explicitly attributed his view of character judgments not to cultural or sub-cultural groups, but to *normal human beings*. As we saw in Extract 72 in Chapter 9, according to DC1, *normal human beings* not only have a reason for everything they do, but they can give a reason for everything they do, such as why they were walking around a particular area on a particular occasion. This characteristic which DC1 attributed to *normal human beings* contrasts with the findings of my (Eades 1988) ethnographic study in southeast Queensland (which includes Brisbane and Cherbourg). Here, "strategies for seeking reasons for actions are indirect" (ibid.: 109) and often ambiguous. Further, there is frequently "no unambiguous linguistic marker of reason", as speakers have considerable personal freedom and privacy in the expression of motives and reasons (ibid.: 109).

These culturally specific presuppositions about *normal human beings* do "substantive ideological work", in Ehrlich's (2001: 76) terms. The DCs presented as common-sense, notions about *normal human beings*, such as that they can give a reason for their actions, and that *swearing* in front of *a lady* indicates a lack of respect for her. In Fairclough's (1989: 33) terms, the DCs used their ideological power to project these assumptions as universal and common-sense.

2.5. About young teenagers in an adult court

One of the most disturbing assumptions which appears to underly language practices in this hearing is that young teenagers can be expected to have the linguistic proficiency and dexterity of adults. As we saw in Section 5 of Chapter 1, linguistic research has found a number of ways in which this is not true, including in the understanding of complex negation and complex questions, as well as asking for clarification in situations involving comprehension difficulties. It has been beyond the scope of this book to deal with cognitive and linguistic differences between adults and young teenagers. However, discourse analysis of certain extracts has highlighted obvious comprehension difficulties, and the inconsistent and insufficient recognition of the fact that the witnesses were not adults.

On the one hand, the DCs asked many simple questions which probably did not cause comprehension difficulties for the boys. But, on the other hand, little was done to address the most obvious source of comprehension difficulty, namely the self-incrimination privilege, as we have seen for example in Extracts 33, 34, 50, 60 and 75, and in Section 4 of Chapter 9. This is unquestionably a tricky right for witnesses to understand, with even the magistrate and lawyers having difficulty with it, as we saw in Extract 57. The magistrate should have been advised that simply repeating the *warning* or slowing his articulation of it would not be sufficient to make such complex legal language comprehensible to the child witnesses who are supposed to be protected by this privilege. Admittedly, there are problems in explaining complex written legal language without presenting a distortion, which could provide the basis for an appeal (as discussed in relation to the language used in jury instructions (for example Tiersma 1999). This case has highlighted the need for a Plain English version of the self-incrimination privilege to be prepared. This could also be used for adult witnesses, as there can be no doubt that the difficulties with the formulation used in this hearing are not restricted to children. While it is unquestionably difficult both to explain and to properly use this right, we have seen that the magistrate was at times less than clear in the directions he gave the child witnesses. Thus, for example, in Extract 34 in Chapter 7, he said to 13-year-old David: *I am directing you to answer it- that is if you have no objection to answering the question.* It seems that the right of a defendant to question the accuser (through questioning by the defence lawyer) overrides any concerns – which arguably should have been held by both the prosecutor and the magistrate – about a child's comprehension of such a contradictory legal directive.

(Socio)linguistic research to date on children in court has paid particular attention to the syntactic structure of questions. In this first detailed sociolinguistic analysis of a single courtroom hearing involving child witnesses, it has been possible to concentrate on larger extracts of courtroom discourse. This has exposed a wider range of linguistic mechanisms to which children may be subject, during the "normal" operation of courtroom rules of evidence. It is disturbing to see that the reliability of the evidence of a child witness has to be tested through linguistic manipulation of memory and interview proficiency, and the trickery that can be used through such mechanisms as complicated entextualisation.

We have seen that there appears to be an assumption that young teenage witnesses can be treated linguistically and cognitively as adults, and this is most clearly evident in the ways in which the privilege *warning* was delivered. But this assumption is directly at odds with the treatment at other times of these witnesses as children, as we have seen in DC1's aggressive rebuking and punishing of the witnesses, discussed in Section 1.2 above.

Certainly the treatment of the young teenagers in the Pinkenba hearing lends support to Chaaya's (1998: 263) conclusion of the need for "a radical rethink of the current procedures for receiving children's evidence". As we saw in Section 3 of Chapter 11, this has happened in Queensland to some extent since the Pinkenba hearing. But the extent to which these new provisions accommodate the vulnerability of child witnesses in any particular case will depend ultimately on the presiding magistrate or judge. What we have seen in the Pinkenba hearing suggests that the independence of the judiciary cannot necessarily be assumed in a case in which a police officer is charged with the abuse of an Aboriginal person. And while the changes to the rules of evidence should mean that child witnesses are rarely cross-examined in committal hearings, they will continue to be cross-examined in trials.

3.   Assumptions about talk in courtroom cross-examination: A summary

Courtroom talk plays a central role in the legal decision-making process. The rules of evidence constrain courtroom talk in many ways, stipulating who can talk when, about what and in what manner. These rules also allow the use of language in ways that can be seen as trickery, as we have seen in the chapters in Parts II and III. Underlying these rules of evidence are a number of problematic assumptions about the ways in which language works. These assumptions have been examined in Section 2 above, and are summarised here. These assumptions about how language works:

1)   allow inconsistencies between the ways in which a witness has told a story on different occasions to be interpreted as lies. But not all inconsistencies are lies. Witnesses may be unable to explain that some inconsistencies are memory lapses or failures. They may also be unable to explain the complex ways in which a story may be told in a slightly different way on different occasions and/or to different audiences.

2)   allow lawyers to change the words used by witnesses, by replacing them with similar words, without indicating that they have made changes. This can then convey a different meaning or impression which the witness is unable to correct. Taking points (1) and (2) together, it is clear that while accuracy is demanded for witnesses, it is flexible for lawyers.

3)   allow lawyers to isolate a witness's words and phrases from the linguistic context in which they were spoken, such as the question the witness was answering, or the utterance in which the particular words or phrases were spoken.

4)   allow lawyers to summarise a story which has emerged from an interview with no acknowledgment of the effect of the interviewer on the story: for example on the way in which the story was told, including what was left out, what was included, and what was emphasised.

5)   allow lawyers to take words or phrases from their cross-examination questions, and attribute them to the witness, as if the expression came originally from the witness. Even if the witness has only given a one-word answer such as *yes* to repeated and harassing questioning, this answer can be replaced by lawyers in their closing addresses, with their own words from the question and reported as if they were the witness's original words. While this is a problematic transformation of evidence, it is particularly disturbing when the witness is vulnerable to suggestibility, on account of such factors as being a child, or coming from a sociocultural group which has a

tendency to answer with gratuitous concurrence in situations of repeated and/or pressured questioning.

6)   allow magistrates and judges to repeat a quotation wrongly attributed to a witness (following points 2–5 above), without any indication that it is not the witness's actual words.

7)   allow judicial decision-making to be made on the basis of distortions of what witnesses have said in their evidence, through the processes outlined in points 1–6 above.

8)   allow a witness's truthfulness to be assessed on the basis of the consistency of their answers to repeated questioning, regardless of the pressure on the witness to provide a particular answer.

9)   allow a court to ignore the social context of a conversation when they interpret it, something which is impossible for people who participated in the conversation.

10)   ignore cultural differences in ways of thinking and acting when drawing conclusions about a witness's character.

11)   allow a witness's previous actions to be distorted and exaggerated, while at the same time holding that distortions and exaggerations are proof of an unreliable witness.

12)   ignore the fact that children, including young teenagers, do not have the same language proficiency as adults. As we saw in Chapter 11, recent changes to the *Evidence Act* have removed this ignorance in a general sense. But the extent to which any particular child witness is protected as a child in the courtroom, ultimately depends on the judge or magistrate, and the ways in which this person may be persuaded to subordinate the child's vulnerability to the rights of the accused.

4.   Aboriginal witnesses in other cases

The focus in this book has been on the mechanisms used in the Pinkenba cross-examination and the assumptions behind these mechanisms. Throughout the book, I have argued that these linguistic details matter: they have served to legitimise police mistreatment of Aboriginal young people, and thus to perpetuate their neocolonial control over Aboriginal people. As this has been a detailed analysis of one case, I have not attempted to analyse how these various mechanisms and assumptions have operated in other cases. The fact that these mechanisms have been allowed and taken as the proper functioning of the criminal justice system, shows just how far the adversarial system can go in cross-examination, as I have argued above. Further, in the chapters in Parts II and III, references to research on particular mechanisms in other courtroom hearings shows that though their use may be extreme in this case, it is not unique to it (for example Ehrlich's 2001 work on presuppositions in pseudo-declaratives in Section 2.3 of Chapter 6).

The witnesses in this case were children, which makes the extreme use of linguistic mechanisms even more disturbing. Recent changes to the rules of evidence which affect children's evidence should lessen the likelihood of such cross-examination of children in the future to some extent (as we have seen in Section 3 of Chapter 11). However, these extremes of cross-examination are still considered legally unproblematic for other witnesses. Further, many of the linguistic practices allowed in the Pinkenba cross-examination (and summarised in Section 3 above) remain unchanged.

While Chapter 4 has analysed some features of Aboriginal English communicative style which have been exploited in the cross-examination in this case, much of the analysis has not treated the Aboriginality of the witnesses as particularly <u>linguistically</u> significant. Thus, for example, I have not argued that lexical perversion (Chapter 5) or the use of metapragmatic attacks (Section 5.1 of Chapter 6) are more consequential for Aboriginal witnesses than for other witnesses. On the other hand, I have argued that the Aboriginality of the witnesses in this case is <u>socially and politically</u> highly significant. That is, a number of linguistic mechanisms which are allowed in cross-examination have been used in extreme ways, because this case is a key struggle in the resistance of the Aboriginal community to the neocolonial control exercised by the police.

However, it is likely that there is an added layer that makes the mechanisms of cross-examination and the assumptions behind them particularly problematic for many Aboriginal witnesses, including the boys in the Pinkenba case. As we saw in the general introduction to Aboriginal English in Section 4 of Chapter 1, many Aboriginal people use indirect ways of seeking information in many situations. The pattern reported from my ethnographic studies in southeast Queensland in the 1980s (e.g. Eades 1982, 1988) is still observable in many Aboriginal communities. Many people are uncomfortable in any interview situation, and feel that *whitefellas ask too many questions*. This contrasts somewhat with many other social groups in Australia, where question-answer routines are part of socialisation from an early age, where the interview is a familiar speech event.

These differences in communicative style are relevant to the assumptions about talk in courtroom cross-examination (discussed in Section 2 above and summarised in Section 3) and the resulting linguistic trickery such as we have seen throughout this book. While these assumptions and linguistic mechanisms can compromise the delivery of justice in any case, some witnesses may be more able to resist them than others. It is likely that a witness with legal training might be fairly well equipped to resist such trickery, while a witness without much experience in interviews might be least able to resist. Many Aboriginal witnesses, then, may be disadvantaged by the fact that they have had limited successful experience in interview situations, whether in the legal context or any other. When we add to this situation, the pervasive cultural difference in the use and interpretation of silence, and the Aboriginal tendency to use gratuitous concurrence, it can be seen that many Aboriginal witnesses can be particularly disadvantaged in courtroom questioning.

In 2005, I observed several Aboriginal witnesses from a country town in New South Wales in a murder trial. The defendant was not a police officer, and indeed this was a case in which the Aboriginal witnesses worked well with police homicide investigators. However, it was alarming to see the extent to which these witnesses' use of apparent gratuitous concurrence was exploited in their cross-examination. For example, it was not difficult for a lawyer to elicit *yes* answers from a witness about how many metres she was from a particular person at a particular time. When this lawyer later exposed an inconsistency in the witness's account of distances, she said *I don't know my metres*, suggesting that her earlier *yes* answers on this topic had been answers of gratuitous concurrence. I also observed the effect of lawyers' apparent ignorance of aspects of Aboriginal lifestyle and culture. Thus, for example, a cross-examining lawyer made much of a young Aboriginal man's evidence that he had gone home late and drunk on a particular night, and had gone to sleep in his car, instead of going inside to his bed. The lawyers' persistent asking about *why* a person would do such a thing, showed his assumption that it was a noteworthy occurrence, which supported his suggestion that the witness must have had a reason other than the one he gave, namely that he was drunk and it was late. The lawyer was from a middle-class professional city background, where it is probably very rare to take such an action. The Aboriginal man lives in a small town in the warmer northern part of the state. In this town Aboriginal housing is typically very overcrowded, and it would not be unusual for someone to sleep in the car, especially when drunk. These are two examples of the linguistic and cultural relevance of the Aboriginality of the witnesses in this case. It is beyond the scope of this book to consider aspects of the social and political relevance of their Aboriginality. In the Pinkenba case, as we have seen, the Aboriginality of the witnesses is socially and politically <u>central</u> to the analysis of courtroom talk, as well as linguistically significant to particular linguistic mechanisms, as we saw particularly in Chapter 4.

5.   The social consequences of courtroom talk

Early sociolinguistic analysis of courtroom talk examined the mechanisms by which power is exercised in the courtroom, focusing particularly on the ways in which witnesses are controlled and coerced by various aspects of the rigid question-answer discourse pattern. More recently, microanalysis of courtroom talk has demonstrated the point made by John Conley and William O'Barr (1998: 138), that this kind of analysis can go beyond an examination of situated linguistic power in the courtroom, and it can be "an extraordinary tool for studying social problems". The most powerful examples are Matoesian's (1993, 2001) and Ehrlich's (2001) studies of courtroom talk which show the ideologies and language practices which legitimise sexual violence against women. These studies have demonstrated the importance of attending to the details of courtroom talk, not limited to individual question-answer pairs, but in larger stretches of talk, as well as in ever-increasing immediate, local, societal and historical events and structures.

It is clear that courtroom talk does not exist in a vacuum, and power relations are not static. Critical sociolinguistics has exposed key mechanisms which enable the reproduction of neocolonial control. Following the framework presented in Section 3 of Chapter 2, this has involved examining "the interplay between agency, structure, constraint and change" (Rampton 2006: 390). The micro-event of the courtroom hearing (which itself comprises multiple micro-events in interactions between the lawyers, the boys and the magistrate – acts of <u>agency</u>) is intricately related to other micro-events in the past 200 years, which together create and sustain the macro-<u>structure</u> of neocolonialism.

In the colonial period, the actions of Aboriginal Queenslanders were subject to much greater control than those of anyone else. For example, as we saw in Section 1.2 of Chapter 3, they were removed by police to reserves where they were forbidden to drink alcohol, required permission to marry or to travel, and were detained for "indiscipline" or "immoral behaviour". The colonial period ended with Aboriginal people being granted citizenship, just 40 years ago in some areas. But despite being entitled to equal treatment, Aboriginal people remain systematically oppressed by the criminal justice system. At the heart of this neocolonialism are specific (and numerous) police removals of Aboriginal people from public places, in contemporary versions of the earlier offences of "indiscipline" or "immoral behaviour". Chapter 3 outlined the ways in which police discretion and over-policing result in these removals. The Pinkenba case was extreme, in that the children removed were not charged with any offence. But removals often result from police charging Aboriginal people with public order offences. We have seen that a central component of the "trifecta" of such offences, which filters many Aboriginal people into the criminal justice system, is the offence of using words which in most other English-speaking democracies would be dismissed as bad manners or rude talk.

But, this book has shown that more is involved than the statutory criminal-isation of actions such as swearing, and the selective actions of police officers. The detailed analysis of talk in the courtroom and the judicial decisions in the Pinkenba case has shown that a central mechanism in the reproduction of neo-colonialism is the continuing construction of Aboriginal people as a *criminal* threat to public safety. In the earliest colonial invasion, Aboriginal people and their lifestyles and use of their land were seen as a threat to the settler's lifestyles and the ways in which they intended to use this land which they had appropri-ated. In controlling and removing this Aboriginal threat, the police force was charged with a powerful and oppressive colonial role. Today Aboriginal people and their use of public space is still seen as a threat to the ways in which many others want to use this space. In particular, public drinking and swearing up-sets many non-Aboriginal people. In controlling and removing this Aboriginal "threat", the police force is still charged with a powerful and oppressive role, which is now neocolonial.

But the powers and actions of police officers do not occur in isolation or uncontested. The Pinkenba courtroom hearing played a pivotal role in both the agency of Aboriginal people and others in rejecting these police powers, and in the counter-agency of people and institutions in legitimising these police powers. We have seen in Chapter 3, that in the months leading up to the Pinkenba event, Aboriginal people had rejected with outrage the police treatment of Daniel Yock, which led to his death. They had rejected the right of police to remove their young people from public places. This agency by Aboriginal people and groups resonated with that of a number of government reports (discussed in Chapter 3), as well as one institution within the state structure, namely the Criminal Justice Commission. In the Pinkenba hearing, the struggle over police control of Aboriginal people moved from the streets, the media and inquiry reports, to the court. Interestingly DC2 made direct reference to this aspect of the case in his closing address. As we saw in Section 1 of Chapter 10, in arguing that the case should not have resulted in criminal proceedings, he said that *social and political issues (ought to remain) exactly where they are*, and he complained that *battles are fought here* [in the courtroom]. But, as we have seen in Chapters 10 and 11, while the Pinkenba case was closed a year after the courtroom *battle* (with the decision of the judicial review), that has not been *the end of the matter*. There can be no doubt that some of the changes introduced through legislation (Section 3 of Chapter 11), the introduction of the Murri Court (Section 2 of Chapter 11), and police recruitment and community policing (Section 1 of Chapter 11) have been influenced by responses to the Pinkenba case. New <u>constraints</u> have been introduced into the criminal justice system, as we have seen in Chapter 11, but these can be ignored by the <u>agency</u> of any particular judge or magistrate, and they leave unchanged many of the linguistic mechanisms exposed in this book. Further, the assumptions about how language works which are at the foundation of courtroom talk also remain unchanged.

We have seen that it was not difficult for the DCs to use conventional courtroom linguistic trickery to gain apparent agreement from each of the boys that they had given their consent to the ride to Pinkenba. If this case of unlawful deprivation of liberty had involved a defendant and a complainant who were adults in a relatively equal power relationship, then this is all that would have been required for a successful defence strategy. But, as we saw throughout the chapters in Parts II and III, much more work was done in the courtroom cross-examination in this case. This was the work of neocolonialism, which both naturalised the actions of the police officers and punished the boys for making their complaint about being taken for a ride by the police. We saw that the DCs defined the experiences of the boys, and constructed them, not as victims of police abuse, but as people who are not *normal human beings*, but lying *criminals* who are a danger on the streets. So successful was this linguistic work that the magistrate used the word *defendant* to address the child witnesses on three separate occasions.

This identity work in the Pinkenba hearing has demonstrated how "microinformation is transformed into macro-representations", to quote Cicourel (1981: 75). The DCs used the cross-examination in this case to construct these three Aboriginal boys as lying *criminals* who are a danger on the streets. This micro-information is about three particular Aboriginal boys, but it also takes up a strong theme in widespread moral panic, and reinforces widespread media macro-representation of Aboriginal young people as juvenile delinquents, and of Aboriginal people generally as a problem for law and order. While the criminal justice system is the major site for the reproduction of neocolonialism, it can only succeed because it resonates with ways of talking about, thinking about and interacting with Aboriginal people in the wider Australian society.

The examination of courtroom talk and neocolonial control in this book has been situated in Australia, with the major focus being on the state of Queensland. Australia is not alone in its experiences of colonialism and neocolonialism, and its courtroom rules of evidence. Indeed, there are many parallels with other former British colonies, such as Canada and New Zealand for example, in the historical processes of colonialism, the contemporary practices of neocolonialism, and the current workings of the adversarial common-law legal system. However, following my argument that the details matter, I have refrained from generalising from Australia to any other specific country.

But this book raises a number of issues which are relevant to future consideration of such possible generalisability. A number of features of the Queensland situation (which are similar, and in some instances the same, as other parts of Australia) are different from other comparable countries. Thus, for example we saw in Section 1.1 of Chapter 3 that the police in Queensland did the work undertaken by frontier soldiers in America. To what extent do such differences in the colonial role of police officers affect contemporary relations between police and Indigenous people? Also looking at early invasion and colonial expansion, we see differences in Indigenous social practices and organisation at that time. For example, the linguistic and social diversity of Aboriginal Australians contrasts with both the hierarchical social organisation of New Zealand Māori, and their linguistic unity. What impact do such differences have on experiences of colonialism and neocolonialism? In examining the agency of colonised people in their struggles with the coloniser, the details of legislative contraints would be central. Related to this are the specific mechanisms, both formal and informal, which Indigenous people have used and use today, to assert the right to equality. According to Malcolm Fraser, a former Prime Minister, Australia is the only *Western country with an Indigenous minority that has no elected representation of any kind* (ABC television news, 26 April 2007). How does this structural difference in opportunities to influence policy and legislation impact on contemporary neocolonial realities? And turning specifically to language and the criminal justice process, a number of questions arise, in considering the generalisability of this study of neocolonialism to other neocolonial situations. For example, is the use of "offensive language" an offence in other former colonies, and if so, how does this offence relate to Indigenous language practices? And does the policing of offensive language particularly target Indigenous people in the same way as it does in Australia? How much variation is there in the rules of evidence, and the related assumptions about language, in common-law neocolonial countries with an adversarial legal system? How are Indigenous identities constructed in public discourse, including the media? To what extent and in what ways are these identities imposed or negotiated? How does the public construction of Indigenous identities interact with their participation in the criminal justice system?

Regardless of the generalisability of this study to other neocolonial situations, it has exemplified a more general concern about the adversarial legal system: in the words of Conley and O'Barr (1998: 138), that "the adversary system is out of control". In the contest between opposing sides, this case was decidedly unbalanced from the outset: on the prosecution side, a relatively inexperienced prosecutor and three Aboriginal part-time street kids, and on the defence side, two of the most highly paid and experienced barristers (at the highest level, that

of Queens Counsel), representing six police officers who had no legal requirement to speak. The prosecutor's reluctance to make objections contributed to an
already very unbalanced contest. This reluctance may be attributed in part to the
difficult position he was in, as a former suburban police officer prosecuting six
members of the "brotherhood" in Ellis' (2005) terms, seen in Section 1 of Chapter 11. And it may also be attributed to his concerns about the power which the
DCs appeared to have over the magistrate – seen for example in Extract 57, and
in the magistrate's apparently subconscious acceptance of the boys' identities as
defendants.

The law is complex, and the stakes are high for accused people. The pre-
sumption that accused persons are innocent until proven guilty beyond reasonable doubt is strongly protected in the adversarial criminal justice process, in
countries like Australia, England, the United States and Canada. But this protection can rely on courtroom rules of evidence which are based on problematic
assumptions about how language works, and which allow linguistic trickery on
many levels. The microanalysis of this hearing has highlighted many of these
assumptions and mechanisms, the linguistic practices and language ideologies
involved.

Given the ways in which cross-examination works, and the easy success
which the DCs had in this committal hearing in destroying the credibility of the
boys and in arguing that they had consented to propositions on the central issue,
it would have been very difficult for a jury to find the police officers "guilty
beyond reasonable doubt". Thus, had the Pinkenba case gone to jury trial, it
would have been most likely to perpetuate the failure of justice which occurred
at the committal hearing, as criminal trials operate with essentially the same
linguistic mechanisms and assumptions as committal hearings. Arguably, then,
the failure of the justice system in this case is part of a wider failure.

Recent changes to the rules of evidence (discussed in Section 3 of Chapter 11) do provide some possibility of reducing the worst aggression of cross-
examination, and of protecting child witnesses to some extent, depending on
decisions by the judge or magistrate. But these changes have done nothing to
address most of the underlying assumptions about courtroom talk – discussed
in Section 2 above and summarised in Section 3 – which have been revealed
in this analysis of the Pinkenba case. This raises the question of whether Australian police can ever be found guilty of a serious criminal offence against an
Aboriginal person. As long as the language practices found in the Pinkenba case
continue to be allowed by the rules of evidence, and the assumptions behind
these practices remain unchallenged, will the neocolonial control of police over
Aboriginal people remain unchecked?

The critical sociolinguistic analysis in this book leads me to question whether Aboriginal people can ever expect justice in cases of police abuse, or whether they will continue to be taken for a ride by the criminal justice system. But more than this, it leads me to also question whether we can expect an end to neocolonial control over Aboriginal people without far-reaching changes to courtroom rules of evidence.

Notes

1. Queensland magistrates are appointed full time, and have legal qualifications and experience, corresponding to stipendiary magistrates in the UK system.

2. The use of the term "traditional" to refer to certain Aboriginal languages and groups can be problematic, especially when used to refer to pre-colonised Australia (e.g. Keen 2004: 1–2). However, it will be occasionally necessary to distinguish in this book between contemporary "traditionally-oriented" and "non-traditionally-oriented" Aboriginal communities. The former label refers to communities in remote Australia, where non-English related languages remain strong, as do a large number of social and cultural practices with strong continuities from pre-colonial times. This is not meant to imply that Aboriginal culture and language are dead in other parts of the country, but rather that they have undergone much more change.

3. Quotations from this hearing are based on my transcription of official tape-recordings. As explained in Section 7, I use italics for any quotation from a spoken source, which includes tape-recordings, and radio and television interviews.

4. At the commencement of his testimony (Transcript, p103), Albert tells the magistrate that his birth date is in April 1981, and that is he now 14. However, given that the hearing is taking place in February 1995, it appears that Albert has miscalculated his age, and that he is still 13 (as asserted by the prosecutor).

5. The term "Anglo" refers to the dominant sociocultural group in Australia, which comprises descendants of early colonisers and convicts from the British Isles.

6. Although *waadjin* generally does not have a derogatory connotation, it is derived from adding the derogatory English word *gin* meaning *Aboriginal woman*, to the English word *white*. (The English word *gin* to refer to an Aboriginal woman originally came from the Aboriginal language spoken around Sydney, where it meant *woman*, and had no derogatory connotation).

7. This title was legally inaccurate, as it was a committal hearing, the first stage in the trial process, but strictly speaking not a trial in itself.

8. In its narrower usage, "forensic linguistics" refers to the use of linguistic analysis as expert evidence in courtroom hearings, as for example in the Stuart and Condren cases, discussed in Section 1.1 of Chapter 2.

9. Some of the ideas in this chapter were first developed in Eades (2004a).

10. However, I am aware of some instances where recording equipment has reportedly malfunctioned, but police have carried out an unrecorded interview and produced a confession. Linguistic evidence about Aboriginal English has been used in recent years in at least two such cases (Ian Malcolm p.c., Amanda Lissarague p.c.), but in these cases it has not been successful in having the confession disallowed as evidence in the trial.

11. I was also presenting similar workshops (on intercultural communication between Aboriginal and non-Aboriginal speakers of English) to a wide range of professional and para-professional workers, including teachers, education administrators, welfare workers, health educators, doctors and prison officers.

12. There is no writing on Aboriginal English and the law which uses the deficit perspective, although it appears to underlie views of a number of legal professionals, who see Aboriginal English as a bad form of English (as discussed in Eades 1995a: 161–166).

13. Foley (1984) was an exception. In his analysis of "Aborigines and the police" he includes sections on "language problems" such as "a superficial fluency in English" (ibid.: 166), "specific linguistic difficulties" such as "omission of prepositions" (ibid.: 168), and "cultural differences" such as the indirect ways of much information seeking (in which he cites my work).

14. In the Rodney King case the criminal justice system failed to convict four police officers for the brutal (videotaped) beating of an African-American man, an outcome which led to street riots in Los Angeles. While the issue of race in the O. J. Simpson case is mentioned in Cotterill's (2003) book (e.g. 12, 16–17, 18, 62), there is no discussion of how the situated contests over power in this trial connect to the wider issues of race in Los Angeles.

15. The rape of a child is different because legally there can be no consent by a child to sexual activity with an adult.

16. Following my use of the term as explained in this section and as consistent with Heller's (2001a) usage, I distance myself from Mey's (1985) Marxist definition. Singh (1996) gives no definition or discussion of the term, although it is in the title of his book. Kress' (2001) use of the term is closer to that of Heller and myself, although he gives no clear definition, and tends to use it interchangeably with "critical linguistics" and "critical discourse analysis".

17. My critical sociolinguistics approach is also influenced by several other related and partially overlapping approaches: Rampton's (2001a) fourth approach to diversity, which he terms the "discourse" approach, Conley and O'Barr's (1998) "merger" of sociolinguistics and sociolegal scholarship, and Pennycook's (2001) "problematizing givens" approach.

18. This book will show how the three boys in this case were taken for a ride by the criminal justice system, literally that night in Pinkenba, and figuratively in the resulting courtroom hearing.

19. The definition of assault in Australian criminal statutes includes "any bodily act or gesture" which "<u>attempts or threatens</u> to apply any force of any kind" to another person without their consent (*Queensland Criminal Code* s245, emphasis added). Thus a person can be charged with assault, because they raised an arm menacingly, for example, without actually touching another person.

20. See note 19 above.

21. Originally a term from betting in which a gambler must select the first three place-getters in a race in order to win, the term is used colloquially in Australian English to refer to "any group of three events, processes, terms, etc., which together make up what is perceived to be a powerful combination" (*Macquarie Dictionary*). It is widely used to refer to the three charges which most frequently criminalise Aboriginal people: public drunkenness, using offensive language and resisting arrest.

22. The reporting of this case in the *Alternative Law Journal* differs from other case reports in that it cites the complete judgment of the magistrate.

23. Cf the "trifecta" discussed in Section 1.3 above.

24. Parts of this chapter build on Eades (2002) and (2003a).

25. Section 2 of this chapter builds on Eades (2006).

26. Cotterill (2003: 64–65) also uses the term "(strategic) lexicalisation" to talk about the "strategic use of lexical choices" in (monologic) opening statements of trials, and in (2001: 293) she uses the term "relexicalisation" to refer to "the recasting of a concept in an alternative lexical representation" in courtroom talk.

27. I cite the *Macquarie Dictionary* in a number of places in this book, not intending to "fix" the meanings of words (cf Fairclough 1989: 108), but rather to check my native speaker intuitions with the results of lexicographical study based on usage, which draws on a large corpus of Australian English texts.

28. DC1 has already used the word *louts* 4 times to Barry in the presuppositions of questions, but no other lawyer and no witness uses the word.

29. It is worth pointing out that each of the lawyers uses the word *friend* on numerous other occasions throughout the hearing, to refer to an opposing lawyer, consistent with Australian legal terminology.

30. My copy of the tape-recorded proceedings is missing the equivalent of 4 pages of official transcript, including this extract. As the level of lexical accuracy of the official transcript appears very high, I feel it is appropriate to cite the official transcript here, noting that Extract 21 does not record pauses, overlaps, latching, emphasis or volume.

31. The overwhelming situation in which Albert is in seems to prevent him from any awareness of what has been described (Langton 1988: 220) as a "supreme stroke of wit", when the swear words used against a police officer by an Aboriginal person are read out in court.

32. All one-word answers of *Yes*, *Yeh*, or *Mm*, as discussed in Section 7 of Chapter 1.

33. All one-word answers of *No* or *Nuh*, as discussed in Section 7 of Chapter 1.

34. Includes answers of *I dunno*, as discussed in Section 7 of Chapter 1. It excludes the small number of answers of the form *I don't know* [something].

35. The official transcript usually gives no name labels. However, when the default structure of Lawyer Question followed by Witness Answer is interrupted, the transcript

labels the speaker, using the labels 'BENCH' (for the magistrate), PROSECUTOR, MR THORPE (for DC1) MR HILLER (for DC2) and WITNESS. However, in this instance, the transcriber has adopted DC1's construction of the witness as a criminal, and indeed as a defendant in this hearing, labelling him as DEFENDANT CARTER.

36. Sentence final *but* is commonly heard in Australian English and some Aboriginal English varieties. It has the same adversative meaning as sentence intitial *but*.

37. Closing addresses are also known as "closing arguments", "final arguments", or "final addresses" in various jurisdictions.

38. With the exception of Extract 97, all of the transcript extract and quotations in this chapter are from the closing addresses and the magistrate's decision. Given the monologic nature of these extracts and the fact that there are no long pauses during these monologues, my transcription of them does not indicate the length of pauses.

39. Transcribed from audio-recording, paragraph numbers added.

40. A more radical kind of Indigenous court operates in several towns in New South Wales, also in cases where the defendant has pleaded guilty to a matter which would otherwise be heard in Magistrates Court. Known as Circle Sentencing, and modelled to a considerable extent on initiatives in Canada and New Zealand, it operates within a restorative approach to criminal justice. In this, it is similar to Youth Justice Conferencing in Queensland, discussed in Section 5 of Chapter 1. Thus, the participation of the victim is considered an important part of the process by which the offender faces the consequences of their criminal act. A major emphasis is on restoring the balance to the community, not simply punishing the offender. Other ways in which Circle Sentencing differs from Murri Court, is in its conduct in a venue away from the courthouse, and in the central notion of the circle. Participants sit in a circle, and the talk goes "round and round" on the issues involved, with circle sentencing hearings typically taking many hours (Potas et al. 2003).

41. I am grateful to Matt Prior for drawing my attention to the Stonechild case.

42. Section 37(c) states: "Deprivation of personal liberty shall not be imposed unless the juvenile is adjudicated of a serious act involving violence against another person or of persistence in committing other serious offences and unless there is no other appropriate response".

43. However, as Matoesian (2001: 208–214, 1993: 221) shows, cross-examining lawyers can still find covert ways of making inferences about a rape victim's sexual history, which can go a long way to discrediting them. (See also Ehrlich 2001: 26–27; Henning and Bronitt 1998.)

44. For example, Ron Finney, an ALS lawyer who had been attending courts in various capacities for more than thirty years at the time of the hearing, told a television interviewer (ABC 1996) that he doubts *there is on record a more extreme example of cross-examination- even with the most heinous of crimes.*

Statutes cited

Australia

Evidence Act 1995

New South Wales

Evidence Act 1995

Queensland

Aboriginal and Torres Strait Islander Affairs Act 1965
Aboriginals Preservation and Protection Act 1939
Aboriginals Protection and Restriction of the Sale of Opium Act 1897
Children Services Act 1965
Criminal Code 1899
Evidence Act 1977, including *2003 Amendments*
Juvenile Justice Act 1992
Summary Offences Act 2005
The Torres Strait Islanders Act 1939
Vagrancy, Gaming and Other Offences Act 1931

International

United Nations Convention on the Rights of the Child 1989
United Nations Convention on the Prevention and Punishment of the Crime of
    Genocide 1948

Cases cited

Crawford v Venardos & Ors 1995 Unreported, Brisbane Magistrates' Court, 24 February.

Crawford v Birchley 2005 Unreported, District Court of Queensland, 17 February.

Couchy v Del Vecchio 2004 Unreported, High Court of Australia, 3 December.

Couchy v Guthrie 2005 Unreported, District Court of Queensland, 17 November.

Del Vecchio v Couchy 2001 Applicant's submission. Queensland Court of Appeal, retrieved on 18 March 2007 from http://boelawyers.com.au

Del Vecchio v Couchy 2002 Unreported, Queensland Court of Appeal, 4 February.

McKinney & Judge v The Queen 1991 Unreported, High Court of Australia.

Mooney v James 1949 *Victorian Law Reports* 22–32 (Victorian Supreme Court).

Police v Shannon Thomas Dunn 1999 Dubbo Local Court, New South Wales, 23 August, *Alternative Law Journal* 25(4): 238–242.

Purcell & Ors v Quinlan & Anor 1996 Unreported, Queensland Supreme Court 14 February.

R v Aboriginal Dulcie Dumaia 1959 *Northern Territory Judgments* 694–699, (Northern Territory Supreme Court).

R v Anunga 1976 *Australian Law Reports* 11, 412–417 (Northern Territory Supreme Court).

R v Condren 1987 *Australian Criminal Reports* 28, 261–299 (Queensland Court of Criminal Appeal).

R v Kenny Charlie 1995 Unreported, Northern Territory Supreme Court, 28 September.

R v Kina 1993 Unreported, Queensland Court of Appeal, 29 November.

References

ABC (Australian Broadcasting Commission)
    1992   *Cop it Sweet*. Four Corners TV documentary 4 March.
    1993   *7.30 Report*. TV current affairs program 30 November.
    1996   *Black and Blue*. Four Corners TV documentary 8 March.
    1999   *Double Jeopardy*. Four Corners TV documentary 19 July.

Abernethy, John
    2004   Inquest into the death of Thomas James Hickey. New South Wales State Coroner's Report Number 287 of 2004 (unpublished).

Adam, Betty Ann
    2005   Deputy chief knew constables were suspects: RCMP investigator. *The Star Phoenix*, 3 March.

Ahearn, Laura M.
    2001   Language and agency. *Annual Review of Anthropology* 30, 109–137.

Altman, Jon and Kingsley Palmer
    2005   Land ownership and land use. In Arthur, Bill and Frances Morphy (eds.), *Macquarie Atlas of Indigenous Australia: Culture and Society through Space and Time*, 142–155. Sydney: The Macquarie Library Pty Ltd.

Amnesty International
    1997   *Australia: Police Brutality against Queensland Aborigines*. London: Amnesty International International Secretariat.

Anon
    1993a   Black sky mirror for mourners. *The Brisbane Courier Mail*, 13 November.
    1993b   Police officer's cover blown. *The Brisbane Courier Mail*, 13 November.
    1994   Finding on youth's death rejected by Aborigines. *The Sydney Morning Herald*, 6 April.
    1995a   Police dumped us: Teen thief. *The Brisbane Courier Mail*, 21 February.
    1995b   "I lied to embarrass police": Teen thief. *The Brisbane Courier Mail*, 22 February.

1995c   Blacks rally to voice disgust. *The Brisbane Courier Mail*, 27 February.

1995d   Public inquiry call on Pinkenba case. *The Brisbane Courier Mail*, 28 February.

1995e   Solicitor slates "thugs" tag. *The Brisbane Courier Mail*, 2 March.

1995f   Outrage at Pinkenba Six "slap on wrist". *Koori Mail*, 24 April.

Antaki, Charles and Sue Widdicombe (eds.)
1998   *Identities in Talk*. London: Sage.

Arnold, Ann
1989   The angry accused. *The Sydney Morning Herald*, 20 September.

Arthur, Jay M.
1996   *Aboriginal English: A Cultural Study*. Oxford: Oxford University Press.

Atkinson, J. Maxwell and Paul Drew
1979   *Order in Court: The Organisation of Verbal Interaction in Judicial Settings*. London: Macmillan.

ATSIC (Aboriginal and Torres Strait Islander Commission)
1997   *Five Years On: Annual/Five Year Report 1996/1997: Implementation of the Commonwealth Government Responses into Aboriginal Deaths in Custody*. Canberra: Commonwealth of Australia.

Auer, Peter
2005   A postscript: Code-switching and social identity. *Journal of Pragmatics* 37, 403–410.

Augoustinos, Martha, Keith Tuffin and Mark Rapley
1999   Genocide or a failure to gel? Racism, history and nationalism in Australian talk. *Discourse and Society* 10 (3), 351–378.

Balogh, Stefanie
2000   Honest cop saw the dark side. *The Weekend Australian*, 15–16 July.

Barton, G.
1889   *History of New South Wales from the Records. Vol 1, Governor Phillip*. Sydney: Charles Potter.

Barwick, Diane
1974   The Aboriginal family in southeastern Australia. In Krupinski, Jerzy and Alan Stoller (eds.), *The Family in Australia: Social, Demographic and Psychological Aspects*. Sydney: Pergamon Press, 153–167.

Barwick, Diane
    1988   Aborigines of Victoria. In Keen, Ian (ed.), *Being Black: Aboriginal Cultures in Settled Australia*. Canberra: Aboriginal Studies Press, 27–32.

Basso, Keith H.
    1970   "To give up on words": Silence in Apache culture. *Southwestern Journal of Anthropology* 26 (3), 213–230.

Bauman, Richard and Charles L. Briggs
    1990   Poetics and performance as critical perspectives on language and social life. *Annual Review of Anthropology* 19, 59–88.

Bealey, Frank
    1999   *The Blackwell Dictionary of Political Science: A User's Guide to its Terms*. Malden, MA: Blackwell.

Bell, Jeanie
    1997   *Talking about Celia: Community and Family Memories of Celia Smith*. Brisbane: University of Queensland Press.

Berk-Seligson, Susan
    2002   Does every *yeah* mean *yes* in a police interrogation? Presentation to the Annual Meeting of the American Association of Applied Linguistics, April, 2002, Salt Lake City, Utah.
    2008   Coerced Confessions: The Discourse of Bilingual Police Interrogations. Unpublished ms.

Biber, Douglas and Edward Finegan
    1989   Styles of stance in English: Lexical and grammatical marking of evidentiality and affect. *Text* 9 (1), 93–124.

Bird, Greta
    1987   Fieldwork in South Australia. In Hazlehurst, Kayleen M. (ed.), *Ivory Scales: Black Australia and the Law*. Sydney: New South Wales University Press, 60–80.

Blackledge, Adrian
    2005   *Discourse and Power in a Multilingual World*. Amsterdam: John Benjamins.

Blackledge, Adrian and Aneta Pavlenko
    2001   Negotiation of identities in multilingual contexts. *International Journal of Bilingualism* 5 (3), 243–259.

Blommaert, Jan
  2001   Context is/as critique. *Critique of Anthropology* 21 (1), 13–32.
  2005   *Discourse*. Cambridge: Cambridge University Press.

Blommaert, Jan and Chris Bulcaen
  2000   Critical Discourse Analysis. *Annual Review of Anthropology* 29, 447–466.

Blommaert, Jan, James Collins, Monica Heller, Ben Rampton, Stef Slembrouck, and Jef Verschueren
  2001   Discourse and critique: Part One, Introduction. *Critique of Anthropology* 21 (1), 5–12.

Bowen, Jan
  1994   *The Macquarie Easy Guide to Australian Law*. 2nd ed. Sydney: The Macquarie Library Pty Ltd.

Braithwaite, John
  1994   Thinking harder about democratising social control. In Alder, Christine and Joy Wundersitz (eds.), *Family Conferencing and Juvenile Justice: The Way Forward or Misplaced Optimism*. Canberra: Australian Institute of Criminology, 199–216.

Brennan, Mark
  1994   Cross-examining children in criminal courts: Child welfare under attack. In Gibbons, John (ed.), *Language and the Law*. London: Longman, 199–216.
  1995   The discourse of denial: Cross-examining child victim witnesses. *Journal of Pragmatics* 23, 71–91.

Brennan, Mark and Roslin Brennan
  1988   *Strange Language: Child Victims under Cross-examination*. 2nd ed. Wagga Wagga: Charles Sturt University.

Briggs, Charles L.
  1993   Metadiscursive practices and scholarly authority in folkloristics. *The Journal of American Folklore* 106 (422), 387–434.

Brown, R, and A. Gilman
  1960   The pronouns of power and solidarity. In Sebeok, T. A. (ed.), *Style in Language*. Cambridge, MA: MIT Press, 253–276.

Bucholtz, Mary
  1999   "Why be normal?": Language and identity practices in a community of nerd girls. *Language in Society* 28 (2), 203–225.

2001   Reflexivity and critique in discourse analysis. *Critique of Anthropology* 21 (2), 165–183.

Bucholtz, Mary and Kira Hall
2004   Language and identity. In Duranti, Alessandro (ed.) *A Companion to Linguistic Anthropology*. Oxford: Blackwell, 369–394.

Butterworths Concise Australian Legal Dictionary
1998   Peter E. Nygh and Peter Butt (General Editors). Sydney: Butterworths.

Callinan, Rory
2004   Terry Lewis sues legal team over his failed corruption appeal. *The Australian*, 13 August.

Cameron, Deborah
1995   *Verbal Hygiene*. London: Routledge.

Carmody, Kev
1995   The young dancer is dead. [song] *Images and Illusions*. Sydney: Festival Records.

Chaaya, Michael
1998   Children's evidence in sexual abuse cases: The need for a radical reappraisal. *Current Issues in Criminal Justice* 9 (3), 262–278.

Chambliss, William J.
1964   A sociological analysis of the law of vagrancy. *Social Problems* 12 (1), 67–77.

Chang, Yanrong
2004   Courtroom questioning as a culturally situated persuasive genre of talk. *Discourse and Society* 15 (6), 705–722.

Charles, Chris J.
2003   The crisis in ATSILS funding. *Indigenous Law Bulletin* 5 (28), 22–23.

Cicourel, Aaron V.
1976   *The Social Construction of Juvenile Justice*. 2nd ed. (1st ed. 1968). London: Heinemann.
1978   Language and society: Cognitive, cultural and linguistic aspects of language use. *Sozialwissenschaftliche Annalen* 2, 25–58.
1981   Notes on the integration of micro- and macro-levels of analysis. In Knorr-Cetina, Karin D. and Aaron V. Cicourel (eds.), *Advances in Social Theory and Methodology: Toward an Integration*

of Micro- and Macro-Sociologies. Boston: Routledge and Kegan Paul, 51–80.

CJC (Criminal Justice Commission)

1992   *Report on the Investigation into the Complaints of Kelvin Ronald Condren and Others.* Brisbane: Criminal Justice Commission.

1994a   *A Report of an Investigation into the Arrest and Death of Daniel Alfred Yock.* Brisbane: Criminal Justice Commission.

1994b   *Report on a Review of Police Powers in Queensland: Volume IV: Suspects' Rights, Police Questioning and Pre-Charge Detention.* Brisbane: Criminal Justice Commission.

1994c   *Implementation of Reform within the Queensland Police Service: The Response of the Queensland Police Service to the Fitzgerald Inquiry Recommendations.* Brisbane: Criminal Justice Commission.

1995   Media release. 3rd March 1995.

1996   *Aboriginal Witnesses in Queensland's Criminal Courts.* Brisbane: Criminal Justice Commission.

1997a   *Integrity in the Queensland Police Service: Implementation and Impact of the Fitzgerald Inquiry Reforms.* Brisbane: Criminal Justice Commission.

1997b   *Reports on Aboriginal Witnesses and Police Watchhouses: Status of Recommendations.* Brisbane: Criminal Justice Commission.

1998   *Policing and the Community in Brisbane.* Brisbane: Criminal Justice Commission.

Clements, Christine

2006   *Finding of Inquest: Inquest into the Death of Mulrunji.* Townsville: Office of the State Coroner.

Coldrey, John

1987   Aboriginals and the criminal courts. In Hazlehurst, Kayleen M. (ed.), *Ivory Scales: Black Australia and the Law.* Sydney: New South Wales University Press, 81–92.

Collins, James

2001   Selling the market: Educational standards, discourse, and social inequality. *Critique of Anthropology* 21 (2), 143–163.

Collins, Randall

1988   The micro contribution to macro sociology. *Sociological Theory* 6, 242–253.

Conley, John M. and William M. O'Barr
   1998   *Just Words: Law, Language and Power*. Chicago: University of Chicago Press.

Conley, John M., William M. O'Barr, and E. Allan Lind
   1978   The power of language: Presentational style in the courtroom. *Duke Law Journal*, 1375–1399.

Cooke, Michael
   1995a   Aboriginal evidence in the cross-cultural courtroom. In Eades, Diana (ed.), *Language in Evidence: Issues Confronting Aboriginal and Multicultural Australia*. Sydney: University of New South Wales Press, 55–96.
   1995b   Interpreting in a cross-cultural cross-examination: An Aboriginal case study. *International Journal of the Sociology of Language* 113, 99–111.
   1995c   Understood by all concerned? Anglo/Aboriginal legal translation. In Morris, Marshall (ed.), *Translation and the Law*. Amsterdam/Philadelphia: John Benjamins, 37–66.
   1996   A different story: Narrative versus "question and answer" in Aboriginal evidence. *Forensic Linguistics* 3 (2), 273–288.
   1998   Anglo/Yolngu Communication in the Criminal Justice System. PhD Thesis, University of New England, Australia *available from author: intercult@netspeed.com.au*
   2002   *Indigenous Interpreting Issues for the Courts*. Carlton, Victoria: Australian Institute of Judicial Administration Incorporated.

Cornford, Philip and Geesche Jacobsen
   2004   Wrong path leads to fiery requiem. *The Sydney Morning Herald*, 18 August.

Cotterill, Janet
   2001   Domestic discord, rocky relationships: Semantic prosodies in representations of marital violence in the O. J. Simpson trial. *Discourse and Society* 12 (3), 291–312.
   2002   "Just one more time …": Aspects of intertextuality in the trials of O. J. Simpson. In Cotterill, Janet (ed.), *Language in the Legal Process*. Houndmills: Palgrave Macmillan, 147–161.
   2003   *Language and Power in Court: A Linguistic Analysis of the O. J. Simpson Trial*. Houndmills: Palgrave Macmillan.
   2004   Collocation, connotation, and courtroom semantics: Lawyers' control of witness testimony through lexical negotiation. *Applied Linguistics* 25 (4), 513–537.

Coupland, Nikolas
   2001   Introduction: Sociolinguistic theory and social theory. In Coup-
             land, Nikolas, Srikant Sarangi and Christopher N. Candlin (eds.),
             Sociolinguistics and Social Theory. London: Pearson Education
             Limited, 1–26.

Cunneen, Chris
   1994   Enforcing genocide? Aboriginal young people and the police. In
             White, Rob and Christine Adler (eds.), *The Police and Young
             People in Australia*, Cambridge: Cambridge University Press,
             128–158.
   1995   Aboriginal young people's experiences in police custody. In Simp-
             son, C. and R. Hil (eds.), *Ways of Resistance: Social Control and
             Young People in Australia*. Sydney: Hale and Iremonger, 115–137.
   1996   Detention, torture, terror and the Australian state: Aboriginal peo-
             ple, criminal justice and neocolonialism. In Bird, Greta, Gary
             Martin and Jennifer Neilson (eds.), *Majah: Indigenous Peoples
             and the Law*. Sydney: The Federation Press, 13–37.
   2001   *Conflict, Politics and Crime: Aboriginal Communities and the Po-
             lice*. Sydney: Allen and Unwin.

Cunneen, Chris, Neva Collings and Nina Ralph
   2005   *Evaluation of the Queensland Aboriginal and Torres Strait
             Islander Justice Agreement*. Retrieved on 1 March 2007 from
             http://www.justice.qld.gov.au/publications.htm

Cunneen, Chris and David McDonald
   1997   *Keeping Aboriginal and Torres Strait Islander People Out of Cus-
             tody: An Evaluation of the Implementation of the Recommenda-
             tions of the Royal Commission into Aboriginal Deaths in Custody*.
             Canberra: Aboriginal and Torres Strait Islander Commission.

Cunneen, Chris and Rob White
   2002   *Juvenile Justice: Youth and Crime in Australia*. Oxford: Oxford
             University Press.

D'Souza, Nigel
   1990   Aboriginal children and the juvenile justice system. *Aboriginal
             Law Bulletin* 9 (44), 4–5.

Danet, Brenda
   1980   "Baby" or "fetus"?: Language and the construction of reality in a
             manslaughter trial. *Semiotica* 32 (3/4), 187–219.

Danet, Brenda, Kenneth Hoffman, Nicole Kermish, Jeffrey Rahn and Deborah Stayman
  1980   An ethnography of questioning in the courtroom. In Shuy, Roger and Anna Shnukal (eds.), *Language Use and the Uses of Language*. Washington DC: Georgetown University Press, 222–234.

Dick, Tim, Jennifer Cooke and Alexandra Smith
  2004   Teenager's death triggers fiery Aboriginal rampage. *The Sydney Morning Herald*, 16 February.

Drew, Paul
  1992   Contested evidence in courtroom cross-examination: The case of a trial for rape. In Drew, Paul and John Heritage (eds.), *Talk at Work: Interaction in Institutional Settings*. Cambridge: Cambridge University Press, 470–520.

Dunstan, R.
  1980   Context for coercion: Analyzing properties of courtroom "questions". *British Journal of Law and Society* 7, 61–77.

Durkheim, Émile
  1930   *Le Suicide.* Paris: F. Alcan.

Eades, Diana
  1982   "You gotta know how to talk … ": Ethnography of information seeking in Southeast Queensland Aboriginal Society. *Australian Journal of Linguistics* (2) 1, 61–82.
  1983   English as an Aboriginal language in Southeast Queensland. Unpublished PhD Thesis. University of Queensland.
  1984   Misunderstanding Aboriginal English: The role of socio-cultural context. In McKay, Graham and Bruce Sommer (eds.) *Applications of Linguistics to Australian Aboriginal Contexts*. Melbourne: Applied Linguistics Association of Australia, 24–33.
  1988   "They don't speak an Aboriginal language, or do they?" In Keen, Ian (ed.), *Being Black: Aboriginal Cultures in Settled Australia*. Canberra: Aboriginal Studies Press, 97–117.
  1991   Communicative strategies in Aboriginal English. In Romaine, Suzanne (ed.), *Language in Australia*. Cambridge: Cambridge University Press, 84–93.
  1992   *Aboriginal English and the Law: Communicating with Aboriginal English Speaking Clients: A Handbook for Legal Practitioners*. Brisbane: Queensland Law Society.

1993   The case for Condren: Aboriginal English, pragmatics and the law. *Journal of Pragmatics* 20 (2), 141–162.

1994a   A case of communicative clash: Aboriginal English and the legal system in Gibbons, John (ed.), *Language and the Law.* London: Longman, 234–264.

1994b   Report to Aboriginal Legal Service Brisbane. Unpublished ms.

1995a   Aboriginal English on Trial: The case for Stuart and Condren. In Eades, Diana (ed.), *Language in Evidence: Issues Confronting Aboriginal and Multicultural Australia.* Sydney: University of New South Wales Press, 147–174.

1995b   Cross-examination of Aboriginal children: The Pinkenba case. *Aboriginal Law Bulletin* 3 (75), 10–11.

1996a   Legal recognition of cultural differences in communication: The case of Robyn Kina. *Language and Communication* 16 (3), 215–227.

1996b   Verbatim courtroom transcripts and discourse analysis. In Kniffka, Hannes (ed.), *Recent Developments in Forensic Linguistics.* Frankfurt: Peter Lang, 241–254.

1997   The acceptance of linguistic evidence about indigenous Australians. *Australian Aboriginal Studies* (1), 15–27.

2000   "I don't think it's an answer to the question": Silencing Aboriginal witnesses in court. *Language in Society* 29 (2), 161–196.

2002   "Evidence given in unequivocal terms": Gaining consent of Aboriginal kids in court. In Cotterill, Janet (ed.), *Language in the Legal Process.* Houndmills: Palgrave Macmillan, 162–179.

2003a   The politics of misunderstanding in the legal process: Aboriginal English in Queensland. In House, Juliane, Gabrièle Kasper and Steven Ross (eds.), *Misunderstanding in Spoken Discourse.* London: Longman, 196–223.

2003b   "I don't think the lawyers were communicating with me": Misunderstanding cultural differences in communicative style. *Emory Law Journal* 52, 1109–1134.

2004a   Understanding Aboriginal English in the legal system: A critical sociolinguistics approach. *Applied Linguistics* 25 (4), 491–512.

2004b   Beyond difference and domination?: Intercultural communication in legal contexts. In Kiesling, Scott F, and Christina Bratt Paulston (eds.), *Intercultural Discourse and Communication: The Essential Readings.* Oxford: Blackwell, 304–316.

2004c   Review of *Language and Power in Court: A Linguistic Analysis of the O. J. Simpson Trial* by Janet Cotterill. *Forensic Linguistics* 11 (2), 293–297.

2006   Lexical struggle in court: Aboriginal Australians vs the state. *Journal of Sociolinguistics* 10 (2), 153–181.

2007   Understanding Aboriginal silence in legal contexts. In Kotthoff, Helga and Helen Spencer-Oatey (eds.), *Handbook of Intercultural Communication*. Berlin: Mouton de Gruyter, 285–301.

Eckermann, Anne-Katrin
1977   Group organisation and identity within an urban Aboriginal community. In Berndt, Ronald M. (ed.), *Aborigines and Change: Australia in the 70s*. Canberra: Australian Institute of Aboriginal Studies, 288–319.

Edwards, Bill
2004   Putuna Kulilpai: Interpreting for Pitjantjatjara people in courts. *The Journal of Judicial Administration* 14, 99–110.

Eggleston, Elizabeth
1976   *Fear, Favour or Affection: Aborigines and the Criminal Law in Victoria, South Australia and Western Australia*. Canberra: Australian National University Press.

1977   Aboriginal legal services. In Berndt, Ronald M. (ed.), *Aborigines and Change: Australia in the 70s*. Canberra: Australian Institute of Aboriginal Studies, 353–367.

Ehrlich, Susan
1998   The discursive reconstruction of sexual consent. *Discourse and Society* 9 (2), 149–171.

2001   *Representing Rape: Language and Sexual Consent*. London: Routledge.

2002a   (Re)contextualizing complainants' accounts of sexual assault. *Forensic Linguistics* 9 (2), 193–212.

2002b   Legal institutions, nonspeaking recipiency and participants' orientations. *Discourse and Society* 13 (6), 731–747.

2005   Trial discourse and judicial decision-making: Constraining the boundaries of gendered identities. In Baxter, Judith (ed.) *Speaking Out: The Female Voice in Public Contexts*. Houndmills: Palgrave Macmillan, 139–158.

2007   Legal discourse and the cultural intelligibility of gendered meanings. *Journal of Sociolinguistics* 11(4), 452–477.

Ehrlich, Susan and Jack Sidnell
    2006   "I think that's not an assumption you ought to make": Challenging presuppositions in inquiry testimony. *Language in Society* 35 (5), 655–676.

Elkin, Adolphus
    1947   Aboriginal evidence and justice in north Australia. *Oceania* 17, 173–210.

Ellis, M. A.
    2005   Letter to the editor. *The Queensland Police Union Journal*, 19 February.

Enninger, Werner
    1987   What interactants do with non-talk across cultures. In Knapp, Karlfried, Werner Enninger and Annelie Knapp-Pothoff (eds.), *Analyzing Intercultural Communication*. Berlin: Mouton de Gruyter, 269–302.

Estrich, Susan
    1987   *Real Rape*. Cambridge, MA: Harvard University Press.

Evans, Raymond
    1992   Wanton outrage: Police and Aborigines at Breakfast Creek 1860. In Fisher, Rod (ed.), *Brisbane: The Aboriginal Presence 1824–1860*. Kelvin Grove: Brisbane History Group Incorporated, 80–89.
    2004   "Plenty shoot 'em": The destruction of Aboriginal societies along the Queensland frontier. In Moses, A. Dirk (ed.), *Genocide and Settler Society: Frontier Violence and Stolen Indigenous Children in Australian History*. New York: Berghahn Books, 150–173.

Fagan, David
    1994   Liaison police blamed over Yock brawl. *The Australian*, 14 May.

Fairclough, Norman
    1989   *Language and Power*. London: Longman.
    1992a   Introduction. In Fairclough, Norman (ed.), *Critical Language Awareness*. London: Longman, 1–29.
    1992b   The appropriacy of "appropriateness". In Fairclough, Norman (ed.), *Critical Language Awareness*. London: Longman, 33–56.
    1992c   *Discourse and Social Change*. Cambridge: Polity Press.

Findlay, Mark, Stephen Odgers and Stanley Yeo
    2005   *Australian Criminal Justice*. 3rd ed. (1st ed. 1994). Oxford: Oxford University Press.

Fitzgerald, Gerald E.
1989   *Report of a Commission of Inquiry Pursuant to Orders in Council.*
        Brisbane: Government Printer.

Foley, Matthew
1984   Aborigines and the Police. In Hanks, Peter and Bryan Keon-Cohen
        (eds.), *Aborigines and the Law: Essays in Memory of Elizabeth
        Eggleston.* Sydney: Allen and Unwin, 160–190.

Forde, Laurie and Susan Forde
2005   Queensland's darkest days. *The Koori Mail,* 18 May.

Foucault, Michel
1991   *Remarks on Marx.* New York: Semiotext(e).

Freed, Alice F.
1992   We understand perfectly: A critique of Tannen's view of cross-
        sex conversation. In Hall, Kira, Mary Bucholtz and Birch Moon-
        womon (eds.), *Locating Power: Proceedings of the Second Berke-
        ley Women and Language Conference.* Berkeley, CA: Berkeley
        Women and Language Group, University of California, 144–152.
2003   Epilogue: Reflections on language and gender research. In Holmes,
        Janet and Miriam Meyerhoff (eds.), *The Handbook of Language
        and Gender.* Oxford: Blackwell, 699–721.

Gagliardi, Jason
1992   Law group sees black injustice: Handbook outlines language prob-
        lems. *The Brisbane Courier Mail*, 13 April.

Gale, Fay, Rebecca Bailey-Harris and Joy Wundersitz
1990   *Aboriginal Youth and the Criminal Justice System: The Justice of
        Injustice?* Cambridge: Cambridge University Press.

Garcia, Angela
1991   Dispute resolution without disputing: How the interactional or-
        ganization of mediation hearings minimizes argument. *American
        Sociological Review* 56, 818–835.

Gardner, Rod and Ilana Mushin
2007   Post-start overlap and disattentiveness in talk in a Garrwa commu-
        nity. *Australian Review of Applied Linguistics* 30 (3), 35.1–35.14.

Garner, Bryan A. (ed.)
2004   *Black's Law Dictionary*. 8th ed. St. Paul, MN: West.

Gee, James
   1990   *Social Linguistics and Literacies: Ideology in Discourse*. London: The Falmer Press.

Gibbons, John
   2001   Revising the language of New South Wales police procedures: Applied Linguistics in action. *Applied Linguistics* 22 (4), 439–469.
   2003   *Forensic Linguistics*. Oxford: Blackwell.

Giddens, Anthony
   1982   *The Constitution of Society*. Berkeley, LA: University of California Press.
   1987   *Social Theory and Modern Sociology*. Oxford: Polity Press.

Goldflam, Russell
   1995   Silence in Court! Problems and prospects in Aboriginal legal interpreting. In Eades, Diana (ed.), *Language in Evidence: Issues Confronting Aboriginal and Multicultural Australia*. Sydney: University of New South Wales Press, 28–54.

Goode, Erich and Nachman Ben-Yehuda
   1994   Moral panics: An introduction. In Goode, Erich and Nachman Ben-Yehuda (eds.), *Moral Panics: The Social Construction of Deviance*. Oxford: Blackwell, 31–66.

Gramsci, Antonio
   1971   *Selections from the Prison Notebooks of Antonio Gramsci*. Hoare, Quentin and Geoffrey Nowell Smith (ed. and trans.). London: Laurence and Wishart.

Groome, Howard
   1995   *Working Purposefully with Aboriginal Students*. Wentworth Falls, NSW: Social Science Press.

Gumperz, John J.
   1982a   *Discourse Strategies*. Cambridge: Cambridge University Press.
   1982b   (ed.) *Language and Social Identity*. Cambridge: Cambridge University Press.
   1992   Contextualization and understanding. In Duranti, Alessandro and Charles Goodwin (eds.), *Rethinking Context: Language as an Interactive Phenomenon*. Cambridge: Cambridge University Press, 229–252.
   2001a   Contextualization and ideology in intercultural communication. In Di Luzio, Aldo, Susanne Günther, and Franca Orletti (eds.),

Culture in Communication: Analyses of Intercultural Situations. Amsterdam: John Benjamins, 35–53.

2001b   Interactional sociolinguistics: A personal perspective. In Schiffrin, Deborah, Deborah Tannen and Heidi E. Hamilton (eds.), *The Handbook of Discourse Analysis*. Oxford: Blackwell, 215–228.

Gumperz, John J. and Jenny Cook-Gumperz
1982   Introduction: Language and the communication of social identity. In Gumperz, John (ed.), *Language and Social Identity.* Cambridge: Cambridge University Press, 1–21.

Gumperz, John J., Tom Jupp and Celia Roberts
1979   *Crosstalk: A Study of Cross-cultural Communication.* (Background material and notes to accompany the BBC film.) London: National Centre for Industrial Language Training in association with BBC Continuing Education Department.

Hagan, Stephen
2005   Our identity tags. *The Koori Mail*, 24 August.

Haiman, John
1998   *Talk is Cheap: Sarcasm, Alienation and the Evolution of Language.* Oxford: Oxford University Press.

Hale, Sandra Beatriz
2004   *The Discourse of Court Interpreting*: *Discourse Practices of the Law, the Witness and the Interpreter.* Amsterdam: John Benjamins.

Hamilton, Annette
1981   *Nature and Nurture: Aboriginal Child-rearing in North-Central Arnhem Land.* Canberra: Australian Institute of Aboriginal Studies.

Harris, Sandra
1984   Questions as a mode of control in magistrates' courts. *International Journal of the Sociology of Language* 49, 5–28.
1989   Defendant resistance to power and control in court. In Coleman, Hylwel (ed.), *Working with Language: A Multidisciplinary Consideration of Language Use in Work Contexts.* Berlin/New York: Mouton de Gruyter, 132–164.

Harris, Stephen
1984   *Culture and Learning: Tradition and Education in North-East Arnhem Land.* Canberra: Australian Institute of Aboriginal Studies.

Haviland, John B.
  1979   Guugu Yimidhirr brother-in-law language. *Language in Society* 8, 365–393.

Hazlehurst, Kayleen (ed.)
  1987   *Ivory Scales: Black Australia and the Law*. Sydney: New South Wales University Press.

Hawkins, Eric
  1984   *Awareness of Language: An Introduction*. Cambridge: Cambridge University Press.

Heffer, Chris
  2005   *The Language of Jury Trial: A Corpus-Aided Analysis of Legal-Lay Discourse*. Houndmills: Palgrave Macmillan.

Hegarty, Ruth
  2000   *Is That You, Ruthie?* Brisbane: University of Queensland Press.
  2003   *Bittersweet Journey*. Brisbane: University of Queensland Press.

Heller, Monica
  2001a   Critique and sociolinguistic analysis of discourse. *Critique of Anthropology* 21 (2), 117–141.
  2001b   Undoing the macro/micro dichotomy: Ideology and categorisation in a linguistic minority school. In Coupland, Nikolas, Srikant Sarangi and Christopher N. Candlin (eds.), *Sociolinguistics and Social Theory*. London: Pearson Education Limited, 212–234.
  2002   *Éléments d'une sociolinguistique critique*. Paris: Didier.
  2006   Communities, identities, processes and practices. Paper presented at Sociolinguistics Symposium 16, Limerick, Ireland.

Henning, Terese and Simon Bronitt
  1998   Rape victims on trial: Regulating the use and abuse of sexual history evidence. In Easteal, Patricia (ed.), *Balancing the Scales: Rape, Law Reform and Australian Culture*. Sydney: The Federation Press, 76–93.

Heritage, John
  1985   Analyzing news interviews: Aspects of the production of talk for an overhearing audience. In Van Dijk, Teun (ed.), *Handbook of Discourse Analysis: Discourse and Dialogue*. New York: Academic Press, 95–119.

Hil, Richard
    1995   Moral panic and juvenile justice in Queensland: The emergent context of the Juvenile Justice Act 1992. In Hazlehurst, Kayleen M. (ed.), *Perceptions of Justice: Issues in Indigenous Community Empowerment*. Aldershot: Avebury, 51–70.

Hiley, Graham
    1996   Native Title Litigation. *Queensland Law Society Journal*, August, 333–334.

Hollinsworth, David
    2005   "My island home": Riot and resistance in media representations of Aboriginality. *Social Alternatives* 24 (1), 16–20.

Holmes, Janet
    1997   Women, language and identity. *Journal of Sociolinguistics* 1/2, 195–223.

Holmes, Janet and Miriam Meyerhoff (eds.)
    2003   *The Handbook of Language and Gender*. Oxford: Blackwell.

Howie-Willis, Ian
    1994a   Buchanan, C. In Horton, David (ed.), *The Encyclopaedia of Aboriginal Australia*. Canberra: Aboriginal Studies Press, 159–160.
    1994b   Family. In Horton, David (ed.), *The Encyclopaedia of Aboriginal Australia*. Canberra: Aboriginal Studies Press, 356.
    1994c   Fogarty, L. In Horton, David (ed.), *The Encyclopaedia of Aboriginal Australia*. Canberra: Aboriginal Studies Press, 373.
    1994d   Native Police. In Horton, David (ed.), *The Encyclopaedia of Aboriginal Australia*. Canberra: Aboriginal Studies Press, 765–766.

Huggins, Rita and Jackie Huggins
    1994   *Talking to Rita*. Canberra: Aboriginal Studies Press.

Hutchby, Ian
    2002   Resisting the incitement to talk in child counselling: Aspects of the utterance "I don't know". *Discourse Studies* 4 (2), 147–168.

Jacquemet, Marco
    1996   *Credibility in Court: Communicative Practices in the Camorra Trials*. Cambridge: Cambridge University Press.

Jakubowicz, Andrew, Heather Goodall, Jeannie Martin, Tony Mitchell, Lois Randall and Kalinga Seneviratne
    1994   *Racism, Ethnicity and the Media*. Sydney: Allen and Unwin.

Jaworski, Adam
  1993   *The Power of Silence: Social and Pragmatic Perspectives.* Newbury Park: Sage.

Jefferson, Gail
  1989   Preliminary notes on a possible metric which provides for a "Standard Maximum" silence of approximately one second in a conversation. In Roger, Derek and Peter Bull (eds.), *Conversation: An Interdisciplinary Perspective.* Clevedon: Multilingual Matters, 166–196.

Johnston, Elliott
  1991a   *Royal Commission into Aboriginal Deaths in Custody National Report: Overview and Recommendations.* Canberra: Australian Government Publishing Service.
  1991b   *Final Report.* 5 vols. Canberra: Australian Government Publishing Service.

Jönsson, Linda and Per Linell
  1991   Story generations: From dialogical interviews to written reports in police interrogations. *Text* 11 (3), 419–440.

Jopson, Debra
  2000   Australia faces year of scrutiny on rights. *The Sydney Morning Herald*, 27 March.

Kearins, Judith
  1991   Factors affecting Aboriginal testimony. *Legal Service Bulletin* 16 (1), 3–6.

Keen, Ian
  1988   Introduction. In Keen, Ian (ed.), *Being Black: Aboriginal Cultures in Settled Australia.* Canberra: Aboriginal Studies Press, 1–26.
  2004   *Aboriginal Economy and Society: Australia at the Threshold of Colonisation.* Oxford: Oxford University Press.

King, Madonna
  1993   State "exercising reverse racism". *The Australian*, 1 December.

Koch, Harold
  1985   Nonstandard English in an Aboriginal Land Claim. In Pride, John (ed.), *Cross-cultural Encounters: Communication and Miscommunication.* Melbourne: River Seine Publications, 176–195.

1991   Language and communication in Aboriginal Land Claim hearings. In Romaine, Suzanne (ed.), *Language in Australia.* Cambridge: Cambridge University Press, 94–103.

Koepping, Klaus-Peter
1977   Cultural pattern on an Aboriginal settlement in Queensland. In Berndt, Ronald M. (ed.), *Aborigines and Change: Australia in the 70s.* Canberra: Australian Institute of Aboriginal Studies, 159–176.

Komter, Marta
2006a   Introduction. *Research on Language and Social Interaction* 39 (3), 195–200.
2006b   From talk to text: The interactional construction of a police record. *Research on Language in Social Interaction* 39 (3), 201–228.

Kress, Gunther
2001   Critical sociolinguistics. In Mesthrie, Rajend (ed.), *Concise Encyclopedia of Sociolinguistics.* Oxford: Elsevier Science, 542–545.

Kriewaldt, Martin C.
1960   Application of the Criminal Code to the Aborigines of the Northern Territory in Australia. *Law Review of Western Australia,* 1–50.

Kubota, Ryuko
1999   Japanese culture constructed by discourses: Implications for applied linguistics research and EFL. *TESOL Quarterly* 33 (1), 9–35.

Kurzon, Dennis
1995   The right of silence: A socio-pragmatic model of interpretation. *Journal of Pragmatics* 23, 55–69.

Labov, William
1972   *Sociolinguistic Patterns.* Philadelpia: University of Pennsylvania Press.

Lacey, Nicola
1998   *Unspeakable Subjects: Feminist Essays in Legal and Social Theory.* Oxford: Hart.

Lakoff, Robin Tolmach
1975   *Language and Woman's Place.* New York: Harper and Row.

Lane, Chris
1990   The sociolinguistics of questioning in District Court trials. In Bell, Allan and Janet Holmes (eds.), *New Zealand Ways of Speaking English.* Clevedon: Multilingual Matters, 221–251.

Langton, Marcia
   1988   Medicine Square. In Keen, Ian (ed.), *Being Black: Aboriginal Cultures in Settled Australia*. Canberra: Aboriginal Studies Press, 201–226.

Larriera, Alicia and Richard Macey
   1991   Government may ban swearing at police. *The Sydney Morning Herald*, 22 February.

Lavery, Daniel
   1992   Review of *Aboriginal English and the Law*. *Aboriginal Law Bulletin* 2 (59), 13.

Lebra, Takie Sugiyama
   1987   The cultural significance of silence in Japanese communication. *Multilingua* 6 (4), 343–357.

Lees, Sue
   1997   *Ruling Passions: Sexual Violence, Reputation, and the Law*. Buckingham: Open University Press.

Lester, Yami
   1973   *Aborigines and the Courts*. Alice Springs: Institute for Aboriginal Development.

Liberman, Kenneth
   1980   Ambiguity and gratuitous concurrence in intercultural communication. *Human Studies* 3, 65–85.
   1981   Understanding Aborigines in Australian courts of law. *Human Organization* 40, 247–255.
   1985   *Understanding Interaction in Central Australia: An Ethnomethodological Study of Australian Aboriginal People*. Boston: Routledge and Kegan Paul.

Loftus, Elizabeth F.
   1979   *Eyewitness Testimony*. Cambridge, MA: Harvard University Press.

Luchjenbroers, June
   1997   "In your own words ...": Questions and answers in a Supreme Court trial. *Journal of Pragmatics* 27, 477–503.

Lui, Gary
   2000   A unique practice. *Indigenous Law Bulletin* 5 (2), 10.

Lyons, Gregory
    1984   Aboriginal Legal Services. In Hanks, Peter and Bryan Keon-Cohen (eds.), *Aborigines and the Law: Essays in Memory of Elizabeth Eggleston*. Sydney: Allen and Unwin, 137–159.

Macquarie Dictionary online
    Retrieved on 10 March 2007 from
    http://www.macquariedictionary.com.au

Maher, Sid
    1993   Police gun threats alleged. *The Brisbane Courier Mail*, 18 December.

Makoni, Sinfree and Alastair Pennycook
    2005   Disinventing and (re)constituting languages. *Critical Inquiry in Language Studies* 2 (3), 137–156.

Malcolm, Ian G.
    1994   Discourse and discourse strategies in Australian Aboriginal English. *World Englishes* 13 (3), 289–306.

Malcolm, Ian G. and Susan Kaldor
    1991   Aboriginal English: An overview. In Romaine, Suzanne (ed.), *Language in Australia*. Cambridge: Cambridge University Press, 67–83.

Malcolm Ian G. and Judith Rochecouste
    2000   Event and story schemas in Australian Aboriginal English. *English World-Wide* 21 (2), 261–289.

Malcolm, Ian G. and Farzad Sharifian
    2002   Aspects of Aboriginal English oral discourse: An application of cultural schema theory. *Discourse Studies* 4 (2), 169–181.
    2005   Something old, something new, something borrowed, something blue: Australian Aboriginal students' schematic repertoire. *Journal of Multilingual and Multicultural Development* 26 (6), 512–532.

Malcolm, Ian G., Yvonne Haig, Patricia Königsberg, Judith Rochecouste, Glenys Collard, Alison Hill and Rosemary Cahill
    1999   *Two-Way English: Towards More User-Friendly Education for Speakers of Aboriginal English*. Perth: Education Department, Western Australia.

Malin, Merridy
    1997   Mrs Eyers is no ogre. In Cowlishaw, Gillian and Barry Morris (eds.), *Race Matters: Indigenous Australian and "Our" Society.* Canberra: Aboriginal Studies Press, 139–160.

Malin, Merridy, Katho Campbell and Laura Agius
    1996   Raising children in the Nunga Aboriginal way. *Family Matters* 43, 43–47.

Maryns, Katrijn
    2006   *The Asylum Speaker: Language in the Belgian Asylum Procedure.* Manchester: St. Jerome Press.

Masters, Chris
    1988   Two confessions. *Page One* TV documentary Channel 10, 9 June.
    1992   *Inside Story.* Sydney: Angus and Robertson.

Matoesian, Gregory
    1993   *Reproducing Rape: Domination through Talk in the Courtroom.* Chicago: University of Chicago Press.
    2001   *Law and the Language of Identity: Discourse in the William Kennedy Smith Rape Trial.* Oxford: Oxford University Press.
    2005a   Struck by speech revisited: Embodied stance in jurisdictional discourse. *Journal of Sociolinguistics* 9 (2), 167–193.
    2005b   Review of *Language and Power in Court: A Linguistic Analysis of the O. J. Simpson Case* by Janet Cotterill. *Journal of Sociolinguistics* 9 (4), 619–622.

Mauet, Thomas A.
    2000   *Trial Techniques.* 5th ed. Gaithersburg: Aspen.

McConvell, Patrick and Nicholas Thieberger
    2005   Languages past and present. In Arthur, Bill and Frances Morphy (eds.), *Macquarie Atlas of Indigenous Australia: Culture and Society through Space and Time.* Sydney: The Macquarie Library Pty Ltd., 78–87.

McDonald, David and Chris Cunneen
    1997   Aboriginal incarceration and deaths in custody: Looking back and looking forward. *Current Issues in Criminal Justice* 9 (1), 5–20.

McRae, Heather, Garth Nettheim and Laura Beacroft
    1991   *Aboriginal Legal Issues: Commentary and Materials.* Sydney: Law Book Company.

1997   *Indigenous Legal Issues: Commentary and Materials*. Sydney: Law Book Company.

Mehan, Hugh
1987   Language and power in organizational process. *Discourse Processes* 10, 291–301.

Meeuwis, Michael
1994   Leniency and testiness in intercultural communication: Remarks on ideology and context in interactional sociolinguistics. *Pragmatics* 4 (3), 391–408.

Meeuwis, Michael and Srikant Sarangi
1994   Perspectives on intercultural communication: A critical reading. *Pragmatics* 4 (3), 309–314.

Mey, Jacob
1985   *Whose Language? A Study in Linguistic Pragmatics*. Amsterdam: John Benjamins.

Mickler, Steve and Alec McHoul
1998   Sourcing the wave: Crime reporting, Aboriginal youth and the WA press, Feb 1991–Jan 1992. *Media International Australia incorporating Culture and Policy* 86, 122–152.

Mildren, Dean
1997   Redressing the imbalance against Aboriginals in the criminal justice system. *Criminal Law Journal* 21 (1), 7–22.
1999   Redressing the imbalance: Aboriginal people in the criminal justice system. *Forensic Linguistics* 6 (1), 137–160.

Morris, Barry
1989   *Domesticating Resistance: The Dhan-gadi Aborigines and the Australian State*. Oxford: Berg.

Mye, G.
1994   Torres Strait Islander. In Horton, David (ed.), *The Encyclopaedia of Aboriginal Australia*. Canberra: Aboriginal Studies Press, 1089–1090.

Nash, David
1979   Foreigners in their own land. *Legal Services Bulletin* June, 105–107.

Ngarritjan-Kessaris, Terry
1997   School meetings and indigenous parents. In Harris, Stephen and Merridy Malin (eds.), *Indigenous Education: Historical, Moral*

and Practical Tales. Darwin: Northern Territory University Press, 81–90.

Nicholls, Christine
1994   Watch your language, eh? *The Aboriginal Child at School* 22 (3), 5–13.

NISATSIC (National Inquiry into the Separation of Aboriginal and Torres Strait Islander Children from their Families)
1997   *Bringing them Home.* Sydney: Human Rights and Equal Opportunity Commission.

Norrick, Neal R.
1997   Twice-told tales: Collaborative narration of familiar stories. *Language in Society* 26 (2), 199–220.

O'Barr, William M.
1982   *Linguistic Evidence: Power and Strategy in the Courtroom.* New York: Academic Press.

Ochs, Elinor
1996   Linguistic resources for socializing humanity. In Gumperz, John J. and Stephen C. Levinson (eds.), *Rethinking Linguistic Relativity.* Cambridge: Cambridge University Press, 407–437.

Ogbu, John U.
1995   Cultural problems in minority education: Their interpretations and consequences. Part One: Theoretical background. *The Urban Review* 27 (3), 189–205.

O'Shane, Pat
1992   Aborigines and the criminal justice system. In Cunneen, Chris (ed.), *Aboriginal Perspectives on Criminal Justice*, The Institute of Criminology Monograph Series, No. 1. Sydney: Institute of Criminology, 3–6.

Parker, Natalie and Mark Pathé
2006   *Report on the Review of the Murri Court.* Brisbane: Department of Justice and Attorney-General.

Pennycook, Alastair
2001   *Critical Applied Linguistics: A Critical Introduction.* Mahwah, NJ: Lawrence Erlbaum.

Peterson, Nicolas, Patrick McConvell, Heather McDonald, Frances Morphy and
Bill Arthur
    2005   Social and cultural life. In Arthur, Bill and Frances Morphy (eds.),
            *Macquarie Atlas of Indigenous Australia: Culture and Society
            through Space and Time*. Sydney: The Macquarie Library Pty Ltd.,
            88–107.

Philips, Susan U.
    1976   Some sources of cultural variability in the regulation of talk. *Language in Society* 5, 81–95.
    1992   Evidentiary standards for American trials: Just the facts. In Hill,
            Jane H. and Judith T. Irvine (eds.), *Responsibility and Evidence
            in Oral Discourse*. Cambridge, Cambridge University Press, 248–259.
    1993   *The Invisible Culture: Communication in Classroom and Community on the Warm Springs Indian Reservation*. 2nd ed. (1st ed. 1983). New York: Longman.
    1998   *Ideology in the Language of Judges: How Judges Practice Law, Politics and Courtroom Control*. New York: Oxford University Press.

Potas, Ivan, Jane Smart, Georgia Brignell, Brendan Thomas and Rowena Lawrie
    2003   *Circle Sentencing in New South Wales: A Review and Evaluation*. Sydney: Judicial Commission of New South Wales.

Pritchard, Sarah
    2000   Facing the wrong way on human rights. *The Sydney Morning Herald*, 31 July.

Queensland Department of Justice
    2000   *Aboriginal English in the Courts: A Handbook*. Brisbane: Department of Justice.

QJAG (Queensland Department of Justice and Attorney-General)
    2005   *Review of the Murri Court: Have Your Say*. Brisbane: Department of Justice and Attorney General.
    2006   *The Murri Court*. Fact sheet C11. Brisbane: Department of Justice and Attorney General.

Queensland Government
    2001   *Queensland Aboriginal and Torres Strait Islander Justice Agreement*. Brisbane: Queensland Government.

Queensland Police Service
   2005   *Aboriginal and Torres Strait Islander and Multicultural Action Plan 2005–2006*. retrieved on 27 November 2006, from http://www.police.qld.gov.au/programs/community/ CulturalAdvisory/actionplan.htm

Queensland Supreme Court
   2005   *Equal Treatment Benchbook*. Brisbane: Supreme Court Library.

Rampton, Ben
   2001a   Language crossing, cross-talk and cross-disciplinarity in sociolinguistics. In Coupland, Nikolas, Srikant Sarangi and Christopher N. Candlin (eds.), *Sociolinguistics and Social Theory*. London: Pearson Education Limited, 261–296.
   2001b   Critique in interaction. *Critique of Anthropology* 21 (1), 83–107.
   2006   *Language in Late Modernity: Interaction in an Urban School*. Cambridge: Cambridge University Press.

Roberts, Celia, Evelyn Davies and Tom Jupp
   1992   *Language and Discrimination*. London: Longman.

Rock, Frances
   2001   The genesis of a witness statement. *Forensic Linguistics* 8 (2), 44–72.

Rowse, Tim
   2005   The colonial encounter. In Arthur, Bill and Frances Morphy (eds.), *Macquarie Atlas of Indigenous Australia: Culture and Society through Space and Time*. Sydney: The Macquarie Library Pty Ltd., 210–219.

Sanday, Peggy R.
   1996   *A Woman Scorned: Acquaintance Rape on Trial*. New York: Doubleday.

Sanders, Jane
   1999   Review of *Youth Street Rights: A Policy and Legislation Review* by Tim Anderson, Steve Campbell and Sheree Turner. *Current Issues in Criminal Justice* 10 (3), 333–336.

Santow, G. F. K.
   2000   Mandatory sentencing: A matter for the High Court? *The Australian Law Journal* 74, 298–305.

Sarangi, Srikant
    1994   Intercultural or not? Beyond celebration of cultural differences in miscommunication analysis. *Pragmatics* 4 (3), 409–428.
    2001   A comparative perspective on social-theoretical accounts of the language-action interrelationship. In Coupland, Nikolas, Srikant Sarangi and Christopher N. Candlin (eds.), *Sociolinguistics and Social Theory*. London: Pearson Education Limited, 29–60.

Schegloff, Emanuel A.
    1991   Reflections on talk and social structure. In Boden, Deirdre and Don H. Zimmerman (eds.), *Talk and Social Structure: Studies in Ethnomethodology and Conversation Analysis*. Cambridge: Polity Press, 44–70.
    1999   "Schegloff's texts" as "Billig's data": A critical reply. *Discourse and Society* 10 (4), 558–572.

Schieffelin, Bambi B., Kathryn A. Woolard and Paul V. Kroskrity
    1998   *Language Ideologies: Practice and Theory*. Oxford: Oxford University Press.

Schiffrin, Deborah
    2006   *In Other Words: Variation in Reference and Narrative*. Cambridge: Cambridge University Press.

Scollon, Ron and Suzanne Wong Scollon
    1995   *Intercultural Communication: A Discourse Approach*. Oxford: Blackwell.

Scott, Leisa
    1995   Aboriginal youth abduction verdict "a travesty of justice". *The Australian*, 28 February.

SCRGSP (Steering Committee for the Review of Government Service Provision)
    2005   *Overcoming Indigenous Disadvantage: Key Indicators*. Canberra: Productivity Commission.

Sercombe, Howard
    1995   The face of the criminal is Aboriginal: Representations of Aboriginal young people in the *West Australian* newspaper. In Bessant, Judith, Kerry Carrington and Sandy Cook (eds.) *Cultures of Crime and Violence: The Australian Experience*. Melbourne: La Trobe University Press, 76–94.

Sharifian, Farzad
    2005   Cultural conceptualisations in English words: A study of Aboriginal children in Perth. *Language and Education* 19 (1), 74–88.

Shea, David P.
    1994   Perspective and production: Structuring conversational participation across cultural borders. *Pragmatics* 4 (3), 357–390.

Shuy, Roger
    1990   Evidence of cooperation in conversation: Topic-type in a solicitation to a murder case. In Rieber, Robert and William Stewart (eds.), *The Language Scientist as Expert in the Legal Setting: Issues in Forensic Linguistics*. New York: The New York Academy of Science, 85–105.
    2005   *Creating Language Crimes: How Law Enforcement Uses (and Misuses) Language*. Oxford: Oxford University Press.

Siegel, Jeff
    1999   Creoles and minority dialects in education: An overview. *Journal of Multilingual and Multicultural Development* 20 (6), 508–531.
    2006a   Keeping creoles and dialects out of the classroom: Is it justified? In Nero, Shondel J. (ed.), *Dialects, Englishes, Creoles and Education*. Mahwah, NJ: Lawrence Erlbaum, 39–67.
    2006b   Language ideologies and the education of speakers of marginalized varieties: Adopting a critical awareness approach. *Linguistics and Education* 17, 157–174.

Silverstein, Michael and Greg Urban
    1996   The natural history of discourse. In Silverstein, Michael and Greg Urban (eds.), *Natural Histories of Discourse*. Chicago: Chicago University Press, 1–17.

Singh, Rajendra
    1996   *Towards a Critical Sociolinguistics*. Amsterdam: John Benjamins.

Singh, Rajendra, Jayant Lele and Gita Martohardjono
    1988   Communication in a multilingual society: Some missed opportunities. *Language in Society* 17, 43–59.

Slembrouck, Stef
    2001   Explanation, interpretation and critique in the analysis of discourse. *Critique of Anthropology* 21 (1), 33–57.

Solan, Lawrence M. and Peter M. Tiersma
   2005   *Speaking of Crime: The Language of Criminal Justice.* Chicago: University of Chicago Press.

Solomon, David
   1993a   A case of US and THEM. *The Brisbane Courier Mail*, 18 December.
   1993b   Chestermann makes appeal over "special treatment". *The Brisbane Courier Mail*, 30 November.

Stephens, Tony and Margo Kingston
   2000   Williams berates judges for stand on NT laws. *The Sydney Morning Herald*, 18 March.

Stevenson, Andrew
   2005   Tears for TJ and unfinished business. *The Sydney Morning Herald*, 14 February.

Strehlow, Theodor G. H.
   1936   Notes on native evidence and its value. *Oceania* 6, 323–335.

Tannen, Deborah
   1994   *Gender and Discourse.* Oxford: Oxford University Press.

Taylor, Brian
   1995   Offensive language: A linguistic and sociolinguistic perspective. In Eades, Diana (ed.), *Language in Evidence: Issues Confronting Aboriginal and Multicultural Australia.* Sydney: University of New South Wales Press, 219–258.

Taylor, John
   2005   Population and patterns of residence. In Arthur, Bill and Frances Morphy (eds.), *Macquarie Atlas of Indigenous Australia: Culture and Society through Space and Time.* Sydney: The Macquarie Library Pty Ltd., 66–77.

Thompson, Don
   1999   Eyewitness testimony. In Freckelton, Ian and Hugh Selby (eds.), *Expert Evidence in Criminal Law.* Sydney: Law Book Company, 647–689.

Thomson, Donald F.
   1935   The joking relationship and organized obscenity in North Queensland. *American Anthropologist* 37, 460–490.

Thorne, Alan
  2005   Migration and Prehistory. In Arthur, Bill and Frances Morphy (eds.), *Macquarie Atlas of Indigenous Australia: Culture and Society through Space and Time*. Sydney: The Macquarie Library Pty Ltd., 38–47.

Tiersma, Peter M.
  1999   *Legal Language*. Chicago: University of Chicago Press.
  2001   Textualizing the law. *Forensic Linguistics* 8 (2), 73–92.
  2006   *Communicating with Juries: How to Draft More Understandable Jury Instructions*. Williamsburg, VA: National Center for State Courts.

Tom, Emma
  1993   March for dancer remains peaceful. *The Sydney Morning Herald*, 18 November.

Trigger, David S.
  1995   "Everyone's agreed, the *West* is all you need": Ideology, media and Aboriginality in Western Australia. *Media Information Australia* 75, 102–122.

Trinch, Shonna L.
  2003   *Latinas' Narratives of Domestic Abuse: Discrepant Versions of Violence*. Amsterdam: John Benjamins.

Van Dijk, Teun A.
  1991   *Racism and the Press*. London: Routledge.
  1993   Principles of critical discourse analysis. *Discourse and Society* 4 (2), 249–283.
  1999   Critical Discourse Analysis and Conversation Analysis. *Discourse and Society* 10 (4), 459–460.

Verschueren, Jef
  2001   Predicaments of criticism. *Critique of Anthropology* 21 (1), 59–81.

Walker, Anne Graffam
  1985   The two faces of silence: The effect of witness hesitancy on lawyers' impressions. In Tannen, Deborah and Muriel Saville-Troike (eds.), *Perspectives on Silence*. Norwood, NJ: Ablex, 55–75.
  1987   Linguistic manipulation, power, and the legal setting. In Kedar, L. (ed.), *Power through Discourse*. Norwood, NJ: Ablex, 57–80.
  1999   *Handbook on Questioning Chilldren: A Linguistic Perspective*. 2nd ed. (1st ed. 1994). Washington, DC: ABA Center on Children and the Law.

Walker, Jamie
1994a   Arrest of the heart. *The Australian*, 6 April.
1994b   Aborigines stand firm on Yock accusation. *The Australian*, 7 April.

Walker, Jamie and David Fagan
1994   Police chief demands apology over Yock. *The Australian*, 6 April.

Walsh, Michael
1994   Interactional styles in the courtroom: An example from northern Australia. In Gibbons, John (ed.), *Language and the Law*. London: Longman, 217–233.
1999   Interpreting for the transcript: Problems in recording Aboriginal land claim proceedings in northern Australia. *Forensic Linguistics* 6 (1), 161–195.

Walsh, Tamara
2003   "Waltzing Matilda" one hundred years later: Interactions between homeless persons and the criminal justice system in Queensland. *Sydney Law Review* 25, 75–95.
2005   Offensive language, offensive behaviour and public nuisance: Empirical and theoretical analyses. *University of Queensland Law Journal* 24 (1), 123–145.

West, Candace and Don H. Zimmerman
1987   Doing gender. *Gender and Society* 1 (2), 125–151.

White, Rob
1994   Shaming and reintegrative strategies: Individuals, state power and social interests. In Alder, Christine and Joy Wundersitz (eds.), *Family Conferencing and Juvenile Justice: The Way Forward or Misplaced Optimism*. Canberra: Australian Institute of Criminology, 181–196.

Whittaker, Paul
1995   Top QC had cocktail of drugs in blood. *The Brisbane Courier Mail*, 11 November.

Wilson, Paul R.
1978   What is deviant language? In Wilson, Paul R. and John Braithwaite (eds.), *Two Faces of Deviance: Crimes of the Powerless and the Powerful*. Brisbane: University of Queensland Press.

Wodak, Ruth
   2001   What CDA is about – a summary of its history, important concepts
           and its developments. In Wodak, Ruth and Michael Meyer (eds.),
           Methods of Critical Discourse Analysis. London: Sage, 1–13.

Woodbury, Hanni
   1984   The strategic use of questions in court. *Semiotica* 48 (3/4), 197–
           228.

Woods, James
   1993   Drop-out in the front line. *The Brisbane Courier Mail*, 25 Novem-
           ber.

Wootten John Halden
   1991   *Report of the Inquiry into the Death of David John Gundy.* Royal
           Commission into Aboriginal Deaths in Custody N19. Canberra:
           Australian Government Publishing Service.

Wright, David H.
   2004   *Report of the Commission of Inquiry into Matters Relating to the
           Death of Neil Stonechild*. Saskatoon: The Commission.

Young, Linda
   1994   *Crosstalk and Culture in Sino-American Communication*. Cam-
           bridge: Cambridge University Press.

Subject index

Name index